TALIBAN

THOMAS H. JOHNSON
with Matthew DuPee and Wali Shaaker

Taliban Narratives

The Use and Power of Stories
in the Afghanistan Conflict

OXFORD
UNIVERSITY PRESS

OXFORD
UNIVERSITY PRESS

Oxford University Press is a department of the
University of Oxford. It furthers the University's objective
of excellence in research, scholarship, and education
by publishing worldwide.

Oxford   New York

Auckland   Cape Town   Dar es Salaam   Hong Kong   Karachi
Kuala Lumpur   Madrid   Melbourne   Mexico City   Nairobi
New Delhi   Shanghai   Taipei   Toronto

With offices in

Argentina   Austria   Brazil   Chile   Czech Republic   France   Greece
Guatemala   Hungary   Italy   Japan   Poland   Portugal   Singapore
South Korea   Switzerland   Thailand   Turkey   Ukraine   Vietnam

Oxford is a registered trade mark of Oxford University Press
in the UK and certain other countries.

Published in the United States of America by
Oxford University Press
198 Madison Avenue, New York, NY 10016

Library of Congress Cataloging-in-Publication Data is available
Thomas H. Johnson with Matthew DuPee and Wali Shaaker.
Taliban Narratives: The Use and Power of Stories in the Afghanistan Conflict.
ISBN: 9780190840600

Printed in India on acid-free paper

I would like to dedicate this book to Lt. Col. John Darin (JD) Loftis, a student, friend, and outstanding military officer who was murdered while helping the people of Afghanistan whom he loved and respected dearly.

I also dedicate this book to Ryan and Courtney, whose love and inspiration maintain me.

CONTENTS

ACKNOWLEDGMENTS

This book was initially conceived at the US Naval Postgraduate School (NPS)'s Program for Culture and Conflict Studies (CCS), which I direct. The research associates and assistants on the program played an indispensable role in the conceptualization of data and notions concerning many of the analyses presented in this book. I would like first to thank Matthew DuPee. I came across Matt's tremendous self-taught knowledge of Afghanistan by reading his articles published on the influential blog, the *Long War Journal*. I found his articles full of data and knowledge concerning Afghanistan that appeared in no other media outlet. It was very evident that he had valuable Afghan contacts and used them extremely effectively. I was so impressed with his scholarship and his writing that I eventually contacted and offered him a research position at CCS and a stipend to enter the MA program in National Security Affairs at NPS. He proved to be an outstanding student, graduating with highest honors, as well as being a tremendous colleague and researcher. His self-initiative, smarts, and outstanding analytic and writing capabilities proved invaluable. He co-authored a number of peer-reviewed journal articles with me and made invaluable contributions to nearly every chapter presented in this book. He now serves as an important Department of Defense Afghan analyst. The country is fortunate to have his services.

I would also like to thank Wali Ahmed Shaaker, an important and well-known Afghan-American poet who was initially hired as a translator for the CCS. I quickly learned that his intellectual tool chest relative to Afghanistan was vast. He basically taught me the essence of Afghan poetry and its many variants, as well as important Afghan poets that we needed to consider in assessing the role of poetry in Afghan IO. Wali's research was critical for those sections of this book that deal with Afghan and Taliban poetry. His transla-

ACKNOWLEDGMENTS

tions of Taliban materials, especially poetry, proved extremely important and are presented in this book. In addition, his support of my field research in Afghanistan proved extremely valuable.

Other CCS members also played critical roles in the research presented here. I would like to thank especially Ahmad Waheed and Amina Kator-Mumbarez. Ahmad, a Kandahari Afghan, now a US citizen, who initially came to study in the United States as a Fulbright Scholar, helped to bring Afghan nuance to almost all of the analyses presented in this book. He served as a CCS Research Associate for over five years, and his contributions to the research presented here were numerous. Like the other CCS members suggested above, his self-initiative and dedication was infectious. Like Matt DuPee, Ahmad served as my co-author for peer-reviewed journal articles on a variety on subjects relevant to Taliban information operations. He translated most of the Pashto materials assessed in this book, including the hundreds of *shabnamah* whose summaries are presented in Appendix B (available online at www.hurstpublishers.com/book/taliban-narratives). Amina Kator-Mumbarez, another Afghan-American, was hired shortly after her graduation from the University of California in Berkeley where she organized important conferences and workshops on Afghanistan. Amina served the CCS as an invaluable colleague, proving to be a very gifted writer and researcher. She, like the other dedicated CCS colleagues, played a critical role in assessments of Taliban IO materials, data collection, analysis, and review. Keely M. Fahoum, a former NPS student, also played a significant role in educating me concerning the early US IO and PSYOP campaigns in Afghanistan. She had a wealth of knowledge concerning early OEF IO and PSYOP, some of which is reflected in this book. Elizabeth (Betsy) Hulme, an outstanding student intern from the University of North Carolina, made valuable contributions during the final push of finishing the book. Finally, I would like to thank Matthew Dearing, one of the first CCS research assistants, for supporting some of the early research relevant to this book.

Very importantly, most of these CCS scholars proved also to be tremendous friends and colleagues and played significant roles in the production of this book on their own time.

This book also benefited from conversations with NPS's Center of Excellence for Information Dominance. I would like to thank especially Professors Hy Rothstein and John Arquilla. I was told that John once stated that the war in Afghanistan would eventually become a "battle of poetry," and I believe the reasoning underlying this statement is quite prophetic and extremely relevant to the major thesis of this book.

ACKNOWLEDGMENTS

Chris Mason, Harold Ingram, Graeme Smith, and Larry Goodson also helped to frame my ideas on many subjects presented here. This group of Afghan scholars regularly communicate with each other and me via emails discussing a variety of important Afghan subjects and personalities. They are also all valued friends. Chris Mason played an especially important role in my understanding of Afghan messaging and narratives, as well as the naiveté of US messaging and information operations.

I would also like to thank all my students at NPS that I have had the opportunity to interact with over the years. Many of these students have had multiple deployments to Afghanistan, and their experiences taught me valuable lessons concerning Afghanistan. In addition, many of my students had unique and real world experience with information operations conducted by both the US and the Taliban that proved important to developing my knowledge and ideas concerning Afghan IO.

The research presented would not have been possible without the data I gathered from numerous individuals interviewed over the course of my research. Such individuals included (please note that position and ranks, where known, reflect those at the time of the interview): Joanna Nathan (Senior Analyst, International Crisis Group), Joe Auger (Local Stability Initiatives Team Leader, DAI), Col. Woodsworth (Canadian PRT), Maj. Perey (Canadian PRT), Karen Swails (USAID officer), Sharif Noorzai, Dr Jouri, Whit Mason (Regional Justice Coordinator, UNAMA), Sarah Chayes, Louis Palu (freelance photographer and journalist), Abdul Bari (tribal elder from Maiwand, Ishaqzai Pashtun), Mohammadullah Barakzai (tribal elder from Panjwayi), Nimat Arghandabi (Head of National Islamic Society of Afghan Youth, Mohammedzai tribe), Qadir Khan Durrani, Alex Strick van Linschoten, three anonymous Kandahari District Taliban commanders, Qari Yousef (Taliban spokesman, southern Afghanistan), Zabidullah Mujahid (Taliban spokesman, eastern Afghanistan), LTC Eric Edin (Commander CJ-POTF), Col. Jeff Jaworsky (TF-Paladin/CJTF IO), Cdr Jon Young (TF-Paladin), LTC Dean Burbridge (CJTF IO), Edward Mooradian (COIC Red Team), Sgt Martinez (2/7 Marines, Helmand), Tom Targus (State Department Political Officer), Bruce Dubee (USDA advisor), Ted Wittenberger (USAID officer), James Fussel (TF Paladin), Dr Jeffery Bordin (Red Team Leader), Alisson Blosser (Assadabad PRT officer), Cdr Dan Dwyer (Assadabad PRT CO), Cpt. Rose (TF Paladin), Cpt. Beasley (EOD), Lt. Matt Myers Assadabad (PRT), MSGT Foreman (TF Paladin), various political party representatives: Sayyaf, United Front, Northern Alliance,

ACKNOWLEDGMENTS

Kunar Governor Wahidi, LTC Paul Donovan (Nangahar PRT Commander), Maj. Brad Adams (TF Paladin), LTC Herb Bilewski (CIED JAF), Maj. Mike Jackson (CIED JAF), Sarah Rahimi (TF Paladin), Chancellor of Jalalabad Medical University, Haji Mohammed Hasan (Nangarhar Provincial Council Representative, Khogiani tribal elder, Sayyef Party representative), Dr Nijra Habib (Nangarhar Provincial Council representative), Abiba Khaker (Nangarhar Provincial Council representative), Lal Agha Kaker (Mayor of Jalalabad, Nangarhar), Nangarhar Governor Gul Agha Sherzai, Masood Ahmad Azizi (Chief of Staff for Nangarhar province), Nujayed Ahmad (Political Assistant, Jalalabad PRT), Fazil Hadi (Speaker of Nangarhar Provincial Council, Sayyaf Party Representative), Mirwais Ahmadzai (Director of Eastern Office, AIHRC), Cpt. John Morash (JIOC Jalalabad PRT), Sean Waddups (Jalalabad PRT Office), Gen. David McKiernan (ISAF Commanding General), Frank Curry (Assymetric Warfare Group, US Army), LTC Robert Spath (CJ POTF), Col. Dietger Lather (CJ POTF), Barbara Sotirin, (Deputy Director, HQUSACE), Bjorn Delaney (Lincoln Group), Todd Wilson (Office of the Coordinator for Reconstruction and Stabilization, US State Department), Brian Goodman, LTC Patrick Kearney (CIED), Christian Harstad (NORNAVSOC), Greg Reichman (CENTCOM), Col. Roger N. Sangvi (Director CJ2 CTSC), Ray Valez (JIEDDO), Alan Yu (Political Officer, US Embassy, Kabul), Paul Fishstein (Director AREU Kabul), Mohammad Yousef (Aschiana), Col. John Agoglia, Ayscha Hamdami (Political advisor, ISAF HQ), Abdullah Amini (Cultural Advisor to COMISAF), LTC Wood (TF Paladin XO), CWO Stephen Pierce, LTC Elders, LTC Jarkowsky, MAJ Dvorsack, Col. Michael Langley, Col. Ronald Sheldon (Senior Mentor and Team Chief, 201st ARSIC-IO), Cpt. Charles Johnson, Afghan MG Rahim Wardak, BG Edward Reeder, Jr (Commanding General Combined Forces Special Operations Component Command, Afghanistan CFSOCC-A), Col. Kevin Davis (Deputy Commander, CFSOCC-A), LTC David Markowski, CWO Steven Pierce, Col. Arthur Tulak (Director USFOR-A Information Operations), Col. Kevin Davis (Deputy Commander, CFSOCC-A), Col. Brian Sweeney (Director of Strategy, J5 Strategy and Plans, CFSOCC-A), LTC Lisa Miller (Task Force Phoenix IO), LTC Greg Elpers (POTF Task Force Siren Deputy Commander), Commander Christopher Hurley (SO2, Key Leader Engagement), Maj. Cas Benavidez (Chief IO Plans, USFOR-A Information Operations), Maj. Katherine Doyle (Analyst, USFOR-A Information Operations, USFOR-A IO Working Group), Michael Innes (JIC), BG

ACKNOWLEDGMENTS

Jonathan Vance (Canadian Commander of Kandahar Task Force) and his HQ Staff, Col. La Croix (Deputy Commander KTF), Col. Hammand (KTF J-5), Col. Burt (OMLT Commander), LTC Paul (Canadian Battle Group Commander), Maj. Kevin McLoughlin (KTF J-5), Ken Lewis (Representative of Canada in Kandahar-RoCK), Ms Renata Pistone (CIDA), LTC Carl Taurren (Canadian Camp Nathan Smith PRT Commander), Ms Deborah Chatsis (Canadian Civilian PRT Director), Maj. Luis Carvallo (Canadian Camp), Nathan Smith (PRT Deputy Commanding Officer), Maj. Claude Villeneuve (Civil Military Cooperation-CIMC), Capt. Roy (CIMIC), Capt. Stepanie Godin (PAO), Maj. Chris Brooke (US PMT Commander), Khalil, Khan Mohammad Jan (Peace and Reconciliation Commission-PRC, Chief, Kandahar), Hajji Mullah Amadullah Khan (Zhari district shura member), Mullah Massoud (former District Chief for Maywand district, Kandahar), Anonymous Panjwaii district shura member, Jorge Silva (freelance photographer and journalist), David Beriain (documentarian/journalist), Anand Gopal (journalist, *Christian Science Monitor*), Ghulam Haidar (Mayor of Kandahar City), Maitullah Qati Khan (Provincial Police Chief for Kandahar), Khan Mohammad Jan (Peace and Reconciliation Commission Chief, Kandahar), BG Edward Reeder, Jr (Commanding General, Combined Forces Special Operations Component Command—Afghanistan, CFSOCC-A).

I would also like to thank various US and Canadian governmental organizations who enhanced parts of the research presented here. Finally, I would like to thank two anonymous reviewers whose constructive criticisms and suggestions have made this a much better book than the one they initially reviewed.

Thomas H. Johnson   Monterey, California, 9 May 2016

LIST OF FIGURES AND TABLES

Figures

LIST OF FIGURES AND TABLES

Tables

FOREWORD

Ambassador (Retd) Peter Tomsen

Throughout history, military strategists have often stressed the importance of motivation in warfare in relation to military might. Napoleon looked back in exile at his military career of victories and defeats to observe: "There are but two powers in the world, the sword and the mind... In the long run, the sword is always beaten by the mind."

A thorough understanding of the enemy, including his will to fight, was highlighted by Sun Tzu, a Chinese strategist who lived in the sixth century BC: "If you know the enemy and know yourself, you need not fear the results of a hundred battles." Sun Tzu and Napoleon must have viewed their guidelines as applicable to all warfare. They have been especially relevant to guerrilla wars in modern times, pitting a militarily stronger side against a determined yet weaker foe on home turf. Vietnam comes to mind in this regard, as does the nine-year Soviet–Afghan war. In both conflicts, the guerrilla's main goal was to mold military and informational operations into a unified, effective strategy to resist and outlast a superpower's will to continue fighting an endless war.

In the end, the US and Soviet withdrawals from (respectively) Vietnam and Afghanistan represented more of a policy failure than a military defeat. The Soviet military in Afghanistan never lost a set-piece battle. After the Vietnam war, a Vietnamese general in Hanoi famously commented "That's irrelevant" when a visiting American retired officer stated that the US had never lost a battle during the war.

Since the initial withdrawal of US Coalition ground combat forces from Afghanistan in 2012, the outcome of the Afghan war has remained in doubt, even though the Pakistani-supported Afghan insurgency—collectively, the Afghan Taliban, the Haqqani Network and Gulbuddin Hekmatyar's Hisb-e-Islami Gulbuddin (HIG)—has gained the upper hand in military and informational areas. The Coalition-backed Afghan National United Government (NUG) suffers from the same ailments that inflicted the South Vietnamese Nguyen Van Thieu government when I served as a District Senior Advisor in the Mekong Delta 1969–70, and later, in 1973, when I returned in the capacity of a ceasefire monitor. Pervasive government corruption, dating back to the Ngo Dinh Diem government and continuing to the 1975 defeat of the Thieu regime, reached down to the district level from elites in Saigon. Vietnamese leaders scuttled free and fair elections. The Vietnamese government's popularity was higher than the popularity of the Communist insurgency in rural areas, but that was only a matter of degree. Most of the rural population just wanted the war to end—a sentiment that appeals to many rural Afghan communities today.

The American experience in Vietnam is not a good precedent for judging what lies ahead in Afghanistan. The two countries are vastly different, as is the regional geo-strategic context that has surrounded each conflict. Still, it bears noting that the South Vietnamese Thieu government lasted three years (1972–5) following the US withdrawal of ground forces. The Moscow-dependent Najib regime in Kabul likewise lasted three more years (1989–92) before collapsing. In both cases, the insurgency had better synchronized, highly sophisticated information operations, with military strategy. Each benefited from a secure rear area to prepare and supply military offensives while—equally important—planning and executing a well-coordinated information campaign in the battle zone. In Vietnam, the insurgency in the South was permanently buoyed by the coming of military age of a quarter million North Vietnamese every year. They were armed with Soviet-supplied weaponry and sent south into a seemingly endless conflict.

In Pakistan, the 3–4 million Afghan refugees have offered a similarly large pool of highly motivated jihadist fighters, accurately described in Professor Thomas H. Johnson's *Narratives* as comprising the great majority of the Taliban leadership, as well as Taliban fighters inside Afghanistan. For over three decades, Pakistan's powerful military intelligence agency, the Inter-

Services Intelligence (ISI) directorate, with funding from Saudi Arabia and support from Pakistani extremist sects, has funneled young Afghan refugees through a network of radical madrasas inside Pakistan preaching obligatory Holy War, to be followed by covert military training in ISI-managed military camps, and subsequent movement to a fighting front, jihad, in Afghanistan. A roughly equal number of Pakistan Pashtuns in poverty-stricken, uneducated families on the Pakistan side of the border continue today to make that same journey under the banner of ISI-created Pakistani religious paramilitary forces—Lashkar-e-Taiba, Jaish-i-Mohammed, Harakat ul-Mujahidin—all on the US government's Foreign Terrorist Organization (FTO) list.

As indicated in this book, nearly the entire propaganda production platform for the Taliban's information campaign carried out inside Afghanistan is located in Pakistan and overseen by ISI: the magazines *Al Somood, In Fight, Shahamat, Elhan, Murchal*; the monthly pamphlet *Srak*; and media studios and video production facilities of *Alemarah*, al Hijirat, and Mana-ul Jihad. Afghan Taliban media spokesmen inside Pakistan provide a Taliban interpretation of events and news releases about developments in the Afghan war to international as well as to local journalists. The media output of other radical Afghan insurgent groups operating from Pakistan—the anti-American firebrand Gulbuddin Hekmatyar and the brutal Haqqani Network—are also disseminated into Afghanistan and internationally from Pakistan, in most cases from the Peshawar region where their leaderships live and freely operate.

When I served as American Special Envoy to Afghanistan (1989–92), Hekmatyar regularly attacked the United States, equating it with the Soviet Union, in his official newspaper, *Shahadat*. *Shahadat* routinely lashed out at me as well for being "an uninvited guest with cheekiness, stubbornness," and "implementing a satanic plan." Today, Hekmatyar's media empire inside Pakistan is considerably larger. In addition to *Shahadat*, it boasts three magazines, a second newspaper, a website, Twitter and Facebook online operations, and an official spokesman. Hekmatyar and the Taliban insurgent media outlets are in close touch with extremist Pakistani and Arab publications, including those operated by al-Qaeda and al-Qaeda affiliates, sharing and disseminating propaganda videos and printed materials with each other across Eurasia.

As is thoroughly documented in the pages of this unique book, the ISI-supported Afghan Taliban, Haqqani Network, and HIG informational campaigns mounted from Pakistan have proven far superior in quality, quantity, and effectiveness to those organized by the American Coalition and the Afghan government. In sum (and expanded on later), "the US military and the

Afghan government have continually failed to offer a credible narrative and stories that resonate with the Afghan people. The Taliban, on the other hand, have crafted a strong, simple, and culturally relevant IO (Information Operations) campaign to energize, coerce, and control the Afghan populace."

Over the past nearly four decades, since the 1979 Soviet invasion, the Pakistan-fueled Afghan insurgency inside Afghanistan has transited through different military propaganda phases. Fluctuating information messaging has been closely aligned with adjustments in military operations and vice versa. As is well-documented in *Taliban Narratives*, the propaganda themes remained basically the same during the Soviet occupation (1979–89) and the post-9/11 American intervention in Afghanistan (October 2001-present). Taliban information operations aimed at mobilizing popular support behind the insurgency, motivating and recruiting fighters, have highlighted:

- The Muslim Brotherhood, Qutbist mandate making it obligatory on every Muslim to conduct violent jihad to defend Islam (the radical Islamist so-called sixth pillar of Islam);
- The call to emulate past Afghan defeats of foreign invaders, with a special accent on ethnic Pashtun historiography, traditions, values, and mythology toward that end;
- Afghan and Pashtun nationalism;
- Foreign sponsorship of an abusive, corrupt Afghan puppet government;
- Warnings to Afghans working in or supportive of the Afghan government and foreign occupiers.

The Mujahidin propaganda campaign during the anti-Soviet war changed along with military objectives when it became clear in early 1988 that the Soviets were leaving Afghanistan. ISI began preparations to install its favorite extremist, Hekmatyar, in Kabul. It shifted the great bulk of financial, propaganda assets, and CIA weapons supplies to Hekmatyar. Simultaneously, it drastically reduced support to major non-extremist Afghan commanders Ahmed Shah Masood, Abdul Haq, Haji Latif, and Ismael Khan. Together, moderate Afghan Mujahidin had inflicted the majority of casualties on Soviet forces during the anti-Soviet jihad. The Soviet departure led ISI to pivot from a defensive to an offensive posture to eliminate or degrade the moderates. On 9 July 1989, a Hekmatyar commander murdered thirty of Masood's sub-commanders in northern Afghanistan. Hekmatyar's radio station in Pakistan blamed Masood. ISI maneuvering disrupted American efforts to investigate the massacre. A month later, Haji Latif, a prominent tribal moderate who had been feuding with Hekmatyar, was poisoned near his base in southern Afghanistan. Many believed that Hekmatyar killed the renowned commander. ISI funds for moderate Mujahidin information operations dried up. ISI cut off support to Ismael Khan and Abdul Haq.

From Pakistan, Hekmatyar's media promoted him as the top leader of the Mujahidin drive to topple the Najib regime which the Soviets had left behind in Kabul. This did not stop Masood from capturing Kabul in 1992 before Hekmatyar's forces could get there. ISI assisted Hekmatyar in bombarding the city, killing thousands. In 1995, Pakistan switched its support from Hekmatyar to the Taliban as the most promising Afghan extremist vehicle to expel Masood from Kabul. By this time, an Afghan Muslim versus Afghan Muslim civil war had replaced the jihad against a foreign invader. The ideological solidarity that had unified the Mujahidin during the jihad was fast dissipating, resulting in a battlefield stalemate.

To gain the initiative and in an unusual departure from the Taliban's radical Islamist messaging, Taliban propaganda featured the "return" of the secular and moderate ex-Pashtun king, Zahir Shah, then residing in Rome. Zahir Shah's popularity throughout most of the Pashtun tribal belt in the south and east gave impetus to Taliban military progress against Masood's Mujahidin forces in control of Kabul. Taliban formations carried aloof huge portraits of Zahir Shah as they marched through Pashtun provinces on the way to the capital. After Pakistani-assisted Taliban assaults forced Masood to abandon Kabul on 26 September 1996, the Taliban's propaganda associating the Taliban with Zahir Shah quickly disappeared, replaced by a stream of religious fatwas establishing the rigid new Taliban order based on a strict, Wahhabi version of Qur'anic law. In early 1997, the Pakistani foreign minister nimbly compared the Taliban's advent to the 1789 French Revolution and announced Pakistan's diplomatic recognition of Mullah Omar's Afghan emirate.

In the wake of the disastrous second Anglo-Afghan war (1879–81), Britain's commander, Field Marshal Frederick Roberts, had suggested that, in the future, the British should seek out internal Afghan allies rather than unilaterally attempting again to invade the country:

- I feel sure I am right when I say that the less the Afghans see of us, the less they will dislike us.
- Should the Russians attempt to conquer Afghanistan, we should have a better chance of attaching the Afghans to our interests if we avoid all interference with them.

A century later, Soviet commanders in Afghanistan would encounter a similar Afghan religious–patriotic uprising reminiscent of the Roman writer Virgil's comment in the *Aeneid*: "Their rage supplies them with weapons." During the Soviet occupation, American Cold War strategists did not need to coordinate arms supplies to the Mujahidin with an informational PSYOP campaign. Afghan fury required no American encouragement. As with the covert weapons supplies to ISI, the Pakistanis ran the propaganda war, building up the al-Qaeda-connected radical Mujahidin groups, particularly Hekmatyar, at the expense of Mujahidin moderates. Washington lost interest in Afghanistan during the mid-1990s following the late 1991 collapse of the Soviet Union.

That left Pakistan with a free hand to shape an extremist sequel to the Afghan war in the form of the Taliban, while keeping outsiders duped or at bay about Islamabad's intentions. US policy-makers ignored warnings from some scholars and diplomats that "Arab terrorist organizations ... could shift their bases to Afghanistan" (Tomsen, *The Wars of Afghanistan*, p. 323). Outsourcing America's Afghan policy to Pakistan backfired. Afghanistan became a launching pad for al-Qaeda attacks on the US, first targeting two American embassies in Africa (1998), then against the warship USS *Cole* off the Yemeni coast (2000), and again on 9/11 directly against the American homeland.

The post-9/11 American military intervention in Afghanistan in October 2001 drove the Taliban and Osama bin Laden's Arab forces back to the Pakistani base areas from which they had emerged after the Soviet withdrawal. As widely accepted in hindsight today, the Pakistani commitment to cooperate in the struggle against al-Qaeda, the Taliban, and Islamist terrorism proved duplicitous. ISI revamped the Taliban. It reorganized three jihadist fronts on the Pakistan side of the Afghan–Pakistani border: Mullah Omar's Afghan Taliban above Quetta in the west, the Haqqani Network in the center, and Hekmatyar's HIG on the western flank. The insurgency's ultimate goal was to outlast the American will to conduct the war. A retired ISI director general predicted that the US would be gone in five years. A group of Pakistani generals decided in a private meeting that it would take ten. The US withdrew its combat forces after twelve years of inconclusive guerrilla warfare planned and supplied from Pakistani safe havens. A large-scale sophisticated Taliban propaganda campaign emanating from Pakistan, detailed at length in *Taliban Narratives*, reinforced the insurgency's gradual expansion to most other regions of the country.

As of mid-2016, some 13,000 American-led Coalition troops are training and assisting the Afghan army and air force and conducting counter-terrorism operations. The Soviet military in the 1980s had only sporadically conducted cross-border air raids into Pakistan. The US adopted a more forward posture, hitting Taliban targets across the border in Pakistan, launching hundreds of drone strikes inside Pakistan's tribal areas, with the silent compliance of Pakistan's military. A drone strike on 21 May 2016 killed Taliban leader Mullah Mansour, traveling by car in Pakistan's western Baluchistan province, undertaken without Pakistani clearance. US Special Forces raids have also periodically covertly penetrated Pakistani territory, including the 2 May 2011 killing of Osama bin Laden, also undertaken without notification to Pakistan.

There is much to be pessimistic about when looking at the situation in Afghanistan today. The Taliban have yet to take over a city and hold it, but the movement has expanded into many rural areas, especially in the Pashtun belt adjoining Pakistan and near Kabul. Haqqani Network suicide bombings rock Afghanistan's capital. The Islamic State is establishing small footholds in the east and north-west. It attempts to create more bases across the Amu Darya in Central Asia. Iran and China oppose the continuing US presence in Afghanistan, as does the Taliban's patron, Pakistan. The Afghan National Unity Government in Kabul is corrupt and inept. Ashraf Ghani is more concerned about keeping American pressure for reforms at arm's length than governing well. The Ghani government's poor image among Afghans reduces its potential to become an effective partner in the critical motivational contest for the Afghan mind. Another Vietnam policy failure is not out of the question.

On the positive side of the ledger, American and Coalition combat forces have been withdrawn. The Taliban message to end the American occupation is less credible. The conflict is now primarily an Afghan war: Afghan extremists based in Pakistan versus the anti-extremist government in Kabul. The Taliban are divided vertically and horizontally, tarnished with being the Pakistani proxy that they are. Soviet ally Najib skillfully divided the Mujahidin for three years after the Soviet departure had weakened the unifying call to jihad. It was the conclusion of the US–Soviet negative symmetry agreement depriving Najib of Soviet arms, not Mujahidin military pressure, that eventually precipitated his regime's collapse in 1992. The US-led Coalition has apparently recognized that Afghanistan is just one theatre in the ongoing struggle across Asia and the Middle East against Islamist terrorism. It is likely to remain committed to a non-extremist outcome in Afghanistan.

Pakistani sponsorship of the Taliban is clearer than ever after the killing of Taliban leader Mullah Mansour. Rumors that the ISI murdered Mullah Omar and suppressed news about Omar's demise for two years after his death had already stoked angry resentment in some Taliban ranks. The ISI's dominant role in choosing first Mansour, then Haibatullah, to be the next Taliban emir, not to mention selecting their deputies, will likely heighten Taliban annoyance about Pakistan's interference in Taliban leadership politics.

Inside Afghanistan, the Taliban record in ruling Afghanistan (1996–2001) has left a bitter legacy among most Afghans, especially the non-Pashtun minorities who make up a majority of the population. Should the Taliban again overrun Kabul, the Northern Alliance of mainly Tajik, Uzbek, and Hazara forces will fiercely resist Taliban expansion north of the Hindu Kush. Backing from Russia, Iran, and India would assist their capability to prevent a Taliban conquest of Afghanistan.

The most important challenges that the US, its Coalition, and Afghan partners must overcome are conveying a persuasive message to the Afghan population to buttress their military strategy; countering Taliban propaganda; and harvesting the many opportunities available to exploit Taliban and Pakistani vulnerabilities. *Taliban Narratives* methodically chronicles how and why the Taliban have to date "won the information war against the US coalition and the Afghan government"—or, paraphrasing Napoleon's dictum, the battle for the Afghan mind. This sobering predicament confronted me during a 2012 military briefing on Afghanistan at a military base in the US. I asked a military officer why the traditional "strategic communications" topic had been dropped from the agenda. "Because it failed," he replied. His answer stunned me. The Coalition's eleven-year information effort, as depicted in Professor Johnson's book, just "did not work."

A fulsome description and assessment of what went wrong with the US attempt to win the hearts and minds of Afghans follows here in the pages of *Taliban Narratives*. Its conclusions and recommendations are based on fieldwork inside Afghanistan over a seven-year period by Professor Johnson and his two colleagues. They interviewed hundreds of Afghans and compiled thousands of documents, videos, and other originally-sourced materials. This book's incisive analysis of Taliban and Pakistani vulnerabilities will prove invaluable in informing a future, more successful US strategy to counter the radical Islamist message, and not only in Afghanistan; for the ideological–military struggle between the majority moderate Afghan Muslims and the radical Islamist brand espoused by the Taliban and its offshoots will continue for decades in the Islamic world.

PREFACE[1]

In mid-September 2001, I was asked by the Office of the Secretary of Defense (OSD) to assist in the formulation of the United States' initial "Information Operations" (IO) campaign in preparation for the US invasion of Afghanistan. The stated policy aim of this invasion was initially to pursue and destroy al-Qaeda, the perpetrators of the 9/11 attacks on the United States. This initial goal would change significantly over the course of the war in Afghanistan to a primary focus on the destruction of the Taliban as well as nation-building. For three weeks I feverishly researched and worked on narratives that I believed would help tell the "story" of why the US military was attacking al-Qaeda and the Taliban in Afghanistan. I was especially interested in the formulation of narratives and stories that I believed would resonate with the Afghan people in a nuanced way.

I had first traveled to Afghanistan in the mid-1980s during the Soviet occupation, and over the course of years I had the pleasure of visiting and meeting many Afghans, both rural and urban, during my numerous trips to the country. Having studied and written on Afghanistan for nearly two decades, I felt I had a fairly sophisticated knowledge of the country and its people. Yet, not expertly knowing their languages hindered my deep structural understanding of certain aspects of the country, cultures, and peoples. Nevertheless, I immersed myself in data and Information Operation's ideas that I believed could be used effectively during our coming invasion of Afghanistan.

I was startled by the frazzled and hectic pace I found in OSD in preparation for our coming operations in Afghanistan. From endless meetings to running into numerous expatriate Afghans I had known for years walking and campaigning in the halls of the Pentagon, I was nearly overwhelmed by the sheer volume and variety of opinions expressed concerning the "best" way to explain our forthcoming actions to the Afghan people.

I was also unprepared for the lack of detailed and nuanced, substantive knowledge among military leaders and OSD personnel concerning the country and people which the US was about to attack. It was very evident that since the US had ended its considerable support of the Afghan Mujahidin and their anti-Soviet jihad (the largest intelligence covert program in US history) and our goal of "bleeding" the Soviets a decade earlier, our government had lost most of its legacy of information on Afghanistan. Moreover, the eventual withdrawal of Afghan support by both "superpowers" created a power vacuum that the Pakistan military had tried to exploit by using their Inter-Services Intelligence (ISI) directive to sponsor the Mujahidin's attempt to overthrow the post-Soviet Afghan government. From the relative importance of the Pashtun community in the governance of the country, to the biases of the Kabuli Afghan elite to the explicit make-up of the Northern Alliance, I was taken aback by the lack of up-to-date, relevant data on Afghanistan within OSD as well as with the military leadership. While I found more sophisticated knowledge concerning Afghanistan within the intelligence community members with whom I interacted, I also found their knowledge of the country lacking in important aspects, especially considering the immense Afghan knowledge I had witnessed in this community a decade earlier. I found myself agreeing with the many critics who argued that after the Soviets withdrew in defeat from Afghanistan in January 1989, the US basically abandoned and forgot about the country. And this had a significant impact on how the US approached their initial Afghan information campaign.

As the date for the US invasion neared, I had flag officers and senior civil servants standing over my shoulder as I prepared PowerPoint slides of possible information leaflets and word documents for possible broadcasts through EC 130E Commando Solo (at the time the US military's only airborne psychological and information operations mission platform). It is actually interesting to note that while working on this initial Afghan information campaign, I was told that the initial air operations against al-Qaeda and the Taliban were supposed to commence on Wednesday 3 October 2001. However, because the initial IO leaflets and Commando Solo broadcasts had not been fully produced and vetted, the start of the war was delayed until Sunday 7 October 2001.

I spent the majority of my time developing messages and narratives aimed at the Afghan Pashtun population. While the Taliban at this time were almost exclusively Pashtun, I believed that the key to our information efforts should be directed at winning the trust and confidence of the Pashtuns, especially those rural Pashtuns I expected would eventually be central to our campaign against al-Qaeda and the Taliban. In my opinion, the key to a successful Afghan IO campaign was to separate the rural Pashtun population from the Taliban and their draconian policies. Indeed, I believed that the best way to defeat al-Qaeda as well as the Taliban was to make them "irrelevant" to the Afghan villager.

From my perspective, the Taliban represented a political bastardization of traditional Pashtun village life. While the *Talib* ("seeker of knowledge, or student" in Arabic) has been an important fixture in society ever since Islam was introduced in the seventh century to the area of present-day Afghanistan, they had never been a formal political entity. For centuries Talibs traveled the countryside as ascetics, often living off the land and tithings from Afghan villagers, in search of religious "truth." The Taliban (plural of Talib) would later become an extremely important part of the Afghan social fabric, running religious schools (madrasas), mosques, shrines, and various religious and social services, and serving as Mujahidin when necessary, but the Taliban had never represented an explicit Afghan political movement until 1994. Moreover, the vast majority of the Taliban foot soldiers had lived most, if not all their lives in refugee camps in Pakistan. Many had never spent time in an Afghan village and were not familiar with many of the key aspects of rural Afghan village politics and culture, including *Pashtunwali* (literally the "way of the Pashtun": the unwritten rules that drive and significantly influence a Pashtun's life, honor, and conflict resolution, especially in rural Afghanistan). The violence of the Afghan civil war after the superpowers left Afghanistan, and the criminality of supposed Mujahidin turned warlords who raped, plundered, and extracted from the war-weary Afghan population between 1992 and 1994, resulted in the political formulation of the Taliban, which was not only a reaction to the criminal warlords, but also represented a reactionary *Deobandi* (a revivalist movement within Sunni, primarily Hanafi) Islamist movement. Many of the early Taliban leaders and soldiers had fought the Soviets in the Yunas Khalis' Hezb-e-Islami ("Party of Islam") party (HIK) or *Harakat-i-Inqilab-i-Islami* (Islamic Revolution Movement) led by Mohammad Nabi Mohammadi.

Due to their combination of fundamentalist Deobandi Islam and Pashtunwali, although many of the Taliban's domestic policies were often based on local customs in the guise of religion, not all Taliban policies were locally based. The Taliban's hostility to orchestrated music and Sufism, for example, was in stark contrast to rural Afghan cultural norms and practices. The Taliban also strictly segregated the sexes (known as *purdah*). While this is an established practice throughout much of rural (particularly Pashtun)

Afghanistan, Afghan urbanites, especially Kabulis, were extremely concerned when the Taliban attempted to push the practice onto the whole country.

According to Islamic scholars and legal experts, most of the Taliban, even senior leaders and clerics, lacked even basic understanding of Arabic and Shar'iah law; therefore, the Taliban's legal code did not adhere to the Islamic legal system that many other Islamic governments practiced. Still, in Afghanistan religion had always been an important contributor to political and social decisions, which is why many Afghans embraced the religiously guided Taliban when they first surfaced to fight the corrupt and greedy warlords. I suspected that the eventual Taliban messages and IO would be heavily focused on their religious beliefs and tenets, but I also realized that the US would gain no credibility by trying to respond to their Islamist messaging. I therefore argued with many involved in our Afghan information campaign that we would have to cede such messaging and IO to our eventual Afghan partners. Of course, the Afghan government never seriously did this during the years to come.

By 2001, while the Taliban were relatively successful in pushing their stated policies onto Afghans, they were never successful in creating jobs, creating or maintaining infrastructure, or establishing meaningful ties with the international community. This inability to bring prosperity and hope to the nation, their draconian policies toward women, along with banning traditional Pashtun pastimes (like music, movies, kite flying, the keeping of pigeons, etc.) caused a significant erosion of Afghan support. In light of this, I attempted to develop narratives that played on these facts.

For example, the first leaflet I developed was aimed at the rural Pashtun community (Figure 1.1). It consisted of a picture I found on the Revolutionary Association of the Women of Afghanistan (RAWA) website that depicted a Taliban member of the Committee for the Promotion of Virtue and the Prevention of Vice, or "religious police," who patrolled the urban and some rural areas enforcing Taliban dress codes and other religious, cultural, and moral "edicts," beating a woman with a car antenna for wearing a burka that revealed the woman's ankles. In the forefront of the picture was a young child viewing the beating with fright in his eyes. Under this disturbing picture I wrote a caption that read: "Is this the future you want for your women and children?" On the reverse side of the leaflet was a picture of al-Qaeda members with the caption: "Drive out foreign terrorists."[2] Here I wanted to play on the relatively xenophobic nature of many Afghans[3] and to suggest that the US war was aimed at foreign terrorists rather than the Afghan people.

An Afghan man's honor and pride (*nang*) is intimately tied to how the women of his family are viewed and treated. It is basically unimaginable for an individual outside the immediate Pashtun family to touch a woman, much less hit or beat her, especially in public. This would be in direct and enormous violation of a Pashtun's honor and esteem (*ghariat*), the most important personal values of a Pashtun, and would demand an immediate act of revenge (*badal*) to regain that honor. This was exactly the reaction I was attempting to engender by this IO leaflet, as well as other IO messages I produced.

I developed this leaflet to be used explicitly in Pashtun areas of Afghanistan, but I also believed that the message would resonate with other Afghan populations. A few weeks after the war commenced, the leaflet was reproduced on the front page of the *Washington Times*, where it was presented as the first leaflet dropped into Afghanistan by the US forces.[4] To my frustration, in the caption that I had carefully crafted to head the leaflet in both Pashto and Dari, the Dari was presented above the Pashto text. While this might seem inconsequential, my response was that to present the Dari translation over the Pashto on the leaflet and then drop it into Pashtun areas was a significant faux pas. "Pashtunwali presents an ethnic self-portrait of the Pashtuns according to which the Pashtuns are distinct from other ethnic groups not only due to their language, history and culture, but also due to their behaviour."[5] Pashtuns take their Pashto language very seriously, and presenting it in a way that appeared to make Pashto "subservient" to Dari was a major blunder. Indeed, presenting a Dari translation on the leaflet, in and of itself, was a major mistake in my view. The leaflet was explicitly developed to be used in rural, predominantly Pashtun areas of eastern and southern Afghanistan. While possibly relevant, I never felt it would be a successful messaging instrument in non-Pashtun areas.

Many have questioned the utility of using leaflets at all in Afghanistan, because of the high illiteracy rates. I was well aware that the literacy rates for the rural Pashtun in the areas I expected the leaflet to be dropped—eastern and southern Afghanistan—was low (5 to 10 per cent), but I expected those literate members of a particular Pashtun village to read it to other community members. This is very similar to how *shabnamah* or "night letters" as well as other types of written information have been delivered to Pashtun communities in these areas for generations. Moreover, I wanted to produce leaflets that could tell a "story" through their visual presentation alone. I believed this leaflet accomplished that goal.

In Fall 2002, I met with a Special Forces ODA team sergeant who had been deployed to southern Afghanistan and we talked about my experience work-

Figure 1.1: Leaflet designed by the author[6]

ing on IO products; he presented me with the actual leaflet that I had designed and was dropped into the country. To my amazement, he claimed that he had personally witnessed Taliban members scooping up the leaflet soon after it was dropped from US aircraft and burning it. I viewed this as an indirect metric that the message I was attempting to send via the leaflet and its narrative was a success. If the Taliban were committed to destroying it, I assumed that it was sending a message which they did not want heard in the Pashtun villages.[7]

My experiences working in OSD on Afghan messaging and narratives heightened my interest in the role of messaging and propaganda generally in Afghanistan. They were also the initial impetus for this book. Over the next few years I gathered responses from numerous students at the Naval Postgraduate School where I teach: when they returned from Afghan deployments they had interesting information and stories to tell, not only about US messaging but also about the Taliban's use of a variety of tools and instruments to influence the thinking and emotions of the Afghan rural population.

Purely on the mechanical or process side of Information Operations, I was told of the significant confusion between IO, Psychological Operations (PSYOP), and Military Information Support Operations (MISO). In the US military, the role of an Information Operations team is to "integrate, synchronize, employ, and assess a wide variety of information-related capabilities."[8] Thus, IO's function is coordinating and facilitating, not doing; unfortunately, throughout the US government, this is a confused topic (there are numerous examples of secretaries of defense, general officers, commanders, and other key personnel routinely using the terms IO, PSYOP, MISO interchangeably). This confusion and misunderstanding of roles impacts on mission effectiveness, particularly that of PSYOP/MISO.[9]

The basic and significant issue becomes unity of messaging and effort. The Taliban do not separate messaging functions: their influence operations/propaganda/strategic messengers, as will be seen below, are often the same people, but this is not necessarily the norm. The US military (and more frequently the Taliban) separate those functions into specialties, and the IO officer's job is to coordinate and synchronize those efforts along with the other capabilities under IO. This sounds good in theory, but it is extremely complicated in practice. Every US Brigade Combat Team (BCT), and the echelon above, have information efforts: they are independently planned and run by each individual unit's IO officer/team; therefore by default the efforts are not synchronized. This is not the case with most Taliban messaging, which is highly coordinated in relative terms. For example, Taliban mullahs regularly coordinate their *khutba* (Friday sermons) in Loya Kandahar.[10] Further confusing the issue is that capabilities under IO, specifically MISO, require very high levels of mission/messaging approval. MISO/PSYOP personnel are trained in this approval process, and US military personnel are also trained to conduct MISO missions. IO officers are not trained to do either, because they are not supposed to be involved; but that does not stop commanders from attempting to task IO officers with messaging, and it does not stop some IO officers from attempting to message. These IO officers might know the target audience's culture and behavioral patterns very well and might create a product that effectively influences behavior; but there is no way for DOD to know that, because the IO officer is not trained to do any of this.

The culmination of this confusion is in DOD officers' training and understanding of influence activities. The vast majority of DOD personnel, even the highest ranking, receive little to no training on the different roles and responsibilities of IO and PSYOP/MISO. Many times, commanders just hear an IO officer say, "Yes, sir/ma'am, we can message this now," and the PSYOP officer says "Well, sir/ma'am, we need to get authority; ensure that this message does not conflict with other messaging in the area, and is approved." Commanders do not necessarily understand the process; they just understand that their mission is not occurring as they want it to. The Department of the Army is now including some additional IO/PSYOP training at the CGSC in Fort Leavenworth, but this is just one component—and the other components receive even less training.[11]

How are military commanders supposed to use weapons/tools correctly if they are not trained in them, if they do not understand the artifacts' roles, and they are routinely mislabeled? As suggested above, and will be elaborated in the further chapters of this book, the Taliban, as well as other Afghan insurgents, for the most part do not face these process or organizational problems. As we shall see, while some Taliban information operations or propaganda are highly centralized and controlled by explicit Taliban organizations, much of this information is decentralized to local commanders and is highly dispersed.

I have also interacted with Naval Postgraduate School students holding explicit and valuable information concerning the Taliban's information campaign. In 2005 one of my students while deployed in Afghanistan had compiled a sizeable collection of Taliban night letters or *shabnamah*. For decades the Taliban and the anti-Soviet Mujahidin before them had used this messaging instrument to instruct and threaten Afghan villagers. I immediately started to collect Taliban night letters through field research and other means and to analyze their explicit messages and narratives. Chapter 5 presents a discussion of the importance of Taliban night letters and an examination of some of the narratives and stories portrayed. Appendix B (available online at www.hurstpublishers.com/book/taliban-narratives) presents a summary of hundreds of night letters across a variety of variables (producer, target audience, message, etc.) to help engender further research concerning this long-tested and frequently-used Afghan messaging technique.

In addition to Afghan field research, I also collected a variety of Taliban messages and narratives while I served in 2009 as a Senior Political and Counterinsurgency Advisor to General Jonathan Vance, Commander of Canadian Forces in Afghanistan (now Canadian Army Chief of Staff). During this time I collected Taliban *taranas* (poetic chants), poetry, DVDs, periodicals, and text messages. I later gathered data on Taliban messaging through Facebook, Twitter, and YouTube. Much of this data will be discussed in the chapters that follow.

My introduction to *taranas* was especially interesting. In Fall 2008, I was interviewing Taliban and Kandahari tribal elders in a hotel in downtown Kandahar. During a break in one of my sessions, I visited the small hotel lobby and witnessed people "blue-toothing" information between cell phones. On further enquiry, I was informed that people were sending Taliban chants/"music" to each other's cell phones. I later found out that this was a regular exercise in southern Afghanistan (Loya Kandahar), but to my surprise I found no NATO/ISAF or US military personnel who had any idea or knowledge of this practice! In fact, I found that the US and its allies were totally ignorant of this Taliban messaging technique. I asked numerous US and Allied PSYOP and IO officers and found that no one had even heard of Taliban *taranas*. Chapter 7 offers an analysis of selected Taliban examples.

The majority of the research presented in this book was conducted over the years 2004–11. During most of these years I conducted considerable field research in eastern and southern Afghanistan, focusing on Taliban messaging. While some might argue that the data and analyses presented in this book are dated, I would vigorously argue that Taliban messaging has not changed significantly over the intervening years and that the findings presented here are still valid and have important implications for US and Kabul policies.

Many of the findings from these research field trips mentioned above will be elaborated in the chapters below, but a number of these findings need to be described in more detail to help present a context for what is to follow.[12]

A central thesis of this book is that information operations and their related stories and narratives should ultimately drive both an insurgent's and counter-insurgent's operations and policies. While data gathered and interviews conducted during my research trips clearly suggested that this was the case for the Taliban, we found that this was not true for the United States, the Afghan government (GIRoA, Government of the Islamic Republic of Afghanistan) or their NATO/ISAF allies. We found that US IO and PSYOP messages were generally too broad and not focused on Afghan cultural nuances, such as Pashtunwali. In contrast, the Taliban's messages are precise, focused and localized, recognizing political and social cleavages in Afghanistan. There is no question that Afghan local politics and the local disposition of the people in the area are very important and that the Taliban play on these dynamics in their messaging.

The Taliban claim patience among their attributes, and impatience among the NATO vanities. They speak of fighting for generations as an honor and a reward from Allah. In fact, this is a common trope of Taliban stories. This is an especially troubling dynamic for Kabul and the international forces. Religious rhetoric is a seemingly important tactical option in the IO campaign that the US and its allies should not have completely relinquished to the insurgents (such rhetoric probably represents 90 per cent of the Taliban's IO battle space).

Another important IO dynamic that was identified by many Afghans we interviewed was that the Taliban are effective at influencing civilians simply due to their daily interaction with people. Mullahs preach about people's daily problems face-to-face and provide an emotional context that resonates with the rural Afghans. Radio programs and billboards—regular US and Afghan government IO instruments—can never have the same effect as such a truly effective whisper campaign. Direct engagement with the population is an extremely significant factor which obviously plays upon the strong Afghan tradition of oral history. Additionally, many Taliban fighters are locals, which of course makes it easier for them to empathize with people because they know the language and culture, as opposed to the international forces' distanced approach. Furthermore, the ability of the Taliban to establish shadow governments and a semi-permanent presence in some areas also helps promote their message. The Taliban have been successful at enforcing justice and Shar'iah law, while highlighting the government's inability to impose law and order. The result is that the local populations are increasingly turning to Taliban courts because they are viewed as more effective and fair when compared to the corrupt official system.[13]

Taliban and insurgent forces have exploited the presence of communication technologies, such as cell phones and text, photo and video imaging capabilities, to expedite the speed of their message transmission. Insurgent websites, such as the Islamic Emirate of Afghanistan (Taliban website) (http://www.alemarah1.org/english1/) and the joint Hezb-e-Islami (Khalis)–Tora Bora Military Front (http://toorabora.com/Pokhto/Filmona/konar.34.htm) were important operating websites during our field research. Each site posted news, battle reports, interviews, commentaries, and the Tora Bora website had five video clips posted, including one that showed a rocket strike against an American CH-47 helicopter in Kunar province. The Tora Bora website also had a significant portion of warrior poetry posted, which is further evidence that the Taliban and other militants were utilizing and exploiting cultural norms to enhance their IO–PSYOP capabilities. This is discussed in detail in the chapters that follow.

The Taliban websites, which are available in several languages at any given time,[14] have taken on an increased sophistication (visually). This was most noticeable in the English version of the sites, which now feature colorful banners and relevant photographs attached to "featured" news reports. The websites are updated several times a day and change URLs frequently to avoid long-term disruption from Western cyber attacks.

In conclusion, let me suggest that a central assumption and a major finding of the research reported here is that the Taliban has won the information war against the US Coalition and the Afghan government. The Taliban's messaging, as will be demonstrated below, is concise, to the point, and uses an effective information discipline that is in tune with the target audiences they wish to influence. Much of their messaging is also supported and funded by the Pakistani military, especially the Inter-Services Intelligence (ISI) directorate. The US as well as their Kabul allies, on the other hand, have blundered greatly in their messaging by basically failing to present narratives and stories that resonate or can be understood by their targeted audiences.

In other words, the United States and its allies have lost the "battle of the story" in Afghanistan. Despite its conventional and technological superiority, the US military lost the battle for the most valuable terrain of all, the trust and confidence of the Afghans themselves; much less their "hearts and minds," that we never had a chance of winning in the first place. Moreover, and intimately connected to the Taliban information campaign, the US and Afghan government have failed to meet the rural Afghan population's basic expectations of improving their lives through good governance and effective security, stabilization, transition, and reconstruction efforts. And this has proved fatal in a war that turned out to be primarily a Taliban rural insurgency wrapped in the narrative of jihad. The Taliban quickly learned how to wage a sophisticated and effective information campaign against the "crusader" invaders and the Afghan "puppet" regime. This was in stark contrast with the initial view of the Taliban in 2001 as a bumbling, technologically backward enemy with few connections with the Afghan people. The Taliban have proved to have an adept understanding of guerrilla warfare strategy and tactics in which "the guerrilla fighter is primarily a propagandist, an agitator, a disseminator of the revolutionary idea, who uses the struggle itself as an instrument of agitation."[15]

While primarily assessing the messaging, delivery means, and central narratives and stories of Afghan insurgents, especially the Taliban and Hezb-e-Islami Gulbuddin Hekmatyar (HIG), this book also assesses US PSYOP and IO operations and compares them to the Taliban's campaign. In my briefs to senior officials responsible for US information and PSYOP operations over the last fifteen years, I have suggested that we include in our messaging allusions to Afghan poetry, folktales, legends, and oral traditions—essentially the kind of sources that the Taliban use in their information operations—but I was basically or at least implicitly told that this was "too hard." Such a response and position, I believe, is one of the central reasons why our efforts were unsuccessful in Afghanistan. We ultimately proved too "lazy" to develop Afghan-resonating stories and narratives that could have complemented our operations and policies in the country.

Finally, let me suggest that many of the analyses presented in this book are extremely relevant to information operations that could be conducted against the Islamic State in Iraq and al-Sham (ISIS), who have adopted a sophisticated information campaign. There is no doubt that the Islamic State militants produce an abundance of highly professional, crafted propaganda in the form of narratives that advertise not only the unforgiving brutality of their operations but also the promise of an "idyllic, pure Muslim life" in areas under its control. They have become masters at producing and disseminating videos, photos, music, messages on social media, electronic magazines, and newspapers to a civilian population living in every Islamic State-held territory. The importance of their messaging is clearly evidenced when the *Washington Post* reports that "senior media operatives [of ISIS] are treated as 'emirs' of equal rank to their military counterparts. They are directly involved in decisions on strategy and territory. They preside over hundreds of videographers, producers and editors who form a privileged, professional class with status, salaries and living arrangements that are the envy of ordinary fighters."[16] The development of counter-narratives is critical to defeating ISIS, and this book suggests some of the ways in which this could be achieved.

In the Acknowledgments section, I name scores of people who have made this book possible; I alone, however, am responsible for any errors in fact or judgment.

1

INTRODUCTION

"Wars today cannot be won without media. Media aims at the heart rather than the body, [and] if the heart is defeated, the battle is won."

Alemarah or the *Voice of Jihad* (Taliban official website),
editor Abdul Satar Maiwandi[1]

"The Muslim community is a subtle world we don't fully—and don't always attempt to—understand. Only through a shared appreciation of the people's culture, needs, and hopes for the future can we hope ourselves to supplant the extremist narrative. We cannot capture hearts and minds. We must engage them; we must listen to them, one heart and one mind at a time—over time."

US Navy Admiral, Michael G. Mullen, Chairman of the Joint Chiefs of Staff, 2009[2]

"When I took a decision or adopted an alternative, it was after studying every relevant—and many an irrelevant—factor. Geography, tribal structure, religion, social customs, language, appetites, standards—all were at my finger-ends. The enemy I knew almost like my own side."

T. E. Lawrence (Lawrence of Arabia)[3]

"The medium is the message."

Marshall McLuhan[4]

Throughout the history of warfare, armed groups have organized, recruited, and extended the duration of conflict by tapping into a myriad of socio-economic grievances, ethno-cultural values, customs, and tropes to help unify their ranks and cultivate powerful doctrines able to withstand opposing efforts to break warrior morale and spirit. The conscious and sometimes sub-conscious effort by armed groups to create and maintain this arsenal of cultural ammunition, referred to here as "narratives," plays an essential part in combat, directly influencing the level of morale, *esprit de corps*, and honor among warriors. The trend of implementing narratives to tap into reservoirs of culture and manpower, especially among contemporary rural-based insurgencies as seen in Iraq, Syria, Burma, and Afghanistan, has largely been misunderstood and under-analyzed.

The primary purpose of this book is to assess the information operations and associated narratives and stories of Afghan insurgents: especially the Taliban and to a lesser extent Hezb-e-Islami Gulbuddin Hekmatyar (HIG), two distinct Afghan insurgent/jihadist organizations.[5] A secondary, but more implicit research goal is to suggest why the Taliban have been so much more efficient and effective in presenting messages that resonate with the Afghan population than have the United States, the Afghan government, and their allies. Chapter 10 explicitly assesses the information and PSYOP campaigns of the United States and compares them to those conducted by the Taliban.

Franz Boas, an early-twentieth-century German cultural anthropologist, suggested that culture, which is intimately related to a society's narratives, is "the system of shared beliefs, values, customs, behaviours, and artifacts that the members of society use to cope with their world and with one another, and that are transmitted from generation to generation through learning."[6] This definition highlights several important concepts that will be central to the assessment of the stories and narratives of the Taliban:[7] first, culture is the shared belief of a self-identified group of people, such as the Taliban; second, culture has a psychological component as well as material manifestations (such as produced artifacts); and third, culture is essentially adaptive and is transmitted through certain processes to others. This operationalization of culture suggests the importance of artifacts as instruments used to transmit Taliban worldviews, or to borrow David Edwards' terminology: the underlying structure of the Taliban's[8] "moral systems" as portrayed by narratives.[9]

A narrative often represents a kind, or series, of "story(ies)" and reflects foundational beliefs that articulate a group's views toward the world. As Turner notes, a "[s]tory is a basic principle of mind. Most of our experience, our knowledge, and our thinking are organized as stories."[10] This is true for peaceful citizens as well as violent insurgents and jihadists. There is ample evidence that such artifacts have an effect on our capacity to recall events, to motivate our action, to modulate our emotional reactions to events, to cue certain heuristics and biases, to structure our problem-solving capabilities, and ultimately to influence our very identity: the underlying structure of the Taliban's "moral systems" referred to above, as portrayed by narratives.[11]

Stories are the "frames" of the narrative or moral systems of a culture or group of people. As well as Turner's insights,[12] there is further abundant literature on this concept.[13] The framing of stories associated with narratives has a critical importance as to how Taliban messages resonate to greater or lesser degrees with target audiences.[14]

To help us understand the gravity of enemy narratives, messages, strategies, and their methods of implementation, this book will present research and analysis on the narratives developed and utilized by Afghan insurgent groups. Throughout the analyses presented, we will attempt to reveal the explicit "story" of the Afghan insurgent information operation artifacts. To do so, I spent many years gathering a plethora of insurgent propaganda material, including statements, *shabnamah* (night letters), websites, publications, DVDs and video segments, insurgent "symbols," and audio files such as insurgent-inspired music and poetry of the Taliban and, to a lesser degree, HIG. In areas where appropriate, examples of other conflict narratives and stories will be used to help provide insight into the powerful use of genres like mythology, lure, music, legends, and poetry in a conflict environment. Efforts have been made to research, analyze, and recommend particular cultural legends and myths within an Afghan-centric framework.[15]

It is important to understand how insurgents in Afghanistan identify themselves, putting aside the obvious limitations of studying their self-produced information materials; it is useful to observe how insurgents attempt to bolster their legitimacy and promote recruitment efforts and community influence. Uncovering how groups such as the Taliban, a decentralized, primarily but not exclusively Pashtun, organization whose roots originate in the southern province of Kandahar, recruit and promote themselves becomes critical, especially as insurgent groups begin to expand and operate in non-traditional battlefields across Afghanistan.[16] Equally important is how such groups can garner support for activities such as IED-emplacement and explosive acquisition through similar messaging campaigns.[17]

An important goal of this book[18] is the assessment of narratives, stories, and associated strategies that the Afghan Taliban have employed to garner support from the Afghan people. To uncover how Afghan insurgent groups tap this wellspring of influence, the research presented here will assess how the Taliban have framed (or "reframed") their ideology post-2001 and what this means for their movement, its organizational structure, and its strategic imperatives. This has allowed for further investigation into the Taliban's message campaign and discovering the power of the stories repeated by them. This research basically seeks to understand what makes Taliban narratives, as well as their stories, resonate with their target audience: the Afghan, especially rural Pashtun, population.

The research presented here also has direct policy relevance to ongoing conflicts in Syria, Iraq, and other conflict regions, by providing a fresh lens for analyzing and ultimately countering insurgent/jihadist narratives. By shedding light on Taliban rhetorical techniques, the research implicitly provides a "style guide" of sorts for constructing counter-narratives that should "connect" with target audiences. In assessing Taliban narratives, this research will attempt to answer several broad questions, including:

1. Do Taliban narratives and stories provide an insight into the conceptual metaphors and other rhetorical techniques that are common in Afghanistan?
2. Does an analysis of Taliban narratives reveal some of the major contours of the Afghan/Taliban (Pashtun) worldview?

Narratives and stories: some theoretical considerations

It is apt to begin this book on Afghan narratives by addressing the basic question of what makes a good narrative. Due to the importance of stories to a group's narrative, it is important to understand what makes a good story. Who better to answer this question than accomplished practitioners of the art of storytelling? Fortunately, many successful writers have recorded their thoughts on this matter. Anthony Trollope, the nineteenth-century British novelist whose autobiography was published posthumously in 1883, argues that "stories charm us, not simply because they are tragic, but because we feel that men and women with flesh and blood, creatures with whom we can sympathize, are struggling amidst their woes."[19] Stephen King strikes a similar chord in his book *On Writing*:

> Book-buyers ... want a good story to take with them on the airplane, something that will first fascinate them, then pull them in and keep them turning the pages. This happens, I think, when readers recognize the people in a book, their behaviors, their surroundings, and their talk. When the reader hears strong echoes of his or her own life and beliefs, he or she is apt to become more invested in the story.[20]

Catherine Ann Jones, a successful playwright and screenwriter,[21] offers the following observation: "Stories written by formulas rarely move us, and consequently fail. They are too generic, not about specific people. This is why true stories are so popular. Knowing the story is true, that it really happened to someone, means it could happen to you."[22]

Annette Simmons, who specializes in group dynamics in the workplace, has written a number of books that focus on the goals and proficiencies of interpersonal communications. In her book *The Story Factor*[23] she persuasively argues how stories demonstrate authenticity, build emotional connections, inspire perseverance, and stimulate the imagination. Nestled in the middle of this book is an absolute gem of a chapter called "The Psychology of Story's Influence." In this chapter Simmons articulates what she calls "the physics of story." She argues that stories are particularly powerful tools of persuasion because they allow you to "tap into your listener's momentum." It is a strategy of pulling instead of pushing; a push strategy "creates another push back." (In other words, it creates resistance.) The goal is to get your audience pulling with you, to create a win–win situation: "Most methods of influence introduce a power struggle where one—influencer or influence—'wins' and the other 'loses.' Story has a quality of graciousness that bypasses power struggles."

A common thread that emerges from the writings of these accomplished storytellers is this: stories will connect if they are about seemingly real people, convincing characters with whom the reader can identify. The Taliban, however, are not writing novels or screenplays; it would be more apt to say that they are producing propaganda and influence documents. According to Garth Jowett and Victoria O'Donnell, "Propaganda is the deliberate and systematic attempt to shape perceptions, manipulate cognitions, and direct behavior to achieve a response that furthers the desired intent of the propagandist."[24] In their book *Propaganda and Persuasion*, Jowett and O'Donnell propose a "ten-step plan of propaganda analysis [that] includes":[25]

1. The ideology and purpose of the propaganda campaign.
2. The context in which the propaganda occurs.
3. Identification of the propagandist.
4. The structure of the propaganda organization.
5. The target audience.
6. Media utilization techniques.
7. Special techniques used to maximize effect.
8. Audience reaction to various techniques.
9. Counterpropaganda (if present).
10. Effects and evaluation.

Many of these variables will be used in our analysis of Taliban narratives and stories.

Some Taliban messaging artifacts, especially night letters, contain historical narratives designed to be read aloud to Afghans who cannot read themselves.[26] Therefore, it makes sense to view them, in part, as speeches. In the introduction to his anthology *Lend Me Your Ears: Great Speeches in History*, former White House speechwriter William Safire offers "ten steps to a great speech": welcome, structure, pulse, occasion/forum, focus, purpose, phrase, quotation, theme, and delivery. The third step, pulse, is worth further mention. According to Safire, "A good speech has a beat, a changing rhythm, a sense of movement that gets the audience tapping its mind's foot... If there is one technique that orators down the ages have agreed to use, it's anaphora, the repeated beginning."[27] This raises the possibility of analyzing the Taliban propaganda—night letters, statements, poems, music—with an eye to cataloging the various rhetorical devices employed. In this vein, this book will examine Taliban poems, songs/chants, and other types of media.

One common rhetorical device is the use of metaphor. Colorful metaphors are often used to embellish the written and spoken word. George Lakoff and Mark Turner have written extensively about the role of metaphor in human cognitive processes. In their classic study entitled *Metaphors We Live By*, they assert: "Our ordinary conceptual system, in terms of which we both think and act, is fundamentally metaphorical in nature."[28] Lakoff and Johnson introduce the useful concept of the "conceptual metaphor," one example being "argument is war." In other words, the language we typically use when discussing argumentation is the language we use when discussing war. Other cultures might have a different conceptual metaphor for argument:

> Imagine a culture where an argument is viewed as a dance, the participants are seen as performers, and the goal is to perform in a balanced and aesthetically pleasing way. In such a culture, people would view arguments differently, experience them differently, carry them out differently, and talk about them differently... Perhaps the most neutral way of describing this difference between their culture and ours would be to say that we have a discourse from structured in terms of battle and they have one structured in terms of dance.[29]

Understanding the conceptual metaphors used by the Taliban and other insurgent and jihadist groups can provide a window into their worldview and can also facilitate replication of their common patterns of thought and discourse in a counter-narrative strategy.

Aristotle's *Rhetoric* is a logical place to turn for further information about rhetorical techniques. William Casebeer (citing an unpublished research paper by Thomas Coakley) makes use of concepts from this classic text:

> *Ethos:* these are appeals the speaker makes to the audience to establish credibility. Essentially, ethos is what a speaker uses—implicitly or explicitly—to ensure that the audience can trust him or her. An example in advertising is an athlete endorsing an athletic product. In war, examples include a history of adherence to law of armed conflict (LOAC) and an assertiveness of willpower.

> *Pathos:* these are appeals the speaker makes to the audience's emotions. An example of this would be an advertisement for tires that emphasizes safety by portraying an infant cradled within the circle of the tire. In war, pathos might be displayed by showing the "average" guy on the adversary's side that the US position is better.

> *Logos:* these are appeals to facts. More doctors recommend toothpaste X than any other brand. In war, there is no greater logic than firepower, but as insurgencies demonstrated throughout the 20th Century, firepower (logos) alone will not win wars, and will win very few arguments.[30]

Casebeer posits seven "narrative strategic principles" as a starting point for narrative analysis. Aristotle is at the heart of the third principle:

> Considerations of ethos, logos and pathos are simplistic. But they are better than not bothering to evaluate the storyline at all. Relative to a target population, an "E/L/P analysis" can provide a baseline for predicting and controlling narrative flow over the course of a conflict.[31]

Patrick Hogan's book on *The Mind and its Stories* presents four hypotheses:

1. "Emotive terms are prototype-based in both eliciting conditions and expressive/actional consequences."[32]
2. "Prototypical narratives—including literary narratives—are generated largely from prototypes, prominently including the prototype eliciting conditions for emotions."[33]
3. "Romantic union and social or political power (including material prosperity) are the two predominant prototypes for eliciting conditions of happiness."[34]
4. "Cross-culturally, there are two prominent structures of literary narrative, romantic and heroic tragi-comedy, derived respectively from the personal and social prototypes for happiness."[35]

In the seventh chapter of *The Mind and its Stories*, "The Structure of Stories: Some General Principles of Plot," Hogan argues that plots are typically "telic" in nature. That is, they "involve a person and a goal."[36] They also have a "causal sequence connecting the agent's various actions with the achievement or non-achievement of the goal."[37]

Donald Polkinghorne provides a complementary perspective. In *Narrative Knowing and the Human Sciences*, Polkinghorne's central argument is "that narrative is a scheme by means of which human beings give meaning to their experience of temporality and personal actions."[38] Polkinghorne suggests:

> Narrative meaning functions to give form to the understanding of a purpose to life and to join everyday actions and events into episodic units. It provides a framework for understanding the past events of one's life and for planning future actions. It is the primary scheme by means of which human existence is rendered meaningful.[39]

Narrative and audiences

Ruston defines a "narrative" as:

> a system of stories that hang together and provide a coherent view of the world. People use narratives to understand how their world works. Narratives contain patterns that fit the data of everyday life (events, people, actions, sequences of actions, messages, and so on), explaining how events unfold over time and how one thing causes another.[40]

It is important to distinguish the terms "narrative" and "messaging." Simply put, "narratives" are a system of cognitive standards within which "messages" are interpreted. For example, American IO Afghan messages make perfect sense to Americans because they are framed within an American narrative that reflects American values. In order to message an Afghan audience effectively, however, messages must be crafted in a way that resonates with Afghans' *own* narratives and stories. This requires an intimate knowledge of the target culture and norms. The Taliban had and have an inherent advantage over the US and its allies, because they craft messages on their "home turf" and with Afghan narratives.

Corman et al. identify two messaging models that were relevant to the information campaign in Afghanistan. From the time of the Cold War, the United States has utilized what is known as the "message influence" model. In this model, one "mind" attempts to influence another "mind" using a series of messages. The goal of the "transmitting mind" is to make the "receiving mind" understand the information in the same way as the originator. Failure of the "receiver" to interpret the message correctly is attributed to noise sources that cause distortion in the message transmission.[41]

An important implication of the message influence approach to communicating is that noise can generally be overcome by either minimizing noise or by *repetition* of the message until it is perceived "correctly." A major problem with this model is that "meaning cannot simply be transferred, like a letter mailed from point A to point B."[42]

This notion about message repetition is especially apt for the Taliban information campaign. Throughout the chapters that follow, the reader will find many narratives and stories presented time and time again. The reason for this repetition bordering at times on monotony is because the Taliban are consistently playing on tropes that most Afghans, but not all Afghans, readily accept; moreover, they represent mechanisms that correlate with Polkinghorne's central argument that stories and narratives represent an attempt to give meaning and relevance to an Afghan's life and actions. Stories are always interpreted within a persistent structure of norms and beliefs (narratives) that will affect the ways that stories and messages are interpreted.

There is an abundance of research that suggests that messages and stories are much more effective when repeated:

> Psychological studies have suggested that repetition can have a positive effect on someone's reception of and agreement with a persuasive argument. J. T. Cachiappo and Richard Petty[43] were two pioneers in this field in the late 1970s and 1980s. They concluded that low to moderate levels of repetition within a message tend to create greater agreement with the message, along with greater recall.[44]

Corman et al.'s second model is known as the "pragmatic complexity model." Rather than focusing on messaging and repetition, this model seeks to alter the fundamental structure of interpretation (the "narrative") among the receivers. In this model, fewer messages are preferred, and actions that undermine the existing narrative are more important. Rather than repetition, messages should vary on a central strategic theme and exploit the nuances and cultural opportunities in the target audience.

Information Operations (IO) and PSYOP

This book focuses on the Information Operations (IO) and PSYOP of both sides in the conflict: both the Taliban and other Afghan insurgents, as well as the US. Hence, it is useful to introduce a few salient points about IO and PSYOP.

The critical challenge for IO and PSYOP programs is to persuade a target audience to engage in a particular behavior that may or may not be culturally normative. IO and PSYOP often use persuasion during situations where "behavior has been modified by symbolic transactions (messages) that are sometimes, but not always linked with coercive force (indirectly coercive) and that appeal to the reason and emotions of the person(s) being persuaded."[45] Persuasion attempts to win the "hearts and mind," or as we prefer the "trust and confidence," of the target audience. These programs frequently rely on the power of verbal and non-verbal symbols and depend heavily on the credibility of threats and promises made by the communicator.[46] When individuals are induced to abandon one set of behaviors and to adopt another, it can be said they were successfully (or unsuccessfully) persuaded.[47] This is the definitive goal of IO and PSYOP.

H. C. Kelman wrote an important article on persuasion which describes the concept of means control as a situation where the persuader is successful because of his or her ability to dispense rewards or punishments.[48] Persuasion pivots on the relative impact of messages. It relies on symbolic transactions between message sender and receiver.

Within the non-verbal realm, there is often room for disagreement as to whether a persuasive act was symbolic.[49] This fact can be exacerbated within an IO or PSYOP campaign that is conducted among a population with extremely low literacy rates and whose non-verbal behavior may differ from that of the communicator; and this is the predominant situation in Afghanistan. Language is a critical part of a persuasive transaction, with non-verbal behavior serving to reinforce or give credence to the verbal messages.[50] There are subtle nuances buried within the linguistics of every culture that can work to a persuader's advantage if he can master the inflective architecture of a foreign tongue. As we shall see in Chapter 10, this was a significant challenge for US efforts in Afghanistan.

Coercive persuasion was a term coined by Edgar Schein after his study of Chinese POW indoctrination. He defined coercive persuasion as "producing ideological and behavioral changes in a fully conscious, mentally intact individual."[51] Another definition of coercive persuasion is offered by Martyn Carruthers: "Coercive persuasion attempts to force people to change beliefs, ideas, attitudes or behaviors using psychological pressure, undue influence, threats, anxiety, intimidation and/or under stress. It is often called mind control and brainwashing."[52] Although most instances of persuasion in IO and PSYOP are not intended to be coercive, nevertheless incorrect or irresponsible messaging techniques can result in coercive communication and intimidate or create fear in the receiver.

IO and PSYOP persuasion efforts often revolve around response-shaping and changing processes. The concept of attitude becomes an intervening variable in the persuasion equation and is often confused with behavior. Attitude is just one factor of the behavior equation. There are two other fundamental variables that are often overlooked or marginalized: the concepts of values and belief. The trifecta of attitude, values, and belief are inseparable, and a change to one element will affect another and have some impact on behavioral outcomes.[53] Attitudes are often unstable and fluid; they can change simply during the process of thinking.[54] Attitudes affect persuasion in four major ways: the orienting of attention to a message; how extensively a message is processed; whether the message is processed in a biased manner; and the resulting behavior (which can be either deliberative or spontaneous).[55] For example, people are more likely to give their attention to something to which they already have an accessible attitude, and so ultimately influence behavior around that object.[56]

Another important concept in IO and PSYOP is "perception management," which includes all actions used to influence attitudes and objective reasoning in foreign audiences. Perception management is also a significant aspect of public diplomacy, PSYOP, Public Information, Deception and Covert Action.[57]

There are four overarching PSYOP objectives of the US in Afghanistan: to isolate the Taliban and other Afghan insurgents from domestic and international support; to reduce the effectiveness of the Taliban and others' forces; to deter escalation by Taliban leadership; and to minimize collateral damage and interference with US operations.[58] In order to obtain these goals, PSYOP must influence behavior. Messages can be aimed at neutral or friendly parties or adversaries, but in all instances IO and PSYOP should project strategic influence.[59] Hence IO and PSYOP attempt to leverage influence to reinforce, reinterpret, or shape foreign perceptions of the US's character and actions.[60] This intent to influence and shape perceptions is very difficult, and for the most part has been only modestly effective for the US, as we shall see below.[61] The Taliban, on the other hand, have been very effective.

Propaganda obviously plays a large role in IO and PSYOP. Propaganda is a specific type of message aimed directly at influencing opinions of people rather than impartially providing information. The word "propaganda" is translated from Latin to mean "things which must be disseminated." The concept of propaganda has acquired a negative connotation referring to false or misleading information. It does not necessarily need to be the case, but incomplete, poorly reasoned or unbalanced perspectives can have negative impacts on the message purveyor. The volume of information also contributes to the reputation of propaganda that usually contains a political message; a propagandist wants the message heard in as many places as possible and as often as possible in order to drown out alternative ideas or reinforce an idea through repetition.

Communications and media literature

To be effective, media like IO and PSYOP must present cohesive messages. In order to be "effective," the media must use proper language that resonates with its target audience. As suggested above with IO and PSYOP, to be effectual media must frame narratives with "stories."[62] Readers who perceive a media story to have a positive slant will usually assume a positive disposition toward that issue. The same applies to stories with a negative slant: readers will adopt a negative disposition and assume that the rest of the public has a negative disposition toward that topic).[63]

Petty, Priester, and Brinol present an instructive "Elaboration Likelihood Model of Persuasion," which argues how media can ignite attitude change.[64] Their main premise is that "it is not the amount or direction of the information per se that produces persuasion, but rather, people's idiosyncratic reactions to this information."[65] As we shall see below, this corresponds closely to the Taliban IO strategy, when they exploited premises of Afghan narratives such as Pashtunwali, and the typical Afghan's view of a proud history of repelling invaders as an integrated tactic to help define many Afghans' perceptions of their environs. Hence, an effective message needs to alter people's "psychological barriers"[66] to the information, rather than merely increasing the amount of exposure to the content. Through cognitive dissonance, people are naturally inclined to warp new, incoming information in a way that suits their previous disposition. Thus, there is a need to prevent cognitive dissonance from occurring, so that people will not be inclined to warp the message which the source is sending. The media or any message purveyor, such as the Taliban, needs to "reinforce a people's already existing attitudes rather than producing new ones."[67]

Petty, Priester, and Brinol suggest that there are five independent variables (or "inputs to the persuasion process") that the media can control:

• Source
• Message (can appeal to logos or pathos)

- Recipient (can be of any level of intellectual prowess, regardless of their cultural or ideological background)
- Channel
- Context (where the message is presented).[68]

Many of these same variables will be used to assess the effectiveness of Taliban as well as US IO and PSYOP.

A central argument of the media persuasion literature is that after there has been an attitude change, for a behavioral change to occur the subject must pull this newly consolidated information from memory and act on it. But for this behavior to stick (i.e. for it to be repeated), there cannot be any negative reactions or negative environmental factors presented post-behavioral action; there must be positive reinforcement for the new attitude and behavioral change to persist into future situations. These points seem very relevant to the Taliban messaging campaign, in part because rural Afghanistan is a "memory-based" society.

Conclusion

The research presented in this book conceives of an insurgency and counter-insurgency as primarily an information war supported by military kinetics or actions. It will be argued that the warring side with the best resonating story or narrative has a tremendous "leg up" on its opponent and will probably win or at least stalemate the conflict. A stalemate for an insurgent, according to Mao, is basically a victory.[69] The purpose of this chapter was to present a series of theoretical considerations especially relevant to what makes a "good" story and narrative. These theoretical considerations will be used both implicitly and explicitly to assess the inherent values of Taliban information messaging and operations. In so doing, this book will examine a wide variety of Taliban information strategies and actual artifacts. Most of these artifacts, the focus of the following chapters, effectively use historical narratives, symbology, and iconic portraits. They are often engendered in emotions of sorrow, pride, desperation, hope, and complaints to mobilize and convince the Afghan population of the Taliban's worldview. These narratives and stories represent culturally relevant and simple messages that are communicated in a narrative and often poetic form that is familiar to and resonates with the local people. This style is virtually impossible for the US and NATO to counter, because of Western sensitivities concerning religious themes that dominate the Taliban narrative space, not to mention the lack of Western linguistic capabilities, including understanding and mastering the poetic nature of local dialects. Nevertheless, there are some general lessons that should have been considered by the West. The US and ISAF should have carefully studied Taliban propaganda and attempted to learn from the Taliban's information operation strategies. Quite simply, the Taliban clearly know what resonates with the Afghan population, and the narratives and stories presented below will clearly reflect this. They understand relevant cultural referents and themes, and of course local traditions. We quite simply do not.

2

AN OVERVIEW OF TALIBAN AND OTHER AFGHAN INSURGENT STORIES AND AN ASSESSMENT OF THEIR MASTER NARRATIVES

Introduction

David Kilcullen's book *The Accidental Guerrilla* argues that "the insurgents in Afghanistan treated propaganda as their main effort in 2005–2006."[1] He characterizes the Taliban's propaganda as a classic armed propaganda, which basically utilizes intimidation as a behavioral control mechanism. The coalition failed to recognize that this armed propaganda was in fact an Information Operation (IO), and not merely "a supporting activity."[2] A major flaw in Western assessments of the Taliban's communications ability is to draw the conclusion that the group's IO campaign is poor or ineffective: Foxley, for example, argues that although the Taliban have "developed to embrace modern technology [its] methods remain crude home-grown"[3] and therefore ineffective.

However, one could, and we believe should, argue the contrary. The Taliban's IO is effective because it is indigenous and relies on traditional tools like *shabnamah* (night letters), *taranas* (chants), poems, and a variety of other culturally effective artifacts. After all, an insurgency is the product of its own culture, with the Taliban being very much part of the Afghan, and especially Pashtun, culture. Kilcullen writes that *shabnamah* are a good example of the Taliban's armed propaganda: they use them to threaten people who do not comply with its rules and it makes "examples of people who do not cooperate: dozens of provincial level officials were killed between 2005 and 2006 as an armed propaganda tool"[4] after receiving such letters. With *shabnamah*, the Taliban were thus able to send the message that it could reach anybody at any time. This book will argue that the Taliban's IO campaign is even more effective, in part because it uses tools that are deeply rooted in the Pashtun culture; thereby it ensures that people will understand the extent of the Taliban's message and take it seriously.

Afghan insurgent groups enhanced and modified their propaganda campaign after 2005 by using a variety of delivery mechanisms. These modes of delivering their messages to target Afghan audiences now extended significantly beyond the rather simplistic, traditional Afghan systems such as *shabnamah*. Groups like the Afghan Taliban regularly exploit digital technologies such as the internet and telecommunications to convey their messages; but more importantly, the Taliban have consolidated and streamlined their strategic communication effort by focusing on Islamic, cultural, and nationalistic themes to solidify the movement's master narrative.

The Afghan Taliban utilize a wide range of message dissemination techniques and platforms, including printed materials, pirate radio broadcasts, official spokesmen, text messaging, their official website, independent but associated websites in Pashto and Dari languages, social networking sites such as YouTube, Facebook and Twitter; as well as conventional means such as *shabnamah*, graffiti, propaganda videos, using preachers (*da'is*) to infiltrate areas and call for jihad, *khutba* (Friday sermons), poetry, *taranas* (poetic chants), and presence patrols and *pattak* (ad hoc security checkpoints). The Taliban even briefly entertained creating an app in April 2016, "Pashto Afghan News—*Alemarah* AMK," a portal into the group's Pashto webpage, but it was removed and banned from the Google Play app store within 48 hours of its appearance.[5]

The Taliban's messaging campaign and its related stories remain relatively simple in the sense that they reinforce easy-to-understand grievances, promote anti-Western sentiments, delegitimize the Afghan government, and attempt to sow fear among the local neutral/undecided population, as well as government supporters, by threats of violence and intimidation. The Taliban mirror a variety of messages that are typical of contemporary Afghan and/or Islamic narratives, but also use a toolkit of messages unique to the Taliban movement, separating their voice from the litany of insurgent and criminal syndicates operating in Afghanistan.

The Taliban identify themselves as the "Islamic Emirate of Afghanistan (IEA)," and view themselves as both protectors of Islam, righteous and uncorrupt, the suitable alternative to the current Afghan regime, and the only legitimate authority able to implement social justice through the implementation of Shar'iah law. Islam, and a Muslim's duty to protect it, is one of the central themes the Taliban use to influence people and gain recruits; it is a powerful motivator among rural Afghans. The Taliban have been able to use Islamic rhetoric effectively to help legitimize their actions, and to help fuel Afghan anger against the foreign forces. Domestically disseminated Taliban messaging varies in the sense that it is often tailored to address local grievances (village/district level) and needs.

Background

Afghan insurgent groups have quickly broadened their ability to disseminate propaganda to the Afghan population and foreign audiences by using the internet effectively and by exploiting the increasing availability of digital telecommunications networks.[6] However, the Taliban continue to use tried and trusted means as well: including low-cost and low-tech delivery systems such as Taliban mullah preachers (*da'is*) to infiltrate local areas and call for jihad, *khutba* (Friday sermons), and official spokesmen able to be reached 24/7 by local and international media outlets. Slickly produced DVDs showing interviews with Taliban commanders, battle footage, and misdeeds carried out by foreign forces and the Afghan government are widely available for sale in Afghanistan's urban cities and bazaars.

While recognizing that the means by which the Taliban distribute their messages is important and a focus of this chapter, the central objective is to make a specific assessment of the Afghan Taliban master narratives and what themes and stories the Taliban have used to support these narratives. As suggested above, narratives serve as a means for societal or group members to interpret and understand their contextual environment. Narratives employ "frames" or stories that represent sub-stories within the larger narrative context. Frames in the form of stories then set the stage for the larger narrative message. In other words, frames act primarily as a mechanism for consistent expression and integration of other stories.

It is important to understand how the Taliban in Afghanistan uniquely identify themselves, putting aside the obvious limitations of studying their self-produced information materials; it is equally useful to observe how insurgents attempt to bolster their legitimacy and promote recruitment efforts.

It is critical to understand how groups such as the Taliban recruit and promote themselves, especially as insurgent groups begin to expand and operate in non-traditional battlefields across Afghanistan.[7] The Taliban are primarily a decentralized militant and political organization, whose roots originate in the southern provinces of Loy Kandahar; the contemporary Taliban movement is an umbrella organization of various militant networks, marginalized tribes and clans, criminal gangs, some of whom pledge allegiance to the core element of the former Taliban government, originally to the late Mullah Mohammad Omar and the so-called Quetta Shura. The years 2015–16 saw an explicit fragmentation of the Taliban after Mullah Akhtar Mansour published in late August 2015 that Omar had died in April 2013.[8] The death of Mullah Omar opened up new tribal and leadership rivalries within the leadership ranks of the Taliban. The killing of Mullah Mansour on 21 May 2016 by a US drone strike in Baluchistan, Pakistan and the selection of Mullah Haibatullah Akhundzada as the new supreme leader, or emir, of the Afghan Taliban will probably heighten Taliban rivalries. Moreover, the role of the ISI within the Taliban ranks, and how many Taliban view this, will be significant to the future maneuverings of the Afghan Taliban. The ISI played a central role in the selection of Mansour[9] and also surely played a critical role in the selection of Haibatullah. How this will impact on Taliban rivalries and factionalism is yet to be determined.

It is interesting that the Taliban named their 2016 summer offensive operations in Afghanistan after their founder and first supreme leader of the group, Mullah Omar; and the Taliban's announcement clearly serves as an information operation statement. As we shall see, the Taliban will use nearly any occasion to spread their narrative and story. Below is the actual announcement of their 2016 Spring/Summer military operations. Note in the Taliban declaration assertions of the "obligation" to fight jihad, the "valor and bravado" of the Taliban, apostate Kabul leaders ("internal servants"), past Afghan military victories against foreign invaders, as well as instructions to Afghan villagers. These are topics and themes often found in Taliban narratives, as we shall see in the following sections and chapters of this book:

[Translation]

"O Prophet, strive against the disbelievers and the hypocrites and be harsh upon them. And their refuge is Hell, and wretched is the destination." 66:9

The Islamic Emirate's armed jihad against the American invasion has completed fourteen years and is now in its fifteenth year. Jihad against the aggressive and usurping infidel army is a holy obligation upon our necks and our only recourse for re-establishing an Islamic system and regaining our independence.

OVERVIEW AND ASSESSMENT

With the advent of spring it is again time for us to renew our jihadi determination and operations. Hence the Islamic Emirate's leadership eagerly announces this year's Jihadi Operation in honor of the movement's founder and first leader, the late *Amir ul Mu'mineen* Mullah Muhammad Omar Mujahid (*May Allah have mercy upon him*).

Under the leadership of the late *Amir ul Mu'mineen* Mullah Muhammad Omar Mujahid (*May Allah have mercy upon him*), Mujahidin pacified 95 per cent of our nation's territory from wickedness, corruption and oppression, and vanquished the maligned and wicked. Then following the invasion, through holy jihad, they defeated the vast multinational coalition arrayed against them, forcing their retreat and *inter alia* filling the annals of Islamic history with deeds of valor and bravado. So we pray to Allah Almighty that through the deceased's blessed name, Operation Omari, He Almighty will consecrate this Operation with strategic victories and cleanse our beloved country from the presence of the remaining foreign invaders and their malignant and corrupt rebel servants.

Operation Omari began across Afghanistan at 5 am today (local time) on the 5th of *Rajab ul Murajab* 1437 (Lunar Hijri) which corresponds to 24th of *Haml* 1395 (Solar Hijri) and 12 April 2016 (Gregorian). The fact that the 5th of *Rajab ul Murajab* year 15 (Hijri Lunar) was the day on which—under the leadership of Khalif Omar al Farooq—the Muslim armies fought and annihilated the vast infidel Byzantine army in the Battle of Yarmouk, so we pray to Allah Almighty that He bless our Operation Omari in a similar fashion and ordain it with great Islamic victories on the battlefield and the unconditional defeat and withdrawal of the foreign invaders and their internal servants.

Operation Omari—which was initiated and planned by the Islamic Emirate's leadership, the leaders of the Military Commission as well as the Emirate's military planners—focuses, with hope of divine assistance, on clearing the remaining areas from enemy control and presence. Similarly the Operation will employ large-scale attacks on enemy positions across the country, martyrdom-seeking and tactical attacks against enemy strongholds, and assassination of enemy commanders in urban centers. The present Operation will also employ all means at our disposal to bog the enemy down in a war of attrition that lowers the morale of the foreign invaders and their internal armed militias.

By employing such a multifaceted strategy it is hoped that the foreign enemy will be demoralized and forced to retreat from our nation. In areas under the control of Mujahidin, mechanisms for good governance will be established so that our people can live a life of security and normalcy.

Simultaneously with the present Operation the scholars, elders, and leaders of the Islamic Emirate will open a dialogue with our countrymen in the enemy ranks to give up their opposition to the establishment of an Islamic government and join the ranks of the Mujahidin so as to safeguard them from the shame and failure of this World and the Hereafter. During the planning of this Operation, the Mujahidin have been unequivocally instructed to implement their operations in such a manner that takes pains to protect civilians and civil infrastructure.

During the span of Operation Omari, in areas including villages and cities where the Islamic Emirate has established its rule, the lives and property of the dwellers will be safeguarded, as is its duty. Therefore we call upon the dwellers of these areas, be they the professional classes or businessmen, not to fall prey to enemy propaganda and not to feel threatened by the Mujahidin. As it is our duty to protect and assist the wronged and helpless, so we will pay particular attention to the freedom of prisoners.

The Islamic Emirate calls upon all the people of Afghanistan and the Mujahidin, that in similar vein to last year's successful Operation Azm, they should fully and in high spirits participate in this year's operations as well so that with the help and mercy of Allah Almighty this present Jihadi Operation serves as the killing blow to the invading foreign forces and their allies and thus our nation is freed from the present invasion.

And nothing is hard for the Almighty Allah.

Leadership Council of the Islamic Emirate of Afghanistan
5th Rajab ul Murajab 1437 Lunar Hijri
24th Haml 1395 Solar Hijri
12 April 2016 Gregorian[10]

The story portrayed in this announcement is:[11]

The Taliban are about to commence a great, new operation named Operation Omari after their late and great supreme leader and *Amir ul Mu'mineen*, Mullah Mohammed Omar. The only way that Afghans can keep the invading infidels, most of whom they have already defeated, and apostate Afghan Government from destroying Islam and the Afghans' way of life is to join the jihad. Joining the jihad is an obligation of all Afghans. This year will see the Mujahidin fight with divine assistance like the most powerful, pious, and influential Muslim caliphs in history. The Taliban will not only defeat their enemies, they will also bring honest and uncorrupted government to Afghanistan, reinstitute Shar'iah law as well as avoiding the harming of civilians or the destruction of Afghan infrastructure. The Taliban plan to attack infidel and apostate leaders in urban areas by assassination and other means and bog down the enemy troops in the rural areas of the country. Over the course of the struggle, sanctified by Allah, Afghans presently fighting with the infidels and apostates and their leaders will join rank with the Mujahidin. The Taliban's supreme goal is to protect and defend the Afghan people and repel the invaders from Afghanistan.

For years, the difficulty in managing an umbrella front consisting of many sub-groups has challenged senior Taliban leadership—many of whom reside in nearby external sanctuaries in Pakistan's tribal areas—and it is most evident in the reissuing of Taliban created field manuals, or *Layeha*. While the Taliban are said to consist of a litany of various committees, commissions, and shuras, the Taliban in effect consist of a few overall governing committees broken down along political, military, and religious responsibilities; while provincial and district level organizations are broken down loosely along military, political, and legal lines of operation.

Equally important is how such groups can garner support for activities such as IED-emplacement and explosive acquisition through similar messaging campaigns.[12] The Taliban tailor their messages to a variety of important actors, segments of society, and even the international community. An overview of these audiences and the Taliban's adjustment in communicating with each supplements the overall analysis presented which defines what the Taliban are saying, how well they are saying it, to whom, and through which means they are communicating.

Key elements of the master narrative: What the Taliban are really saying

The Afghan Taliban movement continues to view itself as a viable alternative to the current Afghan government structure, and refer to themselves as the Islamic Emirate of Afghanistan (IEA): a strategic interpretation that we suspect is meant to invoke a level of authority and legitimacy among its followers. Although it is clear that the IEA's strategic objectives are to evict foreign troops by force from Afghanistan, overthrow the US-supported Kabul government, restore the Islamic Emirate of Afghanistan, and implement Shar'iah law, the Taliban thereby utilize a strategic communication toolkit designed to delegitimize the current government and garner local support for the shortcomings and perceived failures of US and NATO policies in Afghanistan. These overarching themes include:

- Taliban victory in cosmic conflict is inevitable;
- Islam cannot be defeated;
- Taliban are "national heroes" and willing to sacrifice all for Allah and country;
- Afghans have a long and honorable history of defeating invading foreign infidels;
- Foreign invaders as well as their Afghan puppets are attempting to destroy Afghan religion and traditions;

- All Afghans have an obligation to join the jihad against the foreigners and apostates.

In the broadest sense, the Taliban target three distinct social identities which most Afghans share: religious (Islamic), cultural, and political. These three social identifiers are defined further through various dispositions (see Figure 2.1) and each identity is targeted by a variety yet finite number of themes to inform/educate, convince, persuade, and/or coerce the Afghan population into supporting the Taliban movement by disengaging from the Afghan government structure and services and those services provided by US and NATO forces.

The Taliban messaging strategy navigates these three identities and taps a series of recurring themes such as Pashtunwali ("Way of the Pashtun" social code),[13] elements of pride and honor (which also extend to non-Pashtun Afghans), the call for justice, exploiting themes of victimization, independence, and resistance (to "foreign invaders"). The Taliban message campaign articulates these social values through a host of means depending on which audience is being targeted. In general, the Taliban messaging campaign seeks to delegitimize and discredit the previous Kabul regime of President Hamid Karzai and the present regime of President Ashraf Ghani Ahmadzai and NATO forces in Afghanistan. A powerful aspect of the Taliban strategy is the movement's intelligence collection effort at the local level. This effort helps pinpoint specific grievances and accusations pertinent throughout the local community, and the Taliban incorporate these anecdotes into their messages to help increase their influence.[14] This is an area where the US and its NATO allies have had particular problems in generating an information strategy that truly resonates with the local population.

Religious concepts

Religious narratives have been a foundation of the conservative Afghan Taliban movement since its earliest inception and formation during the tempestuous civil war period that engulfed Afghanistan between 1991 and 1996. The Taliban continue to use Islamic piety, based loosely on the strict dogmatic Deobandi interpretation of Islam, to construct a jihadist image that evokes righteousness and greater justification to their violent anti-government military campaign. Deobandi Islam, a conservative Islamic orthodoxy,

Figure 2.1: Taliban narrative targets

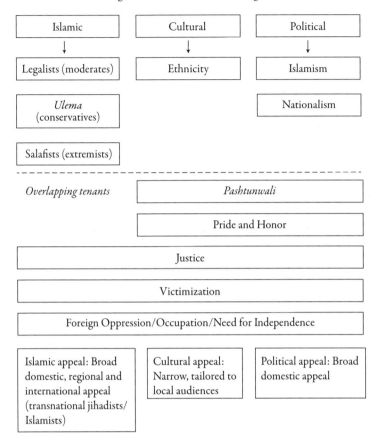

follows a Salafist egalitarian model that seeks to emulate the life and times of the Prophet Mohammed. Within the religious narrative, Islam is used as the primary vehicle and utilizes specific language to target a wide variety of audiences, including local, regional, the global Islamic community, and international audiences.

Jihad: According to the Taliban, jihad is war and is obligatory for all Muslims, particularly Afghans, and must be undertaken against all enemies of Islam such as "infidels," apostates, and those (civilians) who support them. The Taliban produced a *tarana*, or chant, called "Da Kufar sara Jang dai" (Fight with Infidels), which was published on the Islamic Emirate of Afghanistan's website, clearly articulating how the Taliban incorporate religious rhetoric effectively into their messages. Here is an extract:

I and you will definitely win the war over infidels
I and you will definitely win the war over infidels
I and you will win if it is today or tomorrow
I and you will win if it is today or tomorrow
I and you will definitely win the war over infidels
I and you will definitely win the war over infidels
I and you will win if it is today or tomorrow
I and you will win if it is today or tomorrow
O Brothers, please keep your patience high and make your hearts' passion fresh
O Brothers, please keep your patience high and make your hearts' passion fresh
We will win starting from Iraq, Palestine to Arianna
We will win starting from Iraq, Palestine to Arianna
I and you will win if it is today or tomorrow
I and you will win if it is today or tomorrow
I and you will definitely win the war over infidels
I and you will definitely win the war over infidels
I and you will win if it is today or tomorrow
I and you will win if it is today or tomorrow
The fight is tough but it is easy for God
The fight is tough but it is easy for God
As Moses did, we will also win from Pariah [international forces][15]

The Taliban appear to be careful in how they pick the topics to be portrayed in their *taranas* and other message venues, to give an explicit reflection of the values held dear by most Afghans, and by Pashtuns in particular. Simple, culturally relevant information communicated in local dialects projects these messages into the popular Afghan consciousness through topics that resonate deeply with local Afghan communities. The themes portrayed by Taliban chants are relatively unadorned and to the point. The themes are presented through the use of symbols and iconic portraits engendered in emotions of sorrow, pride, desperation, hope, and complaints. Each of these themes and topics is presented in a narrative, and often poetic, form that is familiar to and resonates with the local people.

Islamism: The Taliban's perspective that all Muslims have a duty to protect it is one of the central themes that the Taliban use to influence people and gain recruits. It is a powerful motivator among rural Afghans, who have long believed in jihad when Islam is perceived to be threatened.[16] The Taliban have been able to use Islamic rhetoric effectively to help legitimize their actions and to help fuel Afghan anger against the foreign forces. Most Afghans accept

Allah's divine will, and believe that Allah will punish the oppressor (foreign invader) because Allah is fair and just.

In rural Afghanistan, and even in some urban areas, mullahs hold a near monopoly of power over religion, and they instruct people about what is right or wrong. This association between mullahs and Afghanistan's rural population has developed into a powerful patron–client relationship, and in rural Afghanistan such relationships help define Afghans' day-to-day life. This was not always the case. Before the Soviet invasion and occupation of Afghanistan, mullahs served their communities according to the communities' needs and desires. The Taliban, however, have used the mullahs to present a coordinated narrative to the people. It is even reported that in southern Afghanistan, especially Kandahar, Taliban mullahs coordinate their Friday sermons (*khutba*) to focus on a particular religious, social, or political issue.[17] Undoubtedly, the Taliban have been able to manipulate religion, and have used this manipulation as a powerful weapon in their jihad against the Afghan government and its international allies.

Incidentally, aside from sectarian warfare after the Mazar uprising in 1997 between Pashtuns and Uzbek and Hazara militiamen, anti-Shi'a statements and derogatory ethnic targeting have been a missing element of the Taliban's view of jihad since 2001.[18] However, 2015 did witness some Taliban atrocities against Hazaras.[19] But nevertheless, recent Taliban statements have rarely identified Shi'a as enemies of Afghanistan or "heretics," as radical insurgents in Iraq did during 2004–12, and as Pakistan-based insurgent and terrorist groups have done. In fact, the Afghan Taliban have largely attempted to bypass sectarian and religious divides by using Islam as the unifying factor, particularly the role of jihad. Mullah Omar has repeated this message since being expelled from power in 2001.

- "You should understand that the American plan is never limited to the occupation of Afghanistan and Iraq, but they want to change the whole map of the world by having invaded Afghanistan and Iraq in the heart of the Islamic World. But the Afghans, as defenders of the Islamic *Ummah* and destroyers of colonialist plans, have a well-known history behind." Mullah Omar's Eid message, 8 September 2010

- "I also call on the entire Muslim nation and the Jihadist movements in the world to be aware of the plots of the enemies to cause disagreements between them. They must completely unite their efforts for the liberation and defense of this ruled nation, the victim of injustice." Mullah Omar's Eid message, 19 September 2009

- "Our religion enjoins us to avoid indulging in any kind of activity involving prejudices based on ethnicity. The only bond which binds us is the bond of Islam. Every Muslim is a brother and a friend to one another. We consider every Muslim as a revered soul. Islam views Muslim as a single community. A saying of the Holy Prophet Muhammad (Peace be upon him) related in Abu Dawood instructs as follows: 'Whoever fights for the prejudices of tribe and tribalism, is not one of us.'" Mullah Mohammad Omar, Eid Adha Eve statement, published 12 July 2008.

Shaheed or martyrdom: The Taliban have ascribed the term *shaheed*, or martyr, to any of their fighters killed in combat against international or Afghan government forces, not just those who commit suicide bombings. This belief is based on the trust that those who become *shaheed* will be rewarded in heaven for their action. This is a particularly useful mobilization tool for recruiting suicide bombers from the madrasa networks in Pakistan, including many in North and South Waziristan.

By 2007, over 80 per cent of all suicide bombers in Afghanistan were said to traverse through North and/or South Waziristan before conducting their attack.[20] In nearly all Taliban and Afghan insurgent literature, obituaries of Taliban *shaheed* can be found. Taliban music and poetry has also venerated *shaheed*, especially suicide bombers or the deaths of "famous" Taliban commanders killed in battle. The usage of *shaheed* is not limited to the Taliban, nor is it a new phenomenon. During the Soviet–Afghan war, many Mujahidin fighters were eulogized as *shaheed* following their deaths in combat.[21]

In 2011, a Taliban-produced book entitled *Convoy of Martyrs* was translated after US forces discovered a copy in the Orgun-e area of Paktika province. The book includes advice regarding jihad in accordance with the Qur'an, eulogizes fifteen Taliban fighters killed in combat, and concludes with some warrior poetry. This type of propaganda is prevalent among Taliban periodicals, the website, newsletters, interviews with Taliban spokesmen, and even the official Taliban website.

Shar'iah: Restoring Shar'iah remains a key objective of the Taliban-led insurgency, and is equally represented in the Taliban strategic communication campaign. Simply put, Afghan villagers typically will not ask the Kabul government to help them resolve their disputes because the government is viewed as ineffective, complex, inefficient, and corrupt. This feeling is especially prevalent relative to Kabul's justice system. Some communities view the Taliban as able and willing to resolve disputes quickly and without any persuasion, such as bribery. Taliban leaders conveyed their intentions regarding

Shar'iah during an interview taken at an overrun district (Waigal) in north-eastern Afghanistan's province of Nuristan province in late June 2011:[22]

- "Thanks be to God, the Mujahidin are now in charge of this area, and the people's problems are solved under Shar'iah law. The tribe(s) welcomed us, and now they bring us their problems and we deal with them. They understand that implementing Shar'iah is one of their duties."[23]
- "Smoking is forbidden here; our religious department will punish those who shave and those who intoxicate themselves. Schools and hospitals are open, under Shar'iah law."
- "We will respect the Islamic rights of all people of the country including women; we will implement Shar'iah rules in the light of the injunctions of the sacred religion of Islam in order to efficiently maintain internal security and eradicate immortality, injustice, indecency and other vices; we will strictly observe the law of punishment and reward and auditing in order to bring about administrative transparency in all government departments, The violators will be dealt with according to the Shar'iah rules." Mullah Omar Eid message, 8 September 2010.

Islam: To conclude our survey of religious concepts, Islam is a common influence in that almost everyone in the country (99.5 per cent) is a Muslim, but it would be wrong to infer that this brings unanimity of opinion. While Islam is not a monolithic entity, and in Afghanistan encompasses a wide range of opinions, from reformists, foreign-educated progressives, radicals, Sufis, Salafists, Deobandis, Talibs, to conservative judicial scholars, it is important to note the connection between Islam and jihad, especially in southern Afghanistan. As suggested above, using the call of "Islam under threat" is a prominent theme of Taliban messaging; and the Taliban recognizes that this kind of messaging encourages public and communal action.

> "Our religious and historical enemy has cunningly launched a propaganda drive, spending huge amounts of money in order to gradually strip our young generation of their Afghan and Islamic identity." Mullah Omar Eid message, 16 November 2010

Cultural concepts

Pashtunwali:[24] This term has been variously described as a system of law and of conflict resolution, a body of custom, and a mindset that dictates the way in which Pashtuns operate in their society. It helps define how Pashtuns behave toward each other and how Pashtuns deal with outsiders in order to maintain their identity as Pashtun. The Taliban regularly play on notions o Pashtunwali in their messaging, in an effort to invoke certain tribal more such as those mentioned below.

Pride and honor: Among Afghans, *nang*, or pride and honor, and *gharia* (esteem and pride derived from courage) are the highest personal value. Any infringement on or loss of one's *nang*—any disgrace or embarrassment— prompts a call for an immediate act of revenge. Afghans view the improper trespassing into a village or household, the killing of one's family members, the touching of women outside one's own family, and the hooding and shackling of Afghan males in front of their family members and neighbors as enormous violations to one's honor. Revenge-seeking individuals will usually combine anti-government actions with local Taliban *mahaz* (fronts) to "right their wrong."

This boosts the insurgency's reservoir of manpower with supporters who may not necessarily be ideological/religious fanatics, but rather ordinary Afghans. Afghans refer to these Taliban as *majburi* (forced) Taliban, an indication that these fighters were "forced" into the ranks of the insurgency to defend their honor or to "right" the wrongs of the corrupt local government who habitually abuse and harass local rivals and adversaries (see Appendix A for different "types" of Taliban). The Taliban are apt to exploit these grievances and knowingly tap into this wellspring of supporters for violent activity. References to "errant" air strikes, night raids, compound searches and images depicting the inappropriate touching of women by Coalition forces are the Taliban's most overt messaging to potential supporters, a rallying cry for Afghans seeking revenge, or *badal* ("payback" or restitution): another highly important tenet of Afghan culture.[25] They also refer to their enemies in a similar light. The members of the Afghan National Army (ANA) and the Afghan National Police (ANP) are dismissed as *munafiq* (hypocrite), and others in the Kabul administration are called *ghulam* (slave/servant), *ajir* (agent) and *gawdagai* (puppet).

The Taliban regularly evoke anger as the vehicle needed to avenge dishonor and redress insults to one's pride. Figure 2.2 is an excellent example of how the Taliban try to evoke anger and exploit Pashtunwali and Pashtun concepts of honor, in addition to their trope of the "victimization of Afghans by foreign invaders."[26] This Taliban leaflet shows a female African–American soldier "patting down" or frisking an Afghan woman, but it is very hard to tell from a distance if the American soldier is a woman or a man. The Taliban are obviously suggesting that this is an American man touching an Afghan woman, which would be inconceivable and the ultimate violation of an Afghan's honor (*namus*), pride, and esteem (*ghariat*).[27] Such an action to an Afghan, especially rural Pashtun, would demand immediate revenge.

The translated leaflet caption says it all: "The US evil soldiers are defiling our Muslim sisters, as you can see in the picture." This leaflet portrays not only a culturally powerful message in the frame of the narrative of Pashtunwali, but is also a superb Taliban recruiting tool. This leaflet, in many respects, could be said to be sending the same message but in a more powerful and effective fashion, and of course to a different target audience, as the author's first leaflet developed for OSD that was described in this book's Preface. Also note the leaflet's tropes concerning past historical Afghan victories against foreign invaders, which we have already seen are a common theme of Taliban narratives.

Cultural values and traditions are used by the Taliban to shift public loyalties away from the government. The Taliban narratives attempt to make an emotional connection with Afghans through the explicit use of examples from

Figure 2.2: "The US Evil soldiers are defiling our Muslim sisters, as you can see in the picuture. Despite this our Mukahid Nation keeps quiet. Afghan Muslim Mujahid Nation! Your grandfathers beat the British forces; your father beat the super power Russians! How long will you keep quiet against US? Join the Jihad today against the defilers"

29

Afghan history, and through appeals to Afghan nationalism and Afghan collective memories. The Afghan public is generally proud of their history and their ancestors' performance in defending Afghanistan against foreign invaders over the centuries. This analysis clearly suggests that the Taliban attempts to use and manipulate Afghan culture and traditions. For example, the use of *gila* (complaints), a traditional tool that is tied to Pashtun lifestyle, is often used in their messaging to appeal to subtle Afghan emotions.

> *Leaflet story*: The evil, infidel Americans—a supposed superpower—regularly defile and dishonor our Afghan women. There is an obligation for all Afghans to end their silence at this horrible act and join the Mujahidin and the jihad to regain the honor of our nation, just as our fathers did against the infidel Russians, another superpower.

Resistance and independence: The Taliban repeatedly target local audiences, and to a smaller degree regional Pashtun communities, with themes of resistance and independence. Both themes are not only prevalent among the informal Pashtunwali social code, but also represent an effective communication tool to help create a collective Afghan identity based on shared historical values of repulsing foreign invasions and evoking personal feelings of prestige and honor in the military efforts to resist these incursions. Aside from Islamic/religious rhetoric, the themes of resistance and independence are noticeable in nearly every form of Taliban propaganda and unquestionably represent a cornerstone of the Taliban's overall strategic communication strategy.

"America never ever imagined its defeat, due to its technological advancement, but now everyday it welcomes the coffins of its soldiers and is facing great life and monetary losses. A few years back no one would have conceived that US and its allies would face such resistance in Afghanistan, which would compel their president to beg other countries to provide economic assistance, military equipment and soldiers to combat the resistance; furthermore no one is prepared to bring to light this unique development." Mullah Omar Eid message, 30 September 2008

Justice: The greatest challenge facing successive national governments in Kabul over the past century has been the ability to impose an effective centralized legal code/judicial institutions upon local communities. Historically, local Afghan communities have had their own non-state institutions for regulating behavior and resolving problems. In post-Taliban Afghanistan, the legal system consists of three competing parts: the state legal codes, Islamic religious law (Shar'iah), and local customary law. Customary, religious, and state sectors define their own exclusive shares of authority, but also ally with other actors—a complex relationship that is hindered by insecurity, corruption, and competing interests. The Taliban exploit the central government's inept and inefficient system by offering their own roving form of justice, typically in the sense of a mobile court system, which brings Taliban affiliated *qaziyan* (judges) who are usually bolstered by a Taliban-aligned Islamic scholar (*ulama*). The Taliban utilize this theme especially among domestic audiences, and consistently seek to delegitimize the authority of the central government with this theme.[28]

> "Use your judgment, is it democracy or is it *Bomb-cracy, Qatal-cracy, or Kharab-cracy*? Filling jails with people is what they call their presidency. It is a shame that even though some sold-out Afghans witness everything, they call invading forces as friends." Taliban video by *Alemarah* studio, "Destruction and Reconstruction"

Victimization: Taliban narratives regularly play on the notion that the Afghan people are being systematically victimized by foreign occupiers, who not only want to corrupt and destroy Islam and the Afghan way of life, but also the Afghan people. The Taliban spend considerable time and effort on their attempts to expose US and NATO's collateral damage. The death of innocent civilians resonates enormously for Afghans, who still have vivid memories of terrible and destructive Soviet bombing campaigns. Their official website, *Alemarah*, has an entire section devoted to issues involving the death of Afghan civilians by US and NATO forces. Such issues are also a prominent focal point of Taliban videos and DVDs that are widely available in Afghanistan and Pakistan.

> "Today, this nation is entangled in a complicated trial and an imposed war on the charges of their professing (Islamic) ideology. Every day, men and women of this nation fall prey to the bombardment of the invaders and their children become orphans; miserable people are displaced internally due to the operations and fear of bombardment of the enemy." Mullah Omar Eid Message November 16, 2010.

Political concepts

Nationalism: A key element among insurgent communications is the widening scope of their target audience to include all Afghans (including sympathizers, supporters, and undecided/neutral), avoiding any notions of a purely Pashtun-centric messaging strategy.[29] The communiqués offered by the

Taliban's former Supreme Leader, Mullah Mohammad Omar, depict the evolution of widening the jihad against the government and foreign forces by appealing to all Afghans; later they go as far as asking support from neighboring countries and from Muslims around the world. This trend began soon after the Taliban government was toppled by Coalition forces in 2001, and has remained consistent ever since:

- "Being a leader of Muslims, I accept that jihad against US troops is our duty and everyone who assists Americans in executing their mission is liable to death." March 2003[30]
- Mullah Omar issued a statement saying, "the Americans have tightened their grip on the northern alliance, and the cities of Mazar-e Sharif, Herat, and other northern areas." He also called on "the people and the commanders in the north to free themselves of America's oppression and help the Taliban." 23 October 2004
- "The people of Afghanistan and the Taliban should unite against US and allied forces and intensify their jihad against the foreign occupiers."[31] 6 November 2005
- "Finally I appeal to all Muslims to help their Mujahidin brothers in fighting against the forces of evil, by putting aside their personal interests and desires for power. Now you know your religion and Afghanistan are in danger, so pursue the path of bravery, righteousness, nobility, dignity and generosity by following the footsteps of pious religious leaders and leaving cowardliness, haughtiness, stinginess and the ways of dishonesty by joining *Jihad*." Mullah Omar Eid messages, 17 December 2007
- "The current Jihad and resistance in Afghanistan against the foreign invaders and their puppets, is a legitimate Jihad, being waged for the defense of the sovereignty of the Islamic country and Islam." Mullah Omar Eid messages, 8 September 2010
- "Some internal and external enemies are now speaking of disintegration of the beloved country. They should know that the patriotic countrymen and the Islamic Emirate will never allow anyone to put into practice their wicked plan." Mullah Omar Eid messages, 16 November 2010

Collective memory: Similar to nationalistic appeals, the Taliban and other insurgent groups consistently tap into past conflicts in Afghanistan and urge the recollection of these historic memories in comparison to the current conflict. Coalition forces are usually compared to the Soviet or British army and even German Nazis. Afghans are typically reminded of the hardships faced during the Anglo-Afghan wars, the Soviet invasion, and the success in resisting Genghiz Khan and Alexander's army. The Afghan government is typically compared to unfavorable Afghan rulers and regimes, as the passage below by the late Mullah Omar implies:

- "[There is] no difference between Shah Shuja, Babrak Karmal and the rulers of the present Kabul Administration. All are equal when [it] comes to national and Islamic [betrayal] and treason... Now when the enemy is on the verge of defeat, I would like to remind you that (throughout history) enemies have deprived the Afghans of sustaining the pride of victory following the military defeat of the enemy because the enemies do not leave them to build up a strong foundation and a sole leadership. This exactly happened after the defeat of the Russians. The flames of difference and atrocities engulfed every house of the Afghans. The prolongation of the sufferings of our people and their perdition originate from this factor of not having a sole and strong leadership after the defeat of the Russians. Of course, concoction of collusions and conspiracies added to our failure." Mullah Mohammad Omar, Eid Adha Eve statement, published 12 July 2008.

3

TARGET AUDIENCES OF AFGHAN NARRATIVES AND STORIES

As suggested above, unlike the US-led international Coalition in Afghanistan, the Taliban continually focus and act at the rural, Afghan village level (*kalay*). The Taliban seem to be well aware that the center of gravity of their insurgency, wrapped in the narrative of mandatory jihad, is in the rural hinterland of Afghanistan, and they target their informational messages and propaganda accordingly. Below, we present and assess the target audiences for Taliban narratives and messages.

Local (Dari/Pashto): Taliban and insurgent messaging targeting local constituents is most often published in Pashto, targeting local Afghan Pashtun communities, the traditional wellspring of support for the movement early on and during its rebound between 2002 and 2005. These messages attempt to drum up support and sympathy for the movement by highlighting grievances and animosities against the central government and Coalition presence in Afghanistan. Messages include religious themes (i.e. jihad, martyrdom), cultural, and political themes (i.e. references to anti-colonialism, exploiting local anger over Coalition operations). Considerable Taliban informational efforts are devoted to addressing local issues and concerns.

However, three distinct audiences have been targeted for Taliban messaging: the local population that is undecided/neutral toward the Taliban's cause; the local population that supports or is sympathetic to the Taliban's cause; and those who are opposed to the Taliban's cause and support the current regime.

The Taliban adapts its messaging themes to approach each distinct audience differently, as far as its strategies are concerned.

Local undecided/neutral: Messages are aimed at instructing, persuading, or ultimately intimidating and coercing local constituents into supporting or siding with the Taliban, threatening extreme acts of violence against those "collaborating" with the government, Coalition forces, or foreign NGOs. Some threats force neutral actors simply to vacate the community, village, or area, which helps the Taliban penetrate deeper to establish support and intelligence networks in areas deemed critical to their strategic survival. Often the Taliban will soften the local community by penetrating with a small number of operatives, usually preachers, to gauge the community's attitudes and dispositions, to collect intelligence regarding local grievances, and possibly to offer financial assistance in exchange for cooperation early on. Pro-government supporters or government workers are routinely threatened at this stage, and will be targeted or killed following a warning grace period.

Table 3.1: Local population that is neutral/undecided toward the Taliban's cause

Taliban strategy	Informational/educational, persuasion, coercion
Taliban objectives	To succeed in eliciting a local community's compliance with Taliban demands to end its relationship with the current government structure and to disengage from the influence and outreach of foreign forces.
Narratives used	Islamic, cultural, and political
Major themes used	• Coalition/ISAF forces are exactly the same as the Soviet army that invaded Afghanistan in the 1980s.
	• Coalition/ISAF forces employ the same tactics as the Soviet Army: bombing villages, "killing everyone," targeting civilians because they cannot distinguish between civilians and Mujahidin.
	• Coalition/ISAF speaks of peace and reconstruction but these are lies.
	• Coalition/ISAF simply targets *all* Afghans, spilling the blood of men, women, and children alike.
	• No matter how resourceful and wealthy the United States is, money and superior weaponry cannot defeat the will of the Afghan people.
	• The occupiers despise the values of Islam and attempt to spread Christianity and proselytize for it.
	• The Coalition is facing a military defeat.
	• Morale and resources among the Mujahidin are at an all-time high.

- Afghans have defeated Alexander's armies, the British, the Soviets, and now the US and NATO.
- The Taliban are planning for the future of this country after the occupation "under the shade of social justice of Islam, with economic and social development programs."

Message effectiveness
- Exploiting the failures or deficiencies of the current Afghan government structure, issues of abuse and corruption, and the perceived predatory nature of the Afghan security services.
- Exploiting collateral damage, especially from errant air-strikes or night-raids conducted by foreign forces.
- Portraying US and NATO forces as occupiers and comparing them to colonial occupiers or the Soviet forces, which resonates among most communities.
- Expanding and strategically shaping linguistic delivery capabilities. (For instance, the Taliban disseminated videos of religious sermons spoken in Dari and Pashto, compared to previous offerings only available in Arabic.)
- Afghan media/journalists are being manipulated and leveraged effectively by the Taliban's media commission.

Message ineffectiveness
- Local opposition to terrorism, especially suicide terrorism.
- Redundant and negative messaging campaign induces audience fatigue.
- Contradictory statements between senior and mid-level command (in public addresses, claims of responsibility, on negotiations, relations with al-Qaeda, etc.)
- Taliban attacks against civilians or attacks that maim and kill civilians are extremely unpalatable and unjustified, according to Afghan popular public opinion.

Delivery systems
Preachers, graffiti, *shabnamah*, *khutba* (Friday sermons), poetry, *taranas* (poetic chants), DVDs, and face-to-face interactions.

Local supporters/sympathizers: These messages seek to portray the success of violent battlefield victories and aim to improve recruitment among local communities. By repeating and exploiting local conditions, such as disrespecting Afghan culture, unemployment, corruption, government and international forces' abuse and detention of innocent individuals or collateral damage from Coalition operations, these messages tend to solidify a foundation of support and sympathy among their followers. Greatly exaggerating the battlefield accomplishments of Taliban fronts, messages of this type are usually in the same vein as the messages and statements appearing on the Taliban's website. The Taliban continue to focus on maintaining a high level of morale among their rank-and-file.

Table 3.2: Local population that supports or is sympathetic to the Taliban's cause

Taliban strategy	Informational/educational
Narratives used	Islamic, cultural, and political
Major themes used	• Coalition/ISAF simply targets *all* Afghans, spilling the blood of men, women, and children alike.
	• No matter how resourceful and wealthy the US is, money and superior weaponry cannot defeat the will of the Afghan people.
	• The occupiers despise the values of Islam and attempt to spread Christianity and proselytize for it.
	• The Coalition is facing a military defeat.
	• Morale and resources among the Mujahidin are at an all-time high.
	• Afghans have defeated Alexander's armies, the British, the Soviets, and now the US and NATO.
	• Taliban victory is inevitable and certain.
Message effectiveness	• Messages are delivered with a level of linguistic mastery and resonance.
	• Convincing usage of contemporary folklore, collective memory of past Afghan victories (Soviet–Afghan jihad, anti-colonial jihad).
	• Utilize and exploit shared Islamic identity among Afghans; effectively use cultural tenets of pride, shame, and right-eousness to convey messages.
	• Islamic rhetoric aims to convince participants that their actions in jihad will be rewarded dually in the afterlife if individuals are killed in combat (*shaheed*).
	• Messages are designed to uphold and increase morale among insurgent rank-and-file and leadership.
Message ineffectiveness	• Confusion from inconsistent messaging from leadership, erroneous or competing statements from official spokes-men, or from rival insurgent factions (HIG).
Delivery systems	• *Layeha* ("rules and regulations for Mujahidin" field book), graffiti, DVDs, periodicals, *khutba* (Friday sermons), poetry, *taranas* (poetic chants), face-to-face interactions, internet websites/forums, Facebook, Twitter, YouTube, text messages.

Table 3.3: Local population that is opposed to the Taliban's cause

Taliban strategy	Threats and intimidation, coercion, persuasion
Narratives used	Islamic, cultural, political
Major themes used	• Those who work with the current Afghan regime or international forces are *munafiq* (hypocrites), *zalem* (cruel/tyrannical), *zulum* (tyranny), *ghulam* (slaves/servants), *be-ghairat* (dishonorable, cowardly), *be-ābrū* (dishonor, disgrace, indignity) and/or *gaudagai* (puppets).
	• If you are not supporting the Taliban, then you are supporting the oppressors.
	• You, as a Muslim, must join with the Taliban to evict the invading army so that Shar'iah law can be re-established under the Islamic Emirate of Afghanistan (i.e. the Taliban government).
	• Coalition/ISAF simply targets *all* Afghans, spilling the blood of men, women, and children alike.
	• No matter how resourceful and wealthy the US is, money and superior weaponry cannot defeat the will of the Afghan people.
	• The occupiers despise the values of Islam and attempt to spread Christianity and proselytize for it. The Coalition is facing certain military defeat.
Message effectiveness	• The use of threats followed by violent actions (kidnapping, assassination, murder) can be effective in eroding local support for government structures and services and helps portray the local government as ineffective and powerless.
	• Persuasive messages include referring to local strongmen as Mujahidin to help reach out to those who fought in previous eras in an effort to have them rejoin a "righteous" cause.
Message ineffectiveness	• Message consumption is usually limited, since those opposed to the Taliban do not seek them out and avoid any distributed by the overall Taliban structure.
	• Confusion from inconsistent messaging from Taliban leadership, erroneous or competing statements from official spokesmen, or from rival insurgent factions (HIG).
	• Difficulty in discerning the authenticity of communications from Taliban representatives.
Delivery systems	*Shabnamah* (night letters), graffiti, *khutba* (Friday sermons), face-to-face interactions, and text messages.

Table 3.4: Neighboring population

Taliban strategy	Threats and intimidation, coercion, persuasion
Narratives used	Islamic, cultural, political
Major themes used	• You, as a Muslim, must join with the Taliban to evict the invading army so that Shar'iah law can be re-established under the Islamic Emirate of Afghanistan (i.e. the Taliban government). • Those who work with the current Afghan regime or international forces are *munafiq* (hypocrites), *zalem* (cruel/tyrannical), *zulum* (tyranny), *ghulam* (slaves/servants), *be-ghairat* (dishonorable, cowardly), *be-ābru* (dishonor, disgrace, indignity) and/or *gaudagai* (puppets). • If you are not supporting the Taliban, then you are supporting the oppressors. • The US attacks Muslims worldwide, spilling the blood of men, women, and children alike. • No matter how resourceful and wealthy the US is, money and superior weaponry cannot defeat the will of the Mujahidin. • The occupiers despise the values of Islam and attempt to spread Christianity and proselytize for it. • The Coalition is facing certain military defeat.
Message effectiveness	• Themes highlighting US oppression, aggression toward Muslims, and "the righteous cause of jihad" resonate widely among the regional population. • Persuasive messages include referring to local strongmen as Mujahidin to help reach out to those who fought in previous eras in an effort to have them rejoin a "righteous" cause.
Message ineffectiveness	• Confusion from inconsistent messaging from Taliban leadership, especially regarding pro- or anti-Pakistani government sentiments, erroneous or competing statements from official spokesmen, or from rival insurgent factions. • Difficulty in discerning the authenticity of communications from Taliban representatives.
Delivery systems	• DVDs, periodicals, *khutba* (Friday sermons), face-to-face interactions, poetry, *taranas* (poetic chants), internet websites/forums, Facebook, Twitter, YouTube, text messages, spokesmen, and media influence operations.

Local opposition to the Taliban's cause (i.e. government supporters): Acting government officials, political parties, and their supporters comprise the center of gravity for the current Afghan regime and remain a critical target audience of the insurgency. The Taliban have primarily deployed threats and coercive messages to the strata of government supporters and officials, although persuasion is increasingly used against government supporters and even Afghan National Security Force personnel. Threats of death, beheading, and abduction are being replaced by calls for amnesty if security personnel surrender and disarm to local insurgent fronts, for instance. Non-threatening themes include highlighting or exaggerating the perceived deficiencies and failures of the current Afghan regime and the international military coalition in Afghanistan. Specific language is used to highlight these thoughts, such as referring to the Afghan government as *zalem* (cruel/tyrannical) and those who work for the government as *ajir* (agent), *gaudagai* (puppet), and *munafiq* (hypocrite).

Neighboring countries (Urdu/Arabic): The dissemination of messages and communiqués in Arabic helps to expand the insurgency's support to wealthy areas in the Middle East (i.e. Persian Gulf), where resources and personnel (transnational networks) are sought. Additionally, Arabic spoken sermons and religious texts help to strengthen claims of righteousness and piety among more radical or ideological fighters in Afghanistan. One militant periodical, *Al Somood*, which is also published and linked to the Taliban's official website, is the only Afghan Taliban periodical that is entirely in Arabic.

Urdu published material helps spread inflammatory anti-Western and anti-domination sentiment among the Pakistani Pashtuns and other ethnic groups living in Pakistan. It also provides "battlefield updates" and informs the Pakistani constituency of the unfolding events in neighboring Afghanistan.

International (English, European languages): *Generally opposed to the Taliban movement and its motives*: Messages in English and European languages are quite dissimilar from those published in local and regional languages. English/European written messages attempt to pervert the international perception regarding the conflict in Afghanistan and try to influence local political decisions away from supporting NATO's mission in Afghanistan. Messages attempt to portray the Afghan Taliban movement as a legitimate political organization, and frame its existence around claims of victimization (foreign occupation, suppression, victims of an anti-Islamic "crusade") while reiterating that the group's military and political objectives remain domestic in scope, not international. However, this last point is often refuted by local Taliban fronts who often threaten participating NATO countries and their constituents;

Table 3.5: International population

Taliban strategy	Education, persuasion, threats and intimidation
Narratives used	Islamic, cultural, political
Delivery systems	Internet websites/forums, Facebook, Twitter, YouTube, periodicals, influence operations that target Western and international media outlets

Differences between International Media Statements vs. Regional/Local Articles

International (English)	Regional/Local?
Primarily focus on US foreign policy developments (in Afghanistan); offer few statements directly against the European Union.	Primarily focus on domestic Afghan events, news, actors, and policies. Offer some broader articles focusing on the international Islamic community.
Democracy	Exercise of power/military achievement
Decry "human rights abuses" caused by foreign military operations and collateral damage.	Increased use of nationalistic terms such as the Afghan Nation, "invaders," and "puppet government" while referring to themselves (the Taliban) as Mujahidin.
Describe the West as being the aggressor, and the Afghan population the victim of this aggression.	Almost no use of the term *kafir*, "infidel," whereas this term is frequently used in Taliban night letters at the village and district level.
Indicate that the Taliban movement poses no threat to the international or regional community.	Offer articles concerning the *hijab*/women's rights-related articles (criticize the prohibition of the *hijab* in the West).

also, these claims are not officially sanctioned or broadcast from the recognized Taliban leadership councils or spokesmen.

Conclusion

Having examined and evaluated the targets, the delivery systems and their associated narratives, themes, and effectiveness of Taliban and other Afghan insurgent messaging, the next chapters will discuss in depth each of the key techniques and delivery systems that they use to portray their messages, stories, and narratives.

4

TALIBAN AND AFGHAN INSURGENT MAGAZINES, CIRCULARS, AND NEWSLETTERS

Through a simple but effective communications and public relations campaign, the Taliban have successfully penetrated the "hearts and minds" or trust and confidence of many ordinary citizens throughout Afghanistan. As suggested above, a central target of the Taliban's media campaign is the Pashtun-dominated provinces of southern and eastern Afghanistan where the Taliban have traditionally enjoyed their greatest support, although we have also witnessed this recently in northern Afghan provinces as well.

Afghan insurgent periodicals and newsletters

This section provides a bibliography of Taliban and other insurgent circulars and magazines by identifying their inception, content, length, language, and publication. Many of the magazines are derived directly from the Taliban insurgency, including the Tora Bora Military Front and Haqqani Network; a few others are affiliated with Hezb-e-Islami Gulbuddin Hekmatyar (HIG).

The Taliban magazines and circulars contain myriad amounts of material, and the contents range from interviews and statements of prominent jihadist leaders, to martyrdom obituaries, to commentary on cultural and religious issues, including the rights of women in Islam. In addition, contents often depict battlefield reports, anti-coalition forces rhetoric and propaganda, as well as chronicles depicting the suffering of the civilian population. As a means of appealing to a broader audience, some of the magazines also incorporate poetry, sports, news, and art. Publications range from weekly, monthly, bi-monthly to quarterly. One of earliest and most prominent magazines, *Al Somood*, was allegedly established in 2002; most, however, were generally published after 2004. Furthermore, magazines such as *Al Somood* and *In Fight* are directly affiliated with video studio productions such as *Alemarah* and often recycle images, eulogies, and battle operations produced by the studio. These types of Taliban magazines and circulars continue to proliferate, as many of them have become accessible online and are translated not only into Pashto and Dari, but also into English, Arabic, and Urdu.

The publications released in Peshawar reveal that although the Islamic Emirate of Afghanistan does not directly publish the newspapers, much of the content is extremely sympathetic to the insurgency and serves as Taliban propaganda, focusing heavily on Pashtun nationalism.

The contents within the Taliban magazines and circulars are attempts made by jihadists to reveal their continued presence, as well as an exercise of power. The magazines and circulars typically cover original interviews with current high-ranking Taliban field commanders and Shura leaders, giving eulogies, sermons, or tirades against the US and NATO Afghan policies. There are ample articles and commentary on history, religion, and Islamic issues as well as the coverage of recent political events. As a means of appealing to a broader audience, several of the magazines cater to youth through social media, primarily through Facebook. While most of the magazines and circulars cater specifically to the particular insurgent group's issues, several of the magazines, such as *In Fight*, focus on the Western audience. The objective for *In Fight*, for instance, is to influence international perceptions negatively through the usage of photo essays and by chronicling graphic insurgent raids and suicide bombings on Afghan and Coalition forces. Images typically contain deceased NATO and US personnel's flag-draped coffins.

Taliban origin

Al Somood *(Resistance)*

In September 2002, the Taliban-era Minister of Information and Culture, Qudratullah Jamal (alias Hamed Agha), created the Arabic-language jihadist magazine *Al Somood*. In May 2004, Ustad Mohammad Yasir, a top Taliban ideologue and former military chief for Abdul al-Rasul Sayyaf's *Ittihad-i*

Islami tanzim, took the reins of *Al Somood*. Yasir speaks fluent Arabic and commanded *Al Somood*'s production until his arrest in August 2005. In March 2007, Yasir along with four other Taliban figures were released from prison in exchange for a captured Italian journalist in Helmand province. Yasir resumed his functions in the Taliban but took command of the Invitation Council (Recruitment committee for the Taliban's Quetta Shura) until he was re-arrested in Pakistan on 1 January 2009.[1] Mawlawi Amir Khan Muttaqi, one of the founding members of the Taliban, now runs *Al Somood* and is in charge of the Quetta Shura's Cultural Council (Propaganda wing).[2] *Al Somood* produces original interviews with current Taliban field commanders and shura leaders, including the likes of the late Jalauddin Haqqani, Mullah Berader Akhund, Ustad Yasir, Mullah Abdul Salaam Baryali (a former Kunduz shadow governor), and many others. *Al Somood*'s chairman is published as Sheikh Nasiruddin "Herawi," a *nom de guerre*.

- Content: Interviews and statements of Taliban figures, commanders, and fighters; martyrdom obituaries, poems, and photographs of commanders and martyrs.
- Length: Approximately 50 pages. Color. Includes photographs.
- Language: Arabic. (Analysts note "the simple standard of the Arabic [used] would suggest it is written by those to whom it is a second language, although the cover pages are of a noticeably higher standard.")[3]
- Publication: Every two months.
- Existence: Allegedly established in September 2002; however, consistent since 2008.

Srak *(Beam of Light)*

A monthly pamphlet published mainly in Pashto but includes some Dari material. Its letterhead includes the label "Afghanistan Islamic Literary Association," whose editor is identified as Lutfullah Momand. *Srak*, sometimes misidentified and translated as *Sark*, publishes various commentaries and statements from high-ranking Taliban leaders, most noticeably a lengthy interview with Mullah Berader Akhund during the spring of 2009. *Srak* remains one of the Taliban propaganda magazines with the most content and material, surpassing even *Al Somood* and *Murchal*. *Srak*'s publication address is listed as Khair Khanna Mina, Area 2, Kabul, an unlikely reality since the address is located in a Tajik-dominated neighborhood.

- Content: Interviews and statements by Taliban figures, commanders, and fighters. *Srak* also provides poetry, editorials praising the Taliban, and commentary on religious issues and the history of Islam.
- Length: Approximately 75 pages or more.
- Language: Mainly Pashto, some Dari.
- Publication: Monthly.
- Existence: Since 2004.
- Cover Price: 20 Pakistani rupees.

Tora Bora Magazine

A quarterly jihadist periodical that claims to be published in Nangarhar province (the site of the Tora Bora cave complex), *Tora Bora Magazine* delivers statements and interviews with mid- to high-level insurgent commanders such as Qari Baryal (Kapisa, a commander independent of the Taliban), Sheikh Abu Yaha al-Libi (al-Qaeda), and Mawlawi Saifullah Jalali, an alleged militant commander operating in Kabul. The magazine supports the current insurgency, but is directly associated with the Tora Bora Nizami Mahaz, an offshoot of the Taliban and led by Anwur ul-Haq Mujahid, the son of the late Hezb-e-Islami leader Mawlawi Younus Khalis. *Tora Bora Magazine*'s founder is said to be Ghazi Ajmal and it is edited by Malawi Hatem Tayi.[4]

- Content: Interviews and statements by insurgents, commanders, and fighters. The magazine also offers commentary on religious and cultural issues.
- Length: approximately 70 pages or more.
- Language: Pashto.
- Publication: Quarterly.
- Existence: Since 2007. But its frequency of publication has waned in recent years.

Shahamat *(Courage/Bravery)*

A periodical that appears every two months, *Shahamat* is predominantly published in Pashto, with many of the articles appearing on the *Alemarah* website.[5] Like several other jihadist publications, *Shahamat* lists its publication address in Kabul; it is published by the Taliban front organization the "Islamic Cultural Society of Afghanistan."

- Content: *Shahamat* publishes articles and commentary on history, religion, and Islamic issues and supports the Taliban cause of fighting NATO forces in Afghanistan.

- Length: N/A.
- Language: Pashto/Dari.
- Publication: Monthly.
- Existence: N/A.

In Fight

A photo essay of Taliban-related attacks (taken from reports on the *Alemarah* website), this monthly publication is available in a slick PDF format, complete with color photos taken from a variety of sources, including local press, international media, and military photography departments. This is a monthly publication that began sometime in late 2008. Interestingly, the publication is in English. A typical issue consists of a photo essay chronicling insurgent attacks against Afghan and Coalition forces with heavy attention being paid to imagery of fallen NATO (mostly British) and US personnel in flag-draped coffins. Some photographs seem to be recycled between issues. The magazine does not venerate fallen insurgents like other magazines (i.e. *Al Somood*), and given that it is written in English, this suggests that the magazine is intended solely for Western audiences, in the hope of influencing international perceptions that the war in Afghanistan is going badly and cannot be won (or is not worth the sacrifice).

- Content: Little to no commentary, and when present it is taken from *Alemarah* website reports. Each issue relies heavily on graphic color photographs: primarily a photo essay format that depicts the conflict as the insurgents view it.
- Length: 50–130 pages.
- Language: English.
- Publication: Monthly.
- Existence: Since 2008.

Elham *(Inspiration/Revelation)*

This publication is allegedly published weekly; its chief editor is Salim Sohail. Their publisher is labeled as "Afghanistan's Islamic Cultural Society," the same front behind the *Shahamat* publication.[6] The content includes recycled material from the Taliban's *Alemarah* website. *Elham* is directly linked to the Taliban movement.

- Content: Editorials and battlefield reports previously published on *Alemarah*.
- Length: At least 14 pages.
- Language: Mostly in Pashto but offers some material in Dari.
- Publication: Weekly.
- Existence: Since 2005.

Murchal *(Trench)*

A quarterly periodical published by "the Islamic Emirate of Afghanistan," *Murchal* is one of the longest-running Taliban magazines in Afghanistan. The editor is identified as Mullah Kabir Ahmad Mujahed, and it lists its publication address simply as Kabul.

- Content: Tends to focus primarily on military events happening in Afghanistan.
- Length: Varies.
- Language: Pashto.
- Publication: Quarterly.
- Existence: Since 2006.

Hezb-e-Islami (HIG) origin

Shahadat *(Martyrdom)*

This is the official newspaper of Hezb-e-Islami and is mainly circulated throughout Pakistan's Federally Administered Tribal Areas (FATA). The magazine does not report Taliban attacks and claims, but rather offers messages and statements from Gulbuddin Hekmatyar and attacks attributed to his commanders. *Shahadat* ran its own website, www.shahadatnews.com, which was active until October 2008. Access to the website was broken as of 1 November 2009; it then reappeared on the internet under the name *Daily Shahadat*, accessible at http://dailyshahadat.com/index.php

Tanweer *(Enlightenment)*

Tanweer is a Hezb-e-Islami (Hekmatyar) circular that is published in Peshawar and offers the views of Gulbuddin Hekmatyar and updates from his militant originations activities inside Afghanistan. The late Mohammad Asif Mukhbat, a senior member of HIG, initially ran this magazine. He died of abdominal problems in late May 2011. Mukhbat was also responsible for publishing Hekmatyar's statements and publications.[7] *Tanweer* magazine also carries information regarding the current political situation and offers commentary on Islamic topics.

- Content: Statements by Gulbuddin Hekmatyar, anti-Coalition editorials, interviews with Hezb-e-Islami field commanders.
- Length: 60 or more pages.
- Language: Pashto and Dari.
- Publication: Monthly.
- Existence: N/A.

Mesaq-i-Esaar *(Covenant of Sacrifice)*

A weekly newspaper published in black and white by the Cultural Section of HIG Central Zone Kabul. The newspaper materials are mostly reprints from HIG daily publications of newspapers and website. It is not clear where it is published but it covers HIG propaganda in 8 pages on a weekly basis. Counting the serial number of the newspaper volumes, it appears that the newspaper was founded in early 2007.

- Content: Gulbuddin Hekmatyar statements, HIG military gains, pro HIG political literature and editorials, anti-Coalition and ISAF forces articles, transcripts of interviews with Hezb-e-Islami senior members, religious and cultural pieces.
- Length: around 8 pages.
- Language: Pashto and Dari.
- Publication: Weekly.
- Existence: N/A.

Ihsas *(Feelings)*

A monthly color magazine covering political and social issues published by Zawan Islami Tanzim, a youth wing of HIG.

- Content: The magazine focus is not limited to Afghanistan, but covers the broader Islamic community around the world. It also covers topics such as religious issues, anti-Coalition forces rhetoric and propaganda, and women's rights in Islam and the West. The front cover of its first publication appeared on HIG youth wing's Facebook page. Considering HIG youth wing activities, it seems that the magazine distribution center is in their stronghold Shamshato camp, a prominent Afghan HIG immigrant camp near Peshawar, Pakistan.

- Length: N/A.
- Language: Pashto.
- Publication: Monthly.
- Existence: Since November 2010.

Resalat *(Duty)*

The masthead says that *Resalat* magazine is "a bimonthly independent, jihadi, political and scientific publication. Proprietor of the magazine is the Martyr Asadollah Jihadwal Cultural Centre."[8]

- Content: *Resalat* publishes the views of Gulbuddin Hekmatyar's Hezb-e-Islami as well as commentaries on jihad, Islam, politics; it offers scathing editorials against the Afghan government and the presence of international forces.
- Length: Over 22 pages.
- Language: Pashto and Dari.
- Publication: Every other month.
- Existence: N/A.

Zamir *(Conscience)*

An alleged weekly published by the Association for the Protection of the Islamic Culture in Afghanistan. Little is known about this publication.

Published in Peshawar

Hittin

An Urdu magazine allegedly associated with al-Qaeda and produced by Al-Fajr Media Center. It publishes articles discussing Qur'anic verses and hadiths, justifying martyrdom not only against the United States, but also the Pakistani army.

- Content: Often commentaries on jihad, Islam, politics; it offers scathing editorials against the Pakistani army.

- Length: Over 60 pages.
- Language: Urdu.
- Publication: Once a month.

Wahdat

A daily publication covering politics and security in Afghanistan and Pakistan.

- Content: Covers the political and security situation in Afghanistan and Pakistan; offers editorials and Pashto poetry as well.
- Length: 6 pages.
- Publication: Daily.
- Language: Pashto.

Nawa-i Afghan Jihad *(Voice or melody of the Afghan jihad)*

Affiliated with the Haqqani Network, this publication appears only in Urdu and contains a litany of anti-government and anti-Coalition commentaries, reports, and interviews with top insurgent commanders. The late Jalaluddin Haqqani was interviewed on the use of suicide bombers in a November 2009 issue.

- Content: Publishes insurgent commentary and editorials as well as interviews with known insurgent commanders.
- Length: Approximately 30–50 pages.
- Language: Urdu.
- Publication: Monthly.
- Existence: N/A.

Likwal

Pashto-language magazine offering commentary and editorials that defend the rights of Pashtuns. It specifically covers developments in Pakistan and their impact on the Pashtun people.

- Content: Pashtun issues.
- Length: Approximately 20 pages or more.
- Publication: Monthly.
- Language: Pashto.

Hewad

Periodic newspaper.

- Content: Offers commentaries critical of Pakistani government policies, US foreign policy in Afghanistan and Pakistan, and chronicles the suffering of Pashtuns on both sides of the Durand Line.
- Length: 4 pages.
- Language: Pashto.
- Publication: Daily.

Khabroona

Periodic newspaper.

- Content: Offers editorials regarding US foreign policy in Afghanistan and Pakistan and India's destabilizing role in the region. Also covers sports and arts.
- Length: 6 pages.
- Language: Pashto.
- Publication: Daily.

5

THE TALIBAN'S USE OF *SHABNAMAH* (NIGHT LETTERS)[1]

Shabnamah (or night letters) are an effective means of communication, especially in rural Afghan areas. Night letters are part of the Afghan folklore, which has many functions, especially in a rural illiterate society as found in most parts of rural Afghanistan. According to Louis Dupree, folklore in Afghanistan "explain[s] and justif[ies] the group['s] existence [...] define[s] the ideal personality type, [and] describe[s] interpersonal, in-group and extra-group relations."[2] Night letters are "framing instruments" that present "stories" and serve a number of functions, with social control being one of them.

Opponents to the Afghan regime have often used night letters to mobilize people against the government. The Mujahidin used them during the Soviet invasion to rally support around their insurgency, and now the Taliban send them to villages, at times covertly, to threaten people, call for jihad, and announce a code of conduct for the population to follow. The Taliban benefit from the lack of communication infrastructure and the high levels of illiteracy, because it is hard for people to verify the accuracy of information in the letters or more simply to be exposed to a different discourse or narrative.

One can also argue that the use of *shabnamah* is more than utilitarian for the Taliban: symbolism is also important. Night letters are part of the Afghan tradition and one can assume that people are more receptive to them than to any other/new means of communication that would be foreign to their culture. The use of *shabnamah* is also testament to the Taliban's ability to immerse itself physically in the population, and also psychologically through its ability to use terms and meanings that are culturally close to their audience so as to mobilize or control it.

The Taliban's primary target audience when disseminating *shabnamah* remains the *local population*. The methods and techniques used at the rural, district, and village level remain low-tech and cost-effective but are also extremely potent. Large swathes of these areas, especially in the rural environs, are generally devoid of technological media such as radio, television, internet, landline telephones or printing presses, although this is changing slowly since the US invasion of Afghanistan, especially with the relative abundance of cell phones that are now appearing in the country's rural areas. Nevertheless, in these rural, hinterland areas, the populace is still largely isolated, illiterate, and self-sustaining. Such communities remain vulnerable to Taliban infiltration through low-tech means. The communication methods employed by the Taliban in these areas consist of direct contact (oral communications), radio transmissions, and the distribution of *shabnamah*—crudely written statements posted on walls or doors inside villages, often at dead of night.[3]

Night letters were an effective tool during the Soviet–Afghan jihad, as suggested above, and were quickly reinstated following the Taliban's ousting in November 2001. Interpreting the messages, themes, stories, and intended audiences of these night letters is critical to understanding how the Taliban intimidate and influence community decisions and actions.[4]

Night letters[5] generally address an entire village or district and often threaten violence or death if the demands of the letter are not met. Night letters sometimes "advise" the intended audience, a whole district, village, or influential community leaders, on issues of conduct or warn of an impending attack. Night letter tropes can be summarized as:

- an appeal to past Afghan struggles against "foreign invaders": the Taliban regularly play on how foreign powers have been historically defeated by the peoples of Afghanistan
- the battle between the Taliban and the Karzai or Ghani "puppet" regime and its foreign coalition represents a "cosmic conflict" between the righteous and the infidel. Afghans have a collective religious responsibility to fight the apostates and invaders.
- the Taliban's enemies represent "crusaders" that are promoting Christianity and attempting to destroy Islam
- the power of "martyrdom": brave Afghans will sacrifice themselves to save Afghanistan

- the fight against their enemies involves saving honor
- supporting the enemy is prohibited. The penalty for ignoring the warnings is usually death.

Table 5.1: Thematic lines of operation for night letters

Counter-collaboration: Threats are made against Afghan citizens, entire villages or districts, tribal elders and or other influential personalities, for working with either Coalition forces or the Afghan government. This also includes Afghan security personnel, translators, and "spies."

Counter-education: Threats are made against schoolchildren, their parents, school teachers, principals, administrators, and school facilities.

Counter-reconstruction: Threats are made against construction companies (both domestic and international), laborers, the villages, and districts benefiting from such projects, and the sites of the projects.

Counter-mobility: Threats are made against specific avenues, roadways, bazaars, or other geographic areas. These threats are generally in the form of a warning for citizens not to travel or go near areas during specific time frames due to an impending attack.

Counter-stability: Threats are made against tribal elders, civilians, women, religious personalities, government officials, non-governmental organizations, and political/factional parties.

Table 5.1 presents the general, thematic lines of night letters. As suggested, these Taliban IO artifacts often focus on themes such as counter-collaboration, counter-education, counter-reconstruction, counter-mobility, counter-stability, and explicit tactical military directives.[6]

Given the simplicity, the cost-effectiveness, and the time-tested tradition of night letters in Afghan society, the Taliban are not alone in using them as an underground means of communication and intimidation. Several insurgent groups operating independently, but who support the Taliban's activities to one degree or another, also distribute night letters, sometimes even co-authoring letters. Additionally, there is evidence that criminal elements also try to exploit the fear these messages evoke by forging night letters in the name of the Taliban.

As will be demonstrated below, night letters have played a critical role in the information campaign employed by the Taliban in an effort to establish a popular base for their insurgency, wrapped in the narrative of jihad against the Kabul regime.

Taliban night letter stories and narrative analysis

Night letters, as suggested above, have been a traditional and common instrument of Afghan religious figures, jihadists, and rebels to encourage people, especially (but not exclusively) in rural populations, to oppose both state authority and regulations. Dupree's seminal work on Afghanistan suggests that such "framing" instruments, often in the form of folklore, performed a variety of significant functions to include "social control," where individuals are told by illustration what they should or should not do and what rewards or penalties they will incur for not following these norms.[7] Taliban *shabnamah* are often the modern manifestation of such folklore instruments and serve the same purpose.

Traditionally, storytelling and narratives, especially oral history and *shabnamah*, have been extremely important to the people of Afghanistan as well as to the tribes in the Afghanistan–Pakistan border area. Unique and pervasive themes are found throughout Afghan poetry and literature that resonate with Afghans. In many respects Afghanistan's literature, arts, and music have been critical dynamics for Afghan perseverance and adaptation. Narratives also served an important role in Afghan social mobilization, be it peaceful or violent. This has been especially true when tribal collective actions have intersected with political opportunities.[8] During the British colonialist period, for example, anti-colonial literature encouraged rebellion against the British and their patrons.

As suggested above, night letters and oral stories, as well as narratives, were important instruments used by the Mujahidin against their Soviet occupiers.[9] Resistance literature called for total opposition against the Soviets and their "puppet" Afghan leaders and support for jihad to establish an Islamic order. While a variety of means were used to deliver such messages to the Afghan public, the particularly powerful media, especially in the rural areas, were poems and music.[10]

Below is an example of a widely circulated Pashtun folk poem that was used to transmit a narrative characterizing Soviet-installed Babrak Karmal as a traitor:

> O Babrak! Son of Lenin
> You do not care for the religion and the faith
> You may face your doom and
> May you receive a calamity, O son of a traitor.
> O son of Lenin.[11]

Narratives were also used by the anti-Soviet Mujahidin against King Zahir Shah and the royal family, as illustrated by a popular Mujahidin folk song presented below. This narrative contrasts the sacrifices made by the anti-Soviet Mujahidin with the exiled life of the Afghan king and how he had forsaken his legacy and ultimate rewards:

> You have none of your family fighting in Afghanistan,
> Only the brave are here, you are
> Enjoying life in Italy.
> Wind of the morning, go tell Zahir Shah
> There is no *halwa* [sweetmeat] for you in Afghanistan
> The graves of your ancestors are here,
> But there will be no grave for you in Afghanistan.[12]

Night letters were a particularly useful Mujahidin influence and intimidation technique. In Nelofer Pazira's biographical story, called *A Bed of Red Flowers*, she describes night letters used to coordinate shop closings or other activities designed to create solidarity among the anti-Soviet Afghan population. One activity coordinated by the nocturnal campaign was a concert of "*Allah Akbar*"s (God is Great) shouted from the rooftops of village houses. This created a *levée en masse* effect toward the Soviet invaders, and reminded the secular communists of the unifying power of Islam.

> The next day we are tired but, as if concealing our night's secret from the light of day, we don't talk about *Allahu Akbar*s, until Uncle Wahid arrives with the news. In a silent rejection, all Kabul shopkeepers decided to keep their stores closed yesterday, February 22, 1980; they designated the night as the time to voice that day's protest. An anonymous nightly letter had been spread all over Kabul, asking people to cry *Allahu Akbar* after dark, says Uncle Wahid. For the following two days, Kabul shops remain shut, and for the third night in a row we are standing on the roof, joining in this religious symphony. Until dawn we chant, "God is great." We are all so caught up in this rotation of rhythm and order that no one complains about the lack of sleep ... this is our welcome, Afghan-style, to the Soviet Invasion.[13]

The Taliban have adopted *shabnamah* as a well-tested, cost-effective method of instruction and intimidation. The Taliban regularly post such letters or leaflets during the night, warning of the "wrath" that villages will face if they cooperate with US forces (the "Christian invaders") or the Karzai regime ("a US puppet").[14] The Taliban rely on the educated populace to transmit the *shabnamah* to illiterate villagers. Often these "letters" are pasted to the walls of mosques and government buildings and promise death to anyone who defies their threats or instructions. They are typically aimed at symbols of authority and supporters of the Kabul government, and often read as follows: "Once this government falls, we will be in power. We will have your documents, your résumés, your names and your addresses. We will come and punish you."

The Taliban have thus far been true to their word in sowing doubt and fear among Afghans.[15] As reported by *Time Magazine*:

> Night letters left across southern Afghanistan, the Taliban's stronghold, have slowed government services and brought reconstruction projects to a halt. In Kandahar province, many police officers have quit, and after letters appeared threatening employees, two medical clinics were shut down. In the past two months, insurgents have burned down 11 schools in the region. Night letters warning parents to keep their children home presaged some of the attacks.[16]

The Taliban night letters represent a strategic and effective instrument, crafting poetic diatribes which appeal to the moral reasoning of Afghan villagers. While many of the night letters represent overt intimidation, they also present important insights into who and what the Taliban represent. The quality and use of these letters have impressed professional US Information and Psychological Operation (PYSOP) officers who consider them "eloquent and impressive" and subsequently more effective than the vast majority of US Information Operation artifacts.[17]

Figure 5.1 reproduces a Taliban night letter[18] distributed in Kandahar in 2003 entitled "Message to the 'Mujahid' Afghan nation!" It is a good example of the Taliban's literary eloquence and poetic approach to persuasion, originating in historical intercultural communications found throughout Afghanistan and Iran.[19] This *shabnamah* references Afghanistan's grand history and the threat that Americans and their "cronies" pose to a historically great Islamic Afghan government. The proclamation is addressed to the "Mujahid people" of Afghanistan, intimating the notion that the country itself is engaged in a jihad or lawful war against infidels and an apostate government. The label "Mujahid," as used in this narrative, does not apply solely to the Taliban but rather to the Afghan population as a whole. The message suggests that all Afghans have a role in this campaign against a common enemy of Islam, and Afghans have an obligation to join the fight against the infidels.

The posting is a well-prepared story that helps frame the narrative reflecting on the "illustrious" history of rule of three particular Afghan leaders who harnessed the power of Islam. The first "ancestor and hero" mentioned is Ahmad Shah Durrani (Abdali), founder of the Sadozai dynasty of the Abdali who would establish the Durrani Afghan Empire in Kandahar in 1747. He is

Figure 5.1: Taliban night letter, Kandahar, 2003

د افغانستان مجاهدو لسته پیغام

دافغانستان مجاهدو لسه تاسوپه تاریخ کښی داسلام لپاره بی مثاله خدمت کریدی ـ اودنری

که روسه موپه وارواشکست ورکریدی ـ اوستاسونیکه کا نولکه احمد شاه ابدالی ، محمود

غزنوی ، شهاب الدین غوری ، اونوروقهرمانانو دکاروسره په جهاد کولوکښی دیرینه تاریخ کښی

دی ـ خو افسوس ننورخ یوخود امریکا روزلی غلامان دروښان فکرانوپه نامه د افغانستان

دغیرت دک تاریخ له خاورسره خاوری کر ی نن بیا هم ستاسوبعیان علماء طلباء اودیندار خلکه

په دغه شرائطو کښی خپلی وینی داسلام دخدمت لپاره دکاروپه مقابل کښی ښه نه دی

نوباید تاسوچه فرهیخ ویکری خپل دزره محبت د مجاهد و بجیانوسره وساتی ـ اودنری د

که رو دغلطا اودروغجنو تبلیغاتوپه کښه سره د مجاهد و خلاف تبلیغاتوکولو با ندی

دخپلو بینوخاوری وینه کاندی خدانکده په درخود اخیرت به یونیم ملیون دروسانوسره

مجاهد شهیدان ، اودا سلامی امارت بولکه شهیدان افمین به تاسی نه غاره نیسو دا نه

دنپا لاد ید اد نزد ه د هیله لری چه تاسی نمین دا نده بده کړی هیڅکله طالبان د افغانا نوقتل لری

نه غواړی خود یده منفخ تی دامریکا دعنی نښ په نامه افغانان د مغربی حافظین کړیدی دی

اوکفاند اعزازی چه افغانان به افغانانو قتل کړی اوتاسی کړی به امریکایان دافغانستان د دولت غنه

کښی صلاح سوڅی افغانی چه افغانان ـ خلص بن مسلمانانپه مشاهبی نسه کړی اوتاسی کړ

چه د افغانستان بقای مدنی چه اسلامی نعیات پکښی کید ل نن ښه غوکښی چیا فنو دعبای

دیت ورکل کړی ـ یولو بیا نمین دلخاست دی چه دکانولد همکانی لاس ولخلی وینه

مسؤلیت دمومد دناول اخیرت کښی دمغاروی دنشلام ـ نناد م ، اوسه ،

Figure 5.1

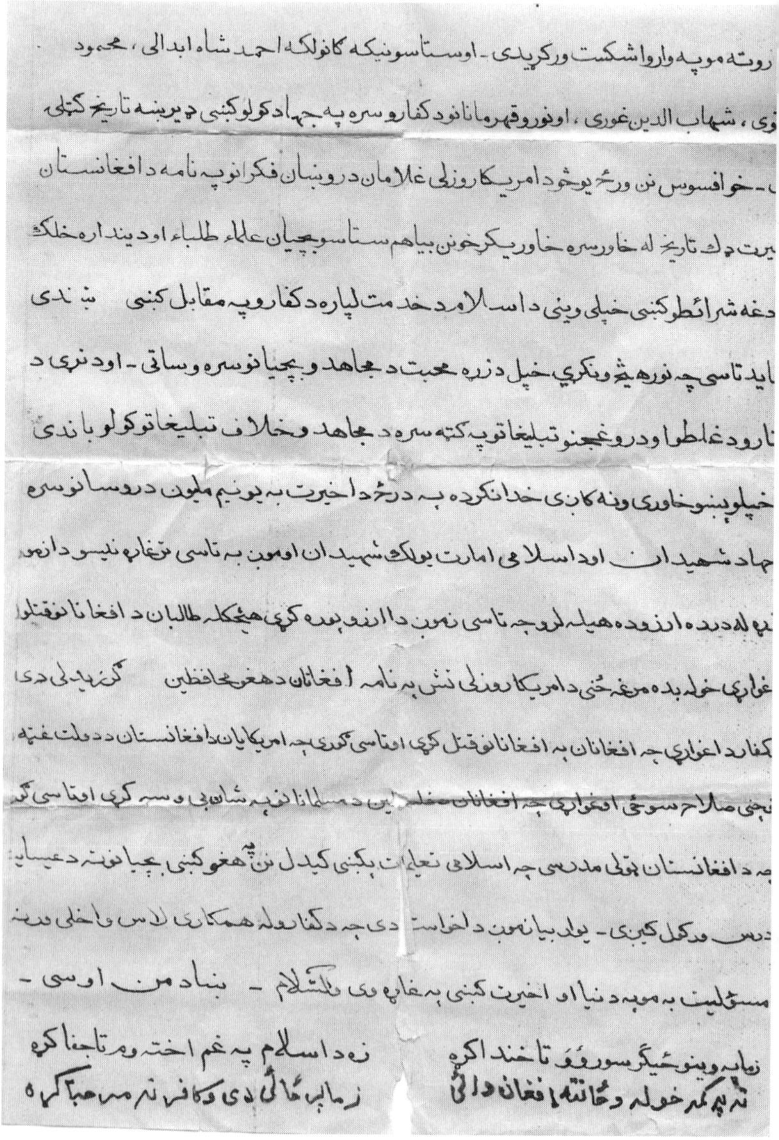
روته موږ په وار وار شکست ورکړیدی - او ستاسو نیکه گانو لکه احمد شاه ابدالی، محمود
وی، شهاب الدین غوری، او نورو قهرمانانو د کفارو سره په جهاد کولو کښې دیر ښه تاریخ کښلی
- خو افسوس نن ورځ یو څو د امریکا روزلی غلامان د روسیان فکرانو په نامه د افغانستان
یرت دک تاریخ له خاورسره خاورې کړ خو نن بیاهم ستاسو ځوانان علماء طلباء او دیندار خلک
دغه شرائطو کښې خپلې وینې د اسلام د خدمت لپاره د کفارو په مقابل کښې ... ندی
باید تاسی چه نوره هیڅ ونکړي خپل د زړه محبت د مجاهدو ځوانانو سره وساتی - او د نړی د
نارو د غلطو او دروغجنو تبلیغاتو په کته سره د مجاهدو خلاف تبلیغاتو کولو باندی
خپلو ښو خاوری وینه کانړی خدا نکړده به د ... د اخیرت به یو نیم ملیون د روسانو سره
جهاد شهیدان او د اسلامی امارت پولک شهیدان او مونږ به تاسی ترغاړه نیسو د
نه له دیده ... هیله لرو چه تاسی ... هیڅکله طالبان د افغانانو قتلول
غواړی خوله بده مرغه ځینی د امریکا روزلی نن په نامه افغانانو د هغو محافظین ... گرځیدلی دی
کفار د اغواړی چه افغانان به افغانانو قتل کړی او تاسی کړی چه امریکایان د افغانستان د دولت
... صلاح سوځی اغواړی چه افغانان ... د مسلمانانو په شانوی وسره کړی او تاسی
په د افغانستان ټولی مدرسی چه اسلامی تعلیمات پکښی کیدل نن ... هغو کښی ځوانانو ته د عیسای
درس ورکول کیږی - ... د اخواستدی چه د کفارو له همکاری لاس واخلی د دی
مسئولیت به موږ د دنیا او اخیرت کښی په غاړه وی والسلام - ... او سی -

زمانه وینو ځیگر سور غو تا خندا کړه — نه د اسلام په غم اخته وم تا جفا کړه
ته په کمر خوله د ځانته افغان دا لی — زمانه ځالی دی د کافر ته مرحبا کړه

Translation of Taliban Night Letter, Kandahar, 2003[20]

Message to the "Mujahid" (freedom fighter) Afghan Nation!

You have served Islam a great deal throughout history and have defeated the non-Muslims of the world. Your ancestors such as Ahmad Shah Abdali, Mahmood Ghaznawi, Shahaabuddin Ghori and other heroes have recorded a great history in fight against non-Muslims, but it is a pity that today some America-trained servants, supposedly bright-minded, have destroyed the honored history of Afghanistan. Today once again your sons, clerics and Taliban and the faithful people in these circumstances are fighting against non-Muslims and are serving Islam. If you don't do anything else, at least support your Mujahid sons and do not be impressed by the false propaganda of non-Muslim enemies. God knows, one and half million martyrs of the jihad against the Russians and one hundred thousand martyrs of the Islamic Emirate of Afghanistan (martyred Taliban) will ask you for the cost of their martyrdom, so we hope that you meet those expectations. They are stopping Islamic education and instead are teaching Christianity to your children. The Taliban never want to kill common civilians, but unfortunately some so-called Afghans have become the supporters of our enemies. Non-Muslims want to kill and pit Afghan against Afghan; in the name of (attacking the) Taliban they are attacking everybody, they are killing Afghans and destroying your houses, and they are destroying Islamic madrasas in Afghanistan. They burn Afghan arms and ammunitions. They want to make Afghanistan as helpless as Palestine. You have seen that in all madrasas (Islamic schools) nowadays they teach Christianity to your children. Once again, we request you not to support non-Muslims, otherwise you will have the whole responsibility here and hereafter.

Be happy

Poem

I was so sad you laughed
I was caring for Islam and you betrayed us
How can you call yourself an Afghan
Instead of me, you supported a non-Muslim

Document 5.1: *Shabnamah story* "Message to the 'Mujahid'
Afghan nation!"

Afghans throughout history have defeated infidel invaders while preserving their Islamic way of life. Numerous Afghan leaders throughout
history, including the father of our nation, Ahmad Shah Durrani
(Abdali), have demonstrated this. The infidel Americans along with
their apostate Afghan puppets are attempting to destroy our nation, our
way of life, and our religion. Your families and clerics and the Taliban,
as well as all faithful Afghans, are fighting these evil people in the name
of Islam. You must support your faithful sons as well the memory of
half a million anti-Soviet Afghan jihadists who were martyred during
our destruction of the Soviet infidel invaders. Beware of the false teachings of the infidels who want to destroy Islam and bring Christianity to
Afghanistan. We see the Americans destroying our schools and killing
faithful civilians as well as our religious "seekers." Afghanistan. They
want to make us as helpless as the Palestinians. If you don't support the
Taliban's efforts, you are not an Afghan but rather a betrayer who will
face punishment forever.

---

considered by many as the "father" of modern Afghanistan. While Ghilzai
members of the Taliban have long disdained the Durranis, Ahmad Shah is
revered by all Afghans. Sykes's *History of Afghanistan* calls Ahmad Shah "a
monarch whose high descent and warlike qualities made him peculiarly
acceptable to his aristocratic and virile Chiefs, as well as to his warlike subjects
in general. In short, he possessed all the qualities that enabled him successfully
to found the Kingdom of Afghanistan."[21]

The second "ancestor and hero" referenced is Sultan Mahmud Ghaznawi, a
young Turkic (non-Afghan) king who ascended the throne around the year
1000 and embarked on Ghaznavid empire-building that represented "one of
the great renaissances of the Early Islamic period."[22] Mahmud was considered
a great general who conducted at least seventeen successful campaigns against
India. According to Dupree: "He added northwest India and the Punjab to
his empire, and enriched his treasury by looting wealthy Hindu temples.
Probably more important, Mahmud's mullahs converted many Hindus to
Islam."[23] Historians, such as Caroe, trace the origin of the Ghilzai nation to
the Turkish tribes of the Ghaznavid empire.[24] Hence, the reference to

Mahmud could be alluding to the glorious genealogy of the Ghilzai, a very important Taliban dynamic during this period.

The early political Taliban of 1994 primarily consisted of rural Pashtuns from the Ghilzai nation[25] with some support from the Kakar tribe of the Ghurghusht nation.[26] The composition of the Taliban has since changed, in many respects, to reflect the local demographics and tribes of the specific areas where they are operating. The Ghilzai are descendants of the great nomad clans (*powindah*) of Sulaiman Khel, and the Aka Khel are the largest Afghan tribal confederation, including the tribes of Sulaiman Khel, Ali Khel, Aka Khel, Taraki, Nasirs, Tokhis, Hotaks, and Khototi.[27]

Much of the original Taliban leadership, including the late Mullah Mohammed Omar, came from the Hotak Ghilzai tribe that held power in Afghanistan in the eighteenth century and for a time even possessed the throne of Isfahan (Persia). The Hotaki Ghilzais under Mir Wais Ghilzai achieved historical fame as the liberators of Kandahar from Safavid control in 1709. In 1722 the Hotaki served as the leading tribe in the invasion of Persia and destruction of the Persian Empire.[28] The importance, remembrance, and implications of such a proud history in tribal Afghanistan stupefy many Western analysts.

Nadir Shah ended the Ghilzai regime in 1737. After the assassination of Nadir Shah in 1747, the Afghans established the first "modern" Afghan government in Kandahar after they elected Ahmed Shah Durrani as their ruler. The Ghilzai have traditionally held a strong animosity toward the Durrani Pashtuns, who took power from the Ghilzai and have held it almost continuously for the last 300 years.[29] The Durranis have provided all of Afghanistan's modern kings, a fact not lost on the Ghilzai. Only four times have the Ghilzai seized national power: in 1721, when Mir Wais took the throne; in 1978, after a coup against Mohammed Daoud by Marxist military officers, who immediately handed over power to the Marxist People's Democratic Party of Afghanistan leader Nur Mohammed Taraki;[30] again in 1996, when Mullah Omar came to power and with the election of President Mohammad Ashraf Ghani in September 2014. Since the demise of Mir Wais Ghilzai and his empire, the Ghilzai have hated the Durranis, their arch-rivals and the tribe of former President Hamid Karzai.

The divisions between Durrani and Ghilzai Afghans have been at the root of centuries of conflict and intrigue in Afghanistan. Such issues were intimately involved in the demographics of Peshawar politics during the anti-Soviet jihad.[31] In fact, a case can be made for the politics of the Afghan war being a virtual Ghilzai affair. Khalq's Ghilzai leaders, Hafizullah Amin and Muhammad Taraki, began the process with the 1978 coup. Khalqi officers, many of who were Ghilzai, dominated the Afghan military forces. Babrak Karmal (with Durrani connections) was replaced by Najibullah, one of the few Parchamis with Ghilzai roots. Except for Babrak Karmal, the great Durrani Pashtun confederation had little representation on either side of the conflict. Khalqi members of the Peoples' Democratic Party of Afghanistan (PDPA) were committed to breaking the established tradition of Durrani rule.[32] Some spoke of the Marxist usurpation and the war as Ghilzai revenge against Durrani dominance. On the resistance side, as suggested above, nearly all the key Mujahidin parties were led by or had strong ties to the Ghilzai. Ethnic rivalry, perhaps more than Islamic ideology, was even responsible for the refusal of the Peshawar parties to accept former King Zahir Shah into Mujahidin politics.[33]

The final "ancestor and hero" reference in the night letter of Document 5.1 is to Shahab al-Din Ghuri of the Ghurid dynasty, who ruled from 1173 to 1206 and controlled the entire eastern caliphate encompassing much of Afghanistan, eastern Iran, and modern Pakistan.[34] His numerous invasions of India and his powerful rule helped construct a widespread and long-lasting historical memory framed by heroism and sacrifice through Afghan generations. Although Ghaznawi and Ghuri were not Afghan by birth, history granted them an Afghan pedigree and the two kings are still honored as heroes. Hence, the Taliban night letter uses the collective historical memory of Afghans handed down through generations to frame their intellectual argument against popular support of the Karzai regime and American forces. The *shabnamah*'s narrative glorifies those who have fought and converted infidels to the righteous path: the goal of the Taliban.

This *shabnamah* also represented a clear challenge to the Karzai regime, its expatriate members, and proffers that "it is a pity that today some American-trained servants ... have destroyed the honored history of Afghanistan." The letter also follows the time-honored Afghan practice of attacking foreign influence: a xenophobic message that has historically resonated with many of the Afghan people, because this is what the Karzai government and the Americans represented in the eyes of the Taliban.

A clear distinction is made between "Muslims" and "non-Muslims" as the Taliban appeal to the "true Islamic believers" and decry the "false propaganda of non-Muslim enemies." The letter appeals to the population's gratitude and appreciation for the "martyrs" of the Soviet occupation and the Taliban's bat-cles during Operation Enduring Freedom-Afghanistan (OEF-A), even citing casualty statistics. The letter states that the Taliban are against killing common citizens, but at times it cannot be avoided. On the other hand, the *shabnamah* argues that supporters of the Karzai regime and the Americans are not "Afghans" and are open targets.

It is interesting to note that this night letter made its appearance during the height of the Demobilization, Disarmament, and Reorganization (DDR) campaign, aimed at ridding the country of weapons and convincing reluctant and recalcitrant regional and warlord militia members to support the Karzai regime. The letter states that "Non-Muslims want to kill Afghans by Afghans while they *burn their arms and ammunitions.*" The author of the letter obviously believes that disarmament is ludicrous while Afghanistan's enemies are "killing" Afghans. During the 1990s there were more personal weapons in Afghanistan than in India and Pakistan combined. "By some estimates more such weapons had been shipped into Afghanistan during the previous decade than to any other country in the world."[35] Afghans and especially the Pashtuns revel in a "gun culture." One of the first sounds that a rural Afghan male infant hears after he is born, immediately after praise to Allah, is the firing of guns celebrating his birth. An appeal against DDR is not only a clear indication that the Taliban tracked aspects of the Bonn Process, especially those that have the potential to impact on their insurgent actions; it is also, more importantly, a recognition that the Taliban understand that taking away a Pashtun's gun is equivalent to taking away his manhood. While the Taliban undoubtedly do not want Afghans, especially their supporters, to give up their weapons and become "helpless," the narrative is appealing to a deeper characteristic that resonates with nearly every Pashtun. Indeed guns are intimately related to the Pashtun tribal code of Pashtunwali and "as a result ... most [Pashtun] males become acquainted with weapons in their early childhood and develop a keen sense of marksmanship."[36] The Pashtun's affinity for weapons has traditionally plagued every state's attempt to enforce its own rule of law in deference to Pashtunwali.

The document does not communicate any direct threat against the US military, but it does insinuate that Americans destroyed mosques and madrasas in order to re-educate Afghan children about Christianity. Such a narrative is presented to create mistrust and apprehension among the Afghan population. Afghanistan is 99.5 per cent Muslim, and religion is and always has been a central characteristic of the Afghan people.

The letter warns that the enemies "want to make Afghanistan as helpless as Palestine." An emphasis on the plight of the Palestinians has been a central focal and rallying point for Islamists for decades. In the past, Islamic struggles outside Afghanistan have not been an explicit mantra of the Afghan resistance. The Mujahidin, for example, had a more immediate and limited goal of liberating Afghanistan from the Soviets and fighting the puppet government they installed in Kabul. "They had no intention or desire to turn their country into a theater or camp from which to wage global jihad against either other Muslim governments or Western states."[37] It is interesting that the Taliban, who in the past have never represented a transnational jihadist organization, would focus on more global struggles, even indirectly in their *shabnamah*.

The letter concludes with a poem that is aimed at invoking respect and striking a chord in the receivers' historical memory. As suggested in Chapter 1, message repetition provides a way to remember facts or messages and enhances the delivery method with emotion anchored in cultural traditions. It is likely that this proclamation was read aloud by an educated village elder to illiterate members of the local populace with an emphasis on the poem at the end of the letter, possibly even reading it twice to allow the audience to experience the power of the poem.

Figure 5.2 presents a *shabnamah* that is an example of a warning letter targeted at the populace of the Kandahar province towns of Ma'ruf and Arghistan.[38] Unlike the night letter examined above, this letter appears quickly constructed and warns the Afghan population against supporting the Americans.

The letter was written in Pashto and warns the residents of Ma'ruf and Arghistan against cooperating with the Americans. It explicitly suggests that the Taliban will kill all those that cooperate with the Americans once the Americans leave. The point is emphasized by asserting that "the Americans will not always be there" to protect those who chose to cooperate. Moreover, the letter states that the Taliban "know" the names and location of collaborators and compare these present-day collaborators with those who were "loyal" to the Russians during the anti-Soviet jihad.

Such a message is typical of messages delivered by Taliban mullahs speaking to rural village elders. They are fond of saying, "the Americans have the wristwatches, but we have the time." The simple message they deliver in person or by night letter such as the one presented in Document 5.2 is one of intimidation: "The Americans may stay for five years, they may stay for ten, but eventually they will leave, and when they do, we will come back to this village and kill every family that has collaborated with the Americans or the Karzai gov-

Figure 5.2: Warning letter to the people of Ma'ruf and Arghistan, Kandahar province

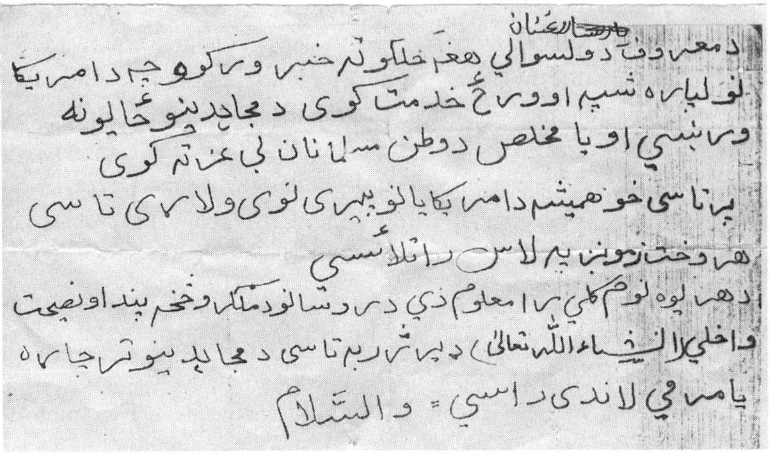

او ارغستان

د معروف د ولسوالي هغو خلکو ته خبر ورکوو چې د امریکا

لو لپاره شپه او ورځ خدمت کوي د مجاهدینو ځایونه

ورښيي او یا مخلص د وطن مسلمانانو بې عزته کوي

په تاسي خو همیشه د امریکایانو پهرې نوی ولاړې تاسي

هر وخت زمونږ په لاس راتلای شئ

د هر یوه نوم کلي را معلوم ذي د روسانو د ملګرو څخه پند او نصیحت

واخلي ان شاء الله تعالی د ډېر ژر به تاسي د مجاهدینو تر چاړه

یا مرمي لاندې راسي = والسلام

Translation of Figure 5.2[39]

We inform those people of Ma'ruf district who serve Americans day and night and reveal the places of Mujahidin to them, or those who dishonor sincere Muslims of the country, that American guards will not always be there and we can catch you any time.

We know the name and place of every person. Learn a lesson from those who were loyal to the Russians. (If God wills) soon you will come under the knife or bullet of Mujahidin.

Document 5.2: *Shabnamah story*

We warn all those apostate people living in the Ma'ruf district who tell the American enemies the Taliban plans or their whereabouts that they not only greatly dishonor faithful Muslim Afghans, but will also meet a dreadful fate by a knife or a bullet. The Americans cannot save you—God wills it—just as the infidel Russians could not save those traitor Afghans who supported and were loyal to their efforts. The Taliban know the Afghans who dishonor themselves and all sincere Afghans by helping the enemies of Afghanistan.

ernment." Such a message is devastatingly effective in these areas where transgenerational feuds and revenge are a fabric of the society. It is also an effective message to keep NGOs and reconstruction activities out of areas which the Taliban control.

If one assumes that the center of gravity for both the insurgency and counter-insurgency is popular support and for the Kabul government to succeed, it must deliver reconstruction, infrastructure, and services to the hinterlands (areas which have thus far received virtually nothing), then the Taliban's strategy has proven very effective. To reiterate, the three fundamental problems in Afghanistan that have allowed the Taliban's re-emergence are:

- the inability of the national government to establish a politically significant presence throughout the country;
- the failure of Kabul as well as the international community to create a secure rural environment, especially in the south, advantageous to even minimal development and reconstruction;
- the unfulfilled expectations of the people in the southern half of the country who have had no meaningful improvement in the lives, despite the fact that they live in an environment where, at the time, one child in five dies before the age of five and 90 per cent of the population lives in conditions little changed since Alexander the Great.[40]

The hinterlands of the east and south remain impoverished wastelands with few schools and roads and little prospect of a better life for the vast majority of the population. A poll conducted in 2005, when this night letter was sent, showed that six out of ten Afghans had no electricity and only 3 per cent had it consistently.[41] Significant change has not happened since this poll was taken, especially in the south, despite the fact that the US has spent considerable money "developing" Afghanistan: in total $113.1 billion, or $10 billion more, adjusted for inflation, than the amount the United States committed in civilian assistance (the Marshall Plan) to help rebuild Western Europe after World War II.[42]

The Taliban are well aware of this and continue to put up obstacles to inhibit Kabul or the international community from bettering the lives of the average Afghan villager. Whole districts in provinces such Helmand, Oruzgan, Zabol, Paktika, Ghazni, Wardak, and Logar (to name but a few) are essentially war zones with virtually no chance of rehabilitating fractured infrastructures: a prerequisite for the US long-standing tactics of counter-insurgency in the country.

Figure 5.3 presents a Taliban night story and its translation from the Wardak province, authored by "the Mujahidin of the Islamic Emirate of Afghanistan." This *shabnamah* is significantly different from the other night letters examined here. The message uses language which mimics that regularly used by transnational jihadist organizations and intimates that the ultimate goal of the Afghan insurgency has a global dimension. This message is in stark contrast with the *shabnamah* presented in Document 5.2 written in 2004. The significant differences between these two letters suggest that the Afghan insurgency had the ambition of morphing into a campaign with more transnational concerns, something that we have not seen.

One theme of the letter is: do not associate with or help the Karzai regime and Coalition forces, or you will be judged as one of them ("One who lends a hand to infidels to transgress [against Muslims] is one of them"). This message of intimidation, as we have seen earlier, is clearly a cornerstone of Taliban night letter narratives.

This letter, like many other Taliban *shabnamah*, has considerably more Islamic references than the narratives assessed above (or below). Juergensmeyer suggests that religious tropes are more likely to play a narrative role if the confrontation between two groups can be characterized as a "cosmic struggle or battle." This is most likely in the following circumstances:

1. If the struggle is perceived as a defense of basic identity and dignity.
2. If losing the struggle would be unthinkable.
3. If the struggle is "blocked" and cannot be won in real time or in real terms.[43]

The first two circumstances are valid for the Taliban. The Taliban view their insurgency/jihad, as evidenced in their *shabnamah*, as a struggle over basic questions of identity and culture: it must be won, and losing is not an option. The third circumstance was probably also valid until mid-2004. Since then, however, the emboldened Taliban insurgency has shown real signs of success since their reconstitution in early 2004.

The *shabnamah* invokes the name of Allah via a standard greeting and begins by rallying the population against the "crusaders" and "their domestic servants." The use of the term "crusaders" is significant. This terminology was often used by Osama bin Laden when he referred to the conflict in Afghanistan as a battle between "a crusader army" and Islam.[44] The use of this terminology suggests that the United States and its allies are waging a crusade against Islam, and this "aggression" is not an isolated conflict, but rather the

Figure 5.3: Night letter, Wardak[45]

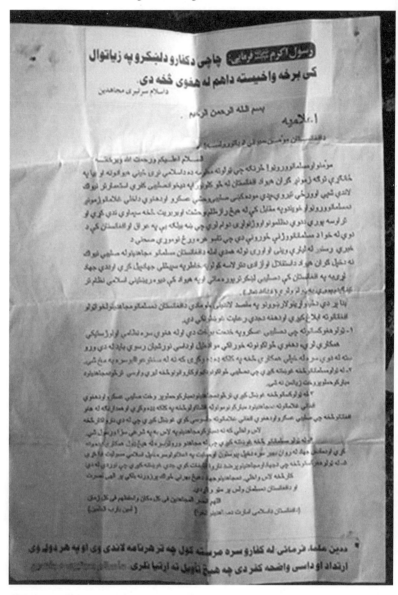

Translation of Figure 5.3[46]

The Prophet of God Mohammed (peace be upon Him) says: One who lends a hand to infidels to transgress [against Muslims] is one of them. By the Islamic Devoted Mujahidin, In the name of Allah, the most merciful and most compassionate

Statement

Pious Afghans, Brave and Courageous People! Accept our greetings. Dear Muslim and devout brother! As you all know, some countries in the Islamic world, and specifically our dear country Afghanistan, have spent day and night under the grip of the crusaders over the last few years. During this time the cruel crusaders' army and their domestic servants have committed grave atrocities, barbarity, and savagery against our innocent brothers and sisters. Their cruelties have not ceased. You have watched and heard of their ongoing savagery in Afghanistan and Iraq, the two best examples that have been exposed by the international media. Therefore, the Afghan Muslim Mujahidin have initiated their sacred jihad to gain the independence of our beloved country from the crusader powers. The jihad will continue until in the end we defeat of the crusaders' army, and establish a pure Islamic State (Inshallah).

Therefore, the Afghan Muslim Mujahidin offer the following related guidelines to help obtain our goals, and earnestly ask all Afghans to respect them seriously:

1. All those who work for and are in the service of the crusader army, cooperate militarily or logistically with them, and carry oil, food and similar things for them: you are strongly warned to stop cooperating with them promptly; otherwise, you will face serious consequences.

2. All those who do business with the crusaders are asked to avoid doing business with them, so as not to suffer during the exalted strike of the Mujahidin on the crusaders.

3. We seriously ask all persons not to expose the holy names of the Mujahidin to the crusaders' army and to their Afghan slaves during the exalted strike of Mujahidin on them, and likewise we ask those Afghans who spy for the Americans and for their Afghan slaves to

stop doing this evil act, otherwise they will be punished at the hands of the holy Mujahidin according to Shar'iah.

4. We ask all Muslims to cooperate wholeheartedly with their Mujahidin brothers and to join their ranks and to support jihad, so as to perform their religious duty properly.

5. We ask all those who spread false allegations against Mujahidin to stop their evil acts. The Mujahid power is not based on any foreign support, it is founded on Allah's blessing and the will of the Afghan Muslim people.

(God grand success to the Mujahid everywhere and always.)

The Mujahidin of the Islamic Emirate of Afghanistan Religious Scholars say: Cooperation with infidels, under any circumstance and for any reason and excuse, in any form, is an open blasphemy that needs no deliberation.

Afghanistan's Devoted Mujahidin.

Document 5.3: *Shabnamah story*

Brave and courageous Afghan Muslim brother, for many years the attacking crusaders have ravaged Afghanistan and other Islamic countries such as Iraq. The crusaders as well as their Afghan apostate slaves have committed savage atrocities against innocent Afghans that have been exposed by the world's media. In response to such barbarity, Afghan Muslim jihadists have fought courageously to free Afghanistan, and the Mujahidin will continue to fight until the crusaders' armies are totally defeated and we can again establish a pure Islamic State. All Afghans working for the crusaders must immediately stop cooperating and doing business with them or they will suffer grave consequences from the Mujahidin. Moreover, all Afghans must immediately stop exposing the Mujahidin to the crusaders or their Afghan apostate slaves. Failure to do this will result in grave punishment sanctioned by Shar'iah. All Afghans have a holy obligation to join and support the jihad. All that we ask is according to Allah's will and blessings.

latest episode in a long chain of conflicts that have been targeted at Muslims. While there is no evidence suggesting that al-Qaeda or an Afghan–Arab wrote this letter, the language used is very similar to the regular terminology used by al-Qaeda. It proclaims a clash of civilizations.

The declaration accuses the "crusaders and their domestic servants" of unceasing "atrocities, barbarity and savagery against our innocent brothers and sisters" in both Afghanistan and Iraq. Both of these conflicts represent, in the eyes of the Taliban, defensive jihads against a Christian onslaught that will continue until the "defeat of the crusaders' army," and "the establishment of a pure Islamic State." The jihad, according to this message, is a collective responsibility of all Muslims and the *shabnamah* instructs Afghans to:

- offer no assistance or cooperation to US or Afghan National Armed Forces or "face serious consequences"
- not divulge the identity ("holy names") of the insurgents
- end the "evil act" of spying for the enemy or "be punished at the hands of the holy Mujahidin according to Shar'iah"
- cooperate and join the Taliban "so as to perform ... religious duty properly"

The letter concludes by suggesting that those who ignore the advice and instructions of the *shabnamah* will be dealt with swiftly without deliberation. Such a response, claims the night letter, has been sanctified by "religious scholars"—a powerful message to Afghans.

Many of the Islamic underpinnings reflected in this *shabnamah* have been a component of the past Afghan resistance movements. For example, Hazarat Shaib or Mullah Shor Bazar (a member of the Mujadidi family) was an important Afghan religious figure whose Ghilzai tribal army or *lashkar*[47] inflicted heavy losses on the British during the Third Anglo-Afghan war of 1919. Hazarat Shaib would later defeat the Afghan reform-minded King Amanullah Khan and assisted Nadir Kahn to overthrow Bacha Saqqao in 1929.[48] Other religious leaders such as Mirwais Khan Hotaki and Mullah Mushki Alam also organized *lashkars* that fought against the British occupation of Afghanistan. And of course during the anti-Soviet jihad, *talibs* (or religious students) regularly fought alongside the Mujahidin, mainly under the leadership of Mohammad Nabi and his Harakat-e-Inqilab-e-Islami and Hezb-e-Islami (Khalis). But none of these movements had explicit global goals aimed at the Islamic *Ummah*.

The role of the Taliban in the larger global Islamist jihad has been a question that has baffled researchers. Most would agree with Fawaz Gerges when he suggests that Afghan resistance has never been focused outside the Afghan border.[49] The message portrayed in the *shabnamah* of Document 5.3, however, indicates that this position could change if the Taliban garner strength and other international events turn against the West (e.g. Iraq, Syria, Libya). There is ample evidence to suggest that the late Mullah Omar appealed to the global *Ummah*,[50] but he as well as the Taliban have traditionally not pursued actions directly and explicitly aimed at this audience.

Figures 5.4 and 5.5 present night letters that represent messages of intimidation against schools and teachers involved in girls' education. The Taliban's strict views against girls' education are related primarily to its views concerning the "protection" of a woman's honor, emanating from the code of Pashtunwali in which women are forbidden to participate in most public events and processes outside their kin group. The authority of the kin is a male prerogative. Gulick describes such kin relations as an expression of the "peril and refuge mentality." He observes that the kin who provide a person with social, emotional, and, if necessary, armed support are also competitors for the same resources. In the case of women, the same brothers and fathers with whom they are so close and who are their protectors are also their executioners, should the males doubt the daughter's or sister's chastity. These are also the relatives who know the person best and to whom he or she is consequently most vulnerable.[51]

The Taliban have consistently pursued a campaign against girls' education by burning schools and attacking teachers. The Afghan Ministry of Education has reported that hundreds of schools have been forced to stop classes: a third of them in the south because of Taliban intimidation.[52] The draconian writs against female education during the reign of the Taliban are well documented and are likely to continue into the future.

Figure 5.4 presents a letter from 2005 found in Kapisa posted to a tree three days before a boys' school in the area was set on fire. The letter was apparently posted by the "Taliban Islamic Movement representative of Parwan and Kapisa provinces" and represents a "warning" against female education. According to Human Rights Watch, other *shabnamah* were also found in the school. The *shabnamah* warns both *ulema* and teachers alike not to attempt to educate girls. It suggests that the Taliban knows who violate this edict and that they will be dealt with appropriately.

Taliban incidents like burning tents and school buildings, explosions near schools, and threats to women teachers are well documented and were a focus of international concern during the reign of the Taliban. Threats such as those

Figure 5.4: Warning from Taliban Islamic movement, representative of Parwan and Kapisa provinces[53]

Translation of Figure 5.4

This is a warning to all those dishonorable people, including *ulema* and teachers, not to teach girls. Based on the information given to us, we strongly ask those people whose names been particularly reported to us not to commit this act of evil. Otherwise, it is they who bear all the responsibilities. They have no right to claim that they have not been informed.

This is to inform all those who have enrolled at boys' schools to stop going to schools. An explosion might occur inside the school compounds. In case of getting hurt, it is they who bear all the responsibilities. They have no right to claim that they have not been informed.

Document 5.4: *Shabnamah story*

Ulema and teachers who are educating girls are dishonorable and acting in an evil, un-Islamic fashion. We know who is doing this and we demand that they immediately stop teaching girls. This is a grave warning to all those dishonorable people not to teach girls. You have been warned and should not be surprised if we seek reprisal. We also demand that boys stop going to schools, because destruction of these schools could happen. You have been warned, so don't be surprised if something happens. If something does happen and someone is hurt, you will be responsible.

---

delivered in the narrative of this night letter cannot be taken lightly. In January 2006 Malim Abdul Habib, headmaster of Shaikh Mathi Baba high school, which is attended by 1,300 boys and girls, was stabbed eight times before he was decapitated in the courtyard of his home in Qalat, Zabul.[54]

The second part of the letter warns students not to go to boys' schools: "an explosion might occur inside the school compounds. If anyone gets hurt, it is they who will bear all the responsibilities. They have no right to claim that they have not been informed." This threat levied at a boys' school that was constructed by a US Provincial Reconstruction Team (PRT) represents an additional indication of the Taliban's strategy of negating most reconstruction and infrastructure development in the Afghan hinterlands.

The *shabnamah* presented in Figure 5.5 is my interpretation of an example of Taliban intimidation directed at a specific individual: Fatima Moshtaq, the then Ghazni province director of education. Threats were apparently directed against Moshtaq because of her role in female education. She was warned that both she and her family were in grave danger. The letter calls on her to resign her position: in the eyes of the Taliban, a position that should never be held by a woman. Similar threats have been directed at numerous government officials by Taliban night letters.

Local education officials in Ghazni blamed the Taliban for scores of the attacks on educational institutions. According to Human Rights Watch during 2004–5, 31 per cent of students officially enrolled in Ghazni schools were girls. In two of the eighteen provincial districts that happen to lie in southern Ghazni and are areas of significant Taliban activity, no girls had enrolled in school:[55] yet another indication that the Taliban intimidation campaign was succeeding.

Figure 5.5: Taliban night letter from Ghazni[56]

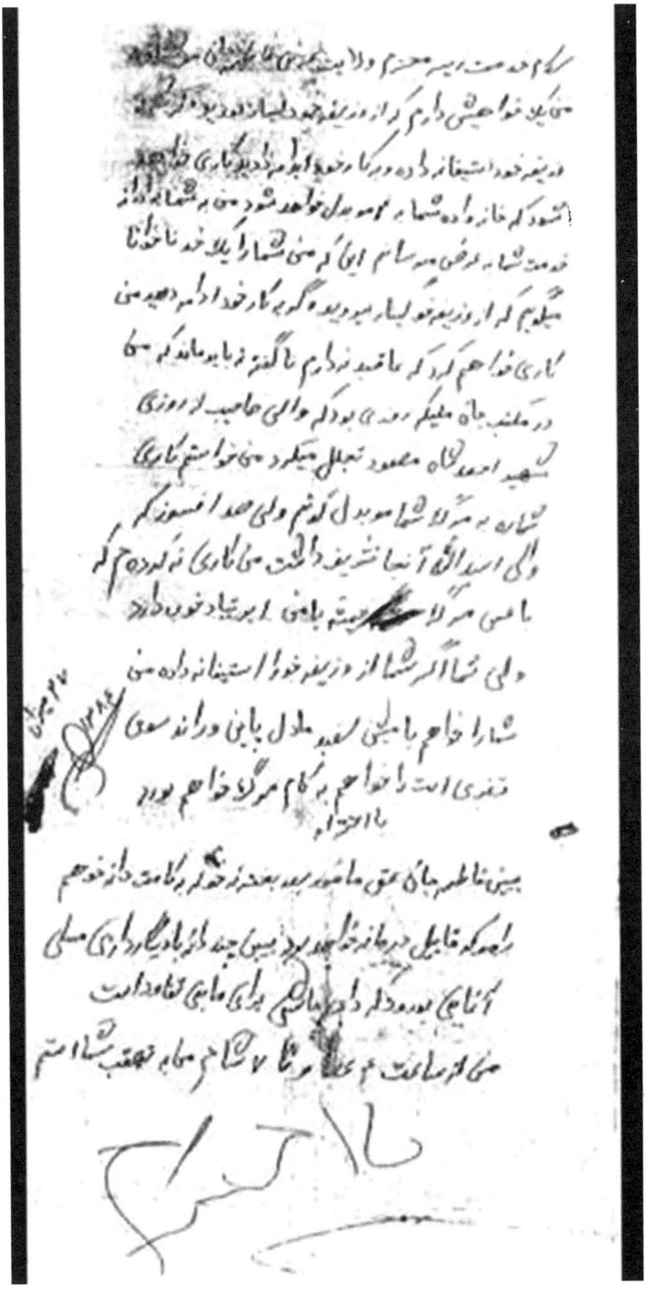

Translation of Figure 5.5

Greetings to the respected director [of education] of Ghazni province, Fatima Moshtaq.

I have one request, that you step aside from your duties. Otherwise, if you don't resign your position and continue your work, something will happen that will transform your family and you to grief. I am telling you this as a brother, that I consider you a godless person. I am telling you to leave your post and if you continue your work, I will do something that doesn't have a good ending. It should not be left unsaid that one day in the Jan Malika school I heard Wali Sahib praise Ahmad Shah Masood. I wanted to transform your life to death and with much regret Wali Assadullah was present there and I didn't do anything to cause your death. But if you don't resign your work, I will attack you to death.

With respects.

27 Meezan 1384 [At the bottom, last paragraph]

Look, dear Fatima, consider your poor employee who will suffer. He was in front of the house, look at how many bodyguards you have, for instance the one who was there, but if you have them, it doesn't matter to us. I was following you from 4 in the afternoon till 7 at night. With respects.

Document 5.5: *Shabnamah story*

This message is meant for Fatima Moshtaq, the education director of Ghazni province. Your actions have demonstrated that you are an infidel and godless person. If you do not resign from your position, harm will come to both you and your family. We have heard that in the Jan Malika School, Wali Sahib praised Ahmad Shah Masood; this is unacceptable. If you do not resign you will be killed. We have already followed you and your employee and will strike when your bodyguards are not present.

Finally, Figure 5.6 presents a 2003 Kandahar *shabnamah* with its translation. After the recitation of a Qur'anic verse ("Jihad is a right in Allah's Path: Jihad yesterday, Jihad until the Day of Judgment"), this proclamation authored by "Jamiat-e Jaish al Muslimin" presents a series of specific actions and instructions that Kandaharis who worked with the Karzai government ("American puppets") were to follow:

- immediately quit your government or NGO job,
- do not use government vehicles and do not go to areas where such vehicles have been damaged or destroyed,
- never go to a feast where government officials are to be present,
- *ulema* as well as community leaders should not attend governmental shuras,
- women and girls are forbidden any educational participation,
- Muslim cars should not use the roads used by government officials,
- do not transport American equipment,
- avoid hotels frequented by Westerners.

These instructions represent an integrated program to obstruct government operations in Kandahar.

The letter of 2003 appears to foreshadow the use of improvised explosive devises (IEDs) and vehicle-borne improvised explosive devises (VBIEDs) as well as suicide bombings, presently a grave concern and a tactic previously unknown in Afghanistan. Despite a quarter-century of war before 2004, suicide attacks in Afghanistan had been relatively rare. "Suicide is not a characteristic tactic of the Afghan people ... they have a cultural aversion to it."[57] Only five suicide attacks, none of which targeted civilians, were reported during the first three and a half years after the Taliban were driven from power in November 2001. This dynamic changed drastically in 2004.[58]

The use of IEDs has demonstrated an unusual level of internal coordination and a growing technological sophistication in the Afghan insurgency. Since the summer of 2004, a variety of guerrilla tactics, including assassinations and kidnappings, have occurred in Afghanistan[59] suggesting that insurgents were borrowing tactics from Iraq.[60] The late Mullah Dadullah, a primary spokesman for the Taliban insurgency in Afghanistan in 2005 and at the time one of the their most combative commanders, claimed that the Taliban had registered 500 Afghans ready to be used as suicide bombers against "the intruders who have occupied our Islamic country" and that Taliban from outlying districts had entered cities to launch attacks. "Now we are going to change our tactics, using a new weapon we did not have in the past, to target US and allied forces ... We will create a big problem for them."[61] His prediction proved to be correct.[62]

Figure 5.6: Night letter from Kandahar[63]

Translation of Figure 5.6[64]

(Arabic Qur'anic verse): Jihad is right in Allah's path: Jihad yesterday, Jihad until the Day of Judgment

Jamiat-e Jaish al Muslemin

Announcement

Date: 24/Moharram/1424 [23 April 2003]

1. This letter aims to address those who are Muslim but work with the current American puppet government, either for money or, assuming they serve Islam, to abandon their jobs immediately.
2. Muslims, do not use government vehicles.
3. Whenever a governmental vehicle is exploded or damaged by any means, Muslims do not go there in order to have a look at the site.
4. Where there is a feast, Muslims should not go there with government officials, because danger may threaten them.
5. Respected Muslim do not go to [illegible] because whoever goes there commits double sins: one, they commit [illegible]; and second, they rescue government officials.
6. *Ulema* and influential leaders of the community should not go to the governmental shura (council).
7. Those women who are teachers, and adult girls who are students, should not go to school.
8. Muslim cars should not use the roads used by government officials' cars.
9. All Muslims should desist from transporting American equipment and oil in their cars.
10. Muslims should avoid going to places where foreigners stay, such as hotels, etc.
11. Muslims should not work in organizations [NGOs], because Americans use those NGOs for their own purposes.
12. Muslims' sons who are working with the current infidel's government should get out of it immediately. Those, whoever, who act in opposition to the above-mentioned rule bear the mortal and eternal responsibilities.

Al-Salaam

Document 5.6: *Shabnamah story from Jamiat-e Jaish al Muslemin*

Jihad is the most important path one can take in life. If you are working for the puppet Afghan government, you must immediately quit your job. No true Muslims should travel in government vehicles because they will be destroyed. All Afghan Muslims must avoid any fests where Afghan puppet officials are present, as well as roads traveled by puppet government officials, because danger will strike them. Afghans should also avoid hotels and other places where foreigners reside. Religious elders and community leaders must also avoid going to government councils. Afghan women must not teach in schools and Afghan girls must not go to schools. Muslim cars should never be used to transport American equipment. Nor should honorable Afghans work for NGOs that are controlled by the Americans or the Afghan puppet and apostate government. If these instructions are not followed, grave mortal and eternal circumstances will occur.

The great majority of the early suicide attacks carried out during 2004–6 appeared to be "outsourced" to non-Afghans, most often to Punjabis from the south of Pakistan and young foreign Islamists recruited from radical groups in the Middle East. Such attacks targeted government officials such as Hakim Taniwal, governor of Afghanistan's Paktia province; during his funeral another suicide bomber detonated an explosive device, killing at least an additional six people. Recent attacks have also targeted US and Coalition forces.

Conclusion

In summary, *shabnamah* are a traditional means of communicating in Afghanistan. As we saw above, the Taliban use them as warnings or instructions to the local population to refrain from cooperating with the international forces or the government. Many of the stories of these letters reference Afghanistan's history and the threat that the international forces pose to the Taliban's Islamic Emirate of Afghanistan and are addressed to the "Mujahid People." The implication of this type of message and story is that all Afghans have a role in the resistance to a common enemy of Islam and Afghanistan and are obligated to fight. Other letters suggest that the Taliban will kill all those who cooperate with the Americans or the Kabul "puppet" government. Some letters, as we say above, even go so far as to target specific people or schools and teachers involved in the education of girls. Much of the effectiveness of these letters is based on the mere presence of the letters themselves. Not only do these letters confirm the presence of Taliban in the area but they are usually accompanied by some direct action as well.

Analysts and observers have argued that "the Taliban are now drawing increasing support from the Afghan population."[65] While it is impossible to evaluate specifically how the Taliban's night letter campaign has contributed to this "support," Taliban narratives have clearly resonated; where their messages have not resonated with the population, the Taliban have compensated by waging an effective intimidation campaign.

The Taliban's *shabnamah* story themes[66] can be summarized as:

- an appeal to past Afghan struggles against "foreign invaders": the Taliban regularly play on how foreign powers have been historically defeated by the peoples of Afghanistan.
- the battle between the Taliban and the Kabul's "puppet" regime and its foreign coalition represents a "cosmic conflict" between the righteous and the infidel. Afghans have a collective religious responsibility to fight the apostates and invaders. Afghans "must not" offer any assistance or cooperation to US or Afghan National Armed Forces or they will "face serious consequences" (threatened death).
- the Taliban's enemies represent "crusaders" that are promoting Christianity and attempting to destroy Islam.
- Afghans must cooperate and join the Taliban "so as to perform ... religious duty properly."
- the power of "martyrdom": brave Afghans must sacrifice themselves to save Afghanistan. The fight against their enemies involves saving honor.

The narratives of the night letters partly represent the preservation of traditional Pashtun values and society, often at the expense of modernity. Night letters used in urban areas by the Taliban, not assessed by the analysis presented here, directly confront some of the ills of modernity, such as alcohol, pornography, and prostitution that are now very visible in urban areas such as Kabul and that the average Pashtun abhors. Recent night letters have targeted urban areas and a more sophisticated campaign against modernity as the Taliban insurgency pushes north—a phenomenon that we have started to witness over the last few years.

The Taliban have deep interests in preserving traditional social structures and organizations and preventing social change. Maintaining the social status quo is an explicit goal of a segmentary society.[67] These root goals and worldviews are clearly evidenced in Taliban *shabnamah* and they severely hamper Kabul's ability to offer social or economic progress as an incentive to accept state authority. Moreover, through their intimidation campaign the Taliban have been able to scare off those few NGOs and humanitarian organizations that could deliver on Kabul's wishes. This has proved to be a brilliant strategy to defy Kabul and the US/NATO counter-insurgency. It has clearly presented a dilemma for the Afghan government as well as US and Coalition counter-insurgency strategies.

Pashtuns value highly their independence and have grown accustomed to it; they have preserved their way of life for centuries, despite the efforts of some very powerful forces to alter it. Although there have been times when parts of this tribal society have experienced short durations of subjugation by alien forces, they were permitted to conduct their lives in accordance with Pashtunwali. Even today, the Federally Administered Tribal Areas (FATA) of Pakistan, predominantly inhabited by the Pashtun, are basically exempt from Pakistani law. Independence is the historical norm for the Pashtun, and the Taliban night letters dwell on this fact. The desire for continued independence is one theme of the *shabnamah* assessed here. The risk of losing tribal independence to "infidels and puppets of the West" outweighs the possibility of improving tribal social welfare or increasing economic opportunities that would probably be gained by accepting state authority. Any concession in tribal independence should exceed any compensation offered in return for submission to state authority. Kabul as well as the US and their Coalition partners have failed miserably to understand this dynamic.

6

THE TALIBAN'S USE OF THE INTERNET, SOCIAL MEDIA VIDEO, RADIO STATIONS, AND GRAFFITI

The internet

The Taliban's official website, *Alemarah*, first appeared on the World Wide Web in mid-2005 and serves as the Taliban's main source of information operation for both domestic and international audiences. It is a simple website but loaded with religious, cultural, historical, and political articulated themes. *Alemarah* publishes detailed and up-to-date situation reports on the Taliban's activities across Afghanistan. It is divided into sections that include Islam, news, commentary, statements, poetry, *taranas* [chants], articles, books, magazines, and a link for the online Taliban Radio, Shar'iaht Voice. Furthermore, *Alemarah* is colored blue and white with labels for the Islamic Emirate of Afghanistan and the Voice of Jihad, together with their logo and a white flag on the front page. Providing Afghan war information in five different languages (Pashto, Dari, Urdu, Arabic, and English languages), it serves as the virtual public relations center to the Taliban and its viewers. Most of the literature on the website is written in simple syntax.

Pashto and Dari sections: The Pashto and Dari sections of the website target domestic Afghan constituents and the Pashto- and Farsi-speaking residents in neighboring countries such as Pakistan, Iran, and Tajikistan. Although many residents in Afghanistan, especially rural, are mostly illiterate and have limited access to the internet, the Pashto and Dari webpages of *Alemarah* are used to facilitate communication with local journalists, the educated community, and to a lesser extent the urban community. The educated population in turn share Taliban messages with people through verbal conversations and other media sources, such as radio, newspapers, television, and other websites. Conversely, the audience living in neighboring countries, namely Iran and Pakistan, has a comparatively wider access to the internet, which provides the Taliban with the opportunity to attract them with inflammatory anti-Western and anti-Afghan government themes in their public relations campaign.

Although only found on the Taliban website, political cartoons are becoming a platform to disseminate general anti-Western sentiments to the Afghan constituency. The cartoon in Figure 6.1 (the first one published on the *Alemarah* website (June 2011) depicts a saw-bladed sword shoved into the throat of an American icon ("Uncle Sam") with text in Pashto that reads: (arrow up) American exit; (arrow down) America stays in Afghanistan.
Urdu, Arabic, and English sections: The Taliban have strategically chosen foreign languages in addition to Dari and Pashto to reach out to some vitally important audiences beyond the Afghan borders. The Urdu language is widely

Figure 6.1: *Alemarah* cartoon, June 2011

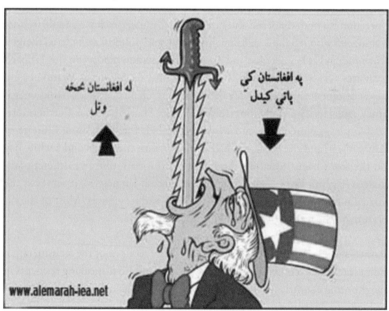

spoken across Pakistan and other South Asian countries, and is also an official language of Pakistan. The presence of this language in the website demonstrates the Taliban's conscious effort to reach out to their supporters within the Urdu-speaking population. In other words, the Taliban's heavy reliance on their Pakistani constituents highlights the need for an Urdu section on the website. The Taliban receive sanctuary, private donations, and—as increasingly exposed by the international media and US military sources—receive state aid and advice especially from the Pakistani intelligence service.[1] Just like the patron–client relationship, those who are actively supporting the Taliban with sanctuary, finance, and ammunition may expect the Taliban to update them on military progress made on the battlefield. In this case, a website is an effective and accessible source for sharing information and establishing communication. Meanwhile, *Alemarah*'s overly exaggerated news and other publications illustrate the Taliban's continuous struggle to placate and impress their foreign audience and supporters with their achievements over Afghan and international forces on the ground. A similar reasoning can be used for the Arabic language presented on the website too.

The Arabic webpage is one of the most updated parts of the website and shows the Taliban's effort at making it attractive with a range of information, including a monthly Arabic magazine called *Al Somood*. It contains interviews with senior Taliban officials, reports on the military operation, Taliban bios, a martyrs' list, and the monthly provincial military operation list.[2] The Taliban understand that the support of Muslim constituents in the Islamic community will assure their legitimacy and success. The Taliban's legitimacy may be acquired by the public's endorsement of the insurgency, and their success will be achieved by the access to generous financial resources in the Arab world; however, the target audience of the English webpage may vary substantially from the Urdu and Arabic pages on the website.

The English language serves as a universal communication tool and so serves as a corridor to convey Taliban messages to the Western world. Most publications are designed to demonstrate the Taliban's power while also conveying the defeat of international forces in the Afghan war. They are used to communicating with the West and maximize local political pressure on ruling governments to end their military presence in Afghanistan. The Taliban hope that excessive expressions of power, fear, and a functioning shadow government will manipulate the West's public perception of the war. A glaring example is the collapse of the Dutch government in February 2010: the first European and NATO administration to fall because of the war in

Afghanistan.[3] Likewise, publishing reports in English help the Taliban to demonstrate the failures of international forces that are continuously making efforts to break the momentum of the insurgency.

Although the number of websites disseminating Taliban statements in English are not as prolific, the Taliban do take the time to create English statements and "war updates" on their official website (www.alemarah.info) and Twitter, as well as some jihadist magazines, such as *In Fight*, a digital photo essay magazine that contains high resolution photos of combat from Afghanistan overlaid with English statements stripped from the *Alemarah* website.

In summary, the Taliban have embraced the use of the internet through their website *Alemarah*. The website has existed under a number of different addresses and has been blocked on multiple occasions, but now moves between service providers. It consists of five language sections: Dari, Pashto, Urdu, Arabic, and English. Its reports list numerous attacks against the US, the Afghan government, and their allies as well as highlighting collateral damage from international air strikes. There are also links to official magazines and sections dedicated to official articles and statements, for example, the Arabic-language magazine *Al Somood*. The magazine is available in PDF format or in hard copy. It covers in-depth articles, military statistics, and interviews with field commanders and leadership figures. In addition, video clips of recent activities are also available. However, unlike some other Islamist websites, *Alemarah* has no discussion forums, although some pro-Taliban forums do operate on an unofficial basis. Another difference from other jihadist websites is its lack of instruction manuals, and it does not link with other groups in other theaters. But like the discussion forums, alternative sites also exist, such as those that report Taliban statements.[4]

Social networking: FaceBook, Twitter, and YouTube

In December 2010, the *Alemarah* website published an interview with the site's editor, Abdul Satar Maiwandi, in which he explicitly stated: "Wars today cannot be won without media. Media aims at the heart rather than the body, [and] if the heart is defeated, the battle is won." This interview was especially interesting because for the first time the Taliban media chief explicitly revealed the venues and objectives of the Taliban's information operations to involve email, texting, tweets, blogs, YouTube, and Facebook. Maiwandi emphasized the importance of both the official Taliban website and expanded use of social media, specifically Facebook and Twitter, to project Taliban messages. While the Afghan government in Kabul is conspicuously absent from social networking sites, the Taliban have become Afghan pioneers in establishing Facebook and Twitter accounts and using them to disseminate their propaganda narratives, especially those narratives and messages targeting Afghan youth and young adults. A few years ago, the Taliban exclusively used a variety of jihadi forums and blogs to discuss their positions and propagate their narratives and self-perceived achievements online. These forums have lost some of their value as social networking sites have come to dominate the market, due in part to their simplicity and the multi-tasking capabilities of the social networking media. The Taliban have taken notice and responded accordingly, and have also shown themselves to be aware of the impact of the media and their role during the Arab Spring.

Before the US invasion of Afghanistan in 2001, there were only 2,000 internet users in the whole of the country; by 2010 Afghanistan had a multitude of internet providers and 1 million users (1,000 per cent growth in the past ten years).[5] According to Mr Amirzai Sangin, then Afghan Minister of Communications and Information Technology, there should be over 2 million Afghan internet users shortly.[6] According to some sources, there are over 155,000 Facebook users in Afghanistan. This number is expected to increase due to vast investment in information technology in Afghanistan.[7]

The Taliban have increasingly used Facebook, where they maintain a relatively large "network of friends" to spread their message to target audiences. Currently over 2,000 members "like" the Islamic State of Afghanistan page, which seems to be the Taliban's official Facebook page; while other Taliban individuals and supporters each have hundreds of friends to share pro Taliban narratives. (As this book was being finalized, Facebook authorities had apparently banned or taken down the most prominent Taliban page. However, it seems that the Taliban continue their publishing and networking under individuals' names.) They appear very flexible and extremely interested in expanding their social media network.

Similar to the Taliban official website, *Alemarah*, Taliban Facebook profiles are loaded with hundreds of Taliban videos, photos, and narratives. Their site provides timely news updates, videos, chants, photos, and conversations on specific topics. Presently the size of the Taliban audience is limited to approximately several thousand people. However, it will most likely increase with the expansion of internet access in Afghanistan.

Even though there are specific pages that regularly disseminate Taliban propaganda, many Taliban supporters separately spread Taliban messages through their individual profiles, to reach out to as many people as possible. Their profiles often carry various al-Qaeda and Taliban-related materials.

Aside from their official Facebook page, there are many individual Facebook pages under various names that share Taliban-related news coverage and propaganda. These sites also assist the Taliban to enlarge their reach and connectivity to their target audience. Likewise, the Taliban have an official Twitter account with over 5,600 (and growing) "followers."[8] Here the Taliban regularly Tweet news updates concerning their exaggerated and propagandized "military achievements," such as: "9 US invaders killed and wounded, two tanks destroyed in Logar battle," "4 puppets killed in clash with Mujahidin," or "Mujahidin kills 12 US–Afghan cowardly troops in martyr attack."

The Taliban have also utilized a network of Twitter accounts to rehash entries made on the *Alemarah* website, and the official Taliban Twitter accounts include the following table.

Table 6.1: Primary Taliban Twitter accounts (as of summer 2011)

User account	Number of followers	Number of Tweets	Status
@Alemarahweb	Over 5,500 followers as of August 2011	Over 1,626 as of August 2011	Active
@Alemarahwebsite	Only 58 followers as of August 2011	Over 384 as of August 2011	Active
@Alemarahmedia	Only 23 followers as of August 2011	Only 36 as of August 2011	Inactive since March 2011
Secondary Taliban Twitter accounts (as of summer 2011)			
User account	Number of followers	Number of Tweets	Status
@Ahmadkhan111	Over 171 followers as of August 2011	Over 180 as of August 2011	Active
@ABalkhi	Over 141 followers as of August 2011	Over 367 as of August 2011	Active
@GhazniwalTariq	Only 36 followers as of August 2011	Only 4 as of August 2011	Inactive since May 2011

Figure 6.2: Screen dumps of the most followed and active Twitter accounts attributed to the Taliban: @Alemarahweb and @adamkhan11. Both accounts were still active on 17 August 2011.

There are several Taliban account managers for the *Alemarah* website: "Dr Tariq" (otherwise known as Azam Tariq), Mostafa Ahmedi, Zabihullah Muhajid, and Qari Yousaf Ahmadi; the pseudonyms or personas of Dr Tariq, Abdul Qahar Balkhi, and Mostafa Ahmedi maintain the network of Taliban Twitter accounts as well.

The Taliban Twitter account, @Alemarahmedia, previously disseminated Taliban propaganda videos via YouTube before the video account was terminated by YouTube in the summer of 2011. The @Alemarahmedia account has been inactive since 10 March 2011, although a few of the YouTube video links posted to this account remain active. The YouTube account (FreedomIsOur1), which has several videos linked to the @Alemarahmedia account, appears to support the Islamic Emirate of Afghanistan, posting a variety of anti-Western and jihad-themed video clips.

Despite early misunderstandings of some technology, such as cell phones and the internet, the Taliban and other Afghan insurgent groups have warmly adopted modern communication and technology to their advantage. The Taliban are aided in the spread of their messages through the lack of meaningful Kabul government (or US/NATO) counter-attacks. The Taliban have capitalized by producing a multi-media strategy that enables them to be a dominant player in the "hearts and minds" battle space, an ironic reality given the ideological foundation of the old-guard Taliban.

DVDs and videos

The Taliban were quick to utilize methods and techniques of message dissemination from other insurgent groups, including using the internet and distributing DVDs with clips showing insurgent attacks, executions, and sermons. The proliferation of Taliban-produced videos was clear by 2006, when a variety of Taliban "media studios" emerged. Most of the early iterations of Taliban-produced videos were conducted by the media arm of al-Qaeda, As-Sahab Media, which in 2006 released speeches attributed to al-Qaeda ideologue Dr Ayman al Zawahiri. Taliban operatives distributed the DVDs for free at first, allegedly scattering them around village areas much like they would leaflets and *shabnamah*.[9]

DVDs are sold in kiosks in both Afghanistan and Pakistan and are given out to journalists (both Western/international and local). The objectives of most of these videos are: recruitment, boosting morale, religious indoctrination, and delegitimizing the current Afghan regime and the international community supporting it. Typical video content includes scenes of militant training and preparation (i.e. showcasing weapons platforms), launching an attack, venerating "martyrs" killed in these operations, interviews with Taliban commanders and/or Taliban religious clerics, and commentary on the Taliban's "state of affairs." Recently, videos of Taliban fighters entering abandoned/decommissioned US and NATO outposts have become prevalent.

Taliban and other insurgent video studio productions

A number of Taliban-affiliated "media studios" have also emerged, and no longer are Taliban propaganda videos solely reliant upon the As Sahab media wing. Studios such as Mana-ul Jihad, al Hijrat, and El Emarah produce and disseminate Taliban videos officially sanctioned by the Islamic Emirate of Afghanistan.

This section provides a glossary of video production units featuring Taliban and other Afghan insurgent groups. It is important to be aware that many of the video producers are in constant collaboration with one another, both regionally and internationally (often overlapping each other with regard to thematic messages), and convey a universal message of jihad against the West, particularly the US. Aside from a few specific studios that focus solely on their particular group

Al Emarah Jihadi studio

Islamic Emirate of Afghanistan

An Afghan Taliban media unit dedicated to the elimination of all foreign troops from Afghanistan and in other Muslim countries. This organization is led by Qari Muhammad Yousuf Ahmadi and Zabihullah Mujahid, who have effectively used social media to unite other Mujahid factions. The video productions are extremely well developed and provide a justification for the jihadi movement. One particular production, *American Reconstruction*, shifted the studio's strategy of propaganda by focusing on the impact of the Afghan–NATO military campaign on the civilian population in Kandahar. Interviews with Afghan locals aimed to depict the carnage by the hands of American soldiers and therefore appeal to locals to join the jihadist movement. English subtitles were provided and languages spoken by the insurgent groups were Dari, Pashto, and English. The studio is also extremely active on Facebook and, similar to As-Shahab, posts eulogies, military operations, and recruitment for prospective jihadists.

Sample video

1) http://theunjustmedia.com/clips/afgha/Jan11/Al-Emara%20Jihadi%20Studio%20Presents%20"American%20Reconstruction"%20In%20English.htm

2) http://theunjustmedia.com/clips/afgha/sep11/Maidan%20Wardak%20Door%20Of%20Kabul.htm

Direct source

1) http://shahamat-english.com/index.php?option=com_content&view=article&id=11211:us-terrorists-horrendous-brutality-and-heart-rending-crimes-in-logar&catid=1:news&Itemid=2

Bot-Shikan

An affiliate of the Islamic Emirate of Afghanistan. Content is often produced in Farsi/Dari.

Secondary source

1) http://botshikan1.blogfa.com/post-8.aspx

Manba-ul Jihad (The Source of Jihad)

A media unit of the Haqqani Network within the Afghan Taliban. The footage often shows raids on US military bases, several bombings targeting vehicles of Afghan, American, and NATO-led International Security Assistance Force (ISAF) vehicles in Khost, Paktia, and Paktika provinces, and suicide bombings in Kabul and Wardak provinces. Other clips show the military training of Afghan Taliban fighters and their recorded wills. The videos further depict scenes from suicide raids.

The Haqqani Network utilizes the Manba-ul Jihad media label, and several notorious videos directly attributed to them include: the 3 March 2008 Sabri district HQ suicide bombing in Khost province; and the insurgency videos showing captured POW US army PFC Berghdal seized by the Haqqani Network shadow governor of Paktia, Mauluvi Sangin.

Sample video

1) http://jihad-e-informacion.blogspot.com/search/label/Manba%20
   Al-Jihad%20%28Emirato%20Isl%C3%A1mico%20de%20
   Afganist%C3%A1n%29
2) http://www.zshare.net/video/53250736869dccb4/
3) http://www.liveleak.com/view?i=769_1224010418

Direct source

1) http://www.jhuf.net/showthread.php?10634-Manba-ul-Jihad-
   Studio-Presents-quot-Da-Jihad-Sungur-quot-%26%231583%3B-
   %26%231580%3B%26%231607%3B%26%231575%3B%26%23
   1583%3B%26%231587%3B%26%231606%3B%26%231711%3B
   %26%231585%3B

Secondary source

1) http://www.crisisgroup.org/~/media/Files/asia/south-asia/afghan-
   istan/158_taliban_propaganda___winning_the_war_of_words.
   ashx
2) http://www.zimbio.com/Bowe+Bergdahl/articles/yy4BBkRXbyq/
   Manba+al+Jihad+Video+Shows+American+Spc+Bowe

Hezb-e-Islami

Affiliated with As-Shahab Media, which publishes Hezb-e-Islami video productions, *taranas*, magazines and books. It has also tapped into social media through Facebook by constantly updating its page and inundating it with HIG propaganda, as well as addressing current events and military operations.

Direct source

1) http://www.facebook.com/pages/ShahabStudio/1076118 42603062#!/profile.php?id=100002186722868&sk=info

As-Sadeqin

A studio belonging to Hezb-e-Islami Gulbuddin Hekmatyar, focusing on recruiting Dari-speaking jihadists.

Sample video

1) http://tanweer.blogfa.com/post-2007.aspx

Tora Bora Nizami Mahaz (Tora Bora Military Front)

A breakaway from Hezb-e-Islami Khalis (HIK), this is a militant group formed by the son of Younis Khalis (deceased Mujahidin commander and leader of a separate Hezb-e-Islami faction), Anwur-ul Haq Mujahid, and currently operating in Nanghahar, Afghanistan. The group publishes its own propaganda magazine, *Tora Bora*, and has its own website, *Alemarah*, independent of the Taliban's primary propaganda source. The Tora Bora Front continues to remain active by periodically updating its website, publishing its quarterly *Tora Bora* magazine, and launching occasional attacks in Nangarhar province. Its potent support base is in Khalis' native district of Khogyani and other dangerous areas such as Pachir Agam and Shinwar.

Sample video

1) http://theunjustmedia.com/clips/afgha/may10/Tora%20Bora%20 Studio%20entitled%20History%20Page%2010.htm

Secondary source

1) http://almanac.afpc.org/taliban

Al Hijrat

An Afghan Taliban media outlet linked with *Alemarah* and Manba-ul Jihad, which often releases footage of Taliban training, martyrdom obituaries, as well as suicide attacks. Typically recycles contents from other production studios.

Taifetul Mansura (Victorious Sect)

A transnational Turkish military group that has joined the jihadi movement in Afghanistan. The Taifetul Mansura spokesman is Suraka Turki. The primary languages used are Turkish and English. Ebu Zer AKA Serdal Erbashi, the former leader of Taifetul Mansura in Afghanistan and a fighter in Chechnya, was reportedly executed by the Taliban after it was discovered that he ordered the death of two foreign fighters on 21 June 2011. The group maintains that its area of activity is in Afghanistan, and that it is not operating at all in Turkey

Secondary source

1) http://occident2.blogspot.com/search?q=mansura

Elif Media (Turkish)

A Turkish jihadi media outlet associated with the German Taliban Mujahidin, and currently supporting the jihadist movement in Afghanistan.

Sample video

1) http://theunjustmedia.com/clips/other/April10/Deutsche%20 Taliban%20Mujahidin.htm

Direct source

1) http://www.alqimmah.net/showthread.php?t=12286
2) http://www.elifmedya.de/

Secondary source

1) http://www.archive.org/details/yardim2-alflojaweb.com

activities, others share videos from other groups and are not focused on one region. This is particularly true for al-Qaeda and Pakistani Taliban.

Many Taliban video productions that are regional often align themselves with internationally-based video production studios to gain superior quality and capability in disseminating propaganda operations and recruiting jihadists worldwide. The numerous languages delivered by these video production studios seek to reach diverse demographics and recruit new jihadists from the Arabian Peninsula, Somalia, and Turkey, to join the movement in Afghanistan. Sympathizers can easily radicalize themselves and ideologues can offer compelling arguments of their struggle, achievements, and devotion to join the movement. Whereas the Taliban video producers can offer the video footage, advanced video producers can create the narrative and emotional appeal to demonize the US and boost jihadist morale.

Taliban spokesmen

The Taliban have learned how to promote themselves expertly through the media. The Taliban have used established contacts with radio, television, and newspaper journalists and they regularly use these contacts to implement their information campaign. In this pursuit, the Taliban have appointed spokesmen as points of contact for the international media and regional press. For instance, two prominent spokesmen are Zabihullah Mujahid and Qari Yousuf Ahmadi. These spokesmen maintain regular contact with the media through email, SMS, telephone calls, and they provide online reports on incidents. Journalists remark that the Taliban spokesmen are available around the clock, as opposed to the government and international representatives. However, at times in the past the international community has received conflicting reports from the spokesmen or ones not associated with the Taliban.[10]

The full-time Taliban spokesmen, Mujahid and Ahmadi, act as mouth-pieces for the Quetta Shura and will also take credit for attacks attributed to the Haqqani Network. It is unclear whether the identities of these spokesmen refer to actual people or a network of spokesmen who make statements under one of the two names.[11] Some semi-autonomous *mahaz* (groups) are represented by their own spokesmen, and some high-level insurgent commanders use spokesmen from a local region representing their group, such as Mauluvi Sangeen's spokesmen identified as Abdullah Jalali and Muhibullah Mahajir, the spokesmen for former Taliban commander Shah Mansoor Dadullah.[12] The local, regional, and Western press can easily contact Taliban spokesmen

Figure 6.3: Photo purportedly showing Taliban spokesman, "Zabihullah Mujahid"

through their email addresses or cell phone numbers, both of which are prominently displayed at the bottom of the *Alemarah* website.[13] "Official" Taliban statements are now found in nearly every major news article written about the Taliban, and newsletters attributed to the IEA are also disseminated from official Taliban spokesmen to international and local journalists working in Afghanistan, all of which are usually translated into English, Arabic, Pashto, Dari, and Urdu.

Shar'iah Zhagh *(Voice of Shar'iah Radio)*

Although the Taliban's main means of message delivery remain relatively simple, such as distributing night letters, word of mouth, and their website, they have repeatedly tried to increase their presence on the radio airwaves in Afghanistan. With a rural population generally illiterate, radio programs in Afghanistan remain a viable method for delivering messages and communicating. However, unlicensed or "pirate" radio broadcasts are essentially an extension of the Taliban's reliance on low-tech means of message transmission.

Most FM radio transmitters are built or purchased in neighboring countries, such as Pakistan, which is also grappling with a wave of unlicensed Taliban radio programs, consisting of basic equipment that can be manufactured or acquired for just a few hundred dollars. In the case of Pakistan, several mobile transmission devices belonging to the Pakistani Taliban have been discovered, confiscated, and destroyed. The low cost and abundance of readily available equipment that can be quickly modified and sent back into the field has made disrupting the pirate broadcasts a challenge in both Pakistan and Afghanistan.

The Taliban movement first revitalized its radio program (through pirate broadcasts) in sporadic bursts since announcing the relaunch of Shar'iah Zhagh (Voice of Shar'iah) from Kandahar, their former stronghold in the south, beginning in 2005. The spotty signal broadcast for over an hour each night was believed to have been transmitted from mobile transmitters mounted on the back of pick-up trucks. In April 2005, then Taliban spokes-man Mufti Latifullah Hakimi told the Pakistan-based Afghan Islamic Press news agency that Radio Shar'iah Zhagh was back on air after a six-month break, although evidence of prior Taliban broadcasts was non-existent follow-ing the termination of the Taliban regime in October 2001. The 2005 broad-cast consisted of an hour's program between 06.00 and 07.00 local time and was broadcast in both Dari and Pashto.

By 2007, similar media reports indicated that Taliban radio programs could be heard in parts of four south-eastern provinces, Paktika, Paktia, Khost, and Ghazni, but local officials said that reception for the programs remained weak. Similarly, during the ten-month Taliban occupation of Helmand's northern district of Musa Qala between February and December of 2007, the Taliban's Voice of Shar'iah could be heard throughout the district. Broadcasts included translations of the Qur'an, calls for jihad, and religious programs. According to a local Taliban spokesman, the radio station had five employees and broad-cast on an FM frequency with the traditional Afghan pattern of morning and evening transmissions.

By 2009, media reporting concerning the Taliban's radio broadcasts had increased, suggesting that the Taliban had attempted to increase their broad-cast capabilities, expanding their coverage area. However, there is little evi-dence to suggest that the Taliban have successfully launched any pirate radio programs since 2009. An additional tool used by the Taliban for broadcasting is the internet. In June 2009, an online version of Voice of Shar'iah was launched via the Taliban Pashto-language website *Shahamat* (Valour) (previ-ously at www.shahamat.org). The internet-based radio service streams news, commentaries, and jihadist songs, and the morning and evening broadcasts are updated daily.

When asked by the Afghan Islamic Press how they set up these radio stations, Hakimi replied: "We imported the equipment from abroad and Afghan engineers here set up the stations." Hakimi added: "The Taliban own three radio stations. One is now reopened and the others will start functioning soon."[14]

During the last decade, media reporting concerning the Taliban's radio broadcasts has increased, suggesting that the Taliban have successfully increased their broadcast capabilities, expanded their coverage area, or the media is just responding to or creating the perception of a trend. Similarly, reports of the Taliban broadcasting two-hour programs in Ghazni province surfaced in August 2009, suggesting that the Taliban have improved their transmission capabilities and are offering more content.[15] In 2005 the Taliban launched the radio station Duond Jokanyanam, and also launched a clandestine radio station that broadcast anti-Afghan government (GIRoA) programs as well as Islamic hymns. It is reported that this radio station, Voice of Shar'iah, broadcasts from Loya Kandahar twice a day: 6–7 a.m. and 6–7 p.m.[16]

Highlights from the Taliban's various broadcast capabilities as of October 2009 follow below.[17] That year was the height of Taliban radio stations; most were jammed soon after, when the US started to halt Taliban radio broadcasts.[18]

Taliban radio in Lower Helmand province

In July 2009, Reuters were reporting on the activities of a British-funded PRT (Provincial Reconstruction Team) radio station at a base in Garmsir, in the south of Helmand province, and said: "Lately, the Taliban have set up their own radio station in the valley, broadcasting from a secret location further south. But it doesn't play music, and the DJs of [PRT's] Radio Garmsir just don't see it as competition."

Radio Shar'iah, Ghazni province

According to Pajhwok, Radio Shar'iah in Ghazni province is a "typical Taliban mouthpiece."[19] In August 2009, Taliban spokesman Zabihullah Mujahid told Pajhwok that the radio station was the most effective communication tool for "the fighters," claiming that the Taliban controlled enough territory in Ghazni to operate the FM radio station "freely." Radio Shar'iah broadcasts in Pashto on 88 MHz FM to the Qarabagh, Giro, and Andar districts. Programs included commentaries, religious programs, poetry praising the Prophet Muhammad, pro-Taliban songs, and exhortations to Afghans "to stay away from the election process."

In August 2009, the Pakistani daily newspaper *Nawa-i-Waqt* reported that Radio Shar'iah's program content was "anti-government." According to Mujahid, Radio Shar'iah could be heard over a 50-kilometer radius from the provincial capital and broadcast from a vehicle parked in a mountainous area. He added that the Taliban had set up similar radio stations in Paktia, Paktika, Konar, and Nuristan provinces.

Taliban radio stations in Khost, Paktia provinces

In August 2009, the Pashto-language website benawa.com reported that a Taliban radio station had begun broadcasting in Khost province. According to locals, it broadcast Taliban announcements and asked people to boycott the upcoming elections. Some residents of Khost province said that the Taliban broadcast had created fear among the population. They also said that they did not know how and from where the broadcast took place. According to the same benawa.com report, Taliban radio stations were active in Ghazni province and in Zormat (a district in Paktia province).

Taliban radio station in Nuristan province

In September 2009, US-based CBS TV news reported from the operating base of a US-funded PRT radio station in the remote Nuristan province that "a battle of the airwaves" had developed locally because, in addition to listening to the PRT radio station, "another villager was listening to a Taliban radio station. They have sprung up around the country as well, broadcasting threats to kill those who cooperate with international forces." CBS reported that US forces admitted that locals could use their new radios (supplied by US forces) to tune into the Taliban, but that, given the choice, Afghans wanted positive information.

Summary of broadcasting

- The Taliban's Radio Shar'iah resurfaced in the spring of 2005 and has increasingly produced "organized" programs, lasting initially an hour and now up to three hours long.

- The programs are broadcast in both Dari and Pashto.
- By 2009, Radio Shar'iah was reportedly being broadcast in Paktia, Paktika, Farah, Ghazni, Helmand, Konar, and Nuristan. In 2007, the program was being broadcast in the southern provinces of Kandahar and Helmand.
- The radio transmission systems are said to be "mobile" and mounted on the back of pick-up trucks. "Engineers" inside Afghanistan are said to aid in the technical aspects of working the equipment.
- Broadcasts include translations of the Qur'an, calls for jihad, and religious programs. Threats against civilians participating in the elections (August 2009) or supporting the government/Coalition are also common.
- No DJs and no music are featured on the Taliban radio programs in southern Helmand. Sometimes poetry, pro-Taliban music or music with no lyrics is played on programs aired in the east (Ghazni).
- The Taliban have further exploited their webpage and now include a Radio Shar'iah webcast that can be heard around the clock. The program is said to be updated daily.[20]
- Local residents seem to be pleased with radio broadcasts in general but gravitate toward stations that play music, and a diverse array of music is even better. Music played during the Taliban era consisted of musical instruments while passages of the Qur'an were spoken.

Ziaullah, a resident of Ghazni's Giro district, told Pajhwok news that he listens to the Taliban broadcasts every night because "he enjoyed listening to songs on the radio." Similar sentiments were also found in Farah province where resident Amir Ahmed said, "The only thing I don't like is the Taliban-style music. I'd prefer to hear some jazz. Something to get us a bit excited."[21]

Graffiti

Graffiti marking the walls of urban and rural compounds and buildings, including threatening messages and pledges of allegiance to Taliban commanders, can be found in both Afghanistan and Pakistan. "Graffiti culture," however, is more prevalent on the Pakistan side of the border, with messages supporting various political parties dotting nearly every available inch of wall space in certain neighborhoods. The Afghan Taliban has used this delivery system inconsistently, particularly in southern Afghanistan and the urban centers of Lashkar Gah, Spin Boldak (Wesh), and Kandahar City. Similar to waving the Taliban's trademark white flag, Taliban graffiti primarily aims to

Figure 6.4: A pro-Taliban supporter standing in front of a display reading "Long live holy fighter Mullah Muhammad Omar" in Killi Nalai, a village near the Pakistan and Afghanistan border, September 2010. Source: AFP.

Figure 6.5: Local residents stand outside a shop ("Maddrassah Petroleum Service") with graffiti reading "Leader of the Faithful Mullah Moammad Omar Mujahed/JAI/ Opinions," on Sunday 8 May 2011, in Pashin, 100 km south of Quetta, Pakistan. Source: Arshad Butt/AP

mark territory friendly or sympathetic to the Taliban's cause and objectives, while offensive graffiti (threatening messages) aims at intimidating or "marking" undecided or pro-government communities.

Conclusion

Many of the areas of Taliban operations and control are ungoverned spaces (at least from a Western perspective) where tribal independence from the state is highly cherished. These areas are primarily inhabited by segmentary societies, such as the Pashtuns. Lindholm's characterization of segmentary societies[22] supports the notion that tribal organizational and normative factors, of the Taliban being quite familiar, impede the establishment of state authority. Segmentary societies differ from other forms of society in that they only tend to unite when they feel that they are losing influence over their own way of life. The Taliban were brilliant at exploiting such sentiments during their initial rise to power in 1994–6, when Afghans were extremely war-weary and seeking to extend control over their lives that had been lost over two decades of war, as well as during the archaic and ineffectual Mujahidin rule after the fall of Najibullah. The Taliban leadership offered stability and the Afghan people welcomed it with open arms (at least until they recognized what the Taliban ultimately represented).

The Taliban use the media presented in this chapter for simplistic objectives such as "forcing the invaders to withdraw" and re-establishing Shar'iah throughout Afghanistan in their strategic communication efforts. It is these two simple objectives that many Afghan insurgent groups subscribe to, challenging Western perceptions that the Taliban employ overly complex or sophisticated messaging campaigns. In fact, it is with their simplistic and easy to follow approach that Afghan insurgents avoid convoluted messaging campaigns that risk alienating their target audience, typically rural, uneducated, and conflict-fatigued Afghans. The simplicity of their strategic aims is similar to their successes soon after their creation in 1994, when they vowed to accomplish (and largely achieved) two highly desired objectives: establishing security and instilling law and order through swift Islamic-based justice.[23]

The Taliban's messaging spectrum and narrative universe are finite, but their information tools are numerous. The number of objectives, messages, and narratives can be identified and framed within a given outline. Henceforth, the Taliban are able to draw upon this information-message/story-narrative-treasure chest and "plug" it into the litany of delivery systems available to them, as we saw in this and other chapters. Despite early misunderstandings of some technology, such as cell phones and the internet, the Taliban and other Afghan insurgent groups have successfully adopted modern communication and technology to their advantage. Video productions, DVDs and CDs, internet web pages, text messaging, Twitter, Bluetooth dissemination of audio and video files are some of the modern delivery systems the Taliban now use to spread their views and statements.

However, despite an aggressive effort from Afghan insurgent groups to exert control over territory, groups like the Taliban still lack the manpower and material needed to impose a large-scale occupation of territory inside Afghanistan. In 2008, the International Crisis Group suggested that the Taliban "still puts out contradictory messages that indicate internal rifts and the diffuse nature of the insurgency."[24] We have seen these rifts definitely materialize in 2015 and 2016.

The Taliban are assisted in spreading their messages by the lack of meaningful government counter-attacks and the proliferation of jihadist messages through local and international media outlets. The Taliban have capitalized on this situation by producing multilingual websites as well as several militant publications and many other media, discussed in this and other chapters, that enable the Afghan insurgents to operate as a competitor in the hearts and minds battle space.

In summary, the use of the internet, social networking, radios, videos, and other storage media as a means to promote the Taliban has allowed the Taliban to speak directly to the population without the need of an intermediary who could edit or censor their message. In addition, this medium speaks louder than published works because of the predominance of illiteracy, especially in Afghan rural society. Much of this media output is not only sold but distributed to journalists as well. The bulk of the content contains archive footage from the fight against the Soviets, videos of insurgent training, attacks on government and international forces, and the destruction or capture of enemy equipment. Finally, the prevalence of mobile phones is one of the most popular ways to pass these images and videos to their Afghan targets.[25]

7

THE AFGHANS' AND TALIBAN'S USE OF POETRY AND *TARANAS*[1]

زه یم زمری په دی نړی له ماڼتل نسته   په هندو سندو په تخار او په کابل نسته

بل په زابل نسته   له ما اتل نسته

امیر کرور (جهان پهلوان)

I am the lion, in this world there is no one braver than me
In India, in Sindh, in Takkhar, in Kabul, nor in Zabul.
There is no one braver than me!

Amir Kror (The world's best wrestler)[2]

"A nation of poets" is how Louis Dupree described the Afghans.[3] Poetry is the central pillar of Afghan literature, with important social and political implications, and the Taliban are well aware of this fact. Afghans use poetry as a tool to communicate feelings and thoughts on a daily and customary basis. Since traditionally there has been minimal presence of print media and a publishing industry, literature in general and folk literature in particular are often shared in oral form, especially in rural Afghanistan. The illiteracy of the great majority of the population certainly reinforces this oral tradition. Thus, written literature has been confined within the boundaries of a few literary circles, primarily in urban cultural centers and educational organizations (i.e. Kabul and other Afghan universities, or the Writers Society of Afghanistan). Realizing that poetry is critical to the process of communication among Afghans, the Taliban have also attempted to use poetry, as will be seen below, as an important component in their information campaigns and storytelling.

Within the past three decades of war and political turmoil, poetry has been greatly politicized in Afghanistan. Numerous collections of poetry concerning political issues have been published either in Afghanistan, or abroad (Iran, Pakistan, Europe, the US and Canada). Subsequently, it has played a prominent role in the expression of political views among Afghans. This chapter examines the intertwined relationship between Afghan politics and poetry, especially from a Taliban perspective.

Poetry is important because it is essentially a spoken, not written art, so it is accessible to those who have not needed to learn to read. Two particular aspects of poetry contribute to its widespread use in Afghan society. One is the rhythm and rhyme embedded in this genre that aids memorization. The other pertains to the unique quality of poetry, which allows deep thoughts, sometimes difficult to comprehend, to be entrenched within a few short lyrics.

The political events of the past four decades have also contributed tremendously to the prevalence of poetry among all other literary genres. War, destruction, and the loss of millions of lives have left deep psychological wounds in the hearts of almost all Afghans. This has given way to the use of poetry as an effective medium to express feelings of sorrow, anger, pride, hope, desperation, and patriotism. Conflict and political turmoil have tremendously contributed to the politicization of poetry in particular, and literature as a whole. Poetry is a window through which one is able to understand the Afghan mind. Afghans memorize specific resonating lyrics reflective of their values, beliefs, and the socio-economic realities of their environment, which can then be used during daily conversations. To make a point, to offer an example, and even to prove a claim, Afghans often refer to and weave a *takbaiti*, a one-liner, or a *do-baiti*, a two-liner, within their speech. In fact, the use of poetry in daily conversation is so prevalent that many lines are synonymous with proverbs and axioms. Unfortunately, these are the critical pieces of communication that are often "lost in translation" during shuras, *jirgas*, and keyleader engagements between US and Coalition forces and Afghan citizens.

Poetry has also played a large role in Taliban information operations. Rural Pashtuns, as we have seen, are a critical component of the Afghan Taliban movement as well as a target of Taliban narratives, relying heavily on oral tradition at the expense of written materials. While some of this reliance is directly related to the lack of literacy, especially in rural Afghanistan, Afghan poetry has traditionally been extremely important to Afghans, in part because poetry relies on spoken language and is figurative in nature. In addition, it is an ideal art to be used when there are few other materials to draw from. Much like *shabnamah*, poetry is used to disseminate news down to the village and individual level, and the Taliban are well aware of this fact.[4]

As previously stated, the late Mullah Omar called on the service of Afghan poets to help support the Taliban's military and political objectives in an Eid statement released around 25 November 2009: "I also urge the committed and sensible poets to preserve the jihadi epics and acts of heroism of Mujahidin in their poetry and literary pieces and generate emotions for independence, honor, national unity, and Islamic resurgence."

- Talib poets portray their anti-government efforts as an extension of the anti-Marxist regime that began in the early 1980s. Comparatively, contemporary and/or moderate Afghan poets tend to focus on *peace* as a theme, reminding the reader of its value and necessity for political unity and the hard work needed in order to achieve and maintain it.
- Their main concern is changing the current state of affairs in the country, which predominantly revolves around the issue of foreign invasion.
- They make use of religious terminology and themes far more frequently than other poets, i.e. jihad, "crusaders" or "people of the cross," martyrs/ *shaheed*, and paradise. In fact, they use religious doctrine to support their arguments in favor of political dissent and military action against the government and coalition forces.
- Cooperation with state is *be-nangi*, a great shame. This is because the regime, in their view, is a puppet of the foreign powers—the infidel invaders. Cooperation with and support of such government means indirect support of the invaders and infidels. This qualifies the Afghan supporter of the state as a *mulhed*, or hypocrite. Some argue that being a hypocrite is a more grievous sin then becoming a *kafir*, or infidel.
- Guilt and shame are two of the emotions that the Taliban authors use to influence their readers' thoughts. The reader must feel shameful because not only is he not taking any action against foreign invaders, but he is also cooperating with the enemy. The reader must begin to act immediately, and participate in the jihad against the infidel—similar to his ancestors who fought against and defeated the Greeks, the Mongols, the Persians, the British, and the Soviets.
- They instigate war and disorder to purify the country of immorality and the religious heresy of the imposed Western political and economic orders.

Below we present Pashto poems written by the Taliban and some of the "stories" they portray, as well as moderate and progressive contemporary poets, all of which are translated and analyzed. This will hopefully help one to gain a better understanding of the way in which Afghans perceive current socio-political realities. A comparative study enables us to understand the manner in which each group differs from (or is similar to) others in reaction to issues and events. The main purpose of this examination is to shed some light on the way in which poetry shapes and mirrors Afghans' world outlook; it should familiarize the reader with the manner and extent to which feelings and thoughts are expressed in poetry among Afghans.

Poetry in Afghan politics

خو چی دا جهان ودان وي   خو چی دا خمکه آسمان وي

خو چی پاتی یو افغان وي   خو چی ژوند په دی جهان وي

تل به دا افغانستان وي

Until there is this earth and sky   Until there is this universe

Until there is life on earth   Until there remains one Afghan

There will always be an Afghanistan

Afghan history is replete with *warrior poets*; in fact, many Afghans argue that any would-be leader, or person wishing to make an impression, needs to write and recite poetry in order to be taken seriously.[5] This last fact may seem utterly foreign to the average Western reader, who would rarely look to their leaders to prove their worth by reciting a few lines of poetic verse in order to prove a point. This fact illustrates just how foreign the Taliban and the people of Afghanistan are to many in the West, and it is for precisely this reason that Westerners should pay attention to the poetry of the Taliban, so that we may extract some understanding of them as well as their target audience.

Put simply, a political poem is one in which political opinion and or patriotic sentiments are expressed. Throughout Afghan history, political activists, politicians, army officers, and journalists have used poetry to convey their opinions and theories on social, political, and economic issues. Statesmen, tribal leaders, and army generals such as Ahmad Shah Durrani and Khoshal Khan Khatak, and journalists and philosophers such as Mahmud Tarzi and Khalilullah Khalili, used poetry to express political opinion and patriotic sentiments. They are often referred to as warrior poets. Being a poet confirmed their intellectual legitimacy, which in turn reinforced their authority as capable leaders. In other words, in Afghanistan politics and poetry are closely intertwined.

This politicization of poetry is a result of many social and political transformations in the past forty years. As politics became intertwined with armed conflict, persecution, and violence, those writers who expressed their political opinions in a direct and emphatic manner became susceptible to imprisonment, torture, and even death. The indirect nature of expression in poetry provided the writer with a relatively less dangerous venue to express discontent with the establishment.

Moreover, poetry has served as a suitable instrument with which to appeal to the readers' religious and patriotic sentiments. Proponents of various social and political movements have attempted to arouse the public's emotions through poetry, and sought to persuade their readers to take action in support of their cause.

Pashto poems by Taliban poets and poets sympathetic to the Taliban

The Taliban, especially in their early political incarnation, were composed almost entirely of Pashtuns.[6] They clearly understand the cultural impact that poetry carried in Afghan society, and they use it deftly in many ways to communicate their messages to existing members, would-be members, the uncommitted bystander, Afghans collaborating with the central government or coalition, the Islamic world, and even to the West.[7]

The Taliban, as suggested above, use poetry to communicate legitimacy and to sanctify the insurgency against the GIRoA and the Coalition.[8] They do so by using three main themes: defense of the homeland against foreign invaders; defense of Islam against crusaders; and for those not so patriotic or pious, by appealing to personal gain in the form of honor and esteem gained through valor and worthy action in the name of the previous two themes. Taliban poetry may also be instructional and is used not only to pass on Islamist/jihadist ideology, but also tactical instruction.

Throughout the Taliban poems examined below, it is clear that several key elements are continuously used as a means of influencing the target audience. Continuous references are made to personal honor and manhood, seeking revenge, defense of the homeland and of Islam, references to invaders/crusaders, foreigners, traitors, the greatness of Afghanistan in world history, and the worldwide fame of the Afghan Mujahid. These ideas are meant to incite the reader/listener in various ways to take action on the side of the Taliban, who portray themselves as the true Afghans and Mujahidin. They play on cultural, historical, and religious elements, which are held very dear to the Afghan in the establishment and maintenance of his personal honor, or *nang*, an element of Pashtunwali.

The main intent of the poetry examined here is for the Taliban not only to justify their war and the manner in which they wage it; but also, and perhaps more importantly, to *sanctify* it not only to the Afghan public, but also to the greater Islamic community. In terms of justifying the war, the Taliban seek to portray the ongoing struggle as a war of honor. They make continuous references to the foreign invader, and historical references to past heroes who have stood up and fought against other foreign invaders, thus putting themselves in the same category as past heroes, and justifying their conflict as one against an aggressive foreign would-be conqueror. It is important to note that this theme resonates to many Afghans due to the long history of invasions by foreign powers such as the Greeks, Mongolians, Persians, English, Russians, and Americans.

The Taliban also make liberal use of Islamic ideology in their poems, playing on the paranoia of jihadists that there exists an ongoing and deliberate attempt by the infidel West to destroy Islam.[9] This is a critical aspect of their information campaign and associated stories, as it casts the Coalition not only as invaders, but as crusaders as well. Furthermore, this theme has a dramatic impact on the nature of the conflict and the actions/tactics used by the Taliban. By wrapping their character as an organization, inclusive of the individual, in terms such as Mujahid, the Taliban affiliates themselves with the greater struggle that the jihadis believe is going on between good and evil throughout the world.[10] Jihadis believe in a global and perhaps universal fight between the forces of Allah (Islam) and the forces of Satan (US and her allies).[11] By using the terms of Islam such as Mujahid and jihad, the individual and the organization become fighters for Allah's cause, and therefore justify their actions.

The Taliban also seek to rationalize their struggle by making it an honorable act. They use terms such as revenge and honor that resonate with their largely original Pashtun audience. These factors, as suggested previously, comprise certain important elements of the Pashto ethic of Pashtunwali, a key aspect of being Pashtun. This factor cannot be lightly overlooked. What is important to understand is how closely related Pashtunwali and the notion of honor are to the identity of the Pashtun. As suggested above, Pashtunwali is so integral to the Pashtun that there exists no distinction between practising Pashtunwali and being a Pashtun.[12]

Furthermore, the Taliban use poetry as a means of instruction similar to how they often use *shabnamah*. Examples of this will be shown to illustrate not only the manner in which the Taliban provide religious instruction, but perhaps more significantly to, illustrate how they use poetry to communicate tactical instruction to their members.

In communicating their main themes with the purpose of justifying and sanctifying their ongoing violence, the Taliban present numerous poetic elements to their audience. As previously stated, the main poetic themes used by the Taliban are defense of the homeland, defense of Islam, and honor of the individual Afghan. The methods used to strike a chord in the hearts and minds of the audience include the use of history and calling the audience's attention to the great past of Afghanistan, including great battles like Maiwand, where, during the second Anglo-Afghan war, Afghan forces inflicted heavy losses on the superpower of the day.[13] The use of this genre is meant to bolster the idea of the Afghan warrior tradition, and several poems refer to the defeat of England, Russia, and America at the hands of the Afghan hero, stating that the Afghan Mujahid is known throughout the world as the one who defeats superpowers. The subtle use of poetry by the Taliban to communicate their ideas to their audience will be further examined below.

The following Taliban poems are expressed within the conventions of *Ghazal*, which is arguably the most popular classical form of poetry, especially in the Pashto and Dari languages. Judging by the types of messages, these poems are no doubt written by poets sharing a belief in the Taliban's cause.[14]

The nuances of language aside, the body of poetry examined reveals several factors of interest. The main purpose of the entire body of poetry seems to be to justify and promote the Taliban's fight against the GIRoA and Coalition forces. It does this by leaning heavily on the following three themes: defense of homeland; defense of Islam; and the gaining and maintaining of personal honor. Here are examples to illustrate how each of these themes is employed to manipulate the target audience.

Taliban poems

> *Mujahid's wish to his mother*
> Mother, pray for me, I am going to *Ghezaa* [the battle] tomorrow
> I am going for Allah's satisfaction, I am not delaying
> Battle has many rewards,
> Allah will give me paradise
> If I am martyred, I'll go to my leader with white face
> I am getting to my trench
> For combating the invader

I like enthusiasm, and will go to the afterlife with enthusiasm
If I don't come back home
This is my will to my father and mother
Don't be impatient; I am going to doomsday with the red shroud
Till the homeland becomes free
All the betrayers will be suppressed
I'll go to the tough area of war with great courage
You became Allah's mercy for us
Now, we all accept you, Abul Fazl
I'll ascend to the sky with great honor

Poem's story: Following the wishes of Allah, I have decided to go to fight the infidel invader. I do this enthusiastically and I am not afraid to die fighting for our noble cause of freedom. Pray for me, Mother, for I do this for our honor and Allah's mercy.

The poet asks his mother to pray for him. He is proclaiming himself a servant of Allah in the Manichean battle taking place between the forces of good and evil. He is fulfilling his duties as a good Muslim, thereby bringing honor to himself, his family, and country. He is fighting the invader of his homeland, making him a good Afghan. This declaration indicates that he believes that his fight is a defensive one, and therefore the jihad that is being waged is defensive in nature, making his actions justifiable and praiseworthy. He refers to himself as a Mujahid, a holy warrior, further justifying his actions and bringing credit to himself and his cause by couching them in Islam. He expresses the desire for all betrayers to be suppressed. The idea of a betrayer indicates that other apostate Afghans and therefore Muslims are helping the invaders. In terms of the language of Islam, apostate Muslims are considered *murtadd*;[15] in terms of Pashtunwali, such Afghans are considered *benanga* (shameless, undignified), possibly the worst insult that can be delivered to a Pashtun.[16] Thus, the poet seeks to use the language of Islam and the cultural values of the Pashtun people to disgrace the Kabul government and anyone assisting them. He proclaims that he is worthy of honor and is assured a place in heaven.

White House!

May you be burnt in red flames, White House
May you be set on fire, burned to ashes, White House
There are black calamities in your stomach, you look white apparently
May you be changed to ruins, White House

Murderers of oppressed tribes live inside you
May you become red with their blood, White House
You are the station of cruelty and barbarism from long ago
May you collapse from the foundations now, White House
You took the faith away from the West lovers
May you become the target of Islam lovers, White House
May Allah fell you down like Bush
May you be plagued with Obama's grief, White House

Poem's story: Foreign invader, America, you will be destroyed because of your brutal cruelty and savagery. Obama will fail just as Bush did, and Afghans will triumph because their cause is just and righteous.

Here the Taliban poet is railing against the US in the language of jihad. He is illustrating to the audience that the White House is the epicenter of evil America. His use of color is interesting throughout, and of course has intended negative connotations. Black calamities in one's stomach may refer to an illness such as cancer, or possibly refer to the Obama family's ethnicity. In Afghan folk symbolism, a black man usually signifies a foreign influence, and "embodies the threat of exogamy in a society where people rarely marry outside of their clan."[17] Furthermore, the poet wishes to imply that the US has murdered and oppressed countless tribes and that those Muslims who ally themselves with the US are *murtadd*.

Screams of forty-one countries reach to the sky

Screams of forty-one countries reach to the sky
As their coffins go out from our land to everywhere
I wonder what might be written as memory on their tombs?
Which nation led them to this end!
This is their policy and democracy's result
Their work in Kabul and Baghdad reaches to trembling
They played with humanity's integrity such that
The brutality and barbarism of history reach to crying
The blow of Afghan sandals with Afghan method
Montazir Zaidi's message reaches to every Afghan
Allah, these are all considered with your mercy and examination
An epic with empty hand reaches to a complete work
We haven't stepped into anyone's house
Inside the house, my message reaches to the big slave

Stop puppetry and lowliness of life
It's impossible that your current position would reach to permanency
As you present a medal to the titled dog
Your insult in dog's shape reaches to the hero Amanullah
Be prepared for Afghan and Allah's accountability
Your name will for sure reach to the garbage can

Poem's story: The world's Islamic countries are in a global struggle against America, the West and their false democracy. Afghanistan and the Taliban will fight with the help of Allah to an epic and a righteous victory. For America, its allies and apostate collaborators will all suffer the fate they deserve and their names will be eternally cursed.

This poet also decries America's influence in the world and suggests the evils of democracy. The forty-one countries are assumed to be the total number of nations in the world that are Islamic. This not only illustrates to the audience that this is a global battle of Islam against the West, but also that Afghans are being victimized by a foreign invader, and thus the Mujahidin are defending Afghanistan for a righteous cause. Once again, anyone working with the US is considered the lowest of the low, on a par with a dog. Such a person will be held accountable for their actions and in the end their name, and consequently their family name, is eternally disparaged. This is a fear tactic employed by the poet to let the "fence sitter" or collaborator know that once the Taliban has won, the betrayer and all of his family will have a day of reckoning; they will be dealt with by Afghans as well as by Allah, illustrative of the idea that Allah is on the side of the Taliban, and by default those working with America and her allies are *kuffar*.

Good news

They are days of the insolent White House collapsing
They are days of the infidels' Coalition collapsing
Signs of disunity are appearing in these forces
They are days of Islamic countries' unity
Bad Abraha has come to ruin our Kaaba
They are days of coming of the green birds
Today as they are burning Ibrahimi nations with fire
They are days of burning Nimrod's forces
The pharaoh of the time has come, killing our children
They are days of drowning the satanic armies
Bush came impudently and wouldn't listen to anyone

His economy is ruined, they are days of happiness
He didn't learn from the example of Gorbachev's defeat
He is disgraced in the world, they are days of shame
Those who would go to their houses in the darkness of night
They are days of escape of the wild forces
They intentionally bombard and then give excuses
They are days of crusader terrorists' disappearance
Invaders, muftis with white turbans
They are embarrassed, they are days of crying
Toward freedom, with the help of the Allah
We are taking firm steps, they are days of hope
Martyrs of the sweet homeland tell us in our dreams
Take revenge, they are days of uprising
The world will be left, don't sell your faith in it, brothers
Hours are waiting for you, they are days of coming
Abidzai wants martyrdom from Allah
Life in this world is enough, they are days of disaster

Poem's story: The audacity of the infidel American and their disarrayed Coalition forces will be totally defeated by a united Islamic foe. The Americans have destroyed their economy, just as the Russians did during their evil and ill-fated attempt to conquer Afghanistan. Like the Russians, the Americans kill innocent children; but the Taliban with the help of all-powerful Allah will seek revenge and defeat the infidels and their false Islamic apostate puppets.

This poem is heralding the eventual collapse of Coalition efforts in Afghanistan. The poet draws the audience's attention to the disunity amongst the Coalition and the unity of the Islamic struggle against the armies of Satan. References are made to the deaths of innocents as if they were intentional acts, further driving the wedge between the Coalition forces and the Afghan populace. The poem illustrates how Afghans defeated Russia and with Allah's assistance will do the same to America and its allies. There is a general call to hold the course, and that the false Islamic scholars who aid the Western invaders will be shamed. The poet calls for revenge, a theme of Pashtunwali; lastly, this poem is a call to arms, stating that martyrdom for this cause is a great and honorable thing.

Pol-e-Charkhi prison

May Allah collapse your wall, Pol-e-Charkhi prison
Fear comes up from your yard again

May your stones and structure be set on fire from hell
You put foreigners' weapons on your shoulders for my death
Once again, the cruel leaders made their daggers red with our blood
Once again, the disgraced brought the Western Satan's tanks
The gown's magician is wandering like a beggar
So that he might be able to find some more forces for my killing
The green parrots of the United Nations got mute (dumb)
The human rights claimers sealed their mouths
We are connected with the principle of enthusiasm, look at our firm determination
We don't have any fear from the deaths and no pain from the wounds
We are going to dedicate our heads to Islam
May death come a hundred or a thousand times on this path
Ahamdi says, o Allah take our revenge from them
Or make us stronger than them so that we'll cut off their heads

---

Poem's story: Pol-e-Charkhi prison is yet another example of the torture and disgrace that the Americans and their apostate puppets have imposed on the Muslim Afghan people. But the United Nations and other "human rights" organizations refuse to face or address the evil of the Americans and their Afghan puppets. The Taliban and faithful Afghan people, however, will stand strong and with the support of Allah will take revenge and end this evil and will drive the evil ones from Afghanistan.

Pol-e-Charkhi prison is an Afghan prison that was originally used by US and Coalition forces to hold captured Taliban and other insurgents (it has since been turned over to the Afghans). This prison is held in the same disdain by the Taliban as Guantanamo Bay and Abu Ghraib. The implication here is that within Afghanistan there exists yet another American institution for torture and murder of the faithful. The poet states that the US can act with impunity, because the world is either too weak, or too afraid to stand up to the US or UN. Moreover, human rights groups have lost their nerve and have turned a blind eye to foreigners' atrocities in Afghanistan. The poet then relates how it is up to the faithful—the good Muslims and good Afghans—to seek revenge for these atrocities in Allah's name, regardless of the number who will die seeking this revenge.

The following poem is extremely interesting. It subtly relates that the poet is no longer a real person. This poem looks directly into the heart of the Pashtun audience and declares that it cannot be a real human being in accordance with Pashtunwali, so long as invaders are within his homeland.

Who am I, what's my duty
How did I come here
There is no house or love for me
I am homeless, without homeland
I don't have any place in this world
They don't leave me to rest
There are shootings and gunpowder here
Rain of bullets
Which direction I should go then
There is no place for me in this world
A small house
I had from my father and grandfather
In which I was very happy
I and my beloved would live
They were great beautiful times
We would sacrifice ourselves for each other
But suddenly a guest came
I let him stay for two days
After these two days passed
The guest became the host
He told me, you came today
Be careful not to come the next day

Poem's story: The Afghan people let foreigners come into their country only to find that they came to destroy the Afghan people and their beloved homeland. Now the foreigners have claimed the country as their own. The foreigners have taken our homes, our lives and now want our entire country, which was once beautiful and was home to people who were always ready to help their neighbors.

This is a poignant lament that the poet is now homeless in a land of warfare. He had all the things in life that a man could need, but he unwisely allowed a guest to stay in his home too long. The guest is a metaphor for foreigners and foreign concepts such as the GIRoA and Jeffersonian democracy. His ancestral home has been taken from him by this guest who now tells the poet—the original host—that he should not visit too long because he is no longer welcome in his own home. The interest here is that it speaks to the Afghan connection to ancestry and homeland. It also reminds the reader/listener that without certain things, a man is not a person, and has no place in the world. Interestingly, the poet raises the question of "what is my duty?" This is particularly interesting as the poet says he has lost his identity. Having lost his ancestral home, he is now no one. He does not know who he is. This is a metaphor for the entire country, and the poet is warning the audience—the Afghan public—that so long as the foreign usurper is within Afghanistan, no Afghan can truly be free, or truly realize his own identity because independence and egalitarianism are such a big part of what makes an Afghan an Afghan. In fact the Afghan has become a servant to the foreign occupier.

In memory of the lost martyr

Your father is looking for you in the mountains
Your mother is looking for you by the sea
They left their sleep to recover the memory
Of which desert or valley you might be lying in
Your father and mother keep your memory alive forever
Your family graves are known in the graveyards
There will always be many flags blowing there
Those who sacrifice their lives for the homeland
The black soul will become gold with their blood
Flowers take color from the martyrs' blood
Ohud and Khandaq's [Prophet Mohammad's battles] mountains are still red
Many years have passed there
Who calls the martyr of the homeland's honor dead?
History writes his name in gold
Tulips are colored with your blood
The atmosphere takes color from it as well
Come and see what happened and what it is
Blood is streaming innocently and changes to rivers
Guesthouses of the Afghans are deserted
O Allah, bring back the previous times
Make trouble for the foreigner and the cruel
So that they won't throw heavy bombs on us
O Allah, accept this prayer from me
Remove this pain and trouble from us ever more
He is sitting in the expectation of your mercy
Khalilzai raised his hand toward you

Poem's story: The fallen martyrs who have defended our beloved homeland are Afghanistan's true heroes that will never be forgotten by their families or country. The martyrs have fought like Mohammad and history will never forget them. We pray for the martyrs and ask Allah to seek revenge against the evil foreigners who have invaded our country and caused the people of Afghanistan so much pain.

This is a prayer to Allah for those who have fallen and remain unfound by their parents. It implies that many fall and remain unclaimed on the battlefield, and even though they are not returned to their family graveyards, they are honored there with many flags. Furthermore, any stain that they had on their souls is now erased because in this struggle against the foreign invader/crusader they gave their lives for Islam and in service to Allah. The fallen martyr is therefore a good Muslim and a good Afghan, worthy of praise, and will be remembered as a hero. Perhaps the intent of this poem is to bolster the courage of the would-be Mujahid who may fear being killed in battle and not being found, claimed, and returned to his ancestral homeland to be properly honored and buried.

Heroes of Islam

Anyone who has an Afghan sword in his hand
He won't resist and escape from the battlefield
The bravery of his sword is obvious to the entire world
The fact that they made the red infidels (Russians) run away from their homeland
It's Islam's soil and has well-trained heroes
That's why they beat the enemy to the ground
This homeland has grown up and trained heroes of the religion
Each of them raised from the cradle by the dedication of their mothers
The entire Muslim world is proud of the Mujahid
Because they have embarrassed the communists in this world
You have banished Lenin's communist system from the world
They have been scattered and the whole universe has laughed at them
Look at our history, what the Afghan has in his background
The English are the great example who have been pushed out of the country
Afghans gave sacrifice for their honor
They have made a revolution, every traitor is shaken by them
Nations are amazed by the Afghans
Since they have beaten a power like Bush
Afghan sons don't have a parallel; hey, o Ahmad Yar
Stop complimenting them, they have won every field.

Poem's story: The Afghan Mujahidin's bravery is the envy of the entire Islamic world. Their bravery drove the Russian invaders from their beloved homeland and eventually destroyed Soviet communism. The Mujahidin also defeated and drove the English from Afghanistan, and are now destroying the invading Americans. The Afghans are the world's great fighters who have defeated all superpowers and are recognized by all for their bravery and heroism.

121

This is a proclamation that Afghans are the heroes of the Islamic world. Afghan mothers instil this heroism in their babies from the cradle, and it is this zeal and bravery that the Mujahid used to defeat the Russians, the English and the Americans (Bush). The poet proclaims that Afghans are revered and honored by the *ulema*, and awed by the rest of the world as honorable fighters. The main theme of this poem is one of national pride, and this poem could serve as a recruiting tool for the Taliban.

This next poem is the lament of a grandfather or a father. He, like all parents, believes his son possesses great potential, and he is crushed when his child falls short, seemingly selling out and shaming not only himself, but the poet and his family as well.

Empty Case

I thought it was an eagle but it turned out a craw
Man wasn't made out of him, and turned out neutral
I trained him with the love of my heart
I wanted to make a heart from him, but he turned out lungs
I thought he had weight in the community
But he finally turned out a light pack of straw
He played with the jihadi purpose
It seems he turned out like the Russians
He danced to US dollars
We said his fortune turned out sinister
Khalis does not complain about anyone else
His own pocket bullet turned out to be an empty case

Poem's story: I thought my son would be a brave and honorable man; this was they way he was brought up. But he gave into the temptation of the blood money of the evil American invaders and he tragically abandoned and betrayed the Afghan people.

The poet suggests that his offspring "sold out" to the Americans. This is a metaphor to shame the target audience. It directly targets those Afghans seen collaborating with the foreign invader. It implies further that some of the offspring (the children, or people) of Afghanistan are less than what they could have been, that they are a disappointment to their fathers. The empty shell case is a metaphor for the weak seed of the father in fathering such a child, and implies shame to the betrayer's family as well. The betrayer is viewed as a man trained in the proud warrior tradition of Afghanistan to fight the invaders, but in the end only playing at jihad, becoming instead a boy dancing for the money of the foreign invader.

The next poem sings the praises of the Afghan warrior. It plays on feelings of national and tribal pride.

I am Afghan *mujahid*
Gun in my hand and dagger under my arm, I am going into battle
I am Afghan *mujahid*, I am Afghan *mujahid*
I may be victimized for my homeland a hundred times
I am Afghan *mujahid*, I am Afghan *mujahid*
I have religion; I have the Qur'an and am under the law of the holy Qur'an
I am Afghan *mujahid*, I am Afghan *mujahid*
Anyone who looks badly at me will see himself lost for ever
Look, I am a known champion of history
I am Afghan *mujahid*, I am Afghan *mujahid*
We have good Shar'iah, and believe in it at all times
Shar'iah is my light and my heart is lit by its light
I am Afghan *mujahid*, I am Afghan *mujahid*
We want a free life, we want universal stability
Because I love truth and hate unjustice for ever
I am Afghan *mujahid*, I am Afghan *mujahid*
We hate the war, but we wage war against war
If war is imposed on us, then I am a man of the field
I am Afghan *mujahid*, I am Afghan *mujahid*
Hey, cruel colonizer, take it from my Qatin
I am taking revenge for my people, I am committed to my promise
I am Afghan *mujahid*, I am Afghan *mujahid*

Poem's story: I am a brave and proud Afghan Mujahid who eagerly goes to battle to fight the evil American invaders. I might be martyred but I have the strength of Islam on my side and history will remember me. I will eternally fight for Shar'iah, truth, freedom, and justice. War was imposed on us, but we will fight and promise to revenge the cruel and evil acts of the infidel invaders.

The poet sings the praises of the Afghan Mujahid. He uses terms that will resonate with the audience, referencing the victimization of Afghanistan at the hands of foreign invaders, the defense of the homeland, and uses Islamic terminology as well. The poet makes the bold statement that he, a Mujahid, follows the laws of the Qur'an. This once again sanctifies not only the individual fighter, but also the cause itself. The poet proclaims that the Afghan freedom fighter is known throughout the world and his name echoes through history as that of a champion. This idea instills pride in the would-be Mujahid. Other ideas put forth by the poet are the correctness of Shar'iah law and the desire for freedom and stability, which can only be attained through making war. Very importantly, the poet states that the Afghan Mujahid does not want war, but since war has been imposed on the homeland (making his struggle purely defensive), he must fight to expel the colonizer. The good Afghan therefore seeks revenge for this wrongdoing and must be committed to undoing it.

Autumn came to you instead of spring, my homeland

Hot wind and rain of fire came on you
Your blossoms of wishes faded in this world
Storm of cruelty and power came on you from all sides
You were tired and exhausted in poverty
The red open-mouthed predatory animal came on you
You had seen cruelties from natives and foreigners
Wars, tensions, murders, and killings came on you
This world has changed to a hell for you, you are burning in it
You were not dead, yet other bullets came on you
You have made many of your son's messengers to paradise
The Satan that has ambushed came from afar on you
They fried you on a fire like a kebab once again
Puppet of Satan came on you with an Afghan name
They brought the army once again, they are not satisfied yet
The big caravan of the time's Nimrods came on you
Abraham's army with arrogance from the West
The line of their tanks and elephants came on you
Your true sons will not give you the built paradise of this world
Leader or Mujahid, a sympathetic Afghan came on you

Poem's story: The Satanic Americans and their apostate Afghan puppets have brought cruelty and murder to Afghanistan but the heroic Afghan Mujahidin will eventually protect our beloved homeland and defeat the arrogant and evil Americans and apostate allies.

In this poem the poet wishes to convey the ruin of the Afghan homeland. He begins with the analogy of autumn, a time of decline having come or been brought to his homeland. Afghanistan has been exhausted and kept in poverty by a predatory animal in the form of foreigners and greedy natives. The far enemy, the great Satan, the US has brought war, death, murder, killings, hell, and bullets on the homeland, setting it afire. Afghan puppets are seen by the poet to be just as guilty of this ruin as the invader. It is these betrayers, false sons of Afghanistan, who brought the multilingual armies of the West, alluding to biblical references of Nimrod's Caravan.[18] The poet concludes that the true son of Afghanistan, the Mujahid, is there to continue to protect it. Throughout, the poet refers to Afghanistan as if a person.

The next poem is another lament at the current state of Afghanistan. Note that the poet lays the blame for this squarely on the shoulders of the Afghan people.

Built prison

Tears dripped on my collar
The history of the Afghan has been defamed
As our turban was high in the world
Today it has descended, my God
Nightingales are crying and remembering their meadow
Foreigners brought autumn to it
They are buying its honor and esteem with dollars
All the competitors unified against it, my God
This mad man is targeting me with stones
They changed my wishes to soil
It's a pity that we are wandering like vagrants
We ourselves did all this to us
Rain of tears pours down my face
When I remember Afghanistan, my God
Poor Afghans are suffering everywhere
There is no one to ask about them, my God
Where can we go, who can we cry to, my God
Say, ruin the cruel ones, my God

Poem's story: While Afghanistan was once a strong and proud country, many apostate, traitor Afghans have sold out to American dollars and corruption and dishonored Afghanistan and their people.

The poet tells us that historically Afghans once held their turbans high, but now they have descended. The metaphorical nightingale of the Afghan people laments the loss of its green meadow at the hands of foreign invaders who have brought a metaphorical autumn (end of prosperity) to the land, whose honor is being diminished by dollars. The poet then puts the blame on the Afghan people for allowing this to hppen, and therefore there is no one to cry to or even blame for this. In this Taliban poem, there are themes of homeland, ruin, foreign corruption, traitors, loss of honor, and a call for action.

The next three poems are all instructive in nature. The first two give guidance to the audience, first in acceptable behavior, and second in what should be the true desires of the good Muslim. The third poem provides instruction to the audience on the validity of using IEDs, and their tactical application.

O, Eid of the trench

You came with peace, o Eid
Joyful and blissful Eid
I welcome your coming
Come all the time, Eid of Tor Ghar [name of a mountain in Afghanistan]
We spent the fasting month in the trench
We would always walk in hunger
Today that you are our guest, my dear
We will surely celebrate you, Eid of Spin Ghar
But don't get upset, dear Eid
Evening is near, Eid
We are moving now to ambush
The Western army is on its way, Eid
If we didn't esteem you
Don't get upset, o Eid
O Eid, they are revolutionary days now
Danger is happening in all directions
Don't complain to the Mujahidin
They are faced with difficulties, o Eid
Faizani is on his way
Launchers are on his shoulder, o Eid

Poem's story: The Mujahidin are fighting honorably to save Afghanistan from the infidel invaders. The Mujahidin fought during Ramadan while fasting. The Mujahidin have to be honorable in fighting the enemy during Eid, and cannot celebrate as they would desire. Fighting evil and danger that is attacking Afghanistan from all directions requires the total attention of the Mujahidin.

This poem is instructive in how it treats the celebration of Eid. The poet says that it is justifiable for the Mujahid to put off his Eid celebrations if he is engaged in battle with the Western army. The poet sanctifies the actions of the insurgent by using the term Mujahid, thereby linking the fighter to Islam, and thus making the fighter's action good, even if he puts aside a mandatory celebration because he is acting for the greater good of Islam and fulfilling God's will. The poet is excusing the Mujahid from strict adherence to Islamic rites.

Inner clothes

Nothing tastes good to the sick
But when they get healthy, they taste everything
Decorate your inner clothes
Trim your outer clothes
Reputation and braveness do not come from clothes
Look to the heroes of Pani Pat [Afghans' battle with the Indians] or Maiwand
Hardships will return to the person who
Did not take his example from history
Virtue is gained through effort
It does not come from simply sitting at home
He will be capable of greatness and leadership
Who has devoted his life to serving
Privilege and manliness come from merit
Not because you are *Ghalji* or *Momand* [names of two Pashtun tribes]
Arrogance decreases with honor and esteem
Patience and modesty grow from them many times over
O dust, who is living in a wealthy palace
Where you had placed yourself in expectation

Poem's story: The true character of a person comes from his internal fortitude and bravery. All Afghans should try to emulate the heroes of the great Afghan victories at Pani Pat and Maiwand. A man's true character is a reflection of his actions and services to fellow Afghans. Don't let arrogance destroy your honor, but always be patient and modest.

Here the poet stresses that it is not the outward appearance that makes a person great. A good Muslim should dedicate himself not to enhancing his outward appearance, but instead focus his efforts on the development of his inner self. He can acquire greatness through service to a greater cause, to suffering hardships for this cause, and by going to battle (a historical reference) for this cause. It is service and hardship that will gain him merit. The poet also says that greatness is not due to tribal affiliation, encouraging potential insurgents to put aside tribal feuds in service of a greater cause. A man can grow his personal honor and esteem from modesty, rather than pride. The poet draws the analogy that the person who seeks to enhance his outer clothes is sick, and once he gets better and "healthy," all things in life will get sweeter.

This next poem deserves close attention, and is a prime example for how poetry is used by the Taliban for instruction.

While crusaders pass

I'll go back to my sweet homeland
When peace comes to my beloved country
We will not go in any other direction
Once Shar'iah is restored there
I go there from time to time
When it is time to farm our lands
When I go there, my friends tell me
They were waiting for the bus when they saw a convoy
Foreigners were at the back, traitors coming ahead of them
The crusaders passed by with arrogance
Like a superior person walking over the poor
The poor all stood aside from them
As if an eagle would come on the birds
One who has little zeal would look at them with anger
He can't do anything to them except sweat down his forehead
But they can't survive a Mujahid at a distance
Spying on them through binoculars
These green-eyed devils would not survive
Going through an ambush
O Janbaz, take revenge for your countrymen on them
He is waiting for when the traitors will come

Poem's story: I am looking forward to returning to my sweet home in Afghanistan once Shar'iah is restored. I am told about the arrogant crusader invaders and their apostate puppet traitors who drive on our roads and make Afghan cars move to the side of the road. But the honorable Afghan Mujahidin will eventually take revenge and ambush the crusaders through the remote use of roadside bombs.

The poet tells of how he will go home when the invaders have been expelled and Shar'iah law has been established. He then relates how the invaders walk with arrogance through the homeland and that the weak tolerate this, but the Mujahid fights back. The poet refers to using IEDs to defeat the enemy and that no foreigner can survive this. Of interest here is the poet's observation of the travel patterns of Coalition convoys, stating that the traitors (Afghans who serve in any capacity with the Coalition, whether it be ANA, ANP, or some other form of collaboration) come first, followed by foreigners: "Foreigners were at the back, traitors coming ahead of them," thus demonstrating a clear knowledge of how Coalition forces move about the battle space. This observation/ instruction is then followed by reference to the use of IEDs when the poet states: "But they can't survive a Mujahid at a distance/Spying on them through binoculars." This statement is interesting in that it not only gives further tactical guidance to the would-be ambusher by instructing him to maintain a distance from the ambush site—enough of a distance to warrant the use of binoculars—but further provides justification for the action by referring to the ambusher as a Mujahid. This reference thereby makes the action of using a remotely detonated IED justified and sanctified, as it is the action of a holy warrior in the defense of Islam and in service to Allah.

The next poem is another example of the theme of defense of Islam.

Every night, somebody hits my door with stones

They hit my knowledge and art with stones
My friends, they hit the sun with stones
I am not hitting them even with flowers, I am surprised
Most of those people hit me with stones
I must be looking so elevated to them
That's why they are aiming so much at my head
Every night, somebody hits my door with stones
The Danish see, and are proud of their wisdom
See the ignorant one; he is hitting the mountain with stones

> *Poem's story*: The ignorant and infidel West is trying to discredit and destroy Islam. Their jealousy of Islam and our purity has even seen the West pursue sacrilegious actions to denigrate the Prophet Muhammad through cartoons and other profane acts.

The poet tells the audience that the thrower of stones is the ignorant West, casting stones at the door of Islam. The poet portrays the West as ignorant, arrogant, and jealous, seeking to denigrate all the best things of Islam, from art, to knowledge, to religion. This is the language of the jihadist. The poet points out that the proud Danish (cartoonists of the Prophet Muhammad) are throwing stones at the mountain of Islam, an act of futility.

Give me your turban

Give me your turban and take my veil
Give me the sword so that the issue can be settled
You sit inside the house; I am going to the battlefield

129

I may either free my dear land, or Karbala will be made again
Don't hide behind nominal masculinity, how long are you going to lie asleep
You sit among the girls, calamity be on your masculinity
Stop these endless stories and don't become so emotional
Your cunning, boasting, and lies make me laugh
That land which has been set on fire still burns
How would you know about widows and orphans
That day will be my Eid and happiness
When the enemy of my religion and land enters the trap of my influence
Someone will rebuild my ruined land and establish the rule of truth
Will such a person rise up? Will such a person appear?
I, Nasrat, am living in sorrow a joyless life
I will know the joy of life once my prayer is answered

Poem's story: If cowardly men will not fight the infidel invaders of our country, I—a woman—will take up the sword. If I am not successful, a large and historic battle like Karbala will eventually free Afghanistan. Cowardly men are natural liars and ignore the enemy's making Afghan women widows and Afghan children orphans. I pray that the defenders of Islam will rebuild our ruined land and re-establish both truth and freedom.

This poem is a prime example of how the Taliban wish to shame men who will not fight. This poet is a young woman who basically is telling any man who will not fight for Afghanistan to put on her veil while she puts on his turban and does the man's work for him. She denigrates this type of man, making him an object of ridicule.

Oblivious Muslim
By Zaheb

Do you have love and affection in your heart or not?	زړه کښی مینه محبت لـري که نـــه؟
Do you have any hope for forgiveness[19] or not?	څه امیـددمغفــرت لـري کـــه نه؟
O! Muslim, you are asleep in oblivion.	!دغفلـت په خوب ویده یې مسلمانه
Do you have the desire for martyrdom or not?	تمنـادشهـــادت لـــري که نـــه؟
When you call Mohammad as your beloved,	خپل جانان چی محـدمحـدبولـی
Do you have the characteristics of Belal?[20]	دبلال غونـدي صفت لـري که نـــه؟
You are proud of the Usman's[21] generosity.	دعثمان په سخاوت باندي خونازکړي
Do you have a generous hand yourself?	ته هم لاس دسخـاوت لـري که نـــه؟
Like Omar[22] who got rightfully angry,	دعمرغونـدي په حقه چي غوسـه شي
Do you have that kind of bravery in you or not?	خان کې داسي شجاعت لري که نـــه؟
The victims look forward to his coming	مظلومـان دي دراتلولاري تـه کوري

Do you have the habit of Khaled[23] or not?   دخالدغونـدي عادت لــري كه نــــه؟

You spent your life with lying and deception.   په دروغ اوبه دوكه دي ژوندون تېركړ

Do you have any interest in truth or not?   چېرته بـاب دحقیقـت لــري كـه نه

Death does not care about anyone O! Zaheb.[24]   !مرک دهیچـاپروانه كوي ذاهبــــــــه

Are you prepared for the day of judgment or not?   تیاری دقیامـت لـــــري كه نـــــــه

Poem's story: If you are a true Muslim, you will fight the infidel crusaders and their apostate allies. Are you true to the wishes and life of Mohammad? Are you a committed warrior willing to defend Islam, like Usman, Omar, and Belal? Are you a brave follower or a liar and deceiver? If you are a coward, you will never reach paradise and will be denied on the Day of Judgment.

This poem asks the reader whether he is a good Muslim. It also warns him that there will eventually be a day of judgment, and that he needs to be prepared for it. Each line asks a fundamental question: Do you believe in ... or do you not? It reminds us of the manner in which an attorney would pose this question to a defendant: Did you ... or did you not? Such questions are designed to appeal to the reader's emotions and give a positive answer. Furthermore, what the poet indirectly asks the reader to do, without actually mentioning it, is to take action. He dares the reader, saying that if he subscribes to the same values that Usman, Omar, and Belal did, and if he is a true Muslim, then he must prove it in practice. He must act in order 1) to prove that he is a believer, and 2) to be saved on the Day of Judgment.

The poet also mentions the names of historic figures that Muslims, especially Sunni Muslims, revere. His purpose is to inspire the reader to achieve the level of nobility that these men did, and to offer role models to relate to and emulate.

Liberty   په گلو كي مي ستـادوینـورنگ لیدلـي دي

By Mawlawi Mohammad Ghafoor Peroz   رنگین چي مي داستایه وینوسنگ لیدلي دي

I have seen the color of your blood in the flowers.   زلـموچـي زمزمـه كړه نغمـه دحریتـه

I have seen the rock become colorful with your blood.   په زړودغلامانوكي مي زنگ لیدلي دي

When the young men began to murmur the melody of freedom   نعره دازادی باندي قربان چي شول سرونه

I have seen the bells ringing in the hearts of the slaves.   دهغومـي قصرونوكي پالنـگ لیدلي دي

Those heads that were sacrificed for freedom.   په روح دازادی باندي ژوندي وي ملتونه

    بې دي روحه مي هرملت ملـک لیدلي دي

    زخمونه كړاوونه جنازې چي پكښې نه وي

    دخولې په څوخبروتاغورخنگ لیدلي دي ؟

I have seen beds made with them in the palaces. پـــروزه ! ازادي داولســـونـــويوه کبنـــه ده

Nations are alive with the spirit of liberty. داحسن مي دتورويه شرنګ شرنګ لیدلي دي

I have seen every nation in destitution[25] without this spirit.

If there are no wounds, hardships, and funerals in it.

Have you seen a movement of only a few [empty] talks?

O! Peroz, liberty is an adornment for the nations.

I have seen this beauty in the clank of the swords.

Peroz attempts to draw attention to the value of freedom. He also justifies paying the ultimate price: sacrificing one's life for attaining it, or its protection. He equates a nation's *liberty* to the human *soul*. Similar to a soul that keeps a body alive, a nation lives as long as it is free. Without liberty the nation dies. He warns that it is not an easy task to fight for and protect one's freedom; it entails suffering and even death. To achieve or protect one's independence, one has to make sacrifices. One may even have to die for this noble cause. This poem is nationalistic in nature; it appeals to the patriotic sentiments of the reader rather than to his religious beliefs.

In Peroz's opinion, freedom is absolutely worth sacrificing one's life for. This is because independence keeps a nation alive, just as a soul keeps a body alive. Therefore, sacrificing one's life is obviously worth protecting and is related to rescuing the life of a nation.

Complaint
By Zaker

My beloved, why did you sell out your love with your beloved one. یاره! ولي مینـه دي له یـاره سـره خرخـه کـــړه

You sold out your promise along with your confessions. تاکـړې وعـده دي له اقـراره سره خرخـــه کـــــړه

The person whom you have won [his heart] with your red blood. چـاچـي دسـروونـویـه قیمت باندي کیلی وه

You have sold out that pearl in return for the thread. هغه ملغلـره دي لــه تـاره سـره خرخـــه کـــړه

It wasn't as light as you assumed. دومره سپکه نــه وه لکــه تاچـــي ورته وکـــــل

You have sold out the sword of your father along with the strike. تـوره دبابـادي لــه ګوزاره سـره خرخـه کـړه

Good, you showed the way to the spring [water] to your competitor. بنـه دي ورتـه وبنـودې رقیـب ته دکودرغـاړي

You sold out our every street along the land. زمورهره کوڅه دي له دیاره ســره خرخـــه کـــړه

You have stamped on all the big sacrifices. څومره ستري ستري قربانۍ دي ترپښنولاندي کړي

وینـه دشهیددي لـه مـزاره ســـــــره خرخـه کـړه

ستړکي مي چي جګي وي دنګ اودغیرت په کور

خونـــــه دتاریخ دي لـه وقـاره سـره خرخـه کړه

!دغــــه د" ذاکر" ددردکیلــــه وه بـــي وفـــاشنا

زمورزخمي سینـه دي له پرهـاره سـره خرخـه کړه

You sold out the blood of the Martyred along with his grave.
The house in which I could hold my head up with pride.
You sold out the house of history along with your honor.
O! My disloyal friend, this was the pain and the complaint of Zaker.
You have sold our wounded chest along with the injury.

This poem is primarily addressing those who cooperate with the government and the ISAF, especially those who used to be members of the Taliban insurgency. To provoke him, Zaker is accusing the reader of being a coward. Breaking one's promise is a sign of spinelessness among the Afghans. He also wants to convince the reader that his desertion of the Taliban has been a great mistake. This is because in return for cooperation with the government, he has lost his moral values. He is selling out the achievements that his ancestors made shedding their blood throughout history. The main objective of Zaker in this piece is to make the reader feel guilty—ashamed of cooperating with the Afghan government.

Traveler Martyred
By Mafton

I am on my way to war, look after me.
Or else you will regret [if you don't look] not watching me leave.

Raise your hands to pray, and ask for my martyrdom.
With tear-filled eyes, look after me.

I am the Majnon[26] of the love of religion and country.
O, deserts, O, mountains, look after me.

I am not a girl, but a brave prince
Of the battleground of jihad, look after me.

If you want to see me, but of course.
Look after me, either on the war front or in prison.

There is a revolution; these are the days and nights of war.
Look after your warrior Afghanistan.

Look after the traveler martyrs
In the dilapidated graveyard.

A riddled shawl [with bullets] colored with blood.
On every tomb look for this sign.

!هله جنک تـه یم روان راپسـي کـوره
!بیابه وروسته کړي ارمان راپسي کوره
په دعاکړه لاس اوچـت شهیدي غواړه
!له ژړانـه ډک چشمـان راپسـي کوره
زه ددین اودوطن عشق کې مجنـــون یم
!دښتي غرونه اوبیابان راپسـي کوره
پیغله نـه یـم زه سرتـبري شاه زلمـی یم
ادمهادحنک مـيدان راپسـي کـوره
!خامخا کـه مي دین غواړي ملکریــه
!یاسنکراویـازنـدان راپسـي کـوره
انقلاب دی دجنکونـوورځپي شپـي دي
!خپل جنکي افغانسـتان راپسي کوره
هلتـــه یـــادمســـافروشهیدانــو
!هغه خرپـربقبرستـان راپسي کـوره
یوسـوري سوري پټکی رنګین په وينو
!پرهرقبـردانبنبـان راپسـي کــوره

The poet, Mafton, is a journeyman, but not an ordinary one. He has made a decision to travel to the battleground. From there on, he is certain that he will either be a martyr or become a prisoner. He will eventually travel to heaven. The poet is sure that he will not return from the war. He does not characterize victory in jihad in a conventional sense, as the defeat of the enemy. His goal is to become a martyr while defending his religion and country.

It is time for jihad

By Mawlawi Mohammad Yonos Khales Nabi Khel[27]

The autumn's wind has arrived in the territory of red flowers.
Vouchers have taken the place of nightingales.

This is the territory of Islam and of Islam's followers.
There is no place here for the coming of strangers.

Now that the looters have placed their looting claws on it.
O! Muslim, it is time to shed some red blood.

Today if we be frightened by the real martyrdom.
For God's sake, we will not be free from the claws of the foreigners.

Come on! Rise and turn your backs on them, and turn your faces toward religion.
Placing even one step behind is not appropriate for the Muslim.

Pick up a sword and a shield, and jump to the battleground of jihad
Don't be hesitant any more to bring death upon them.

Today, the time of the test [of courage] for the Muslim has arrived. The Muslim does not have permission to procrastinate.

بيادخزان بادراغي په سيمي دسروكلو
څکه نوکارغانوخاي نيـولي دبلبلو
داداسـلام سپه داسلام دپروانوده
دي کې څه ځای نشته داغيارودراتلو
اوس چي غاصبانوپري دغصب پنجي ايښي دي
وخـت دي مسـلمانه ، دسرو وينـو تـويـولـو
نن که وبره ولرو، رښتينيتني شهادت څخه
خدايوخلاص به نه شو،دردیوله منګولو
هلي راولاړ شئ دوی ته شاادودین ته مخه کړئ
نه ښايي مسـلم تـه يو قدم دشـاته تـللو
واخلئ توره اوسپراود جهادمبدان ته ودانګئ
مه کوي صـرفه نوره، ددوی په مرګ وهلو
نن په مسلمان دامتحان موقع راغلي ده
نشـته مسلمان تـه اجازه د ځنډولو

The poet's purpose here is comparing the foreigner to a vulture and thus demonizing the enemy. This vulture has taken hold of the Muslims' territory with his claws. This line of argument connects the Muslim with a specific space, offering a tangible reality to the existence of his reader who belongs to a Muslim nation. He also refers to the foreigners as robbers. For this reason, he deems the killing of foreigners not only legitimate, but also necessary and urgent. Therefore, all Muslims must take up arms immediately and free themselves from the claws of the foreigners. This poem appeals to the religious beliefs of the reader as much as it does to his nationalistic sentiments.

Closing One's Eyes
By Amanzoi

You pointed to the past, you forgot the present.
There is chaos all over the country; you have closed your eyes on the north.

You gave the criminal many titles.
You closed your eyes on justice being trampled.

Next to and with the Cross you raised a drink.
You didn't think about it, you closed your eyes on its sin.

The *Shaikh* and *Morshed*[28] sat on the rank of the invader.
You closed your eyes to fourteen years of trouble.

The country's young girls are colorful with new colors.
You have closed your eyes on their pants,[29] and jacket and shawl.

From the beginning it wasn't like this, music was all *haram*.[30]
Today a new fatwa[31] has been imposed; forever you closed your eyes.

Not only blind and deaf, but also the Mullah became a democrat.
He closed his eyes on his old promises.

Watch out, Amanzoi, so your pen does not go astray.
Your enemy is a sorcerer; he will close his eyes on your writing.

Amanzoi pretends to be speaking to a person such as a government official. He explains a dire social and political situation. But in fact he is having a monologue not with a government representative, but with the ordinary Afghan. Amanzoi attempts to convince his reader that the state is a weak and unjust entity incapable of governance. He makes this claim based on two main factors: first, the government does not have the capacity to serve the public; and secondly, its actions are contrary to Islam.

Pashto poems by moderate and progressive contemporary poets

خوابه خوب لیدلی

وطن جوړیږی خو په تنک عزم او ایمان جوړیږي
په قربانۍ د شخصي کبو او د خان جوړیږي
په یوه ستوري رڼا نه راځي تیاره دنیا کې
دادیرستوري چې یوځای شي روڼ آسمان جوړیږي

I have had a sweet dream

The country will be built, but with strong resolve and faith;
It will be built by sacrificing one's self-interest.

With one star there won't be light in the dark world;

دتش یو لاس نه ټک نه خیژي اونه کیږي کوم کار
لاسونه ورکړئ سره یو شئ بیا جهان جوړیږي

When many stars get together, then the sky will be brightened.

هر یو مشکل ته پیدا شویدی یو لار د خلاصون
هر یو بیار په دوایي د طبیبان جوړیږي

From only one hand no sound will arise, and nothing can be done;
Put your hands together, unite, then the world will be built.

طاهري یاره ما بیکاه دیر خوابه خوب لیدلی
سوله راځي او زمونږ گران افغانستان جوړیږي

For every problem there is a way to a solution;
Every sick person will be cured with doctors' medicines.

شکرالله طاهری

Taheri, my friend, last night I saw a sweet dream: Peace is coming, and our dear Afghanistan will be built.

Shokrullah Taheri

This poem is a hopeful and optimistic message. The poet encourages the reader to focus on the reconstruction of Afghanistan. But he also reminds the reader that this is no easy task. Rebuilding the country requires strong resolve, faith, and sacrifice. In addition, using relevant examples, Taheri tries to convince the reader that without unity it will be impossible to reconstruct Afghanistan. Even though the reconstruction is a difficult task, there is no problem that does not have a solution. This assertion coincides with the English saying that "where there's a will, there's a way."

O! my country, in your love

O! my country, in your love I sacrifice my life.
I am the kind of young man who wants your progress.

ای وطنه ستا په مینه کې
ای وطنه ستا په عشق کې زه تیر تر خپل خانه یه
ستا چې ترقي غواړي زه هغسي ځوان یه

O! my country, you are the graveyard of our mother and father.
I am the servant of a shrine like you.

ای وطنه ته یې هدیره د مور او پلار زمونږ
ته لکه زیارت زه مجاور ستا د استان یه

I will not give one speck of your soil in return for the whole world.
I sacrifice my life and belongings for one fistful of your soil.

یوه ذره د خاوري ستا په درست جهان ور نکړم
یو موټ له خاوري ستا په سر او مال قربان یه

I will sacrifice my head, but not a piece of you.
That is why I am famous by the name of Afghan in the world.

تیر به شم له سر لیکن نه ستا د یو کړیږي نه
ځکه چې دنیا کې مشهور شوی په افغان یه

There is no other good fortune like the one that I, Malang Jaan, have seen myself.

نشته داسي بخت لکه چې ما ملنگ جان خپل ولید
شپږ ورځي دا ستا په غیر کې پروت خوشال خندان یه

I am happy and laughing in your embrace, day and night.

Malang Jaan

This is a poem about patriotism. In this piece there is no mention of jihad or martyrdom, the inclusion of which, as seen above, is typical of Taliban poetry. This poem also demonstrates the poet's desire for progress and reconstruction of the country. Malang Jaan seems to be optimistic about the future. However, he emphasizes the importance of making sacrifices to achieve success. The nationalistic element of pride is also salient in this piece. Malang Jaan likens the country to a shrine, or sacred place. The public in general perceives the shrine with reverence, and it bears a special symbolic significance among the Sufi Islamic school of thought.

Who do we want?

We want the kind of person who would unite us in one room.
We want the kind of person who would heal our wounds.

The kind of person who would rescue a homeless and lonely Pashtun
From the taunting remarks of others.

The kind of person who would make one climb down the mountain, from the war front, And from the tank, and gather us all in one basket.

The kind of person who would destroy the imposed wall which stands between us,
And make me a brother with my brother.

The kind of person who could transform a gun and a sword into a pen
And discourage us from war.

The kind of person who would mend our torn collars,
And make us all the children of one mother (motherland).

To rescue the victimized heart of *Attak* from the foreigners,
And turn the power of the bully into water,
That is the kind of person we want.

Ajmal Attak Yosofzai

This piece is not just about the criteria that the author sees necessary for selection of a leader, but also about what Pashtuns need in order to restore the lost glory of the past. Yosofzai portrays the Pashtuns as the ethnic group that has been victimized throughout the years of war. In this poem, he is in search of a leader who could change the undignified social and political status of Pashtuns from its current state. Indirectly, he is asking the Pashtuns to refrain from fighting against each other, and unite. Additionally, there is emphasis on the need to replace the gun and sword with a pen: in other words the poet highlights the importance of knowledge and learning for restoring this lost identity. He maintains that Pashtuns are the sons of one mother (Afghanistan) and therefore they are brothers. The conclusion he draws is that they should not fight each other but become united. Yosofzai's poem entails a list of the essential values that play an important role in engendering peace and progress among Pashtuns. Note that this poem focuses on the importance of national unity among Pashtuns as an ethnic group, not *all* Afghans. This is a clear example of how ethnic sentiments continue to remain pronounced among some, or perhaps many Afghans.

بدخشان تر کندهاره	From Badakhshan to Kandahar
له هرات تر ننگرهاره	From Heart to Nangarhar
پکتیا نه تر مزاره	From Paktia to Mazar
له جوزجان تراسماره	From Jawzjan to Asmar
همه واړه زما کوردی	All together is my house
مسلمان ئی زماوروردی	Any Muslim is my brother
له بولان تر حیرتانه	From Bolan to Hairatan
له اټک نه تر شیرخانه	From Attak to Sherkhan
تورغوندی نه تر چتراله	From Torghondi to Chatral
همه کور دی دافغانه	It is all the house of the Afghan
زماهر یوو دستړکوتوردی	Each one is the light of my eyes
مسلمان ئی زما وروردی	Any Muslim is my brother
صفاري اوکه سوري دی	If it is Safari or Sori
طاهري اوکه لودي دی	If it is Taheri or Lodi
هوتکي،که ابدالي دي	If it is Hotaki or Abdali
دافغان د متو زور دی	They are the power of the fist of Afghan
مسلمان ئی زما ورور دی	If he is Muslim he is my brother
فداحمد نومیر	Feda Muhammad Nowmir

While Ajmal Yusofzai addresses only Pashtuns as an ethnic group, this piece by Feda Nowmir focuses on the nationalistic notion of "Afghanness." He recognizes people from other parts of the country as his brothers. He argues that the fact that all Afghans are Muslims is reason enough for all Afghans to be considered a nation. Nowmir sees Afghanistan as the home of one nation, regardless of people's ethnicity or geographical location.

The following is another example of a Pashto poem that advocates nationhood among all Afghans. This piece by Abdul-Bari Jahani gives precedence to nationality, rather than ethnicity as the main pillar of one's political identity. Born in Kandahar, Jahani is arguably the most famous contemporary (living) Pashto poet among Pashtuns (south and east) in particular, and among Afghans in general.

کندهار دئ که لغمان دئ وطن زما دئ   If it is Kandahar or Laghman, it is my homeland.

که پنجشیر دئ که واخان دئ وطن زما دئ   If it is Panjsher, if it is Wakhan, it is my homeland.

که تاجک دئ که اوزبک دئ یو افغان دئ   Tajiks and Uzbeks are all Afghans

د دې خاوری هزاره ترکمن زما دئ   This soil's Hazara and Turkmen are all of my own.

عبدالباری جهانی   Abdul Bari Jahani

Comparative analysis

A comparative analysis of poems written by the Taliban and those published by moderate and progressive poets[32] reveals obvious differences in their perceptions of the political affairs in the country. However, authors from both groups share a common ground within the boundaries of which the authors share their thoughts and feelings with the reader, hoping to entice the reader/ listener to subscribe to his views of the Afghan social and political realities. Each struggles to appeal to the reader for certain commonly accepted morals (i.e. religious beliefs, patriotic sentiments, desire for justice, etc.). The following are the main disparities between Taliban and moderates' views expressed in the poems assessed here:

Taliban	Moderates
1) *Taliban* poets portray their anti-government efforts as an extension of the anti-Marxist regime that began in the early 1980s.	1) Tend to focus on *peace* as a theme, reminding the reader of its value and necessity for political unity and hard work in order to achieve and maintain it.
Their main concern is changing the *current* state of affairs in the country, which predominantly revolves around the issue of foreign invasion.	2) They emphasize the importance of working towards a future that is prosperous and peaceful.
2) They make use of religious terminology and themes far more frequently than the moderates, i.e. jihad, people of the cross, martyrs, paradise. In fact, they use religious doctrine to support their arguments in favor of political dissent and military action against the government and Coalition forces.	3) Their poems possess a nationalist flavor. They often incorporate vocabulary such as "nation," "Afghan," and "unity." In general, they look beyond the boundaries of religion and ethnicity. However, this is not to say that they ignore religion or ethnicity altogether.
3) Cooperation with the state is *be-nangi*, a great shame. This is because the regime, in their view, is a puppet of the foreign powers: the infidel invaders.	4) Although they do not explicitly encourage people to cooperate with or support foreigners' presence in the country, they do not condemn their

139

Cooperation with and support of such government means indirect support of the invaders and infidels. This qualifies the Afghan supporter of the state as a *munafiq*, or hypocrite. Some argue that being a hypocrite is a graver sin then becoming a *kafir*, or infidel.

4) Guilt and shame are two of the emotions that the Taliban authors use to influence the reader's thoughts. The reader must feel shameful because not only he is not taking any action against foreign invaders, but he is also cooperating with the enemy. The reader must begin to act immediately, and participate in the jihad against the infidel: just as his ancestors fought against and defeated the Greeks, the Mongols, the Persians, the British, and the Soviets.

5) They instigate war and disorder to purify the country of immorality and irreligiosities imposed by Western political and economic orders.

existence in Afghanistan either. Many do complain about the country's "dependence" (political, economic) on foreigners. However, they do not aim to instigate resistance against the "foreign occupation."

5) These poets in general convey a sense of hopefulness regarding the future. They seem to believe that with hard work, and a united nation, it is possible to achieve peace and prosperity.

6) They see disorder and war as eminent dangers to Afghanistan's future.

Conclusion

Two particular aspects of poetry contribute to its widespread use in Afghan society. One is the rhythm and rhyme embedded in the genre, which aids memorization. The other pertains to the unique quality of poetry that allows deep thoughts, sometimes difficult to comprehend, to be entrenched within a few short lines.

Poetry has an exceptional place within Afghan culture and society, and the Taliban play on this fact. Condensing deep thoughts and emotions within just a few words, and expressing them with elegance and flow, has meant that a Taliban poem's can be used as a communication device. In the West, on the other hand, it is the longer essays and novels that have played a pivotal role in shaping literary discourse around philosophical issues. It is important to understand and appreciate why poetry occupies such a significant space in the psyche of the Afghans.

Poetry in Afghanistan plays a huge role in communicating thoughts and ideas from person to person. Understanding this fact, the Taliban uses poetry to communicate the legitimacy of their actions, and to sanctify the ongoing insurgency. As illustrated in the numerous examples and their associated stories, the Taliban has three major themes that it employs to accomplish its goal: defense of the homeland against foreign invaders; defense of Islam against crusaders; and appeal to personal gain in the form of honor and esteem. Furthermore, they make excellent use of other aspects of Afghan culture by playing on feelings of national pride, the code of ethics of Pashtunwali, and even shame. Poetry resonates so greatly with the Afghan and Pashto people that the Taliban also employ it as a means of indoctrination and tactical training.

Through poetry, the Taliban can continue to deliver messages to the people that the Coalition is nothing more than the latest in a long line of invaders of the homeland. Furthermore, they seek to portray the Coalition as crusaders bent on the destruction of Islam. It is against these two beliefs that the West will have the greatest struggle. As the Taliban has demonstrated, they fully understand how powerful poetry is in communicating messages to the people of Afghanistan.

Taranas *(chants)*[33]

Similar to poetry, *taranas* or poetic chants play an important role in Taliban communication with local populations. The chants are communicated in the local language and traditional style and often represent a manipulation of Afghan traditions, narratives, collective memory of events, and culture to serve Taliban interests. These chants, like poetry, are melodic with memorable tunes, often with repeating passages that have a tendency to stay in people's consciousness. The chants are easily memorized, due to their rhyme, rhythm, lyrics—much like the advertising jingles that permeate other countries' radio and television.

In many areas of Afghanistan, especially those with a significant Taliban presence like Loy Kandahar, Taliban chanting has flourished.[34] For example, many Kandahari music shops that used to sell various types of music audiocassettes and musical instruments have begun since the 1990s to supply Taliban chants to the market. Undoubtedly such dynamics are partly pragmatic in light of the fact that Kandaharis (and other Afghan urbanites) have been tortured and imprisoned for listening to or participating in other forms of music. In some cases, a number of local singers/musicians have decided to sing Taliban chants, while others have migrated to other countries because of their well-founded fear of Taliban prosecution.[35] Essentially, the Taliban have been largely responsible for the spread of such chants, which have not only become a source of entertainment for many but also a key component of the Taliban information and propaganda war. These chants have also become a powerful Taliban tool for "instructing" and intimidating the Afghan population.

In June 2009, as the author sat in a hotel lobby in downtown Kandahar City, he witnessed individuals "blue-toothing" what appeared to be music from one cell phone to another. Upon further enquiry, he discovered that the "music" being transferred between cell phones was actually Taliban chants. While aware of the importance of folklore and music to Afghan culture and traditions, the author was unaware of how pervasive Taliban jihadi chants had become in southern Afghanistan. On further reflection, he suspected that these chants were just another piece of a very sophisticated (and often misunderstood) information campaign that the Taliban had pursued for years at the expense of the United States and NATO. Taliban information operations and narratives have long used cultural identifiers, historical memory, familiar icons, and schemata; it made perfect sense that the Taliban would also use a type of musical refrain in the form of chants to present their message to target audiences.

This section offers a descriptive analysis of Taliban music and messaging in the form of chants and the stories they reveal that were circulating in the Kandahar region in the summer of 2009. Through a review and analysis of actual Taliban chants, this assessment argues that Taliban chants are another link in a long chain of sophisticated information operations used to reveal the stories, rationale, and "road map" of the political and social goals the Taliban wish to achieve. These chants follow a rational, discursive, and iconic form designed to mobilize and convince the Afghan population of the Taliban's worldview.

Afghan music

Historically, music has always been an integral part of Afghan culture and traditions.[36] It is especially important to recognize that Afghan songs in the form of chants are of course closely related to poetry, an intimate aspect of Afghans' daily life. "Generally, [Afghan] music implies the use of instruments and song refers to poetry. Early music was basically in the form of hymns and sacred chants, the focus was on the underlying text, and so it was often classified as literature, not music."[37] Traditional songs and chants are part of the fabric of Afghan society, with people often singing and chanting as a central part of ceremonies associated with weddings and other celebrations.[38] Many of these chants and songs are often drawn from Sufi texts and poetry. Indeed, despite negative reactions from some parts of Afghan society to music and especially musicians, mystical Sufi orders have always held music as critical to many of their religious rituals.[39]

All types of Afghan music were drastically affected when the Taliban came to power in 1996.[40] The Taliban not only viewed music as a distraction from serious and important life matters, they also viewed most music as *haram* based on their particular interpretation of Islam. This view of music has also been upheld and enforced throughout the Pashtun areas of western Pakistan, particularly in Swat and the Khyber-Pakhtoonkhwa (NWFP) Province since the Taliban became prominent in the area.[41] Many mullahs, who are conservative religious figures, also disapprove of music despite the fact that Pashtun culture has its own traditional music and musical instruments such as *rabab*, *dohol*, *shawm*, and double-headed frame drum.

The Taliban viewed musical instruments as tools of *Shaytan* (Satan). They did, however, apparently allow the use of the frame drum—the *duff*—because they believed that other Islamic traditions allowed the use of this instrument during certain religious and personal celebrations and ceremonies. Hence, as distinguished British ethnomusicologist John Baily suggests, "the Taliban were not against all forms of music, and they certainly permitted religious singing without musical instruments."[42] The musical expressions of Taliban chants and *taranas* were allowed. According to Baily, the Taliban *taranas* are constructed in "the melodic modes of Pashtun regional music, nicely in tune, strongly rhythmic, and many items have the two-part song structure that is typical of the region. There is also heavy use of reverberation."[43]

Analysis of Taliban *taranas (chants)*

As suggested above, chants play an important role in Taliban communication with local populations. The chants are communicated in the local language and traditional style and often represent a manipulation of Afghan traditions, narratives, collective memory of events, and culture to serve Taliban interests.

The chants are very similar to certain types of Afghan poetry that are regularly memorized and recited by Afghans. Afghan poems, much like the chants assessed here, are wrapped in deep emotions and thought; the language of poetry in Afghanistan is the language of *wazn* (balance or rhythm), and *qafia* (rhyme). Abiding by the many other rules of poetry, *badee* (rules of creating a poem) and *arooz* (the art creating balance and flow in poem), each verse of a poem must maintain a specific *wazn*, and continuity in *qafia*. The combination of the two adds a melodic effect to the lyrics.[44] This obviously has important implications for their resonating narratives as well as their basic propaganda value.

As will be demonstrated below, theses chants often portray the ongoing events of Afghan life. Pashto and often Dari languages are mostly used in a simple and traditional form that resonates with Afghan locals. We find it particularly interesting that the chants are gaining the attention of an increasing number of Pashtun youth, especially in (rural and urban) areas where the Taliban have substantial presence.[45] Nonetheless, the Afghan government and security forces do not seem to take the chants seriously, perhaps because the chants are not viewed as a direct threat to the country's stability. Instead, they probably consider chants as part of the local entertainment.[46] It should also be pointed out that none of the US military or government personnel that the author spoke to after his field research had ever heard of Taliban chants.[47] This might explain why there is little, if any, news on the seizure of audiocassettes or CDs, or of any effort to curb business related to the supply of recordings of chants. Within this permissive environment, the Taliban eagerly and regularly distribute chants to the population. The Taliban chants are widely available in books and Taliban magazines,[48] or on audiocassettes, CDs, cell phone ring tones, various internet web pages,[49] and even on YouTube.[50]

In an effort to assess the meaning and impact of Taliban chants, we sought and obtained a series of chants that were circulating around Kandahar in the summer of 2009,[51] all of them vocalized in Pashto, and then translated them into English.[52] Below, we present the actual narrative of each chant, followed by a brief analysis of its meaning and its potential impact on the Afghan population.

As mentioned above, all of the chants assessed here were found in Loy Kandahar, and it is assumed that the primary target audience was the local Pashtun population. In assessing the meaning and impact of Taliban chants on Afghan target audiences, we have been forced to make certain generalizations concerning this population's own narratives, and their view of local political, religious, and social environments. We recognize that Afghan identity and belief systems are multifaceted and dynamic, and are layered by language, residence, tribe, clan, family, and *qawm* (among others), with each playing an important role in an individual Afghan's worldview.[53] *Qawm* (solidarity or affinity group)[54] membership is particularly important to chants and narratives because *qawms* are based, in part, on patron–client relationships that in turn are central to the nature of resonating subjects or narratives for a typical Afghan:

> No single concept is more important to Afghanistan's internal conflicts than that of patron–client relationships and the patronage networks these create... The importance of patronage relations extends to the *battle of ideas* in Afghanistan. Afghans are exposed to many different and often competing sources of news, but there is a tendency to follow the views of the provider of patronage or other Afghans that they desire to emulate.[55]

While we are not suggesting an "ideal" or reductionist Afghan view of the world, we have been forced to generalize across the target population in assessing the meanings and impact of the chants on the Pashtun.[56] The Taliban, in their construction of these chants, have clearly calculated the intended informational impact based on their own assumptions about what resonates with their target audience, and we have attempted to do the same here, albeit tentatively, for this analysis.

Afghan Mulk Angrizan (Afghan region foreigners)

Chant 1

O Afghan, the British (foreigners) are present in your country.

They are your yesterdays' (past) enemies whom your ancestors defeated, and then they ran away. Today, they are the rulers who dominate your soil (country). [repeated chorus]

Today, they have come under the slogan of friendship and rehabilitation of your country. [repeated]

The spies are present in your country. Your yesterdays' (past) enemies are present in your country.

They have invaded your country again. They intend to kill you. [repeated]

The murderers of your ancestors are present in your country.

They hit you with huge bombs, cruise missiles, and napalm bombs. [repeated]

Those people are present who pretend themselves to be your friends, but they are your previous enemies.

Be careful, O Afghan, do not be deceived and do not be segregated from your goal. [repeated]

Otherwise, Christians will be present [in your country].

The world's biggest thieves have come to our country, and look! They are all Westerners. [repeated]

Your history's purchasers have come to your country.

The prospects and desires of *Siddiqi* (poet) will be accomplished. They will be accomplished at the right time and date when once again the Afghan conquerors are in power.

O Afghan, the British (foreigners) are present in your country.

They are your yesterdays' (past) enemies whom your ancestors defeated, and then they ran away. Today, they are the rulers who dominate your soil.

Tarana's story: Our brave ancestors defeated the British after they invaded our beloved land, yet they and other foreigners have come again to spy on us and are attempting to destroy the Afghan way of life. They were cowardly murderers when they originally invaded our country and they have come again as "friends," but their real intention is to murder innocent Afghans and try to take over our beloved country. Don't be deceived by them, they want to destroy Islam and replace it with Christianity. But just like our brave ancestors, we will defeat the British and other foreigners who will eventually run from our country in defeat. It is the obligation of all Afghans to fight and destroy the invaders.

Analysis: This chant clearly targets the segments of the general Afghan civilian population who make up the Taliban's main recruiting pool. This chant touches on a variety of serious issues that are dear to Afghan history, culture, and lifestyle:

• Foreign invasion (All foreigners in some parts of Afghanistan are referred to as "British");

- Foreigners want to bring Christianity to Afghanistan;
- The cowardly nature of foreign invaders ("They were defeated and then they ran away");
- Defeat of British Empire by Afghan fighters ("ancestors defeated");
- Fight against invaders ("Do not be deceived and do not be segregated from your goal").

This chant also focuses on the mistakes and contemptible behavior of foreign forces in Afghanistan ("they pretend to be your friends; they intend to kill you"), behavior that is in direct contrast with the Afghan value of being a straightforward "friend" or "enemy." Foreign invasion has historically been a very sensitive topic among Afghans, and the above chant repeatedly plays on this foreign invasion message in an effort to draw the attention and support of the public. The chant's reference to past Afghan struggles against foreign invaders is a theme that we have regularly seen in other Taliban narratives.

The vast majority of Afghans recognize personal freedom and national independence as core values, and the Taliban understand the significance of this. But the chant does not merely play on these Afghan sensitivities; it also explicitly invites Afghans to join the Taliban's war against the current influx of foreign "invaders" by encouraging nationalism and playing on nationalistic sentiments.

There is little argument that most Afghans are very proud of their nation's history. And some of this pride relates to the fact that Afghans in years past have defeated some of the world's dominant powers, including the Soviet Union and Great Britain. In fact, this narrative of defeating "superpowers" is arguably one of the most effective motivational tools used to provoke Afghans against foreign forces, and is regularly used by the Taliban today.[57] We suspect that the Taliban often mention British forces because the British were long viewed as interlopers; moreover they are part of the present NATO "occupying" force, so the British can be used to represent both past colonial powers' attempts to exploit ("purchase") Afghanistan and the present "invading/ occupying" ISAF foreign forces. This Taliban chant presents the foreign forces as the "murderers" of Afghans' ancestors in an apparent attempt to revive a sense of revenge (*badal*) amongst their target audience against the foreign forces. Meanwhile, the Taliban chant reminds the Afghan public about their ancestors taking revenge and defeating the British.

In this *tarana*, the Taliban also emphasize a very common and consistent message found in other pieces of Taliban propaganda: Islam is at risk with the presence of international security forces in Afghanistan. The call to arms against a "threat to Islam" has been an extremely powerful incentive for Afghan communal action, and has historically been used to motivate Afghans—including even non-Pashtun elements of society who can be mobilized under the banner of Islam—to take action against foreign invaders. The Taliban portray invaders as representing a "cosmic" threat[58] to the survival of Afghan's religion and way of life. They want to project the argument that an Afghan is not a true follower of Islam if he does not rebel against foreign invaders. Taliban messages describe foreign forces as cruel and inhumane invaders who do not respect Afghan culture and religion, and who do not deserve the respect of Afghans. This chant plays up allegations of foreign forces' brutality by referring to foreigners' use of aerial bombs, cruise missiles, and napalm bombs to kill and maim Afghans. These examples are offered as evidence to prove that US and ISAF forces are neither friends nor protectors; that the foreign forces came to slay Afghans and to dominate the country[59]— not unlike the Soviet occupation forces, whose widely acknowledged atrocities against Afghans are still fresh in popular memory. These messages powerfully exploit Afghan emotions by touching on painful historical and more recent collective memories.

Ultimately the chant tells Afghans that the Taliban are strong enough to defeat the enemy and to regain power. But the Taliban admit that they must have the support of the Afghan people to succeed.

Aghyar Ashna *(Stranger friend)*

Chant 2

Should I complain about a stranger or should I complain about my friend? I don't understand, I don't understand, should I complain about the world or should I complain about myself? [repeated chorus]

The councils are held under my enemy's command. Decisions are taken by disqualified people in the council. They accept plenty of dollars to kill me.

Should I complain about his children or should I complain about their father?

They conspire to murder me with the advice of strangers. Some cowards in our country were celebrating my murder, as if it was Eid's eve. [repeated]

Should I trust their regrets or complain about his laughter?

My meat was being cut and you [pro-government Afghans] were pouring salt on them. My meat was being cooked in the skewers of brutality.

Should I complain about a butcher or should I complain about you?

I could hardly breathe because of my wounds and pain in this desert. I was treated like a stranger guest that suffered from pain and no one offered me treatment. [repeated]

Should I complain about a doctor or whom should I complain about?

I have become crazy about true love and have become like burned rue. I am burnt on the beautiful candle of Islam. [repeated]

Should I complain about our own traitors or complain about the world?

I am screaming for justice and recall past times. Where is the security that I was happy with?

Tarana's story: Foreign invaders have invaded our country and have been joined by cowardly, apostate Afghans who accept the blood money of the foreign invaders to murder us and destroy our country. But I have faith in Islam and know that we will get our justice and security, just as our forefathers did.

Analysis: This chant has two central objectives:

• To recruit new fighters, and
• To undermine the Afghan government.

It consists of a series of melodic refrains interestingly based on the Pashtunwali concept of *gila*, which means to complain about something important. In this chant the Taliban use Pashtun tribal mores not only to "connect" with their target audience (Pashtuns) but also to argue against the people supporting the Afghan puppet government ("councils are held under my enemy's command") and international forces. In this very emotional chant, the Taliban complain about the pro-government Afghans' cruelty, while

149

explaining how righteous and innocent the Taliban are. The chant suggests that the current conflict has been imposed *on* the Taliban, and that they are the victims of this war ("I am screaming for justice").

It is instructive to note that the Taliban have established a series of "shadow" justice systems throughout the country that are highly popular in adjudicating land (*mezaka*) and water disputes as well as criminal cases. Using Shar'iah law, a Taliban judge can settle a case in a few hours without bribes— unlike many of the formal Afghan government courts. While these Taliban courts may not administer the kind of justice preferred by Kabul or the West, it is swift and perceived as just by most that use them. This is especially the case when property disputes are involved. In southern Afghanistan many villages as well as city dwellers go to the Taliban court to settle such land disputes, that are often quite contentious and a serious source of local instability.[60] The shadow courts actually give a certain degree of legitimacy to the Taliban. The Taliban have also established an ombudsman system that local populations can use to report an abusive local Taliban commander or other complaints that are then forwarded to an independent authority for resolution.

Most Afghans—particularly southern Afghans—will agree that the complaints (*gila*) voiced in this chant by the Taliban are legitimate.[61] This chant not only challenges people to oppose a corrupt, incompetent ("disqualified people in the council"), and brutal government and the people that support it ("traitors"); it also slams government corruption ("they accept plenty of dollars to kill me"), the foreign dependency of the Kabul regime, and injustice. The Taliban call their battle a pure Islamic movement ("the beautiful candle of Islam"), and call the Afghan government a puppet regime that only serves foreign countries that aim to dominate the entire country and kill Afghans.

This chant not only attempts to play upon Afghan's Islamic affinities, but also to discredit the Afghan government as being un-Islamic. The government is introduced as evil, corrupt, and unable to provide justice. By doing so, it is clear that the Taliban recognize that ownership and independent decision-making are important parts of Afghan and community tradition. In addition, the Taliban accuse the current Afghan government of killing Taliban fighters in return for money from foreigners: actions that directly contradict Afghan ownership and independence. In other words, to local Afghans this chant suggests that Afghan government officials are killing their own citizenry to serve foreigners. Likewise, the chant argues that *Jirgas* (councils) called together by the government are held with the advice and support of foreigners who are ruling the country by proxy.

Lastly, the Taliban reminds the Afghan public about the past justice and security which existed while they ruled over Afghanistan ("I am screaming for justice and recall past times. Where is the security that I was happy with?"). The phrase is an attempt to gain public support by drawing people's attention to the Taliban's past performance while implicitly comparing the Taliban's past with the instability and insecurity under the current Afghan government, which is itself under the authority of the US and its allies.

Volleyball, football, and cricket

Chant 3

O youth, quit volleyball, football [soccer], and cricket. Take the Rocket-Propelled Grenade launcher [RPG] on your shoulders. [repeated chorus]

Play with human heads instead of playing with balls. [repeat]

Quit kids' games; take the RPG on your shoulders. [repeat]

You look good with the weapon and Moswak [herbal tooth brush] but not chewing gum and chocolate.

Purchase every worthless human for free (Kill the enemies.) [repeat]

You will soon defeat the enemies. You only need to put some more efforts defeating them.

Behead by using the sword those people who open the country gate to the strangers. [repeat]

Walk beside Ayubi [poet]. Don't be late, not even for a minute! [repeat]

O youth, quit volleyball, football (soccer), and cricket. O youth, take the RPG on your shoulders.

Tarana's story: Afghan youth must accept their responsibilities and give up their trivial pursuits, such as sports and candy, and join the righteous jihad against the infidel invaders. The youth of Afghanistan will be successful and defeat the foreign invaders, but this will take dedication and immediate action.

Analysis: This *tarana* is specifically written and sung to recruit Afghan youth to join the fight against the foreign invaders. The chant implicitly encourages Afghan youth to regain their *nang* (honor) by focusing their attention on important matters (defeating and killing the foreign invaders) instead of wasting time ("don't be even late for a minute!") on "kid's games" and trivial pursuits such as "gum and chocolate."

That the Taliban have chants that target a specific demographic says a lot about the sophistication of their overall information campaign. Chants such as this are aimed at influencing specific age groups of locals (under 25)—a major recruiting pool for the Taliban—as well as the jobless and uneducated. The Taliban understand that many Afghan youths spend their free time playing different sports ("volleyball, football (soccer), and cricket"). In general, the most popular Afghan sports are soccer, cricket, and volleyball. Due to a series of recent successes by Afghan sports teams in the international arena,[62] the numbers of Afghans who participate in these sports and sports fans have increased tremendously. This increased popularity has had a directly negative impact on Taliban recruitment, and the Taliban recognize this. In an effort to reach local youth and convince them to stay away from activities that do not correspond to the needs of the Taliban, the Taliban have included this topic in their chants.

As is apparent in this chant, the Taliban use various symbols and icons that fit Afghanistan's war-torn situation by talking about Rocket-Propelled Grenades (RPGs), fighting on the battlefield, and killing the enemy. Specifically, the RPG was one of the most well-known weapons used during the war against the Soviet Union. The RPG was widely available during the war, and Afghan Mujahidin became quite accomplished at using RPGs to destroy Russian tanks, military vehicles, and pro-communist Afghan forces. In past centuries, the sword was the most well-known weapon in Afghanistan, but it has more recently been replaced by the AK 47 (Kalashnikov) and the RPG. Therefore, the Taliban use these symbols of "modern" Afghan warriors in an attempt to motivate Afghan youth to become "real" champions by joining the Taliban in their fight against the foreign invaders.

Arman-Khodaya *(Wish-Allah)*

Analysis: This chant has two objectives:

• To create sympathy for the Taliban among the Afghan public, and
• To fuel people's sentiments against foreign forces.

Chant 4

O Allah, it is very sad that our innocent youths are colored with blood [martyred].

It is very sad that our village is (full of sorrow), covered with dust. [repeat]

O Allah, it is very sad that this dust and ashes come from the (dead) flower plant. [repeat]

O Allah, it is very sad that the [innocent Taliban died] innocent lamps of love fell down. [repeat]

It is very sad that despite the resistance of young flowers, they are falling down [the Taliban dies].

O Allah, it is very sad that the blood flow shakes our young plants.

O Allah, it is very sad that our innocent youths are colored with blood.

It is very sad that our companions' gatherings (*Majlas*) are destroyed.

Life is full of tasty honey.

O Allah, it is very sad that their red blood (loss of life) brought harsh life to the community. [repeat]

It is very sad that the grey huts of love carry the coffin of desires.

O Allah, it is very sad that our innocent youths are colored with blood.

It is very sad that my prospects and desires are unachievable, only Sakhi Bacha (poet) is crying.

O Allah, it is very sad that sorrow shakes our country. [repeat]

O Allah, it is very sad that our innocent youths are colored with blood. [repeat]

Tarana's story: Foreign crusaders are martyring innocent Afghan youth as well as our hero Taliban. The foreigners not only kill honorable and brave Afghans, they are also here to destroy our villages and way of life. But we will win if the people join the just Taliban cause.

This chant focuses on the sadness of the dead youth ("innocent youth," "dead flower plant") and commemorates young slain Taliban fighters ("despite the resistance of young flowers, they are falling down"). The target audience of this chant appears to be both the Taliban and the Afghan public. The chant implicitly introduces the Taliban as "freedom fighters" and attempts to create sympathy for the Taliban among the public. The chant also suggests how valuable the lives of the Taliban are for the country's prosperity. This chant aims to give emotional support to the Taliban in an attempt to explain the importance of each Taliban fighter's life in the community and their struggle to free the Afghan nation ("it is very sad that their red blood (loss of life) brought harsh life to the community"). These chants are meant to create a high level of local public support, particularly for the relatives and villagers of the fallen Taliban fighters. Generally, the Afghan public tends to be very sympathetic to a dead or "martyred" Afghan, even if he is viewed as an enemy.

This chant is also intended to prompt people to side with the Taliban against the foreign forces. One traditional Afghan way to attract popular support is to be humble in the invitation for assistance while at the same time keeping open the door for a participatory struggle. The Taliban encourage all Afghans to join their war against the enemy: "It is very sad that our companions' gatherings (*Majlas*) are destroyed." Also, they convey a message, through this chant, that this holy war is unwinnable without the participation and cooperation of the public: "It is very sad that my prospects and desires are unachievable."

Ay Ghrabi Shamara *(O Western dragon)*

Chant 5

O Western dragon! Where will you go when we shut all the ways? [repeat]

O Western dragon! You have an opportunity to run away now. Hurry and get out of Kabul so that you won't regret when you are captured. [repeat]

O Western dragon! Where will you go when we shut all the ways? You will leave like a handicapped Russia and you will never gain victory. [repeat]

O Western dragon! If you want to stay healthy, hurry up and apologize for your actions. [repeat]

O Western dragon! Where will you go when we shut all the ways?
The Afghans cannot be deceived; they are intelligent.
O Western dragon! You will be ashamed and you won't be able to recover. [repeat]

O Western dragon! Where will you go when we shut all the ways?
This country is a flower in the turban of Asia. This nation is a great champion.
This force will make you lose your direction.

O Western dragon! Where will you go when we shut all the ways?
This country belongs to Ghazi Abdullah. [repeat]
O Western dragon! This is the residency of Ahmad Shah Baba.
O Western dragon! Learn from this poetry.

O Western dragon! Where will you go when we shut all the ways?

Tarana's story: America and NATO, you have the opportunity to save yourself, but you must leave Afghanistan immediately or you will suffer the same fate as other foreign invaders such as the Russians. If you don't leave immediately you will have no escape; you have no chance of conquering us. History has demonstrated time and again that Afghanistan cannot be defeated. We are the champions of Asia and we will not only repel your invasion but totally destroy you.

Analysis: This *tarana* is an exercise of power by the Taliban and a warning to US and NATO military forces ("Western dragon") in Afghanistan to leave the country while they are still able ("you have an opportunity to run away now. Hurry and get out of Kabul so that you don't regret when you are captured"). The target audience is the Afghan public, although this chant is composed of a series of ultimatums to international forces. In fact, via this chant, the Taliban suggest Afghanistan's degree of power and influence in the region ("this country is a flower in the turban of Asia"). In addition, this chant claims that the Taliban will soon regain power and defeat their enemies by invoking past Afghan victories ("you will leave like a handicapped Russia, and you will never gain victory"). Similar to other chants, the Taliban want to empower their supporters' morale by reminding them of Russia's defeat in Afghanistan and the courage of Afghan national heroes (Ghazi Abdullah, Ahmad Shah Baba) fighting various invading armies throughout history.

While the Taliban were in power, they rarely honored past national heroes because this did not explicitly serve their interest and goals. During their rule they considered themselves the real and superior Afghan heroes, in part because they were ready to sacrifice everything for religion and country. However, more recently, they have increasingly used the names of past Afghan heroes in their chants, especially those who fought foreign invaders in past conflicts. Honoring national heroes' achievements and their struggles to defend the country against foreign invaders is a tactic the Taliban now uses to connect to the general public. This tactic also reflects a nationalistic pride:

- By suggesting that Afghanistan "is a flower in the turban of Asia" and a "great champion."
- By invoking the legend of Ahmad Shah Durrani ("Ahmad Shah Baba," Ahmad Shah the "father"), the founder of the Durrani Empire, and the founder of modern Afghanistan, as well as Abdullah Shah Ghazi who tradition suggests was a famous commander and conqueror during the Afghan-Anglo wars.

Afghans generally and fondly recall past historical "victories", and the Taliban continually play on this by recalling past victories in an effort to engender pride and confidence in their target audience.

Ay Mujahid *(O Mujahid)*

Analysis: This chant focuses on praising and honoring the Mujahidin[63] (aka, Taliban fighters). Interestingly, the Taliban's former ambassador to Pakistan, Mullah Salaam Zaeef, now under house arrest in Kabul, stated that the group refers to its own forces not as Taliban but as Mujahidin, because only one in ten fighters is a true Taliban, while the rest are "ordinary Afghans."[64]

This type of *tarana* appears to have two central objectives:

- To provide moral support and encouragement to the Taliban, and
- To assist in the recruitment of new fighters.

To achieve these two objectives, this chant claims that there are four central benefits of being a Mujahid:

- You become a hero to the people ("you are champion and courageous. You are our beloved man; you are our pride in the world");

Chant 6

O Mujahid fellow, you are a champion and courageous man.
You are our beloved; you are our pride in the world. [repeat chorus]

The enemies hear the fearful sound of your sword that won't let them get sleep and relax.
You are the thunder to every brutal enemy.

You devoted yourself and suffered difficulties for the sake of Allah.
You have defended your bunker with the cost of your blood.
You are a recorded champion in history.

The country's deserts exist because of your braveness.
The deserts are colored with your blood and look like red flowers.
You are the beauty of the country and protector of the whole book of the Qur'an.

You are very famous for your bravery and everybody knows about you.
I am proud of your heroism; you are the solution to our problems.

O Mujahid fellow, you are a champion and courageous man.
You are our beloved man; you are our pride in the world.

Tarana's story: Our beloved Mujahidin are the courageous heroes of the world. All the unjust and the brutal enemies of Afghanistan fear you. You fight and are willing to sacrifice everything for your people and Allah. Enemies run from you and your braveness and the whole world loves you and knows that you are brave and heroes to all righteous and just people.

- You make history and become a historical figure ("You have defended your bunker with the cost of your blood. You are a recorded champion in history...You are very famous for your bravery and everybody knows about you");
- You become a servant and protector of Islam ("You devoted yourself and suffered difficulties for the sake of Allah... The deserts are colored with your blood and look like red flowers. You are the beauty of the country and protector of the whole book of the Qur'an);

- You provide protection to the community ("You have defended your bunker with the cost of your blood ... you are champion and courageous").

All of the aforementioned qualities have immense value in the Afghan culture and community. Moreover, all these qualities offer moral-related benefits. The Taliban are attempting to suggest that new fighters are not being offered material benefits such as salary, pension, and promotion; rather, in the eyes of the Taliban, the benefits include the protection of their communities and religion.[65] The Taliban recognize that helping and defending the community is very important to the Afghan public. They regularly play on the fact that the Afghan government has been unable, in most instances, to provide for the protection and defense of the Afghan people. The Taliban portray themselves as ready to provide that security and protection to the Afghan people and to Afghanistan without any foreign support and backing. Their objective is to impress the public by stressing their hope for a secure Afghanistan following decades of war. They know that a large percentage of the Afghan population is extremely war-weary.

Interestingly, the chant suggests that a key advantage of joining the Taliban is that it allows one to become a "recorded champion in history." This claim resonates with the Afghan population's narrative of a proud history complemented by ancestors and historical figures that were great warriors and conquerors. Thus, this chant invites the Afghan people to follow and build upon their ancestors' struggle to protect the country from foreign invaders. Afghans are generally emotional by nature, and pride themselves in being strong and brave. Chants such as this serve as a reminder of their proud, collective history and invoke memories of their elders and ancestors in defending their territory from invaders. This chant also reinforces the Taliban claim that NATO security forces are foreign occupiers of Afghanistan.

As we have seen in other chants, the Taliban use the appeal of Islam for recruitment and to legitimize their actions. Taliban narratives, in conjunction with the Mullah status of many Taliban, allow the Taliban to leverage their religious authority and teachings in support of their cause. Mullahs are an important source for providing narratives, information, and guidance to village populations. Therefore, the public, and especially the rural Afghan, is increasingly under the Mullah's sphere of influence. A large majority of local Afghans are religious, but cannot read religious books and teachings; they rely on the Mullah (who is often illiterate himself) to teach and interpret for them the Islamic narrative.[66] The religious status and influence of Taliban

Mullahs as a powerful authority to guide the local population should not be under-estimated.

Badan Zakhmi *(Wounded body)*

Chant 7

My entire body is wounded. The wounds are colorful. O Allah, please assist the Taliban's madrasas. [repeat chorus]

We are holding the martyr's shawl and pray for him.
After his (Taliban) death, he left his family behind.
There is nobody to take care of him.

The Islamic nation does not take the lessons [responsibility to assist us.]
O Allah, we only need your treatment.

All the cruel infidel nations oppose him.
O Allah, the Taliban defends your religion.
O courageous Afghan, please be brave [join us.]

O Allah, please be kind to us now.
My "Ayobi" prayer is for one whose body is wounded.
This is a shame for our descendants.

My entire body is wounded. The wounds are colorful. O Allah, please assist the Taliban's madrasas.

Tarana's story: Please, Allah, protect and save our madrasas, students, and the Taliban. We mourn our fallen Taliban. Foreign invaders who have wounded Afghanistan threaten Islam. All Afghans need to join the Taliban and the jihad and save Afghanistan from the infidel invaders.

Analysis: This chant mourns the death of a Taliban, and asks Allah to help and save their madrasas. Attracting support and creating sympathy for the Taliban fighters appears to be the specific objective of this chant. Similar to other chants, this *tarana* illustrates that the Taliban are the true followers of Islam because they sacrifice themselves for the sake of Allah and seek assistance only from Allah. The chant further implies that although war has cost Taliban their lives, they are still determined to seek assistance only from Allah because they are true believers of Allah and Islam.

They also claim in the chant that they are the sole protectors of madrasas, referencing the religious schools that provide Islamic religious instruction, while also complaining about the Afghan people for their reluctance to join the Taliban. Furthermore, the Taliban do not only state that the motivations behind this war are divine, but also claim that Islam's fate is reliant upon their survival. The Taliban invite people to join and support their cause because Islam is at risk, a common narrative that we have seen in other chants.

Bagh-Baghwan *(Stranger-gardener)*

Chant 8

It was a blooming garden of flowers but the stranger gardener took over this garden.

Every flower's leaves fell down because the autumn is a stranger. [repeat chorus]

All the deserts, stones, and plants look forward to seeing their lovers (Taliban).
We have not seen yet the red lips of those lovers. [repeat]

Tarana's story: Foreign invaders are trying to destroy Afghanistan, but as in the past, the Taliban will eventually destroy the foreigners and reclaim our beloved homeland.

Analysis: This chant represents an iconic metaphor about how Afghanistan—portrayed as a beautiful flower garden ("blooming garden of flowers")—is being destroyed by foreign forces, portrayed by a "stranger gardener." Afghans generally have an affinity for flowers and gardens and this chant plays on this empathy.[67] The chant's story concentrates on how a foreign invasion is leading to the destruction of the once prosperous and peaceful Afghanistan, while at the same time they all wait for their "real lovers" (Taliban). The chant holds foreign forces responsible for all the misery in the country. It argues that Afghanistan was at peace in the past, but the outsiders have devastated everything. It also conveys a message to the people that they are the true caretakers of the country, and that they will soon take control of Afghanistan.

Ghaleem pa Kaano *(Enemy by stones)*

Chant 9

O Lord, people stone me because of my love for you. The sons of Nomudiaan stone Ezrayel [Angel.] [repeated]

Analysis: This chant targets the Afghan public and justifies Taliban actions as "holy warriors." This short but effective chant portrays the Taliban as pure Muslims who suffer all kinds of problems for the love of Allah ("O Lord, people stone me because of my love for you"). Meanwhile, it claims that all those people who oppose the Taliban, including the Kabul government and the international forces supporting the government in Kabul, are evil. The Taliban often refer to the Karzai government and international forces as the enemies of Allah because of their opposition to the Taliban, who claim to fight in the name of Allah. The Taliban are ever vigilant of the notion that most Afghans are highly religious, and this chant plays on those emotions by highlighting Islam as core of the Taliban life-style.

Gulan Paasha *(Toss flowers)*

Chant 10

Please come, dear friend, and throw flowers on my grave. I lie on deserts so please come always. [repeated]

Analysis: Although this chant is not fully copied from its original version, the context of the song is obvious. The Taliban believe, as suggested by previous chants, that they are national heroes who are often "martyred" as they attempt to protect their country and people. This chant encourages people to visit shrines dedicated to dead or martyred Taliban: typically a Sufi tradition, and outlawed under the previous Taliban regime because shrine visitations pre-date Islam. This chant suggests an interesting turn of events, possibly meaning that either the Taliban have become more politically adaptable in their percep-tion of Islam and more flexible about their tolerance of traditional cultural norms, or possibly because this *tarana* was created by a more localized, non-ideologically aligned segment of the insurgency who reflect more traditional Afghan values. In sum, this chant may represent the true face of local resist-ance in Afghanistan comprising indigenous Afghans who are less influenced by the radical interpretation of Islam subscribed to by neighboring Pakistani Taliban fronts, than by ancient traditional customs and Sufi influences observed in rural Afghanistan.

Afghans generally have a high level of respect for the shrines of national heroes, influential figures, and religious leaders. Moreover, nearly every village, town, and city in southern Afghanistan has a shrine visited by local Afghans for a variety of reasons. They often go to pray beside the graves of deceased ancestors. Many local Afghans believe that some shrines hold the key to solv-ing problems faced by individuals and communities today. For example, Afghans often go to shrines to ask for help for their sick children or relatives, to pray for better family relationships, or to ask for increased economic oppor-tunities and wealth. It is also common for Sufi and Shi'a Afghans to visit simi-lar shrines in the Pashtun areas of Pakistan. The observation of this tradition on the Pakistan side of the border has drawn heavy criticism and resentment from the Pakistani Taliban who habitually bomb and kill visitors to such shrines, as witnessed during an early July 2010 attack against a Sufi shrine in Lahore, Pakistan that killed 37 and wounded 180 others.[68] In summary, this chant plays on people's affinity for shrines, and implicitly asks Afghans to consider the Taliban as national heroes whose only purpose is to save the Afghan people from outsiders and foreign invaders: a central justification for their war against the Afghan government and international forces.

Jama ki da dosthai *(In the clothes of friendship)*

Chant 11

The enemies have come in the shape of friends.
They look like human beings but they are wild animals.

The act of disuniting people stays in their blood.
Their messages look like flowers but they are full of poison.
They have come under the banner of friends but they are murderers.

I have always made the destiny of this country.
I have brought happiness and beauty to my country.
They have come under the name of sympathy but they are muggers.

They are Jewish but half of them believe in statues.
They are [pre-Christianity Zoroastrianism] believers who came from East and West.

The enemies have come in the shape of friends.
They look like human beings but they are wild animals.

Tarana's story: Beware of foreigners, who claim to be friends of Afghanistan but are actually infidel, murderous crusaders who want to divide our people and destroy our country.

Analysis: This chant, like the others we have analyzed above, challenges the presence of international forces in Afghanistan by focusing on the notion of false friends.

Generally, Afghans take the issue of friendship very seriously. They have a tendency to respect those who call themselves friends of Afghanistan. In this chant the Taliban claims that foreigners:

- Appear as "friends" but they are really "wild animals," "murderers" and "muggers";
- Present messages that "look like flowers" but are really "full of poison."

This chant tells the people to beware the international forces because they are insidious, false friends. The Taliban often use terms such as "disunity," "unreal or false friends," and "deception and non-believers" in their propaganda narratives. If we carefully assess these terms, we will be reminded of Afghanistan's former invading powers (the British Empire and Soviet Union). Afghans recall that Soviet forces consistently referred to themselves as "friends to the Afghan people" while they bombed and raped Afghans. Indeed, there are many common local stories concerning this topic that nearly all Afghans have heard numerous times. This chant reinforces these stories and may be aimed at creating suspicion of all foreigners who offer friendship but are perceived as not having fulfilled promises since 2001.

Pashtun Mayaan *(Pashtun lover)*

Chant 12

Be brave and get your gun, those are not Pashtun who fight at the house like a fox.

Get the sword of your ancestors because the infidels have come to our innocent Afghanistan.

Please protect Haji Mullah Dadullah because the Taliban are proud of him.

Get your swords and let's be united. All the streets are full of nonbelievers. My country is my belief.

Whoever further destroys our country, Allah may give them punishment in hell.

I am with the Taliban because it is the army of Islam and I want to impress Allah.

The mother of martyr cries while his coffin is carried by the angels of the sky.

Allah says that our brothers are alive, the Taliban are colored with blood.

Tarana's story: Proud Pashtuns, get your weapons and guns and fight the foreign infidel invaders, just as the honorable and martyred Mullah Dadullah and your forefathers did. The infidels are everywhere and are here to destroy our country. The Taliban are the defenders of Islam and will die, if need be, defending Afghanistan and Islam.

Analysis: We received this chant as part of a video that showed the chant being sung by a local Afghan singer at a picnic. The video is significant in that it indicates that the Taliban have been able to spread some of their chants using local singers. Weekend picnics like the one displayed in the video are very popular in Afghanistan, especially for urban Afghans who leave the city—

Kandahar in this instance—to picnic in rural village areas. We find it very interesting that local singers who are often hired to entertain at these picnics would sing a Taliban chant that implicitly indicates the presence and influence of the Taliban in the area.

Although this chant seems like a mix of various other chants, it still presents very powerful messages about the Taliban and their jihad against international security forces. For example, this chant encourages Pashtuns to use their courage and honor ("Get the sword of your ancestors"), central components of Pashtunwali, to protect Afghanistan from the non-believers' invasion. The chant also includes requests for Afghans to join the jihad and to protect Mullah Dadullah (a slain Taliban commander known for his brutal and inhumane battlefield behavior). Familiar refrains about the righteousness of the Taliban, the proud history of the Afghans in expelling infidel foreign invaders, and the power of Islam and the Taliban are also prominent in this chant.

Taliban Nasheed *(Taliban ode)*

Chant 13

I will defeat Khalilzad's red brothers. I will defeat American and British forces. I will be neither tricked nor deceived. [repeated chorus]

I have power in my arms to defeat these forces. [repeat]
I want to announce today that I will break the teeth of Westerners. [repeat]
The outsiders live in Kabul and I publicly say that I will defeat American and British forces. [repeat]
I will come down from the bunkers with power and dignity. [repeat]
I will destroy pharaoh's residency in these valleys. [repeat]

I will break crusade and crusaders.
I will defeat American and British forces.

Tarana's story: It is inevitable that the Afghans will defeat the Americans and British and their apostate Afghan allies. The Taliban will not be tricked or deceived; we will come from all regions of Afghanistan to destroy the foreign crusaders.

Analysis: This chant is recorded as background sound for a video of Mullah Dadullah Mansour and his fighters.[69] It is sung in a way that demonstrates Taliban power, and to let the public know that they will defeat their enemies. The video shows Mansour visiting a suicide bomber training camp and giving a speech to very young trainees at the camp. It is an emotional and motivating chant that focuses on giving moral support to fighters. The chant primarily focuses on the idea that Taliban victory over American and British forces is inevitable.

Interestingly, the chant also refers in the opening refrain to former Presidential Special Envoy and US Ambassador to Afghanistan 2003–5, Zalmay Khalilzad. The chant insinuates that Ambassador Khalilzad was allied with the "communists" in Afghanistan, invoking the Soviet experience in Afghanistan ("I will defeat Khalilzad's red brothers"). We suspect that this chant might be referring to a specific group of Taliban that operates in regions within the British and American forces' areas of responsibility (e.g. in Helmand province). Alternatively, the American and British forces may also have been invoked in this chant, because they are well known today by most Afghans across southern Afghanistan.

Taliban Reciting Nasheed (Ode)

Chant 14

Women fought on the battlefield because they wanted to scarify for the sake of Islam.
The Muslim is reliant upon Allah. The war is for Allah (there is no other God but him). [repeat]

In the war of Uhud, our beloved prophet got injured.
The war is for Allah (there is no other God but him). [repeat]

Analysis: Although we only have a portion of this chant (we obtained it as part of a video), the main theme of the chant is jihad. The video shows a group of Taliban singing this chant with Arab fighters watching them. This is the only chant we have heard that refers to women's role in defending Islam. We suspect the term "women" is used either to persuade males to join the jihad, or to seek the involvement of women in Taliban military operations.

The chant suggests that the fight against the Afghan government and international forces is a "war for Allah." Hence the message to the Afghan people is that there is only one worthy motive behind this war, and that is to serve Islam. This chant implicitly dismisses a notion held by many that the Taliban fight for power and wealth, a charge often leveled against the Taliban.

Conclusion

This analysis of Taliban chants and their associated stories suggests that the Taliban carefully pick the topics to be portrayed in their *taranas*. The chants are seemingly developed explicitly to reflect values held dear by most Afghans, and by Pashtuns in particular. It is also interesting to note that many of the narratives and topics presented in the chants are also featured in other types of Taliban propaganda, such as night letters. Unlike Western information operations campaigns in Afghanistan, which seem to try to cover a multitude of topics and issues, the Taliban have limited the topics that their chants and other propaganda artifacts address.

Simple, culturally relevant messages communicated in local dialects project these messages into the popular Afghan consciousness through messages that resonate deeply with local Afghan communities. While the chants analyzed have focused on a variety of key topics, including Afghan history, religion, and tradition, the specific themes the Taliban *taranas* address are limited in scope. The chants' and stories' overarching themes include:

- Taliban victory in cosmic conflict is inevitable;
- Islam cannot be defeated;
- The Taliban are "national heroes" and willing to sacrifice all for Allah and country;
- Afghans have a long and honorable history of defeating invading foreign infidels;
- Foreign invaders as well as their Afghan puppets are attempting to destroy Afghan religion and traditions;
- All Afghans have an obligation to join the jihad against the foreigners and apostates.

The themes portrayed by Taliban chants are relatively unadorned and to the point. The themes are presented through the use of symbology and iconic portraits engendered in emotions of sorrow, pride, desperation, hope, and complaints. Each of these themes and topics is presented in a narrative and poetic form that is familiar to and resonates with the local people. When one listens to the chants, their rhythmic and melodic form is immediately apparent.

Islam, and a Muslim's duty to protect it, is one of central themes the Taliban use to influence people and gain recruits; it is a powerful motivator among rural Afghans. As we have seen in earlier chapters, the Taliban have been able to use Islamic rhetoric effectively in their chants to help legitimize their actions, and to help fuel Afghan anger against the foreign forces. Most Afghans accept Allah's divine will, and believe that Allah will punish the oppressor (foreign invader) because Allah is fair and just. In rural Afghanistan, and even in some urban areas, mullahs hold a near monopoly of power over religion, and they instruct people about what is right or wrong. This association between mullahs and Afghanistan's rural population has developed into a powerful patron–client relationship. The Taliban have used the mullahs to present a coordinated narrative to the people. Undoubtedly, the Taliban have been able to manipulate religion, and have used this manipulation as a powerful weapon in their jihad against the Afghan government and its international allies.

The analysis of these chants and stories also suggests that cultural values and traditions are used by the Taliban to shift public loyalties away from the government. The analysis clearly suggests that many of the Taliban chants attempt to connect emotionally with Afghans through the chants' explicit use of examples from Afghan history, and through appeals to Afghan nationalism. The Afghan public is generally proud of their history and their ancestors' performance in defending Afghanistan against foreign invaders over the centuries. Chants that focus on these sentiments remind Afghans of past foreign invasions (by Great Britain and the Soviet Union), and suggest the ignoble motivations of the foreign invaders: "they may appear as friends but they have more sinister motives."

The analysis clearly suggests that the Taliban attempt to use and manipulate Afghan culture and traditions through their chants. For example, the use of *gila* (complaints), a traditional tool that is tied to Pashtun lifestyle, was used in a number of the chants. In addition, the Taliban have used chants to appeal to subtle Afghan emotions.

Some of the chants posit that the Taliban are actually victims rather than perpetrators of war. These chants portray the Taliban as an innocent and humble people, while simultaneously portraying US and ISAF forces as evil and reckless invaders. The Taliban also use metaphors in their chants to send indirect messages to the Afghan people, aligning themselves with Afghan traditions. At the expense of over-generalization, Afghans frequently communicate indirectly, using idioms and poetic expressions when they want to complain about something without directly or explicitly stating their concerns. For example, in the chant "*Bagh-Baghwan*," we saw how the Taliban compared a blooming garden of flowers with Afghanistan, and a strange gardener as the foreign forces.

All of this begs the question, was there ever a realistic way to counter Taliban chants and other Taliban narrative expressions? The simple answer, as we shall see below, is that countering Taliban narratives is an extremely difficult and often almost impossible task for the West, because of sensitivities concerning religious themes that dominate the Taliban narrative space. This, in addition to the relative lack of Western linguistic capabilities, especially the understanding of local dialects, makes the countering of *taranas* extremely difficult.

Songs and chants are important mechanisms for storing and sharing Afghan memories, and a thorough understanding of these cultural artifacts as well as Afghan history could play an important role in helping to win the trust and confidence of the Afghan people. A more nuanced understanding of these elements is essential to building influential communication bridges from the West to the Afghan population. Taliban chants and other narratives evidently work effectively because of their simplicity, cultural relevance, iconic symbology, and rhythmic repetition.

8

THE *LAYEHA*, THE TALIBAN CODE
OF CONDUCT[1]

Introduction

This chapter assesses the Taliban's *Layeha* or "codes of conduct," and in so doing offers valuable insights into the Taliban's objectives and key strategies, and their attempt at consolidating the movement at the tactical and operational level. The codes of conduct also reveal overt and concealed clues into the psyche of the Taliban leadership and their information campaigns. Moreover, the codes highlight the Taliban's weaknesses, fears, and vulnerabilities. Finally, the *Layeha* also represent a sophisticated Taliban information operation artifact.

The Taliban's code of conduct manifesto, "Rules and Regulations for Mujahidin," offers critical clues into how the Taliban intended to operate as well as how the movement was structured according to the Taliban, and represents a component of the Taliban strategic communication campaign. It also suggests a catalog of weak points, vulnerabilities, and fears that are entrenched within the Taliban organization and its top echelon of leadership. A thorough examination of the document reveals the Taliban's attempt to wage a guerrilla campaign implementing a rudimentary population-centric strategy, while calling upon elements of Pashtunwali and Shar'iah law into the doctrine as well.

While there is a rich scholarly literature on the Taliban,[2] relatively little has been written concerning the Taliban's *Layeha* or "codes of conduct" that they issue periodically for their cadre.[3] We propose that although there are clearly limitations to the analytical use of Taliban *Layeha*—parts of these documents, as posited above, relate to a kind of public relations or information operations exercise[4]—these codes of conduct clearly suggest clues concerning the psyche and perspective of Taliban leadership, as well as insights as to how the Taliban see themselves and their organization.

What the Taliban presented in their latest manifestation of their *Layeha* was unlike the usual media or political assessments of the Taliban's strategic positions and tactics. This document depicts a sense of urgency and offers details as to how the Taliban, as an organization, planned to pursue their short-term objectives and also make it serve as a propaganda narrative against the Kabul regime.[5] The Taliban continues to expand,[6] but struggles in many respects to maintain its command and control authority as well as its "ideals" and "core principles." Moreover, after the announcement of the death of Mullah Omar, the Taliban has fractured into at least two factions. The movement, at least at the tactical and district level, seems to be suffering from a variety of dynamics including greed, predatory behavior, and criminality. Self-prescribed treatment for these dilemmas, if this *Layeha* is to be believed, comes in the form of consolidation, loyalty, obedience, structure, professionalism, tolerance, lawfulness, and unity.

This chapter examines what the *Layeha* implies about Taliban objectives, strategy, information operations, and organization.[7] It is premised on the assumption that deconstructing the *Layeha* provides important clues into the Taliban's organization following the capture of several of its political and military elite in 2009 and 2010, as well as other recent changes in the organization. For example, the rise to power of younger, more aggressive and militarily capable commanders, such as Mullah Abdul Qauyum Zakir and his deputy Mullah Abdul Rauf Alizai,[8] and their power struggle with old-guard Taliban leadership was partially evidenced in the 2010 *Layeha* and will be assessed below.

29 May 2010 issue of Layeha

The Taliban first issued their code of conduct manifesto in Spring 2006. They reissued the code in May 2009 and again in late May 2010. The Taliban's most recent code of conduct manifesto[9] is significantly different from the 2009 edition. The May 2010 *Layeha* included major modifications as compared to earlier versions, including an additional chapter and 18 new "articles" (rules). The reissuing of the *Layeha* came at an important juncture in the Afghan conflict, especially in light of the seizure and detention of several leading

Taliban leaders since January 2010, including the "Deputy Imam," Mullah Abdul Ghani "Berader" (he was later released by the Pakistani ISI), who, interestingly, was mentioned seven times in the 2009 *Layeha*.[10] It is hypothesized that the restructuring of the Taliban Quetta Shura following a series of high-profile arrests and the targeted killings of "365 high-ranking and mid-level insurgent commanders and mid-level Taliban leaders" between May and August of 2010 prompted many of the changes observed in the 2010 *Layeha*.[11] It is also interesting to note that the largely absent voice of Mullah Omar had become more apparent by Fall 2010, possibly signaling that some commanders had lost (or were losing) faith in the Taliban's then-supreme leadership.[12] Some even claimed that Mullah Omar was basically under house arrest in Pakistan, or at least tightly controlled by the Pakistani intelligence services.[13] The ultimate role of Omar in the operational and strategic posture of the Taliban at the time of the publication of the *Layeha* was critical to a whole series of issues, including the feasibility of Taliban negotiation and/or reconciliation with the Kabul regime, which had become a major focus for Kabul as well as within certain sectors of the US Afghan policy community.

Although the publication of the *Layeha* was perceived among some Western analysts as political theater, the document does provide important clues as to how the Taliban intend to operate in the developing security environment, as well as how the movement had been restructured—all according to the Taliban's leadership perspective. As will be seen below, the document reveals the Taliban's attempt to wage a guerrilla campaign in concert with a rudimentary population-centric strategy; including the important creation of a complaints commission: a shura that investigates suspected abuse of Afghan civilians by Taliban leaders and their fighters. It appears that the Taliban have become particularly sensitive to local perceptions and increasingly relied upon traditional "population-centric" lines of operation to consolidate their battle for "hearts and minds" of the Afghan populace and especially the southern, rural Pashtun.[14] All of these apparent Taliban positions also have powerful information operation implications.

As in the past, the Taliban remain conscious, and vulnerable, to the damage done to the movement's political capital by the incorporation of criminals (*Taliban-e duzd*) into the movement during the "open door" recruitment policies enacted in 2003. Infighting among Taliban factions was another key concern, something that has been recorded steadily over the past few years[15] and has been explicitly witnessed in 2015. The Taliban are exerting tremendous efforts to rectify issues concerning abuse and criminal activity by Taliban commanders and, as will be seen below, dedicated several new articles in the *Layeha* to deal with these issues. Such efforts definitely have IO implications, because many organizations and personnel associated with the Kabul regime are widely viewed as massively corrupt, and even criminal, by a significant majority of Afghans.

Tribal and communal conflicts were also of particular concern, and the Taliban exerted considerable efforts to mitigate these issues by creating effective mediation council and dispute resolution mechanisms, usually termed "shadow courts," which were critical to achieving local support and sympathies.[16] The 2010 *Layeha* paid particular attention to the importance of these judiciary councils and outlined the accepted way for Taliban fronts to create, utilize, and manage these systems. The Taliban judicial system is also an important subject of their information campaign.

Methodology

The analysis of the *Layeha* presented below is based on a qualitative content analysis of the 2009 and 2010 documents. This analysis was primarily interested in categorizing and comparing the statements presented in each of the two published *Layeha*. Particular research attention was devoted to analyzing differences in content and themes. The Table of Contents of each document was carefully compared and similar sections were systematically assessed in an effort to identify changes in scope, intent, and focus between the two documents. This analysis was then complemented with previously obtained documents, including interviews with top Taliban leaders published in jihadist leaflets, magazines, and websites, as well as the *Layeha* of 2006. The research objective was to assess changes as well as similarities in the Taliban's own statements as presented in the two manifestos, concerning their strategy, tactics, and goals.[17]

Before presenting the content analysis of the May 2010 *Layeha* and comparison with the 2009 "code of conduct" below, we first compare the structure of the 2010 document with its predecessor. We will then present an analysis of the 2010 *Layeha* and compare it to the 2009 document. Finally, we will examine the Taliban's organizational construct as presented in the 2010 *Layeha*. This organizational case study will demonstrate how the Taliban have adopted portions of the *Layeha* in actual practice.

Structure of the 2010 Layeha as compared to the 2009 manifesto

Table 8.1 presents a comparison of the Tables of Contents of the 2010 and 2009 *Layeha*. The code of conduct manual offers a structured approach using a chapter format with numbered "articles" listed below each chapter subheading. As evidenced in Table 8.1, the Tables of Contents of the two documents were very similar. Ten of the fourteen 2010 section topics were the same as 2009. New topics suggested by the 2010 Table of Contents as compared to the 2009 document were:

- Decisions Pertaining to the Surrender of Opponents and Giving Invitations to Them;
- Health Related Issues;
- National Issues;
- Advice.

While many of the sections of the 2010 *Layeha* were similar to the 2009 document, the 2010 *Layeha* nevertheless represented a significant expansion of instructions (although not necessarily a replacement) as compared to the originally released 2006 Taliban *Layeha*.[18] The 2009 *Layeha* was mentioned in the foreword of the Taliban's much longer 2010 version, which contains 14 chapters and 85 articles (or rules).[19] In the 2010 *Layeha*, the Taliban leadership asked its operators to abandon all previous modes of operational doctrine, including the 2009 *Layeha*, and abide by the new set established within the code of conduct.

Table 8.2 presents an overview of the thematic changes evidenced in the 2010 *Layeha* as compared to the 2009 version. As suggested in the table, out of the 85 articles in the 2010 *Layeha*, 47 were repeated from the 2009 *Layeha*, 14 were modified/altered, and 24 were new (18 of which are new additions, 6 are additional articles to replace the omissions from the 2009 *Layeha*). At least 17 out of the original 30 *Layeha* were repeated in the 2009 manifesto. The following analysis is focused on types of variations found in the Taliban's latest iteration of the *Layeha*, and provides insight into the Taliban's overall strategic shifts, alterations in Taliban command and control structures, and the Taliban's perceived adaptation to the ongoing and fluid security environment unfolding in Afghanistan. Similar to the US military force structure in Afghanistan at the time, the Taliban have undergone serious leadership changes between 2009 and 2010, and obviously since; these changes, many caused by Coalition operations against senior leadership elements as well as some arrests of senior Taliban leadership in Pakistan, had a seemingly significant impact on the Taliban's group cohesion and political objectives. An examination of the 2010 *Layeha* strongly reflects these dynamics relative to thematic changes in the document.

Table 8.1: Tables of Contents of 2010 and 2009 *Layeha*

2010 *Layeha*	2009 *Layeha*
1. Decisions Pertaining to the Surrender of Opponents and Giving Invitations to Them;	1. Security;
2. Regarding Prisoners;	2. Regarding Prisoners;
3. Regarding Spies;	3. Regarding Spies;
4. Enemy's Logistics and Construction Activities;	4. Enemy's Logistics and Construction Activities;
5. Captured Enemy Equipment (War Booty);	5. Captured Enemy Equipment;
6. Regarding Commissions (i.e. Mujahidin Organization);	6. Mujahidin Organization;
7. Internal (Personal) Issues of Mujahidin;	7. Mujahidin Personal Issues;
8. Education and Training;	8. Education and Training;
9. About Departments and Companies;	9. Regarding Mujahidin Organization;
10. Health Related Issues;	10. Local Personnel Topics;
11. National Issues;	11. Prohibited Items;
12. Prohibited Items (Forbiddance);	12. Recommendations and Focus Regarding These Rules and Regulations;
13. Advice;	13. The conclusion is summarized by a poetic statement by Mullah Mohammad Omar, titled *God Give Us Victory*.
14. Recommendations about the Code of Conduct.	
15. The conclusion is marked by a small speech of Mullah Omar, called *Dear Grateful Mujahidin Brothers*.	

Analysis of 2010 Layeha

The 2010 edition, as previously suggested, was much longer and covers in greater detail more strategic and tactical concerns than the earlier *Layeha*. Significant additions were made to chapter 7 ("Internal Issues of the Mujahidin"), with 10 new articles added, and a new chapter 10 entitled "health-related issues" was included.[20]

There were suggestions that the Taliban were attempting to moderate their behavior, after events in Sangin district in Helmand, where the Taliban

Table 8.2: Overview of 2010 *Layeha* thematic changes

Repeated (47)	Alterations (14)	New Additions (24)	Omissions (6)
• Guerrilla fundamentals • Prohibited behaviors such as torture, kidnapping for ransom, home invasions, and accepting bribes • Recommendations for suicide attacks • Ordering fighters to blend in with the local population	• Properly dividing war booty • Construction and logistics activities • Decision-making on captured Afghan logistics personnel	• Rules for Provincial and District Commissions • Rules on health services	• Condoning attacks against NGOs • Narcotics

shadow governor was replaced several times in 2012 because of brutality;[21] but this was clearly not universally recognized or followed by all Taliban and Taliban groups. Code stipulations such as "protection offered to any government official, worker or contractor captured by the Taliban" have been cited to suggest a "softer, kinder" Taliban, but this was not a new doctrine.[22] This rule was previously outlined in the Taliban's 2006 *Layeha* and is also a widely accepted tenet of Pashtunwali.[23] Obscene battlefield atrocities, such as beheadings, the murdering of women, and the mutilation of Afghans working for the government and NATO forces were still occurring. The Taliban repeated their prohibition of cutting "ears, nose, and lips" (chapter 12, article 70 of 2010 *Layeha*). However, in practice, the Taliban have continued the practice of mutilating Afghan citizens, severing ears and noses, and often beheading Afghan villagers (including women) and security forces.[24] Hence, one needs to ask if such pronouncements are mere IO propaganda or actual policy pronouncements. The appeal by Taliban leadership to end this unpopular battlefield conduct remained a major bane to the Taliban's political capital, especially when they were linked to heinous acts like the carving out of a villager's eyes in Kandahar province back in 2008 and the execution of a pregnant woman in Badghis province in August 2010.[25]

The content analysis of the main themes of the 2010 code of conduct suggests that the main purpose of the reissuing of the *Layeha* in light of the restructuring of the Taliban's leadership infrastructure was:

- A continued focus on network communication, consolidation and control;
- A focus on the quality of jihadist operations;
- A recognition of the importance of public support;
- To ensure jihadist operations do not negatively impact the Taliban's political capital;
- An attempt to convince the local population that the Taliban—not the local Afghan government, local security force, local militia, or even a rival insurgent faction (e.g. Hezb-e-Islami)—is the real power in that specific region;
- To convey the new construct of the Taliban provincial leadership, namely the importance and structure of political commissions, the Taliban's proverbial "silver bullet" in defeating the government of the Islamic Republic of Afghanistan by creating an effective and legitimate parallel government that responds to the social, political, and security needs of the people;
- To incentivize Afghan government personnel not only to defect to the Taliban, but to be rewarded as newly "high-ranking Mujahidin" if they kill a top government official or Coalition soldier or if their actions create an environment where the Mujahidin can kill a high-ranking official or Coalition forces;
- To loosen the command-and-control parameters on executing captured government officials, clerics, commanders, and elders.

It appears that the 2010 manual's target audience was the provincial and district leadership (many of the *Layeha* are directed at them), and stressed the importance of obedience and the chain-of-command in conjunction with the larger Taliban administrative bodies (provincial commissions). The 2009 version seemed to target "group leaders," tactical-level Taliban commanders in charge of *dilgai* (local cadres) numbering 10–15 members. It also outlined the organizational responsibilities of both the district and provincial-level command apparatuses. Interestingly, the 2010 *Layeha* only scantily refers to the Taliban's then supreme leadership, Mullah Muhammad Omar (*Amir ul-Momineen*)[26] and his Deputy, who goes unnamed unlike the 2009 version where Omar's then most trusted deputy, Mullah Abdul Ghani "Berader," was referred to frequently.[27] Berader was arrested by Pakistani authorities in Karachi sometime in January 2010 and later released to great fanfare. In the 2009 manifesto, Mullah Omar was referred to six times and his deputy six times; in the 2010 version, Mullah Omar was referred to eleven times and Berader seven times. In previous versions, Omar is referenced three times, Berader not at all.

A significant addition to the 2010 edition of the *Layeha* was a directive concerning Taliban access to medical facilities. The Taliban at the time reportedly maintained several clandestine medical clinics throughout southern Afghanistan, such as those in Helmand's Garmsir district. Additionally, wounded Taliban/insurgents had also been treated regularly at the Italian NGO clinic [Emergency], then in Lashkar Gah, Helmand.[28] This directive was most likely aimed at curbing Taliban fighters from abusing their access to such medical provision, because they sent their relatives and friends to seek treatment from these facilities for non-combat-related injuries and ailments. This stricture could also be advice from foreign sponsors, such as elements of the Pakistani security establishment, who reportedly established medical facilities close to the Afghan–Pakistan border to treat wounded Taliban.[29]

"Guerilla fundamentals," an important addition to the 2009 *Layeha*, are largely repeated in the new version. In the 2009 *Layeha* these fundamentals included:

- "The Mujahidin must have a good relationship with all the tribal community and with the local people, so that they are always welcomed and are able to get help from local people."
- "The Mujahidin should forget about tribal or language differences. The Mujahidin should not fight among themselves. Prophet Hazrat Mohammad says, 'Those people that fight each other because of language or tribal differences, they are in the wrong path' (chapter 319). If you are living under the one flag and fighting under the same flag, then the language or tribal differences should not be important."
- "The Mujahidin should always have the same uniform (read 'dress') as the locals because it will be difficult for the enemy to recognize them, and also to make it easy for the Mujahidin to go from one location to another."[30]

The dismissal of the importance of a particular tribe reflects the Taliban's preference (in recent years) to have members, especially "foot soldiers," from all tribes living in a particular locale. Downplaying the differences of tribes as reflected in the above codes reflects the strategy that the Taliban had adopted since around 2004–5.

The 2010 *Layeha* gave special attention to article 62 in chapter 11 [National issues] which referred to two other articles [articles 46 and 76]. Article 62 was presented as a cardinal rule regarding legal/judicial matters and states:

If the regional residents ever present a request to Mujahidin with the aim of judicial resolution for rights or other conflicts, then not every group's leader holds the authority to intervene in public affairs. Although only the provincial commander, the district head or his deputy can take the petitioner's request application into consideration and according to the procedures, initially in collaboration with the mediators, the issue should be resolved with peace and organized *Jirga* in such a way that it does not contradict the sacred Shar'iah. If reconciliation or *Jirga* consultation is not possible, then in case of availability of courts, they should proceed to the court and if a court doesn't exist then in that situation the procedures in agreement with the scholar's points of view should be followed.

It is interesting to note that the Taliban in this *Layeha*, as demonstrated above, referred to themselves as Mujahidin. Mullah Salaam Zaeef, the Taliban's former ambassador to Pakistan now under house arrest in Kabul, stated that the group does not refer to its own forces as Taliban, but as Mujahidin, because only one in ten fighters is a true Taliban, while the rest are "ordinary Afghans."[31] While many of the Mujahidin of the anti-Soviet jihad (1978–89) joined the Taliban in the early 1990s, it should not be forgotten that many of the Mujahidin, especially those allied with Jamiat-e-Islami, Shura-ye Nazar, and various Shi'a *tanzim*, formed an anti-Taliban bloc called the United Islamic Front for the Salvation of Afghanistan; they were the principal enemy of the Taliban after they came to power, and were their opponents in the brutal Afghan civil war of 1994–2001.[32]

Significant differences: 2010 vs. 2009 doctrine

Although the Taliban had incorporated more than half of the prior *Layeha* into their new manifesto, it is important to note which rules were modified or removed altogether; additionally, which rules were added: namely just additional caveats and explicit details to particular rule sets (i.e. more detailed rules for prisoners, the creation of provincial commissions, and dividing war booty). Rules that were added to the 2010 doctrine are listed below, followed by noteworthy deletions from the previous *Layeha*.

Actions prohibited by the Taliban (chapter 12) remain mostly unchanged from the 2006, 2009, and 2010 *Layeha* except this important modification:

- 2010, article 69: "Youngsters (those without beards) are prohibited from living in Mujahidin residencies or administrative centers."
- 2009, article 50: "Youngsters (those without beards) are not allowed to be taken on jihad."

The importance in this modification was not so much the Taliban's acceptance of child soldiers, but the prohibition of them from Taliban sleeping quarters. Male-on-male sexual activity, especially that of man-on-child abuse (known locally as *bachabauzi*, or "child's play"), is a practice that allegedly rose to prominence throughout the past forty years of conflict.[33] Most Afghans view *bachabauzi* as a grave social injustice, and even the Taliban movement itself prides itself on the widely held narrative that the event that prompted Mullah Omar and his small band of *talibs* to take up arms against the warlords was the tank duel that ensued between two commanders who were fighting over the right to own a young dancing boy.[34] The issue is so contentious that Afghan laws also prohibit the young from dwelling in Afghan police and military barracks.

Kidnapping and the criminalization of the Taliban remained a major vulnerability to the Taliban organization and how they were viewed among certain Afghan communities.[35] Article 73 of the 2010 document expressly prohibited kidnapping for money. The continuing focus on kidnapping and other criminal activities in the *Layeha* would seem to suggest that the senior Taliban leadership was fully aware of the negative reactions garnered by local communities regarding the movement's involvement in kidnappings, extortion, mutilations, bribery, and attacking educational systems and students. Nevertheless, 2010 saw a major increase in kidnappings in Kandahar City and other locations.[36] It is strikingly apparent that the Taliban organization(s) had severe problems with banditry, extortion, bribery, and all-out criminality within their ranks.[37] Opportunistic predatory behavior was interfering with Taliban tactics and strategy, and corrupting the organization from the district level upward, likely infecting provincial-level leadership as well.[38] Media reports from summer 2012 speculated on a financial drain of the "central treasury" that was partially caused by corrupt and greedy tactical and district-level commanders who helped bleed resources for their own self-interests and caused inner-Taliban rivalries based on economic domination of specific territories, specifically within Zabul province;[39] evidence of this phenomenon also existed in nearly all areas where insurgent groups were operating.

The 2010 Taliban doctrine highlights a directive by Mullah Omar written on the back page of the manifesto. Table 8.3 presents this statement as well as his statement in the 2009 document. As evidenced in the table, Omar's 2010 statement was nearly identical to 2009's, with one addition (highlighted in Table 8.3): this included the emphasis on "consultation" before jihadi operations were carried out, a further indicator that the Taliban were striving to consolidate command-and-control capabilities throughout the battle space, highlighting the importance of the many new additions to the *Layeha* regarding provincial commissions and quality of operations.

Table 8.3: Mullah Omar statements in *Layeha*

Layeha 2010 statement by Mullah Omar	*Layeha* 2009 statement by Mullah Omar
Dear Mujahidin,	Dear Mujahidin,
1. Your intentions and all other activities must match the policies of almighty God and the Prophet Muhammad.	1. Everything you do should be according to Islamic Law and only for God.
2. Stand firm like steel in front of the enemy, any incidents or propaganda should not shake your resolution.	2. Stay like a rock to face the enemy and never go back.
3. Love your Mujahidin brothers and your own people. Keep the brotherhood and firm honest relationship with people so that the enemy cannot penetrate to divide you to obtain its sinister aim.	3. Keep good relationships with your friends and the local people, and do not let the enemy divide/separate you.
4. *All of your jihad activities and operations must encompass consultation, carefulness, contrivance and cleverness.*	4. Always be careful during your operations.
5. No one should use personal animosity, inferiority complex, or carelessness to punish someone.	5. Do not give anyone difficulties because of your personal issues.
6. Safeguarding the wealthy and the ordinary people is the basic responsibility of the Mujahidin. All of you are to fulfill these obligations responsibly and do not allow those ambitious, armed, and material-loving individuals to abuse people and waste their wealth for their own personal gains.	6. This is our mission: to keep people and their property safe. Do not let those people who love money take away people's property and cause them problems.
Amir ul-Mominin[40]	Amir ul-Mominin

Financial matters as well as extortion appeared in several other rules throughout the 2009 manifesto as well as the 2010 document, and have important Taliban IO implications:

- "Taking money in order to forgive someone is prohibited."
- "When we mention that we need a 'guarantee' from someone, we are saying that a trusted person should provide a guarantee. We are not talking about property or money."

- "When you capture drivers, contractors, or soldiers, releasing them for money is prohibited."
- "If an Afghan National Army soldier is captured, the Imam or Imam's Assistant will make the decision whether to kill him, to use him for a prisoner exchange, or exchange him for money."[41]

In Pashtunwali, money is often a means of settling disputes, or forgiving a transgression between individuals or clans. It is a measure of conflict resolution that has been an established process in Afghanistan for thousands of years.[42] Afghanistan's customary criminal norms are based on restorative justice rather than retributive.[43] In Pashtun communities, this means that a culprit is asked to pay *poar*, or compensation money, to the victim or the victim's family and to ask for forgiveness rather than spend time in a prison. This underlying custom of seeking apology and eliminating enmity is known as *nanawati* among Pashtuns and *'uzr* among other communities. Even within the doctrine of Shar'iah law, this type of "blood money" payment is also prevalent and is known as *diyat*. In respect to the Taliban's prohibition of taking *poar*, the Taliban were preventing a traditional practice among Pashtuns, Tajiks, and other ethnic groups in Afghanistan.

Apparently in anticipation of having Afghan government employees and others switch sides and join the Taliban (likely as a response to the increase in US and Afghan government support for often unsuccessful reconciliation programs for the Taliban and other insurgents), the 2010 code of conduct included a series of new rules as to how to handle such events or government desertions. These, like other rules presented above, have important Taliban IO as well as "story" connotations:

- "The people who surrender and regret their past deeds will have to return the money or properties in case they have snatched the money or properties while they were working with the infidels or their slavish government."[44]
- "Those who quit the puppet government and join the Mujahidin should not give him a place in their lines until they develop satisfaction about the person. In case of giving a place to such a person in their lines, the Mujahidin will have to obtain the approval of the provincial commander."[45]
- "If a person quits the opposite camp and is unable to defend himself, it is not justified to kill him until it is known if he plans to join the Mujahidin or attack them."[46]

Although there had not been reports of significant members of the former Karzai regime or government workers "switching sides," a 16-man Afghan police unit did defect to the Taliban in Khogeyani, Ghazni, an explosive and unstable area south-west of Kabul.[47] The mere fact that a series of new rules addressing such a contingency was added to the 2010 *Layeha* is interesting in its own right. It was probably an indication of the confidence that the Taliban had in early 2010 that their side would eventually be victorious. These rules might also indicate the Taliban recognizing that Pashtuns historically have been very willing to change sides, especially if they think the other side will eventually be victorious.[48]

While the last few years have witnessed concentrated Taliban attacks on US and NATO supply lines in both Pakistan and Afghanistan,[49] 2010–12 witnessed considerable concern in Washington concerning the intensity of Taliban attacks on coalition logistics and supply convoys.[50] The 2010 code of conduct explicitly addressed such dynamics and contractors and others involved in US/NATO convoys and logistics:

- "For those contractors who deliver and supply oil, resources, or other material, and build governmental centers for the infidels or their slave administration ... and drivers supplying the enemy with goods who are captured, the death penalty should be pronounced if the judge has solid proof in regard to their involvement.[51]

The seriousness that the Taliban assigned to supply convoys was suggested by the penalty that they ascribe to those proven guilty of being associated with convoy work—death. Like the 2009 *Layeha*, the 2010-reissued version had a special set of rules of conduct concerning construction and logistics activities. The rules assigned specific responsibility to Taliban leaders (provincial authority *only*) who attacked and seized contractors' construction equipment or vehicles and what was to be done with captured construction personnel. Again, there were special instructions for Taliban fighters not to obtain and loot convoys for their own self-interests.

- "Burning a private vehicle which transports material to the infidels or provides other services to the infidels is lawful, but it is forbidden to spare them in exchange for money or use them for any benefit."[52]
- The Taliban "have the right to kill" men who use "vehicles which transport material to the infidels. The rules assign specific responsibility to Taliban leaders (Taliban judge or in the absence of a judge, a Provincial Shadow Governor)."[53]

The 2010 *Layeha* also published new rules concerning construction and logistics activities:

- "When it is confirmed that contractors ... are transporting oil or other equipment ... the Mujahidin should burn their resources and they (contractors) should be killed."[54]
- "When it is confirmed [that] contractors are providing laborers and workers to the enemy ... [they] should also be killed."[55]

These rules further suggested the importance that the Taliban apparently placed on logistics, convoys, and especially oil transport by the types of penalties proffered for those found supporting such activities. This is especially interesting in light of the fact that a number of new more "moderate" rules in the 2010 code of conduct pertain to penalties and prisoners. For example:

- "Mujahidin are not allowed to torture any prisoner with hunger, thirst, heat, cold even if these prisoners deserve death ... nobody is allowed to pronounce punishment decisions except the Imam, deputy Imam, and the judge. The district judges are not allowed to pronounce death sentences without the approval of the provincial judge. However, if a provincial judge is not yet appointed, then pronouncing death sentences or other type of punishments will be the authority of the governor."[56]
- "As there are so many Shar'iah obligations linked with execution, if Mujahidin intend to execute a criminal person ... Mujahidin ... must ... inform his relatives about his date of execution."[57]

As in earlier *Layeha* (2006, 2009), the 2010 document had a section and a series of specific rules devoted to war spoils or "booty." "Booty" was defined as "property captured from infidels during war."[58] All money or other commodities captured by the Taliban during combat was to be split between participants. One-fifth of such spoils were to be expended by the provincial commander, and the remaining divided amongst "those Mujahidin who fought." Rule 28 states that before a battle begins, the relevant Taliban commander should record the "names and particulars of the [participating] Mujahidin" to aid in the "distribution of booty."[59] Money or property that was obtained by means other than combat, according to the *Layeha*, was to be distributed to the *Baitul Maal*, the "central treasury," which is a Taliban organization for distributing commodities and goods amongst the people as well as the "Mujahidin." Although hardly a serious attempt by the Taliban to institute Hezbollah-type social welfare programs, the author has seen "community ledgers" written by the Taliban that documented names, ages, and other descriptors of local individuals supportive of the Taliban and their military activities. Programs that benefit the people, at least in the eyes of the

Taliban, were also reflected in the new rules concerning war spoils of the 2010 *Layeha*:

- "If Mujahidin carry out fighting against infidels in a village and if the villagers also participate in the fighting, then they will have a share in the booty."[60]

The benefits the Taliban offered villagers have been a major theme of their efforts to win over sympathy and support from local communities. Having an explicit rule that suggested that locals who participate with the Taliban in fighting "infidels" would reap rewards (in the form of war spoils) was an attempt to gain the trust and confidence of the local Afghan population. While the Taliban explicitly stated that none should accept cash for transgressions, they leave an opening for provincial authorities to accept money. This aspect could be emphasized to show the hypocrisy and corruption of Taliban leaders: hoarding money for themselves.

Both the 2009 and 2010 *Layeha* attempt to expand and reinforce the success of the Taliban shadow court system, which represents a parallel legal system that is acknowledged by local communities as being legitimate, fair, free of bribery, and swift. The Taliban shadow justice system is easily one of the most popular and respected elements of the Taliban insurgency by local communities, especially in southern Afghanistan.[61] The author witnessed this first-hand in the Panjwayi district of Kandahar where there existed no formal, operable justice system to adjudicate criminal cases or extremely important civil disputes involving water and land rights. Disagreements over land (*mezaka*) and water were (and are) presently a serious source of social instability in the district. Such disputes were quite frequent because of a complicated and convoluted system of landownership and inheritance that had been aggravated by decades of violence and malfeasance by predatory local officials. Attempts to resolve these disputes or claims through the channels of the Afghan government's formal justice system can take years and significant monetary bribes. The Taliban have effectively exploited this situation through their shadow justice system once housed in Zangabad (Horn of Panjwayi).[62] Using Shar'iah law, a Taliban *qazi* (judge) can settle a case in a few hours without bribes. While this court may not administer the kind of justice preferred by Kabul or the West, it is swift and perceived as just by most that use it. This is especially the case when property disputes are involved. Many villages as well as city dwellers go to the Taliban court to settle such land disputes. The shadow court system actually gives a certain degree of legitimacy to the Taliban and strongly enhances their political capital.[63] The elders' account of how the legal system is organized and how it functions matches the 2010 Taliban code of conduct rule on justice exactly. These codes concerning justice also play an important role in Taliban IO stories.

Organizational analysis of the Taliban movement: internal issues of the Mujahidin

Important information can be obtained regarding the organizational force structure of the contemporary Taliban movement through the examination of the new articles in the 2010 *Layeha* chapter concerning "Internal issues of the Mujahidin." The *Layeha* identified how the Taliban plans to increase its efficiency and popularity in rural environs and zones of conflict by the creation of *walayat-kommsyon*, so-called "provincial commissions," which are investigative councils designed to ensure the interests of the local population and maintain order within the Taliban's provincial force structure. Chapter 6, "About Commissions" (articles 34–39), and chapter 7, "Internal Issues of the Mujahidin" (articles 40, 41, 42–50, 58), and chapter 11, "National Issues" (article 62), indicate the Taliban's methodology to be used to create provincial commissions. The encouragement to create district-level commissions, which are managed by a district governor and his deputy, is also critical in organizing and directing the Taliban's activities at the village and area level. The *Layeha* advised its provincial governor to help create these councils and seek out well-respected leaders and deputies who have civil service skills to help with political and social causes, rather than having two military commanders in charge of Taliban governing duties.

Since the issuing of the 2010 *Layeha*, US and Afghan forces carried out a protracted series of operations aimed at dividing and conquering elements of the Taliban's senior leadership. The Pakistani arrest of [Deputy Imam] Mullah Abdul Ghani "Berader," several ranking members of the political and ideology committees, and the killing of scores of other senior leaders within the Taliban's military and political committees in 2011, led to a restructuring of the Taliban leadership. An analysis of the *Layeha* chapters dedicated to the creation and maintenance of the Taliban's provincial-level force structure led to the construct the Taliban organizational structure presented in Figure 8.1.

The Taliban's vision of a provincial command and control structure is centered around five entities: the provincial governor, the provincial council, the Shar'iah court, the district commission, and the district governor and his deputy. The provincial command and control infrastructure remains loyal to and under the management of the hierarchal leadership of the Taliban Quetta

Figure 8.1: Provincial military force structure of the Afghan Taliban

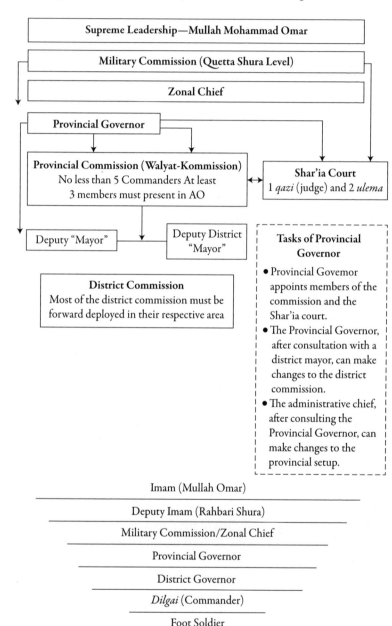

Table 8.4: Responsibilities of the Taliban chain of command[64]

Responsibilities of Taliban command and control apparatus			
Zonal chief	*Provincial governor*	*Provincial commission*	*District governor*
Has the authority to make changes in the provincial command structure after consultation with the governor.	Responsible to form a provincial- and district-level commission and Shar'iah court system.	Comprises at least five members, three of which must be present in their area at all times.	Must appoint a deputy to serve as a civil works/social outreach representative for the Taliban.
Coordinates regional military activities of the Taliban.	Has the authority to make changes in the district command structure after consulting with the district governor. If a disagreement ensues, the case is then passed to the zonal chief.	If any issues arise between the Taliban and local residents, the commission will investigate the matter and help resolve the situation. If the commission cannot resolve the issue, it must be investigated by the zonal chief.	In conjunction with the district commission, he ensures no spies, thieves, or criminals enter the ranks of the Taliban.
Oversees Taliban operations nationwide and makes strategic decisions accordingly.			If the district governor or group commander suspects any Taliban member of repeatedly breaking the *layeha* rules, they must refer this case to the provincial council who will investigate the matter and consult with the provincial governor.
Must occasionally send delegates to the provinces to assess the strength of the provincial command structure.		Ensures no spies, thieves, or criminals enter the ranks of the Taliban.	
Investigates cases of abuse committed by a district governor, his deputy, or a *dilgai* commander.		The provincial commission conducts a monthly survey of the Taliban fighting in the province to ensure they are abiding by the *Layeha* and are being effective.	

Shura, whose regional military council and respective *rais-e-thazema* ("zonal chief") relay strategic decisions and requests from Mullah Omar to the provincial leadership (Figure 8.1); Table 8.4 details the explicit responsibilities of the Taliban chain of command.

Noteworthy Code of Conduct deletions

A number of articles were omitted or significantly altered from 2009's *Layeha* as compared to the 2010 version. For instance, one of the major differences was the reconfiguration of the decision-making process as applied to captured Afghan logistics personnel. The previous strictures recommended "any construction companies that repair infidel foundations or bring oil to the infidels—after the Mujahidin warn them and they do not stop working for the infidels—will be captured and taken to the provincial authority, who has the right to decide their fate."[65] The new directive ordered Taliban fighters to kill the logistics drivers on sight and burn their vehicles; if the drivers were captured alive, they must be tried by a Taliban judge for their alleged involvement in supporting the Coalition and the Afghan government and subsequently would be sentenced to death if found guilty. Additionally, the new rule 26 indicates that any contracting firms who were providing laborers to the Coalition should also be targeted and their personnel shot on sight. These measures offer the glaring evidence of an organization whose main aim is to separate the state from the people and the people from the international community, by ordering the summary execution of such "collaborators."

Previous *Layeha* included scathing commentary against NGOs operating in Afghanistan and justified the targeting and killing of unarmed NGO field personnel. The 2009 and 2010 manifestos did not include any mention of international NGOs nor did it promote the targeting and killing of their personnel; primarily because many residents find the services provided by such organizations to be somewhat useful, especially healthcare services, food distribution, and agricultural assistance. The removal of NGOs' death warrants also offered the Taliban a level of plausible deniability when they do commit such atrocities; although several examples from 2010 onward indicate that the Taliban are still deliberately targeting and killing NGO personnel. For instance, the Taliban claimed responsibility for the execution of ten international NGO personnel in a remote forest of Badakhshan on 7 August 2010: a grim reminder of the Taliban's intentions despite the barring of such rules in its code of conduct.[66] According to the Afghan National Safety Office Third Quarterly

Report, between January and September 2010, 25 NGO workers were killed in Afghanistan compared to 17 who were killed over the same period in 2009; and the deliberate targeting of de-mining personnel had also increased.[67]

Conclusion

The purpose of the 2010 *Layeha* was to establish an operational order and retain discipline within the Taliban movement and promote their IO narratives and stories. This was probably an attempt to solidify the movement in possible preparation for the future withdrawal of international forces beginning in 2011, or in case acceptable political offers were presented by the central government's newly established "High Peace Council" tasked with reaching out to Taliban networks for potential reconciliation measures. This analysis suggests that the Taliban remain most concerned with: chain of command principles; preventing the fragmentation of the various Taliban networks; obtaining and maintaining political capital by winning "hearts and minds" of local residents; ensuring enough fighters remain engaged in combat; and galvanizing the perception that the Taliban represent a capable, desirable, and fair alternative to the current political establishment.

The content of the Taliban's 2010 *Layeha* exposed specific weaknesses regarding the Taliban movement: their obsession with group cohesion and consolidation, unifying the command and control structure, issues concerning communications, and the difficulties the top leadership (the late Mullah Omar and his Rahbari Shura) had in coordinating with fighters at the district and provincial level from their safe haven in Pakistan. Reissuing strictures that prohibited group members from "taking money" to forgive someone, "guaranteeing" someone in exchange for money or property, and outlawing the practice of kidnapping people for money indicated that the Taliban leadership continued to worry about losing political capital from low-level members engaged in criminal behavior.

"Additionally, it is widely known that the Taliban's 'central treasury' had been drained numerous times due to false claims from Taliban commanders requesting payment for attacks they did not commit or to 'replace' war equipment under false pretenses."[68] The punishment for criminality (rule 36) is immediate banishment (Pashtunwali element of ostracizing) from the group and future prohibition from joining any other Taliban factions unless the individual pleads for forgiveness, which was a fairly light punishment. One possibility was that the Taliban, although a resilient and redundant organization able to regenerate its rank and file somewhat easily, were finding it challenging to regenerate as quickly as they did in the past, due to an increase in Coalition, Afghan and Pakistani military offensives in the years 2010–12.

This brings up a second major implication: the 2010 *Layeha* laid out numerous specific duties, most of which were directed at provincial military force structure and its district-level chain of command, and the heavy reliance upon the provincial- and district-level commissions, investigative bodies tasked with ensuring "good behavior" and hearing the complaints of the local population against local Taliban officials. This was the Taliban leadership's attempt at solidifying its political legitimacy and thwarting the proliferation of criminality among its commanders and foot soldiers at the level. It is obvious with the inclusion of "guerilla fundamentals" as well as the late Mullah Omar's statements at the conclusion of the *Layeha* that the Taliban remained strategically concerned about the movement's image among the populace. In step with public perceptions, the Taliban prohibited the videotaping of executions, outlawed all forms of torture, ordered those sentenced to death to be shot (not beheaded) (rule 21), and strictly avoided the tactic of cutting off noses, lips, and ears (rule 70).

The Taliban have suffered politically from engaging in barbaric, ultra-violent, and un-Islamic methods such as beheadings and mutilating civilians. While this method may have short-term advantages in garnering support from certain foreign donors or outbidding among competing insurgent groups, it has had detrimental long-term strategic effects on Taliban efforts at gaining public support among rural communities. This analysis suggests that media reports framing the Taliban as criminals, a hostile entity vehemently against education, rapists, bandits, or kidnappers has had an effect on the decision-makers within the Taliban's upper echelon. The fact that protecting civilians and their property was a tenet from Mullah Omar himself signifies the ire that civilian casualties caused among local communities.

As the past has shown and 2015 explicitly experienced, Taliban factions are susceptible to tribal rifts, rivalries, and conflicts, as much as any non-insurgent Pashtun community may be. This can mean the difference between a safe haven and a hostile environment regarding areas intended for penetration and expansion. Nearly sixteen years have passed since the US-led attack against Afghanistan ended the Taliban's former regime, yet the Taliban has failed to represent a plausible replacement to the current political establishment, presenting itself as no model candidate for state-building experiments.[69] However, despite the Taliban's effort to portray its organization in a certain light—as a structured, orderly hierarchy with efficient information flow and doctrine—

this does not represent the Taliban in a realistic sense. The 2010 *Layeha* clearly dictated that the military chain of command, and political commissions designed to hear the will of the people, ultimately refer back to a military committee of the Quetta Shura for guidance. Clearly designed political and social mechanisms—such as a hierarchal political and ideological committee or public services committee operating at the Quetta Shura—were not mentioned in the *Layeha*. In the final analysis, the assessment here suggests that the Taliban were simply repeating the same mistakes as in the past, overly focusing on military objectives and intra-organizational functions, while failing to capture the true will of the Afghan people.

9

HEZB-E-ISLAMI GULBUDDIN (HIG)
PROPAGANDA ACTIVITIES

Having assessed a large variety of Taliban information operation artifacts and dissemination methods, we will now turn our attention to assessing the IO and associated strategy of another central Afghan insurgency group: Hezb-e-Islami Gulbuddin (HIG).[1] HIG has long been one of Afghanistan's leading insurgency groups and radical Afghan political parties. Indeed, HIG is one of Afghanistan's three major insurgent groups and continues to produce propaganda materials and issue statements against the Afghan government despite public statements indicating that HIG is willing to participate in political negotiations with the Afghan government. In comparison to the Taliban's information campaign, HIG has produced propaganda that is often better written and intellectually more sophisticated than much of the Taliban's information. HIG's IO venues have increased over the past years, particularly during the group's high-level delegation visit to Kabul in March 2010.[2] In 2010, HIG launched a new website called *Oqab* (Eagle) presenting information and propaganda in both Pashto and Dari. This website served as HIG's official communication hub and offered various types of propaganda materials, including dozens of online books written by its supporters as well as Gulbuddin Hekmatyar. The website is no longer available and has been currently replaced by a blog forum, which also contains a plethora of HIG materials and content.

HIG continues to recruit fighters and maintain its influence over the activities at the Shamshato refugee camp located near Peshawar, Pakistan. HIG has recruited many of its foot soldiers from this large refugee camp. What distinguishes the Shamshato refugee camp from other camps is that it is under the direct control of Gulbuddin Hekmatyar and his followers and has been for years. The 64,000 inhabitants of the camp have access to "schools, medical facilities, mosques, madrasas and a crime-free security offered by HIG."[3] HIG publishes two local newspapers (*Shahadat* and *Tanweer*) for the refugee camp that serve as important fora for propaganda dissemination.[4]

Historical analysis of Hezb-e-Islami Gulbuddin (HIG)

The Soviet occupation of Afghanistan inevitably served as the catalyst for the jihad against foreign invaders and the birth of some and expansion of other Mujahidin factions, including Hezb-e-Islami Gulbuddin (a resurgent militia of Hezb-e-Islami and the former Mujahidin Tanzim party). Originally one of the leading fronts of dissent in Afghanistan during the 1970s, Hezb-e-Islami emerged as the leading Mujahidin resistance organization throughout the 1980s Soviet–Afghan war and a favorite of Pakistan's ISI. Although the party itself split into several competing organizations before the Soviet–Afghan war began, Hezb-e-Islami Gulbuddin, as the name suggests, was and is led by the notorious Islamist warlord and former prime minister of the Afghan Mujahidin government, Gulbuddin Hekmatyar. Even during the 1980s, HIG excelled at media interaction, strategically communicated with the Afghan refugee community in Pakistan (especially, the Shamshato refugee camp near Peshawar and camps in Iran), and widely published and disseminated propaganda materials throughout the region. The rigid and hierarchal structure of Hezb-e-Islami allowed the group to maintain some coherence over the course of the past forty years and is indicative of the group's re-emergence following the international community's involvement in Afghanistan post-2001.

As suggested above, during the anti-Soviet jihad in Afghanistan, HIG had a prominent propaganda and IO machine that included the production and dissemination of *shabnamah*, magazines, and other media products:

> The pro-Hekmatyar Afghan News Agency (ANA) was headquartered in an Inter-Services Intelligence (ISI)[5] building in Islamabad. There, HIG and ISI propagandists worked side by side to roll out pro-Hekmatyar tracts. The Pakistan ISI played a major role in nearly all facets of early HIG information operations and worked "side by side" with Gulbuddin's propagandists until HIG lost ISI favor to the Taliban in 1994.
>
> ANA was the most voluminous Hekmatyar mouthpiece in his ISI/Saudi well-lubricated media network, reporting, usually shrilly, near-daily condemnations of

the US, his Afghan critics, especially the three moderate Peshawar parties in the Afghan Interim Government (AIG, February 1989-April 1992), his bombardments (ISI supplied and assisted inside Afghanistan) of the Mojaddidi and Rabbani-Masood interim regimes in Kabul after Najib's overthrow.[6]

During the Afghan Civil War, which began soon after the Soviets withdrew from Afghanistan, there was brutal fighting between various Mujahidin forces all vying for power in Kabul. While Hekmatyar was prime minister of the Mujahidin government that had overthrown Mohammad Najibullah Ahmadzai, the "Marxist" president and "Soviet puppet" 1987–92, in mid-1992 he conducted fierce rocket attacks on Kabul, killing thousands of civilians, and his ANA[7] continued to push out HIG propaganda:

> ISI trucks carrying rockets, ammunition and other armaments ferried supplies to Hekmatyar's base camps south and east of Kabul. Hekmatyar's ISI-assisted ANA news agency in Islamabad and his newspaper in Peshawar, *Shahadat*, published articles glorifying his murderous rocket barrages against Kabul's 2 million inhabitants.[8]

HIG, which is currently one of the largest militant groups in Afghanistan, continues to use the same rhetoric against the US and its allies as it did against the Sardar Mohammed Daoud Khan Afghan regime (1973–8). Unlike other Mujahidin parties, however, HIG's primary focus has been based on propaganda production and dissemination within its own ranks. Besides using other media sources, HIG has focused on operating its own printed media, schools, university, and large gatherings to expand its sphere of influence among the Afghan population, particularly among Afghan refugees living in countries neighboring Afghanistan since the early 1980s.[9]

Although both Hezb-e-Islami Gulbuddin and the Taliban are currently fighting a common enemy, their gestation and operational strategies differ significantly. It is worth noting that high-ranking HIG members were and continue to be much more educated than their quasi counterpart, the Taliban. Much of the leadership of HIG emerged from the University of Kabul in the early 1970s and radical, urban intellectuals complemented this leadership. In 1994, the Taliban emerged as the force against groups such as Hezb-e-Islami and eventually seized control over 90 per cent of Afghan territory. HIG was one of the major enemies of the early Taliban, and like many other former Mujahidin groups, the Taliban defeated HIG, and its leader, Hekmatyar, took refuge in Iran.[10]

The collapse of the Taliban in 2001 and the presence of international military forces in Afghanistan ultimately resulted in a pseudo relationship and collaboration between HIG and the Taliban along the lines of "an enemy of an enemy is a friend". However, HIG makes a conscious effort to distance itself from the style of ongoing military operation that induces major civilian losses, whereas the Taliban are notorious for such brazen attacks. Furthermore, whereas the Taliban have been quite resolute in abstaining from serious peace dialogues with the Afghan government, recent HIG visits and official messages indicate that HIG is more amenable to engaging in a peace negotiation with the current Afghan government. In order to establish a better relationship and gain legitimacy from the Afghan population, HIG makes a concerted effort in addressing some of the ailments of the Afghan people, as evidenced by its public statements, as will be seen below.

Information operations of Hezb-e-Islami Gulbuddin (HIG)

Hezb-e-Islami Gulbuddin (HIG) utilizes a wide range of delivery systems to maintain its political influence and to publicize its official position regarding social and political events unfolding in Afghanistan. The group regularly uses official spokesmen, *shabnamah*, as well as the internet and printed media (host newspapers, newsletters, books, magazines) and videos to convey its statements and policies to the Afghan populace and international community. HIG's strategic communications attempt to address political, cultural, and religious themes in a more structured, organized, consistent, and clear format compared to other insurgent movements active in Afghanistan. HIG messages often portray sympathy toward civilians, government employees, and public property, while its most offensive messaging is usually reserved for the international community, namely NATO and the United States.

A statement attributed to Gulbuddin Hekmatyar during Eid 2011 highlights the important differences between HIG and Taliban communication strategies:

> I advise Mujahidin to concentrate on a real enemy. Do not get busy in other wars [meaning internal fighting]. When you load your rifle, your intention should be firing at your real enemy's red chest. Don't let people in your *leeki* (military fronts), who harass people, don't have Islamic manners, don't respect Islamic rules, fuel rivalries and dispute among Mujahidin, and disunite Mujahidin. Also, don't let them carry out explosions in mosques, Madrassas, schools, health clinics, bridges, offices, public facilities and areas that harm people. They [those people] have other plans than focusing on destroying military power of a real enemy. Avoid explosions that hurt civilians. Don't kill government civilian employees such as teachers, judges, Mullahs, Engineers, doctors, reporters and other civilians. Do not force

people to pay *usher and zakaat*. Only the Islamic government has the right to ask for *usher* and *zakaat* in return of providing security for its people. Encourage people to pay Mujahidin *usher, zakaat*, and charity voluntarily.[11]

These are powerful stories that HIG has repeatedly presented to the Afghan populace.

Printed media[12]

Two of the main sources of statements from HIG are online and printed newspapers/newsletters: *Daily Shahadat* (Martyrdom) and *Tanweer* (Enlightenment).

Daily Shahadat (Martyrdom): Unlike other media sources related to the Afghan insurgency/jihad, the HIG newspaper and website, *Daily Shahadat*, is designed to target audiences from a variety of backgrounds and age groups. The website is divided into different sections which explicitly address adolescents, children, editorials, poetry and literature, articles, books, magazines, and useful links. *Daily Shahadat* conveys various HIG social and political messages while publishing current news on domestic and international issues with particular emphasis on topics related to the Global Muslim Community (*Ummah*). A central focus is the military operations in Afghanistan, events related to Palestinians, and conflicts in other Muslim countries. The official party newspaper of HIG, it is designed to target audiences from all educational backgrounds and some certain age groups. The website is colored green, portraying the HIG's party flag color, while the newspaper hardcopy is printed in black and white. Although the website often becomes unavailable online, it can usually be found at http://dailyshahadat.com/index.php

Tanweer (Enlightenment): *Tanweer* is a HIG monthly, published in Peshawar and offering the views of Gulbuddin Hekmatyar and his organization on Afghanistan, as well as its activities inside the country. Based on analysis of several volumes of magazines, it appears generally designed to include commentary on current political events, religious and social articles, HIG monthly military/battlefield achievements, and official statement and narratives. A number of recent magazines also include a chapter from a book called *Bible Da Islam pa Rana Ki* (Bible in the light of the Qur'an) authored by Hekmatyar.

- Length: 60 or more pages.
- Language: Pashto and Dari.
- Publication: Monthly.

Interestingly, the magazine is published in both Dari and Pashto in an attempt to reach a wider general Afghan audience. It is estimated that approximately 40 per cent of *Tanweer's* content is published in Dari and 60 per cent in Pashto.[13] The typical table of contents for *Tanweer* suggests the importance of the following issues and themes:

- Editorial (*paigham tanweer*) (politically themed);
- Complaints and suggestions section (readers' comments);
- Religious teachings (multiple);
- Interview, official statement, or book excerpt attributed to Gulbuddin Hekmatyar;
- Interviews with a Hezb-e-Islami military commander;
- Pashtun culture (including literature/grammar lessons);
- Regional coverage (e.g. Western world and Israel; Open Letter to Obama);
- Martyr list of HIG personnel killed in Afghanistan and their biographies;
- Khpalwak Afghanistan (Independent Afghanistan) publishes their political statements (primarily anti-Western sentiment) within *Tanweer*.

HIG's use of printed media in the last few years has resulted in a considerable increase in HIG's propaganda activities. This surge in HIG's dissemination of stories and narratives began during (and immediately after) their "peace delegation" trip to Kabul in March 2010.[14]

Shabnamah *and spokesmen*

Like other insurgent groups active in Afghanistan, HIG use *shabnamah* to communicate with local audiences, usually at district and village level, but occasionally at the provincial level as well. Some speeches attributed to Gulbuddin Hekmatyar are also neatly reprinted and disseminated as *shabnamah*, including bi-annual Eid statements.

HIG relies upon official spokesmen to relay messages to local and international media sources, but also allows its lower-level commanders to speak to the media. Engineer Haroon Zarghoon is widely regarded as the chief spokesman for HIG, while a number of lesser-known regional commanders occasionally serve as spokesmen for district or provincial-related messages and incidents. Zarghoon rarely, if ever, appears in public, and no actual image of him is currently available online or in print. But other high-ranking HIG officials, like Ustad Qareebur Rahman Saeed, who serves as the senior representative to Europe; Mohammad Daud Abedi, the HIG representative to

Figure 9.1: HIG spokesmen and representatives

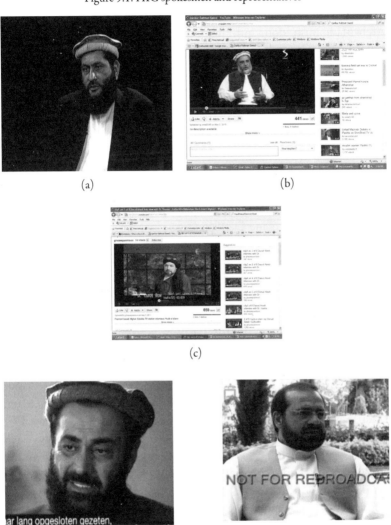

(a) Eng. Qutbuddin Helal, Ariana TV interview, 2007 (broadcast from US) (b) Ustad Qareebur Rahman Saeed, Shamshad TV interview, 2010 (broadcast from Afghanistan) (c) Mohammad Daud Abedi, Noor TV interview, May 2011 (broadcast from US) (d) Dr Ghairat Baheer, Canvas TV interview, September 2011 (broadcast from Belgium) (e) Eng. Mohammad Amin Karim Tolo TV interview, May 2010 (broadcast from Afghanistan)

North America; Eng. Mohammad Amin Karim and Dr Ghairat Baheer, members of the HIG delegation to Kabul to discuss HIG peace proposal with the Afghan administration; and Eng. Qutbuddin Helal, the deputy political director of HIG, occasionally offer official statements to local and international media outlets.

Lesser-known or locally active HIG spokesmen include Sher Agha for Nuristan province,[15] Qari Mansoor for Nangarhar,[16] and Zubair Siddiqui for Kunar province;[17] all have provided statements to Afghan press organizations regarding military activities attributed to HIG.

Internet activities

In 2010, a new website called *Oqab* (Eagle) was launched by HIG, sharing information in Pashto and Dari languages; by May 2011 it had been shut down. *Oqab* served as HIG's official hub of communication and dissemination for several books written by HIG commanders, including several allegedly written by Gulbuddin himself.

Oqab published a variety of statements, commentaries, and directives that represented the official HIG view, as well as news updates on war and political activities. Up until 4 March 2011, the website was able to offer services in English and Arabic languages, with tabs for both languages. At the top of the website was a Dari poem and logo showing a cavalry on the map of Afghanistan holding a green flag with a *Kalema Shahada* (There is no god but Allah, and Muhammad is His messenger), the first of the five pillars of Islam. Most importantly, it shared with its audience many books authored by Hekmatyar himself and HIG members. Loaded with poetry, audio and video *taranas*, and video clips on HIG fighter operations across the country, the website was still in the process of expanding when it was disrupted and taken offline. It was formerly accessible online at http://www.oqab1.com/

Tanweer weblog is another web-based outlet that disseminates HIG propaganda and literature. This blog, under the name *Dostdaraan-e-Watan*, publishes HIG official messages, statements attributed to Gulbuddin Hekmatyar, members' articles, videos, pictures, Hekmatyar's interview transcripts with the media as well as the weekly newspaper *Mesaq-e-Esar*. It carries almost as much information as their websites. Some of the literature present in the blog suggests that several senior HIG members contributed to writing for this blog. According to its archive dates, it seems that *Tanweer* weblog became available online around 2006.

Figures 9.2A: (above) and 9.2B (below): The above logo of *Zawanano Islami Tanzim* appeared in one of the HIG Facebook accounts.

HIG on Facebook

HIG appears to disseminate its propaganda on Facebook as well. Beside various Facebook accounts under people's names, Shahab Hezb is their official Facebook page for sharing HIG propaganda on a daily basis. Content includes military news, HIG statements, and photographs depicting atrocities blamed on US and NATO forces as well as photos of HIG fighters, commanders, and those HIG fighters killed in battle (*shaheed*). After studying their activities on Facebook, it seems that HIG propaganda on social networking sites is handled by its youth wing, *Zawanano Islami Tanzim*. This group, probably based in Shamshato camp in Peshawar, is active at connecting with Afghan youths and HIG media products.

DVDs and videos

Like the Taliban and other insurgent groups operating in Afghanistan, HIG also uses digital technologies other than the internet to convey political and military messages. These formats include DVD and internet-based video dissemination methods, such as YouTube (users Huryat786, Tanweer7866, Tanweer 786, Oqaab08, Ghazy66, and ZAZAI11). HIG also uses its own media label (*Shahadah*, or martyrdom). The videos are heavily reliant upon imagery, including montage sequences of still photos showing American forces in Afghanistan and Iraq, and are usually accompanied by background music (*taranas*).

In a video uploaded to YouTube on 10 November 2010 entitled "Stay for another little while, O you: the martyr who has no grave," HIG presented footage of one its fighters preparing for a suicide attack. The nine-minute video is accompanied by a *tarana* urging Muslims to prepare to conduct suicide attacks to achieve the status of a martyr. Although no date is presented in the video indicating when it might have been made, the footage appears to be cut from multiple sources and depicts various suicide bomb attacks in Afghanistan. A date stamp of 6:27 indicates that the footage was probably recorded on 27 June 2007 and possibly shows the individuals who launched a car bomb attack against a security convoy in western Kabul on that same date.

The video is a rather crude attempt at replicating the preparations of a suicide attack, and the only audio soundtrack is a *tarana*. Unlike Taliban-produced videos, this video lacks personal statements from the bomber, and no further information on where or when the attack occurred and what it

Figure 9.3: Stills from HIG video "Stay for another little while, O you: the martyr who has no grave"

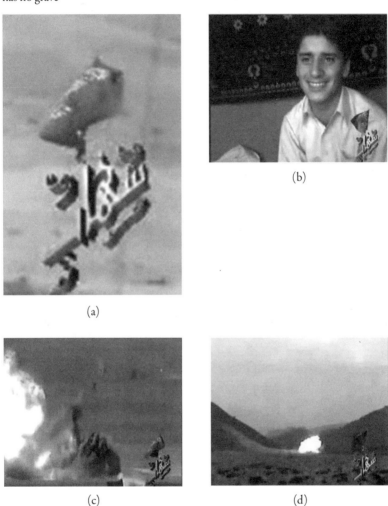

(a)

(b)

(c)

(d)

a) *Shahadah* is the media label of HIG. The green flag is the iconic symbol of *Hezb-e-Islami*. b) The video, which was unaccompanied by audio other than a music track, features suicide bombers greeting other militants before launching their attack. c) The video shows several car bomb attacks against alleged security targets, such as military convoys, although they are never close enough to be photographed. d) The video also recycles suicide-attack footage from other militant networks, including some Taliban attacks previously produced under the *Manba ul Jihad* label.

Figure 9.4: Stills from HIG video "How large is the caravan we have?"

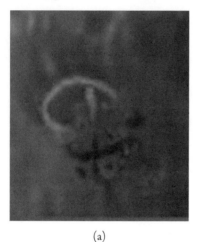

(a)

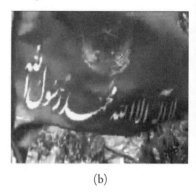

(b)

(c)

(d)

a) *Shahab* (Arabic for a shooting star) is another media label attributed to HIG. b) The iconic green flag of *Hezb-e-Islami* is prominently displayed throughout this video. The militant group's Imam leads his "caravan" of fighters over rough terrain while bearing the flag. c) The producers of this video appear to be extremely mindful of operational security, blurring out the faces of all individuals in the video except the group's religious leader (shown top right). d) The masked militants wear green Kalima headscarves bearing the Islamic testification of faith while being led in prayer by their imam (face uncovered). A voice-over sermon by Maluvi Shah Mohammad is presented in both Dari and Pashto.

might have accomplished. Other HIG videos, such as "Shaheed Habibullah Shahab Hekmatyar," a video eulogy to a slain relative of Gulbuddin Hekmatyar uploaded in June 2011, and "How large is the caravan we have?" are similar in that they lack any dynamic audio tracks or audio taken at the scene.[18] Instead, they are accompanied by a single track, a *tarana*, and the images are usually long, somewhat roughly cut together shots or still images presented in a montage sequence.

While HIG periodicals and websites are sophisticated, well-written, and articulate, HIG-produced videos seriously lack both quality and creativity.

Major political themes of HIG propaganda

The themes of HIG's IO activities and stories have concentrated on promoting a number of consistently focused political tropes, such as:

- Protecting civilians (exploiting collateral damage by Coalition and Afghan forces and even the Taliban);
- Coalition forces are facing an imminent defeat in Afghanistan;
- Political discussions about a permanent presence of foreign forces and military bases in Afghanistan.
- Implications of the parliamentary and presidential elections;
- The HIG peace proposal.

Collateral damage: the failure to protect civilians

Civilian collateral damage is a primary issue of HIG propaganda and an issue that it attempts to condemn in very strong words.[19] Civilian casualties have become a very sensitive topic among the general Afghan public, and HIG seems to attempt to distance itself from the kind of ongoing insurgent operations that result in major civilian loss: attacks which are usually carried out by groups like the Taliban, the Haqqani Network, and the Islamic Movement of Uzbekistan (IMU).

Unlike the Taliban, HIG rarely claims responsibility for attacks that cause civilian deaths. As an example, in a statement to the residents of Loy Paktiya (Greater Paktiya),[20] Hekmatyar admired his followers while also confirming the sacrifices made by the people of Loy Paktiya in the jihad against the Soviets. This typical HIG statement discussed three major issues: the need for the public to support the Afghan insurgents and need for unity among them;

the encouragement for people to wage jihad; and instructions for avoiding killing civilians and destroying public properties.

It should be noted, however, that HIG has also inconsistently claimed responsibility for a number of attacks in which Afghan civilians have died. One case in point is when HIG spokesmen claimed the deadly attack against the Finest Supermarket in the heavily guarded Wazir Akbar Khan section of Kabul on 28 January 2011. A suicide bomber detonated himself in the crowded food store after engaging the armed security guards in a shoot-out, killing eight people, including five Afghans from the same family.[21]

Similarly, HIG claimed responsibility for the high-profile execution of ten Western aid workers traveling through a remote valley in northern Afghanistan on 5 August 2010—as did the Taliban through their spokesman Zabihullah Mujahid, although Taliban commanders from Nuristan later denied that their fighters attacked the convoy of aid workers. A spokesman for HIG contacted the Afghan media outlet *TOLO News* and said that the ten medical workers were killed because they were "spies" who "had gone to the province for espionage."[22] A similar statement was given to the Afghan media outlet *Pajhwok News* by self-proclaimed HIG spokesman Qari Mansoor, claiming that HIG killed the foreign aid workers on suspicion of their working for NATO forces.[23] HIG and Taliban spokesmen regularly offer competing claims of responsibility for attacks for purposes of prestige and fear among the populace.

Following a series of Taliban attacks on soft targets killing hundreds of civilians across the country in March 2011, HIG published the statement below:

Greetings to the pious and brave Mujahidin

HIG Leader Eng. Hekmatyar message to pious and patriotic Mujahidin [people] of Loy Paktiya

In the Name of God, Most Gracious, Most Merciful

I pray for pious and heroic Mujahidin to further succeed. I hope Paktiya, Khost, and Paktika's heroic Mujahidin keep their courageous ancestors' history alive and transform this region into robust jihadi trenches once again. Increasing attacks and resistance against the crusade armies indicate that God willing, our desires will turn into reality. Hence, Mujahidin from Loy Paktiya will be recognized as the leading people of Islamic jihad. In the past jihad, Loy Paktiya was an unbreakable active trench. The predominant population had actively participated in Jihad and had suffered martyrdoms and injuries. It is an honor and pride for the courageous public to have actively contributed in the continuous Jihad. God grant martyrs higher grades in paradise and grant victories to brave warriors. They certainly made all Mujahidin proud and their turbans' *shamley* up.[24]

I congratulate the pious and Mujahed nation of Loy Paktiya. I pray God to empower your Jihad and make you victorious. Loy Paktiya's Mujahidin are appreciated because they have avoided internal disputes and maintained unity. They have turned their attention toward real enemy and have avoided such military operations that lead to civilian casualties and the destruction of public property. They have ignored wrong and satanic fatwas[25] of those abrasive clerics who justify internal conflict and military operation causing civilian loss.

I wish success to the pious victors of Loy Paktiya. I wish glory to Loy Paktiya; a firm trench of Mujahidin.

Hekmatyar[26]

Invading forces are losing the war in Afghanistan

Another primary focus of HIG's IO involves HIG's exaggerated claims of the capabilities of its forces and the damage it "inflicts" on foreign forces. Their websites, newspapers, and magazines consistently publish reports and analyses of the "successes" of HIG fighters in their actions against foreign and Afghan forces. This type of information is generally aimed at achieving three goals:

1) It boosts the morale of HIG supporters and forces.
2) It attempts to encourage financial supporters and donors to support its political and military actions.
3) It demonstrates the power and influence of HIG and demonstrates the strength of HIG's position especially relative to the balance of power with other insurgent groups.

These objectives are evident in the following HIG news articles.

Fighting between Mujahidin and invaders in Jowzjan: 13 foreign and government soldiers killed Shaburghan, Jowzjan (Mujahidin News Sources)

13 foreign and domestic soldiers were killed. Reports from Jowzjan province inform about fighting between Mujahidin and foreign forces. Yesterday, the battle started around 10 am and continued for two hours. According to the report, during this heavy fighting, Mujahidin's RPGs destroyed 2 Tanks and 4 Ranger Cars [Pickup trucks]. In addition to that, 13 foreign and domestic soldiers were killed. Mujahidin also seized GPS, one box of *dehshaka* bullets and different types of ammunition. It has to be mentioned that two Mujahidin were martyred during these few hours of fighting.[27]

American forces withdrew from number of districts

03–01–2011 Asad Abad, Qalat (News Sources)

> NATO forces led by the US transferred the authority of some districts to government forces. Based on the reports from news agencies, the former deputy head of NATO forces, Lieutenant General David Rodriguez, said that the security responsibility of Arghandab, Maizan, and Dai Chopan are transferred to government forces and foreign forces have left these districts. This was announced in a gathering held in Qalat yesterday. According to another report, the spokesman for NATO forces, Gen. Josef Blotz, announced in a gathering in Asad Abad of Kunar province yesterday to reporters about the exit of their forces from Pechdar district and officially transferred security responsibility to government forces.

> Gen. Blotz and Gen. David Rodriguez, however, didn't say about the relocation of these foreign forces. Anyhow, this is an excuse for fleeing and evacuating foreign forces from Afghanistan because of Mujahidin attacks and fighting.[28]

Permanent Presence of the United States in Afghanistan

Afghan politicians are presently discussing and weighing the potential option of US permanent bases in Afghanistan. HIG was among the first insurgent group to react to this issue through its propaganda artifacts. For example, they condemned such a plan and questioned the basic legitimacy of the Afghan government for even raising the issue:

HIG Europe office statement and story on US permanent military presence in the country

> In the name of God, the most merciful, the most compassionate. As the US military forces have been facing heavy resistance from our brave nation and suffer growing financial and human loss, they search for honorable exit of their forces; however, there are rumors spread by the puppet government about their desire to negotiate the permit for building permanent invading forces bases. It comes at a time when neither the puppet government nor handpicked parliament has such authority to take this shameful and dishonorable decision on the fate of our brave and proud nation. HIG, on behalf of Mujahidin and the nation, will not allow anyone to cut such a deal with invaders that will lead to lasting slavery and invasion in order to stay in power. HIG is determined to continue its peaceful struggle until all foreign invaders withdraw from Afghanistan and we regain independence of our country.[29]

Parliamentary and presidential elections

Parliamentary and presidential elections and the controversies surrounding them have become a topic given considerable attention by the HIG propaganda machine. Per their general narrative, HIG has taken a softer approach to participation in elections. In fact, many HIG members have been elected to the Afghan parliament. While HIG statements condemn such elections as illegitimate, unlike Taliban propaganda, HIG does not warn the Afghan public to refrain from participation in the election. It also criticizes defected HIG leaders who officially operate under the new constitution and serve as part of the government with a prominent presence in the Afghan parliament.

Although recent Afghan elections have been marred by widespread corruption and dispute among candidates, HIG is concerned that the continuity and improvement of such events may eventually lead to increased government legitimacy and public participation. HIG, on one hand, tries to delegitimize and disrupt elections, while on the other hand it softens its communication toward the ordinary people:

> HIG is stronger, robust and a united *Tanzim*. Those [HIG members] who joined the Kabul administration are just a handful of people. Their position does not represent our code of conduct and objections to participation under the strangers' hegemony. No honest and loyal member of HIG would participate in an un-Islamic government supported by strangers. HIG officially reject such elections under the authority of invading forces and does not participate in it.[30]

HIG peace proposal[31]

Beginning with the anti-Soviet Jihad, HIG has historically been recognized as one of the most violent and opportunistic groups among Mujahidin *Tanzims*. In an apparent effort to deflect some of these negative views and restore the group's reputation as well as to differentiate itself from other insurgent networks such as the Taliban, HIG has expressed a certain level of flexibility in their views toward negotiations, particularly in negotiating "peace" with the Kabul regime. In the past, both the Taliban and HIG have offered similar preconditions for peace talks—the complete withdrawal of foreign forces prior to any negotiations. However, HIG has redefined its demand and apparently accepted the announcement by the US of an expected withdraw as opposed to the previous demand of the complete removal of foreign forces before such talks could even begin. The Taliban, however, retain a rigid demand of a complete withdrawal of foreign forces before meaningful discussions can take place.

HIG devotes considerable effort to statements, articles and news reports covering events concerned with peace talks, especially events involving their own envoys. HIG senior officials have publicly appeared on numerous local media outlets in Kabul discussing peace talks and negotiations.[32] Such visits with Afghan senior officials and politicians bring substantial attention to the insurgent group by prominent Afghan media sources both inside and outside the country. To engage with a wider audience in the Afghan community, HIG official delegates even appeared in interviews with several Afghan television channels targeting the Afghan diasporas in the West.[33]

A prominent narrative of these interviews is that HIG is not waging an offensive war as much as resisting un-Islamic foreign forces that have invaded Afghanistan. Hekmatyar and his followers have attempted to introduce HIG as a more noble Islamic political organization as compared to the Taliban, in an attempt to establish ties with the population and increase Gulbuddin's influence. Many of these efforts are also an attempt by HIG to rebuild Hekmatyar's public image and redirect blame away from him as the lead culprit in the destructive Civil War battles that killed tens of thousands of civilians, ruined Afghanistan's infrastructure, and destroyed Kabul between 1991 and 1994.[34]

While the Taliban's reputation has often been sullied due to incidents targeting civilians, HIG attempt to build momentum and public support by focusing on negotiations and ending the conflict. The following are the key points of the HIG peace proposal and call for negotiations with the Afghan government and international forces:

> HIG requests all political and civil society groups through its national contract [peace proposal] to reach an agreement granting Afghanistan's independence.

> HIG will strengthen national unity and provide an opportunity for Afghans to choose their preferred leadership and establish administration according to their belief and trust. Foreign forces should begin withdrawing and complete the process in 6 months. During this period, they should stay in the military bases and leave population centers and cities.

> Transfer all security responsibilities to the ANA and ANP. Foreign forces under no circumstance have the right to carry out military operations, house searching and arresting suspects.

> Transfer power to an interim administration that is acceptable to all rival sides. If other sides do not agree to establishing interim administration, there should be

reforms in the current government; however, the current government should avoid having people who are controversial, corrupt, traitors, infidels or accused of war crimes. Also, leaders of all three institutions [government, parliament, and justice] should be neutral and avoid fighting in favor of any group.[35]

As suggested above, recent years have witnessed a political dialogue between the HIG representatives and the Afghan administration (at various levels). These discussions have become a major point of discussion in the local media, including the HIG official newspaper *Daily Shahadat* (Martyrdom). It is also interesting to note that many of these discussions have appeared in the adolescent section of *Daily Shahadat* and associated website, possibly indicating that a number of young HIG members were suspicious or unclear of their party's move toward political settlement with the Afghan administration.

To provide more details and inform its supporters, HIG leaders have articulated arguments and narratives in support of the peace talks while stressing their continued opposition toward foreign forces in the country. In an article written by HIG member Mukhlisyar, he explained how HIG used this opportunity to introduce its organization as a peaceful movement.[36] His article included the following arguments:

1. Justifying HIG's peace dialogue.
2. Portraying HIG as a peaceful and patriotic group.
3. Exercising HIG influence over the people.
4. Defending the HIG leadership stance on the Afghan conflict and indicating that US/ISAF is the primary enemy of HIG.
5. Attempting to sabotage US involvement through the discussion of the prominence of US-caused civilian casualties.
6. Persuading Afghan National Security Forces to turn against ISAF and suggesting that Afghan public support for ISAF/US forces no longer exists.

Major religious and cultural themes of HIG propaganda and stories

HIG's propaganda activities are focused on a number of religious and cultural themes such as:

• We are fighting crusaders;
• Islamic government is our purpose;
• Pashtunwali;
• Afghan history.

Beside politically oriented messages, HIG propaganda is replete with religious and cultural stories and narratives. HIG focuses on disseminating religious messages, as does the Taliban, that involve terms such as "crusades." Branding the current insurgency as a religious war has been a fundamental propaganda effort that insurgents have made against Coalition forces. The following statement by Hekmatyar describes how HIG labels their fight as jihad for God and Islam, calling coalition forces "crusader armies":

> My advice to Islamic *Ummah* (Nation) is to keep strengthening your patience. Do not lose your trust in God's indispensable victory. Do not follow other imperfect paths but continue with [the perfect path of] jihad. You should be confident that God the all-powerful will grant us victory over Satan's forces. The crusader armies will face defeat.[37]

In another statement, an Islamic government is argued as the only solution to honor and stability, while disapproving of the current government and calling it un-Islamic and unelected. According to HIG, Islam will only come into existence and dominance when foreign forces leave the country: "Afghans will celebrate their independence day at the time when all the foreign invading forces leave our beloved country, [when the] Islamic flag is waving over the country, and [when] we have our elected Islamic government. Without Islam, neither will one enjoy real freedom nor will he achieve honor and stability."[38]

HIG also utilize Pashtunwali themes that are common across Afghanistan. For example, consider the following HIG statement: "One who protects himself by others [strangers], his house keys are in possession of *Pradai* [strangers]. They are not ashamed of humiliating and disgraceful living under strangers' airplanes wings. His *Ghairat* never arises when these forces [foreign troops] kill his tens of innocent countrymen on a daily basis. They violate their *Namous* and *Ghairat*."[39] Afghans across all ethnicities have some specific traditions in common: *Namous*, *Ghairat*[40] and strangers are key themes culturally sensitive to all ethnicities in Afghanistan. HIG selectively choose these themes to resonate with every Afghan citizen throughout the country.

HIG repeatedly uses the historical event in Maiwand[41] in its narratives and propaganda to evoke nostalgia among the Afghan population and to draw parallels between its fighters and those Afghans who—during the second Afghan-Anglo war—destroyed British forces in Maiwand in July 1880.

Conclusion

HIG is an influential insurgent group operating throughout Afghanistan and its propaganda operation continues to address relevant Afghan issues. In the

> *Typical HIG story*: "Today, the crusader forces' flags led by US and Britain are waving in our country. They give us *Paighour*, they test our *Ghairat*, and threaten our religion, sect, independence, and freedom. Look, invaders transform their Afghan slaves into freedom and democracy champions and these slaves praise their superiors as freedom fighters and [people of] reconstruction; likewise, they call rascals, thugs and terrorists our freedom fighters, the Mujahidin. They speak to our nation and Mujahidin exactly the same as Shah Shuja did 90 years ago and the Russians did 22 years ago. History is repeating itself again and it puts a heavy burden for a war of independence on our shoulders. It [history] requires us to revive our memories of Maiwand and Jagdalak and prepare for another great and historic jihad."[42]

past decade, it has increasingly focused on many issues Afghans consider critical for their country's situation. As suggested above, all of HIG's information operations are aimed at not only improving HIG's image in the political arena, but also building a direct connection to the Afghan people.

The manipulation of topics like avoiding civilian casualties and the promotion of potential negotiations with the Kabul regime have been key elements in HIG's attempt to attract Afghan popular support. Their strong statements on protecting the civilian population, condemnation of civilian loss, and the focus on peace talks have attempted to gain HIG political advantages in the Afghan war. HIG clearly understands the significance of propaganda and its implications for its future.

In summary:

- Throughout its history, HIG has specifically focused its Information Operation on eastern and central Afghanistan by infiltrating universities, schools, media, government institutions, as well as other "elite" institutions, and establishing political associations within the institutions that are vehemently supportive of HIG.
- HIG's statements and apparent primary political concerns have concentrated on permanent US military bases in Afghanistan, Afghanistan's Parliamentary and Presidential elections, and the HIG Peace Proposal.
- Religious and cultural messages revolve around themes such as jihad, crusade, Afghan history, and Pashtunwali that resonate with the Afghan public.

- HIG-produced videos depicting insurgent operations against government and NATO forces have increased visibility on a variety of HIG-affiliated websites and social media websites.
- The daily newspaper *Daily Shahadat* (Martyrdom) regularly provides updates concerning HIG activities. This information is regularly published in other print media as well as on the internet, such as in HIG's monthly magazine *Tanweer* (Enlightenment) and online books.

10

THE UNITED STATES' AFGHAN INFORMATION AND PSYOP CAMPAIGN AND A COMPARISON TO THE TALIBAN'S CAMPAIGN

Introduction

For the past sixteen years, the Unites States has striven to achieve an explainable victory for Operation Enduring Freedom-Afghanistan (OEF-A),[1] the moniker given to the US government's counter-terrorism campaign in Afghanistan.[2] Despite early success in the effort to overthrow the Afghan Taliban regime, which, to the surprise of many, took only approximately eight to ten weeks in late 2001, since then the US and its NATO allies have struggled to define the parameters of the war. In fact, many have argued that the US has failed to define meaningful future strategies for Afghanistan, Pakistan, and Central Asia.[3] Another critical problem that has plagued US polices in Afghanistan, as will be argued below, is that the US has never had a story or narrative that would resonate with the Afghan population.

In 2009 the US adopted counter-insurgency (COIN) tactics in Afghanistan.[4] One way to conceptualize COIN, as posited in Chapter 1, is that it is an information war supported by military kinetics. Yet even before COIN tactics were adopted in Afghanistan, where strategic communication efforts—including information operations (IO) and psychological operations (PSYOP)—are a critical component, US strategic communications efforts had been consistently critiqued since the beginning of the war. The initial US strategic communication effort during the onset of the war in October 2001 was the deployment of millions of crudely made leaflets which were dropped all over Afghanistan,[5] but they soon suffered when resources were diverted to the US mission in Iraq, beginning in 2003. The US IO leaflets campaign did improve over the years, as we shall see below, but leaflets are only rarely productive and may actually prove counterproductive. Afghans were often afraid to hold onto them or pass them around in fear of the Taliban catching them with one.[6] Most Afghans are illiterate: nationally 61.8 per cent and much higher in the Afghan rural areas.[7] Thus, for leaflets to be useful, they must be understandable in picture format alone. However, if the imagery is not properly vetted, it can also be used as IO against the deployer if picked up by insurgents. The US strategic communication efforts would continue to face serious challenges throughout the campaign and struggled to compete with the often superior master narrative and approaches by the Afghan Taliban (see Chapter 2), which expertly maximized religious and cultural values.

The first portion of this chapter examines the genesis and permutations of the US effort to communicate strategically with the Afghan population—the most important target audience of the Afghan conflict. While this chapter focuses on US strategic communication efforts in Afghanistan, it should be noted that the Afghan battle space became more complicated when in December 2001 the US-led Coalition became the International Security Assistance Force (ISAF): a NATO-led security mission in Afghanistan established by the United Nations Security Council. Although the main purpose of ISAF was to train the Afghan National Security Forces (ANSF) and assist Afghanistan in rebuilding key government institutions, ISAF elements also engaged in armed conflict with the myriad of Afghan insurgents. The ISAF mission, which concluded in December 2014, also employed a wide range of strategic communication efforts, often in parallel to US efforts.

Additionally, this chapter compares the overall US effort with the robust propaganda campaign employed by Afghan insurgents to counter US messages and the presence of foreign forces in Afghanistan. The US strategic communications strategy in Afghanistan often lagged behind the effective and powerful narratives consistently employed by Afghan insurgents, of which the most effective master narrative belonged to the Afghan Taliban.[8]

The final objective of this chapter is to assess some actual US IO and PSYOP artifacts and their associated stories (or lack thereof).

The Afghan Taliban movement continues to view itself as a viable alternate to the current Afghan government structure, and refer to themselves as the Islamic Emirate of Afghanistan (IEA): a strategic interpretation that we susɔect is meant to invoke a level of authority and legitimacy among its followers. t must always be remembered that Afghanistan's population is estimated to ɔe 99 per cent Muslim,[9] and Islam plays a critical role in all Afghan life. This therefore has an immense impact on the IO battle space in Afghanistan. So the vast majority of Taliban stories and narratives are based on their vision of Deobandi Islam and the jihad. This means that the US knows that it has no credibility with the Afghans relative to these topics. Moreover, the Afghan government has also been reluctant in countering the Taliban's Islamic messaging. Thus, the US and Kabul basically have conceded 90 per cent of the IO battle space to the Taliban.

The Taliban's strategic objectives are to evict foreign troops from Afghanistan, to overthrow the US-supported Kabul government, to restore the Islamic Emirate of Afghanistan, and to implement Shar'iah law; for these ends, the Taliban utilize a strategic communication toolkit designed to delegitimize the current government and garner local support by demonstrating the shortcomings and perceived failures of US and NATO policies in Afghanistan. As will be seen below, the United States and NATO-ISAF have had a very difficult time "countering" these narratives.

The US goes to war in Afghanistan

The US responded swiftly following the devastating and unprecedented terrorist attacks in New York City and Washington DC on 11 September 2001. A US-led Coalition attacked Afghanistan on 7 October 2001 to remove the Afghan Taliban regime, which had refused unconditionally to hand over Osama bin Laden, the mastermind of the 11 September attacks. The US-led Coalition also sought to target and destroy the al-Qaeda network, a global terror franchise that had used Afghanistan as its base for planning and operations.

During the onset of the war, the US employed conventional PSYOP, such as dropping millions of crude leaflets with messages seeking to gain local support in overthrowing the Taliban regime and preparing the local population for the presence of foreign troops.[10] The messages were heavily influenced by the 11 September terror attacks, and many of the PSYOP products even incorporated images of the burning World Trade Center, shocking visuals that were lost on many rural Afghans who had never seen such Western buildings. A poll taken in September 2011 found that "Some 92 per cent, or 25 million people, said they were unaware that terrorists had flown planes into the World Trade Center on 11 September 2001, sparking the invasion of their country.

They called it 'this event which foreigners call 9/11' and had no idea what i
meant."[11] This being the one central basis for the US Afghan military operations, the US information campaign was a non-starter. It meant nothing to the
Afghan population, who were the target of the US IO mission.

The US-led invasion of Iraq in March 2003 further degraded the US effort
in Afghanistan and resulted in a substantial decline in the capability of the US
PSYOP Task Force (POTF) in Afghanistan during this time period.[12]

The US relied upon a fairly consistent set of strategic communication
themes between 2001 and 2006:

- The War on Terror is right and just;
- Coalition forces come in peace;
- Al-Qaeda and the Taliban are enemies of the people of Afghanistan;
- US forces are technologically superior (difficult to sell when it comes to
  collateral damage);
- There would be monetary rewards for providing information about Taliban
  and al-Qaeda leaders;
- There would be monetary rewards for turning in weapons;
- The Afghan government is legitimate;
- Afghan National Security Forces (ANSF) serve the people of Afghanistan;
- Democracy will benefit the people of Afghanistan.[13]

But the Afghan population, and especially the rural population, had little
knowledge of or interest in most of these themes. Also, importantly, these
themes were never couched in stories or framed in narratives that were coher-
ently presented to the Afghan population.

Much of the effort during this time was dedicated to messages intended for
the Afghan population, and even in 2007 the Afghan population remained
the most important target audience, yet the US did not seem to know how to
motivate their support. By contrast, senior insurgent leaders and rank-and-file
insurgents were, respectively, ranked seventh and eighth in terms of the most
important target audiences:[14]

1. Afghan population
2. Afghan government
3. Government and military of Pakistan
4. Pakistani population
5. Governments of ISAF Troop-Contributing Nations (TCNs)
6. Populations of ISAF Troop-Contributing Nations (TCNs)
7. Enemy leadership (AQ, Taliban, criminal networks)

8. Taliban rank-and-file
9. Governments of Central Asia
10. Central Asian populations
11. IGO and NGO community
12. US domestic audience

In 2007, the US in conjunction with NATO-ISAF revamped its effort to streamline the strategic master narrative and emphasized the following themes and stories:

1. The government of the Islamic Republic of Afghanistan, NATO-ISAF, and the US are committed for the long term to ensuring a democratic, stable, peaceful Afghanistan that is inhospitable to terrorism. The Afghan people can rely on its allies, including the US government and NATO, to stay the course.
2. Success in Afghanistan over insurgency, terrorism, violent extremism, and trafficking in narcotics is critical to the security of the Afghan people, the United States, our NATO allies, its regional neighbors, and the international community.
3. Afghanistan's security, reconstruction, and development needs remain large but the country has come a long way since the overthrow of the Taliban, and the government of the Islamic Republic of Afghanistan continues to make progress.
4. Success requires a comprehensive approach that includes security and stability as well as reconstruction and development.
5. The Taliban are a destructive force that target innocent Afghan civilians. They engage in criminal activity and brutal tactics for their own gain and cannot offer long-term security, stability, or development for the people of Afghanistan.[15]

The US strategy and these stories were problematic at various levels, including an inability to present or articulate them to the Afghan population in an intelligible manner. Most of the time, the stories and overall narrative failed to resonate with a vast majority of the Afghan population; the narratives and messages were seemingly tailored to the urban, educated, or elite elements of Afghan society, rather than the rural population, which comprised 75 per cent of Afghanistan's overall population. Moreover, the United States was relatively ignorant about Pashtun culture and cultural dynamics that would have greatly enhanced US IO efforts.[16] For example, the United States never came to grips with what the term jihad meant to the average Afghan, especially among residents in southern Afghanistan,[17] for whom it meant broadly any defensive effort to protect Islam from outside invaders and negative influences. While historically this often implied armed actions, in many instances it merely meant following the faith and one's personal Islamic virtue ("greater" jihad in Islamic teachings) and supporting those who were battling for Islamic righteousness. The US never understood these nuances. In a broader indictment of US IO efforts, then Chairman of the Joint Chiefs of Staff Admiral Mike Mullen, for example, said that for "US efforts in Afghanistan and elsewhere to send a positive message about US military action and development efforts, [it] hurt US credibility when they do not coincide with what the populace sees on the ground." Mullen's criticism came as US officials acknowledged that the US was losing the war of ideas against its Taliban and al-Qaeda enemies.[18]

Recognizing that they were clearly losing the information war and the "hearts and minds" of the Afghan population—to use an often-cited COIN term—the NATO-ISAF Strategic Communications Framework for 2011 sought to reset the key communications themes as the US and NATO prepared to move forward with the process of transition and developing a long-term partnership between Afghanistan and NATO. The new objectives and narratives included:

1. Communicate that stability in Afghanistan is crucial to global security and that NATO-ISAF will never again allow Afghanistan to become a launching pad for international terrorism.

The stability of the country and the deaths of Afghan civilians had become a major issue for Afghan President Hamid Karzai and became an important point of contention between the United States and Karzai. In 2009, under the command of US General Stanley McChrystal, the US and ISAF implemented directives limiting the use of airpower to curtail the perception that coalition airstrikes were causing a significant number of civilian casualties in Afghanistan. Shortly after the directives were implemented, US Army Colonel Francis Scott Main assessed that the "inability of PSYOP and strategic communications to address this perception of excessive [casualties] had restricted one of the most effective kinetic tools available to the coalition."[19]

2. In coordination with the government of the Islamic Republic of Afghanistan, explain and gain support for transition.

Ten years into OEF-A and the Bonn Accords, the Afghan government was still facing charges of massive corruption and lack of "democracy" and transparency. Transparency International produces a yearly "Corruption Perceptions Index" (CPI), and Afghanistan has always been judged as one of the most corrupt countries in the world, just behind North Korea and Somalia.[20] The Afghan rural population had become extremely antagonistic to Kabul and this, in turn, had significant implications for US COIN efforts throughout the country. US night raids, for example, became a rallying point for not only Karzai but also rural Pashtuns throughout the country. These operations had multiple layered effects. First, the operations offended the village and its elders when men of military age were taken from the home without a perceived reason. Second, entering the home of a Pashtun without permission dishonors the owner. If his wife is home and another man enters, Pashtun culture considers this rape, thus dishonoring the entire family. Third, the district and provincial governments were often unaware of these operations. The inability of the Afghan government to notify or step in as an intermediary both delegitimized the authority of the government which the US was trying to strengthen, and set the people against their representatives.[21] Finally, such operations presented crucial and important IO to the Taliban every time they were conducted.

3. Generate the active support of the Afghan people, the GIRoA, Troop Contributing Nations' (TCNs) populations and international community for the ISAF mission.

As suggested above, a variety of US tactics had disturbed the Afghan population, especially those in rural Pashtun areas. Moreover, perceptions and the exploitation of US collateral damage had turned many Afghans against the US and Kabul. Indeed, the death of Afghan innocents as a result of US, ISAF, and Afghan security forces had become a major recruiting tool for the Taliban and associated groups.

4. Promote NATO's long-term commitment to Afghanistan in close coordination with GIRoA.

After decades of war and years of OEF-A, the populations of many NATO countries started to question the wisdom of a continuing combat presence in Afghanistan. The theme of NATO's long-term commitment became an important IO theme, but its ultimate resonance with the Afghan population was questionable.

5. Communicate progress against ISAF campaign objectives and priorities, articulated in theatre-defined measures of effectiveness.

Theatre-defined Measures of Effectiveness (MOEs) for IO and PSYOP were a continuing problem for OEF-A. Much of this was due to the basic lack of knowledge of Afghanistan and the Pashtuns, in particular, by members of the US Coalition. The United States and its NATO-ISAF partners spent much of their time in discussions with Afghan elites and Afghan technocrats at the expense of listening to the needs and desires of rural Afghans. This was especially problematic considering the rural insurgency that this war represented.

6. Diminish support for the insurgents and criminal patronage networks that are detrimental to the ISAF mission and effective Afghan governance that commands public confidence.

Criminal elements and Afghan drug mafias quickly became associated with the Taliban. Groups such as the Haqqani Network were as much criminals, if not more, than the insurgents.[22] These criminal networks preyed on the Afghan population and helped to increase corruption in a wide variety of ISAF and US development efforts and other policies.[23]

The core strategic message at this time emphasized the partnership between the US, NATO-ISAF, and Afghanistan: "This mission is essential for our shared security. Our strategy is sound, our long-term commitment is solid and with our Afghan partners we will succeed."[24] Themes had also been redefined to help promote and achieve the overall strategic communications objectives.

Following the conclusion of the NATO ISAF mission mandate in late 2014, the subsequent NATO-led Resolute Support Mission Afghanistan (RSMA) began on 1 January 2015. Its objective was to "build on the achievements made by the now completed ISAF mission while officially and formally recognizing Afghan Security Forces' growing capabilities and their assumption of full security responsibility for the future of Afghanistan."[25] But even here the realities did not match the messages that the US were propagating. Several tribal leaders we interviewed in Kandahar City in July 2008, for example, suggested that the Afghan Nation Police (ANP) units operating in the districts of Kandahar were generally "corrupt" and were viewed negatively by local communities and travelers. The ANP, these leaders suggested, were engaged in drug trafficking, drug use, abductions, rape, and "terrorism."

The Resolute Support Mission operates under a training and advising directive that supports four Lines of Effort (LOE): Posture the Force, Protect the Force, Complete Afghan Security Institutions/Afghan National Defense & Security Forces (ASI/ANDSF) Development, and Support Political Transition. The four LOEs are further focused on eight specific areas of concentration known as Essential Functions (EFs):

EF1: Multi-year budgeting and execution of programs
EF2: Transparency, accountability, and oversight
EF3: Civilian governance of the ASI
EF4: Force generation
EF5: Sustainment
EF6: Strategy and policy planning, resourcing, and execution
EF7: Intelligence
EF8: Strategic communication

The Resolute Support Mission EF8 comprises a train, advise, and assist framework that seeks to create a consistent message among Afghan institutions such as the Afghan Ministry of Interior and Ministry of Defense.

There are two components of the Resolute Support Mission EF8. One, Public Affairs and Strategic Communication, combines government relations, media communication, issue management, and information dissemination, and is managed through the Government Media Information Center and the Cross Ministry News Desk. The general Afghan population and Afghan government are most likely the intended audience for these efforts. The Government Media Information Center serves as a means to coordinate, produce, and distribute accurate and timely information, as well as providing training for Afghan communicators and a venue for press briefings. The Cross Ministry News Desk is an information nerve center comprising representatives from the Ministries of Defense and Interior, the National Directorate of Security (NDS), and the Independent Directorate of Local Governance (IDLG). The Cross Ministry News Desk allows these representatives to coordinate and disseminate press releases and official statements about Afghan security operations and activities.

The second component of EF8 is EF 8.2 Information Operations and Afghan Information Dissemination Operation/Special Information Forces, which focuses on countering and disrupting insurgent communications through messaging at the national level. This includes the relatively standard message dissemination techniques such as billboards, leaflets, and radio and TV spots that are most likely intended for insurgent leadership, insurgent rank-and-file, and the local Afghan population.[26]

Strategic messaging to insurgents

US efforts at the tactical and operational level of strategic communications were intended to influence targeted insurgents and insurgent leadership nodes, with the most common desired effects including: undermine morale, counter-propaganda, exploit fissures, disrupt wider support network, and disrupt supply network. But most of these efforts proved ineffective. We have seen no evidence that these efforts had any significant impact.

In order to understand the United States approach to information operations and strategic communications in Afghanistan, it is critical to assess these approaches relative to strategies and means of IO communication used by the Afghan Taliban and other insurgent/jihadi groups. IO strategies and tactics cannot be viewed in isolation. All such communication is dyadic and it is critical not only to understand target audiences but also the IO approach used by these actors to counter or inhibit US/NATO-ISAF efforts.

Taliban's effective messaging and their insurgency/jihad as compared with the US messaging and counter-insurgency

As suggested throughout this book, the Taliban have a concise, effective information discipline that is in tune with the audiences they wish to influence. We would submit that the US Coalition never totally understood this, and this lack of understanding had a negative influence on what turned out to be an ineffective counter-insurgency doctrine in the information domain. The Taliban are not invincible on the information battlefield. They have weaknesses that could have been exploited by an aggressive information campaign, but this was not to be. The US Coalition messaging system was primarily a passive one that tried to discredit the Taliban among the Afghans through ill-formed attempts to make Afghans realize the superiority of the Coalition cause. This strategy did not work, in large part because the US had no message or story to tell that made a case in a way that the Afghan population could understand or believe.

In Afghanistan, as in most asymmetric conflicts, there is a marked difference between the motivation levels of the actors in conflict. When strong actors decide to fight against weak ones, it is typically in pursuit of a limited set of objectives relevant to national policy, but seldom viewed as vital to the national interest of the stronger party. Even if such conflicts are viewed as vital to the strong state, a protracted conflict will often change this view dramatically. Thus the weaker but determined American Continental Army, Algerian ALN, Viet Cong, and many others overcome their much stronger adversaries, as the protracted conflict causes the strong actors to re-evaluate the overall value they place on the object of the fight. Statistically, the weak actors in asymmetric conflicts will win when the strong actor employs a conventional strategy of direct military engagement against the weaker actor's strategy of attacking the fighting will of the strong actor. Using historical data of asymmetric conflicts, Arreguín-Toft shows that the weaker forces win by a margin of 28 per cent when this situation exists.[27]

In light of this "motivation disadvantage," the task of the weak actor is to remain credibly in the field while the strong actor's determination wanes. To remain in the field, the weak actor must have at least the tolerance, at best the support and participation, of the people. And a stalemate is a victory for the weaker state. Mao, the master of asymmetric warfare, built his guerrilla campaign around the political mobilization of a disgruntled peasantry who gave his irregulars shelter and sustenance. Similarly, Castro and Guevara were able to aggravate the schisms between the people and the regime with only a handful of determined guerrillas.[28] The weak actor will thus capitalize on the strong actor's impatience,[29] while nurturing his vital shelter among the population. This nurturing is achieved through an effective means of communicating with the population that provides this support. The challenge for the US in Afghanistan was to develop a strategy for defeating the insurgent *narrative* just as decisively as the enemy's *capability*. Unfortunately, this was never done.

A central purpose of information operations, as suggested throughout the chapters of this book, is to influence the decision of a target or affect a decision in support of a given objective. This requires communication to a specific audience. Moreover, in order for a messaging campaign to be effective, the messenger must have an intimate understanding of the audience for the message, as this group's interpretation of the message will occur within the narrative framework constructed by the group's experiences and biases. Information campaigns must be designed to communicate effectively to a wide range of audiences. Each audience group should be approached and engaged with unique tactics. As we have seen, since at least 2008, the Taliban have developed a sophisticated capability for IO directed at Western audiences, publishing English language websites, complete with appropriate idiomatic expressions that indicate participation by native English speakers.[30]

Communication lies at the heart of the insurgent effort in an asymmetric conflict. In any conflict, two competing actors can attack the opponent's capability through conventional operations, or they can attack the will of the adversary through unconventional operations. The Taliban attack US and their Coalition capabilities through guerrilla attacks against conventional targets, but they must know that this will not bring victory. The Taliban's only hope of victory rests in attacking the Coalition's will to fight. Attacking the will happens through communication. This communication can take several forms: it can often look like kinetic operations, like a terrorist's car bomb, an assassination, or roadside IED. This is communication to the adversary and is designed to break the will of the enemy. Suicide attacks are designed to showcase the difference in motivation that exists between the Taliban and the United States. The message is perfectly tuned for the Western audience: "Do you see how determined we are? You don't want this nearly as much as we do, so why not give up now?"

The Taliban messaging strategy seeks to recreate a national identity and expand their political capital by tapping shared values and customs and exploiting collective experiences of the past, such as the anti-Soviet jihad. While it is difficult to counter the Taliban's propaganda, it is not impossible given the inherent vulnerabilities inherent in the Taliban's overall strategic communications strategy. Themes indicative of weakness in the Taliban's strategy include: insurgent attacks against civilians, or insurgent attacks that inadvertently kill and maim civilians, allegations of the Taliban abusing and brutalizing the local population, the well-known ties between the Afghan Taliban and foreign intelligence services (Pakistan's ISI), and Islamic opposition to terrorism, especially suicide terrorism. Similarly, while the Taliban messaging campaign is consistent, the strategy is primarily a negative one, playing on the perceived failures of the international community and Afghan government to restore law and order, enforce justice, and to complete construction and development projects. The Taliban's messaging campaign fails to offer viable solutions or alternatives to the current situation, other than threats of more violence and destruction—a strategy that promotes the notions that the Afghan government, the United States and NATO are ineffective in governance and security; but it also limits how deeply public support can ultimately be reached.

Yet the US efforts have not significantly attempted to play on these vulnerabilities with their messaging efforts. The US IO and PSYOP planners struggled with crafting and processing an appropriate response, not only because of bureaucratic red tape, but also because the quality of the message would not have compared to that of the Taliban forces. It is highly unlikely that a large part of the US IO or PSYOP forces would have an intimate grasp of Afghan history or an understanding of the cultural nuances buried within references to early rulers, in order to craft letters or poetry on a par with that of the Taliban forces. In order to prepare work that resonates with a historically aware population, message architects must have extensive and accurate cultural intelligence and be fluent in the minutiae of Afghanistan's history, politics, religion, society, and militant activity. Cultural intelligence is one aspect that was much needed to lay the groundwork for an effective and powerful US IO and PSYOP campaign.

There was a fundamental lack of cultural literacy among US military members as a whole at the beginning of OEF-A. And, quite frankly, it has not improved much since. Especially in the early stages of OEF-A, there were few Afghanistan cultural and area "experts." And until the US military's Foreign Area Officer (FAO) Program was expanded, there was little effort on an institutional scale to create a cadre of active duty military officers and enlisted members who could master high-demand languages and cultural cognizance and who could serve as capable message architects and advisors to construct successful US messaging campaigns. In addition, the process of crafting truly nuanced messages and stories proved to be impossibly demanding in this context: the time crunch meant they were too rushed, and without a proper cultural aptitude they failed to create clarity within the message and indirectly sabotaged the campaign altogether. Finally, it took years after the start of OEF-A for the Department of Defense to make the heavy investment needed to create IO and PSYOP leaders who were culturally fluent, could speak Pashto or Dari, master the political/social and historical aspects of Afghanistan, and could make basic predictions of behavior that were accurate and truthful. A lack of intelligence (cultural and operational) about the target audience greatly hindered the OEF-A effort.

US messaging leaflets in Afghanistan[31]

Early IO efforts during OEF-A

The leaflet campaign conducted by Operation Enduring Freedom-Afghanistan provides a useful case for comparing US messaging and IO strategies with those of the Taliban. This section will examine cultural messaging efforts used during the operation, especially during the early phases of OEF-A. A general lack of cultural awareness and perspective, especially in the early years of OEF-A, hindered the US IO campaign and created significant challenges for US PSYOP and IO personnel supporting the campaign. As we shall see, leaflet messaging distributed throughout Afghanistan at the start of the US invasion failed to resonate with the Afghan population and often resulted in a muddied objective for military IO and PSYOP. And yet over 80 million leaflets were dropped over Afghanistan from October 2001 until March 2002.[32] Theoretically, that represents almost four leaflets per Afghan citizen!

The options for delivering messages depend on available means of transmission and other matters, including the target audience for the messaging. Geographic barriers, linguistic diversity, and extremely low literacy rates challenged message architects during the run-up to OEF-A. This created a particularly difficult challenge for cross-cultural communication. Messages would have to be conveyed primarily through images on leaflets, simple written phrases, or radio broadcasts. In order to convey behavior-generating communiqués, message crafters would have to be particularly adept at employing cultural symbols, frames, and recognition of behavior through still images. It was believed that each part of the message delivery, from transmission to reception, would have to be saturated with well-placed cultural imagery. In order to prepare an effective leaflet campaign, OEF-A planners would have to possess current and accurate cultural intelligence. In addition, a grasp of geo-ethnic and linguistic distribution would be vital in order to get the right message to the right group. The problem of low literacy rates and subsequent watering down of OEF-A messaging would surface as a major problem for US PSYOP planners when the Taliban responded with eloquent and culturally indigenous night letters distributed to educated members of rural villages to read to the illiterate members of the group.[33]

Putting the right message in the right place at the right time was a challenge for IO and PSYOP campaigners. There were many cases of leaflets being dropped into the wrong locations, which affected the resonance and impact of PSYOP and IO efforts in the area. Moreover, there was little coordination between the geographic targets and timing of maneuvers. Some Special Forces (SF) teams reported complaints from rural Pashtuns as to why all the "litter" was being dropped on their village and what it meant.[34] Such Afghan sentiments clearly suggested that the US efforts were not persuasive and not having their desired impact on the Afghan target audiences.

At the start of the conflict, there were few cultural advisors available to preview leaflets, and close scrutiny by CENTCOM and Joint Special Operations Task Force (JSOTF) created challenges to message architects. Moreover, in the early stages of OEF-A there was limited US knowledge concerning Afghan psyche and culture nuances.[35] Most of the early data available to US IO personnel on Afghan tribes, history, culture, and regional influence came from books purchased prior to their deployment.

The hasty initial OEF-A IO and PSYOP campaigns were certainly detrimental to the overall goals of the war planners, primarily due to a failure in the cultural framing of the leaflet operation. The messages that OEF-A military planners wanted to send were not overly difficult to incorporate into leaflets, but the problem manifested itself primarily through a lack of effective cross-cultural communication and inaccurate geographic targeting as well as lack of knowledge as to how messages would be viewed and interpreted by the Afghan target audiences. Military operations began on 7 October 2001, but leaflets were not dropped until 15 October because of high winds.

The first leaflets of the campaign were dropped to prepare the Afghan population for an impending US military invasion. Planners wanted to create a message that told Afghans what to do when US forces arrived, how to avoid harm during the bombing raids, and not to stand under food drops.[36] Other messages targeting the Taliban and co-located al-Qaeda operatives were dropped without pre-testing and geographic coordination. The failure to coordinate leaflet drops with military maneuvers became counterproductive as the conflict wore on. Although the initial "blind" leaflet drops could have had a limited effect on the Taliban, the progressive campaign began to run in cross-purpose to the action on the ground.[37]

Time was not just a factor in the lead-up to OEF-A, but also hampered IO and PSYOP efforts on the ground during the conflict. There were problems in the product approval cycle between the JSOTF and the IO and PSYOP planners on the ground. When the PSYOP cadre prepared campaigns that needed to be distributed quickly, either in response to a Taliban information operation or in reaction to a US military maneuver, the "request–approval–delivery cycle" did not even meet deliberate planning requirements.[38] There was a distinct lag on the part of the JSOTF to respond to tactical needs in the field.

Inadequate message crafting and the failure to grasp the nuances or, in many cases, even the basics of Afghanistan's culture became a major and significant problem for the military and civilian IO and PSYOP:

> Delivered as aerial leaflets (carpet bombing), [the leaflets] were recovered by local Afghans, a great many of whom could not read. Often, the leaflets were presented to the most educated local villager for interpretation, who would render a judgment of the "rewards" and "threats" as stupid, and regarded them as an insulting level of literature. The villagers, esteeming the educated villager, generally adopted his interpretation and attitude. Westerners tend to be condescending toward non-literature-based cultures. Cultures that do not primarily rely on written words often compensate with poetry as a memory tool to retain narratives …[they] also interpreted the Western style of directness as flat, lacking social elegance and intellect. Regardless, they were the intended audience, and our messages fell flat.[39]

The level of cultural intelligence prior to and even during the initial campaign fell short of adequate and could not compete with the Taliban information campaign which made use of its indigenous grasp of local, provincial, and national themes to render their messages more powerful to their audience. In contrast to the elementary and cartoonish OEF-A IO campaign, the Taliban IO operation was a strategic and effective effort to craft poetic diatribes that appealed to the moral reasoning of Afghan villagers. The messages were viewed as eloquent, impressive, and were subsequently more effective than the US IO campaign.[40]

A major problem with the initial OEF-A leaflet campaign, as suggested above, was a failure to absorb accurate and timely cultural intelligence. But there where other significant problems: for example, there was a milieu of expatriates and Afghan urban elite, especially Kabulis, serving as informal advisors to IO campaign[41] who had not lived in Afghanistan since the Soviet invasion in 1979. Moreover, the targets for the bulk of this early IO campaign were the rural Pashtun population or supporters of the Taliban and al-Qaeda, and most of these Afghan expatriates had never been exposed to or had little knowledge of this target population.

Additional problems involved the lack of pre-testing leaflet messages that might inform relevant personnel as to messages probably failure or success. This resulted in many of the messages being deployed that not only failed to resonate with the target audience but, in some instance actually alienated or insulted the target audience. There were also no formal feedback mechanisms or "measures on merit" available to assess the success or failure of a particular message.

Early phases of OEF-A leaflets

A critical analysis of the initial OEF-A leaflet campaign exposes the key problem with the initial IO and PSYOP campaigns: the lack of knowledge concerning Afghanistan's people, society, and culture. It is important to note that not all the leaflets dropped during the beginning phases of OEF-A were culturally insensitive or insufficient; but most were, and a sample of these leaflets demonstrates the US's poor cross-cultural communication. The most glaring factor, which hinders most cross-cultural dialogues, is that each communicator assumes that the other looks at the world exactly as he or she does.[42] That is, while a message might make perfect sense to an American writing it, this surely does not guarantee that the Afghan recipient will understand it at all. It ultimately comes done to the point made in Chapter 1, that a person's perspective will be intimately tied to the narrative that drives how they view and interact with their environment and the stories that make sense to them.

Figure 10.1: Partnership leaflet[43]

If the objective of the IO and PSYOP campaign is to induce or create behavior, then the message should resonate culturally and communicate some type of instruction to the recipient. The following samples of leaflets were dropped in the initial OEF-A leaflet campaign and provide examples of successful or unsuccessful cultural messaging.

Figure 10.1 shows one of the first leaflets dropped during OEF-A, leaflet AFD10c, "Partnership." The front of the message in Pashto and Dari reads, "The partnership of nations is here to help," while the back of the leaflet reads, "The partnership of nations is here to assist the people of Afghanistan." The leaflet has an image of what appears to be a Coalition soldier shaking hands with an Afghan male.

Figure 10.2: Peace and partnership leaflet[44]

یك افغانستان متحد

صلح و شگوفانی بار میآورد.

یوه متحده افغانستان تاسی ته

سوله او نیکمرغی راوړي.

This is an example of an effective and somewhat neutral leaflet. There is no specific behavior implied, only that the placement of the Coalition male in an equal stance with the Afghan male as well as shaking hands creates the impression of a man-to-man bond between the two. The Afghan male garb is comparable to that which is found in parts of some rural Afghan provinces (a wool pakul hat that is quite popular in Afghanistan), and the message is a fairly simple one. The perception shaping strategy for this leaflet was simply to create awareness and a sense of partnership between Coalition forces and the Afghan population. An important aspect of this IO artifact is that it communicates the message visually: the message is clear from the image, regardless of text.

Figure 10.2 shows a leaflet with text that translates as "A united Afghanistan offers peace and prosperity." This leaflet is an example of poor and even confusing cultural messaging. Copies of these leaflets were brought to Coalition forces by Afghans thinking that the dove was a type of chicken and that the leaflet was a coupon that entitled them to a free bird from the "Partnership of nations."[45] The symbol of the dove and olive branch originates from a Biblical story of Noah and the ark and does not resonate with a large part of the Afghan population. Although the dove and olive branch are widely understood in the Arab Middle East as a symbol of peace, this is primarily because of the history of interaction with the Christian minority. Afghanistan has been overwhelmingly Sunni Muslim for centuries, and has had no exposure to Christianity to relate the picture of the dove with the concept of peace. The other problem with the leaflet is that the Afghanistan flag in the backdrop has horizontal stripes, whereas the official flag has vertical stripes. A crucial mistake such as this makes one doubt the amount of basic research in preparing the leaflet. This was not the only instance when the Afghan flag was depicted incorrectly, as will be seen below. There were at least two other instances where a similar error was reproduced. Although some Afghans may not have noticed the error, it is evident that any preparation and research done for this leaflet fell short. But most importantly, the images have no cultural meaning for the audience.

Figure 10.3: Mullah Omar as a dog and bin Laden playing chess with Afghanistan, #AFD-51c[46]

Figure 10.5 is a leaflet depicting Osama bin Laden in traditional Arab clothing holding a chained leash attached to a dog with Mullah Omar's head. The message on the front of the leaflet reads, "Who really runs the Taliban?" The back of the leaflet depicts bin Laden playing chess on a board representing Afghanistan and moving chess pieces with heads of Mullah Omar. The text reads, "Expel the foreign rulers and live in peace." There are several aspects culturally problematic with this leaflet. First, the fact that there is a dog in the picture fosters a nearly inaccessible attitude among many Afghans. Dogs are considered unclean by most Afghans, and depicting one near any Muslim is an insult to Islam. When one Afghan calls another a "*spay*" or dog in Pashto, it means a fight is soon to follow. The fact that the dog's foot is resting on the outline of Afghanistan sends an even more culturally insensitive message about how the Coalition forces see Afghanistan. The vast majority of rural Afghans have absolutely no knowledge of the geographical shape of Afghanistan. Gilles Dorronsoro, author of *Revolution Unending*, opines that this leaflet was definitely ambiguous when distributed by non-Muslim forces.[47] The back of the leaflet is not offensive, but appears culturally irrelevant. The Taliban banned chess during their rule, and although educated Afghans may know how to play and enjoy the game, the more rural population would not be familiar with the concept or follow the meaning of the leaflet. This side of the leaflet does not send a message effectively, and appears for the most part culturally misinformed. There is not any particular behavior being encouraged by the document, but the intention was of perception management strategy in persuading the Afghan people that Arab foreigners are controlling the

Figure 10.4: American family and Afghan family[48]

236

Taliban. The cultural message from this leaflet is strategically ineffective and possibly offensive.

Figure 10.4 depicts an Afghan family and an American family with the caption "Friendship." A total of 2,540,000 copies of this leaflet were disseminated throughout Afghanistan until September 2002.[49]

This leaflet is a regrettable example of cross-cultural miscommunication and a counterproductive IO story. There are various significant problems with it. First, the Afghan family depicted in the photo does not appear to be Pashtun, the key center of gravity of the Afghan conflict, to use a Clausewitzian term.[50] The second and most damning problem with the leaflet is that the vast majority of Afghan families would never take a photo of their female members' uncovered faces and show it to strangers. While such a leaflet makes "perfect sense" to Americans, sharing a picture of a wife or daughter would be an extremely dishonorable act for any rural Afghan, especially Pashtun. As explained in Chapter 2, it would be inconceivable for an Afghan to show a picture of a female family member, because this would ultimately be a violation of an Afghan's honor (*namus*), pride, and esteem (*ghariat*). As demonstrated throughout this book, for an Afghan man to maintain his honor as defined by Pashtunwali correlates directly with his ability to protect/control his *zan* (women of his family).[51] One possible cultural message seemingly conveyed to an Afghan receiving this leaflet is that you and your family should become like the American family. This creates the possibility of a misperception by the Afghan population that Coalition forces are in Afghanistan

Figure 10.5: World Trade Center leaflet AFD 189[52]

to unveil Afghan women (many of whom who live in a state of *purda*) and make everyone look like Americans. This is regrettably a culturally ineffective message; in fact, the evidence is that this leaflet and its message were counter-productive: it did much more harm than good.

Finally, as mentioned before, the leaflet originators are displaying their ignorance of the Afghan flag: the stripes should be vertical with a gold crest in the center. A new leaflet was eventually issued with the correct flag design, but not before millions of these embarrassing leaflets had been dropped into Afghanistan. To have such an IO artifact deployed without accuracy checks by people with knowledge of Afghan culture highlights one of the central problems the US faced with its intial IO campaign in Afghanistan. That is, the US IO and PSYOP personnel had not taken time to learn about Afghan culture and what would resonate with the Afghan people.

Figure 10.5 is another example of an IO leaflet that may make sense to the average American, but means virtually nothing to most Afghans. This leaflet depicts the destruction of the World Trade Center and reads, "20 September 1380 (Persian Calendar). World Trade Center. The Coalition Forces came to arrest those responsible for the terrorism against America. They also come to arrest anyone that protects them. More than 3,000 people in the United States of America were murdered in these attacks."[53] The major problem with this leaflet is in the selection of the visual image: first, it is a rather abstract depiction of the horrors of that day; and second, most Afghans have never seen a skyscraper or could even understand its concept. How can they decipher a billowing red flame as an attack on someone else's 110-storey building? Moreover, as noted above, polls in Afghanistan suggest that very few Afghans had any knowledge of the 9/11 attacks and what they meant.[54] Hence this leaflet, which had the critical objective of trying to explain why the US and NATO invaded Afghanistan, could never hope to convey the rationale for the invasion in one rather indecipherable image.

Figure 10.6 depicts four men, three of which are identified and one that is not. The front of the leaflet says, "The Taliban's reign of fear" and continues on the back, "...is about to end." The men have writing on their head coverings identifying them, although the fourth is an unknown Taliban male. The man on the left, identified as [Mullah] Mutawakkil, was working with the US forces and served as the Taliban's foreign minister. As suggested by Gopal, "Maiwand native Mullah Mutawakkil ... [s]urrender[ed] to US forces, making him one of the highest-ranking Talibs in American custody. In fact, Mutawakkil's defection was only the latest in a rush of Taliban officials look-

Figures 10.6: Front of leaflet, depicting Mutawakkil, bin Laden, Haqqani and unknown Taliban male, AFD 56[55] Back of leaflet, depicting the same men with faces of death

ing to switch allegiances."[56] He had been identified by bin Laden as an enemy, and picturing him in a leaflet as a target showed the lack of research conducted about Mutawakkil and his position within the al-Qaeda/Taliban network.[57] It was probably a mistake to identify someone working with the US as a target for destruction and apparently an enemy of bin Laden.[58] It appeared as though the US were doing bin Laden a favor by targeting Mutawakkil for death.

The leaflet includes a fourth man with no identification, which would confuse Afghans who could not know who he was. The black turban is often worn by Taliban, but not in all cases. So any Afghan male wearing a black turban who was not Taliban might expect from this message that he could be targeted for killing.

While urban Afghans with televisions might be able to recognize one or two of the faces depicted on the leaflet, most rural Afghans, especially those who could not read the leaflet's written message, would not recognize them. Moreover, the choice to show the four men's skulls on the back of the leaflet is bound to cause ambiguities. Some Afghans believe in mystical *jinns* who have "fiery bodies [and] are intelligent and imperceptible" and are able to appear in various shapes and colors.[59] And maybe the developers of this IO leaflet should have been aware of this possible cultural interpretation when they made their assumptions of what a particular visual image would signify to their intended audience.

Figure 10.7: Eid wishes and dates, a common food used to break the Ramadan fast, AFD89[60]

Figure 10.7 is the last leaflet from the early phases of OEF-A that we will present and analyze. This leaflet, unlike most of the previous leaflets assessed, is actually an example of a positive and effective cultural message. The leaflet states, "Noble people of Afghanistan, Eid Mubarak,[61] We wish that God will accept your prayers and fast. Have a blessed holiday. People of America." Dates are a common food used to break a Ramadan fast, and passing Eid wishes to Muslims throughout Afghanistan is a positive message indicating that Americans celebrate with Afghans and respect the religious traditions of Islam. Dates were also air-dropped with the leaflets, to accentuate the well wishes delivered with the document—a very creative IO tactic,[62] because although common in Afghanistan, dates are still a luxury item. The only trouble was that many rumors ran through Afghanistan that "everything Americans touched or ate was cooked in pork fat," which is forbidden by

Islam;[63] so if indeed the dates were "tainted by pork," they could not be eaten and might actually be *haram* ("unlawful").

While we only evaluated a small sample of the many IO leaflets used in the early phases of Operation Enduring Freedom, the leaflets assessed are fairly representative of the ones created and deployed.[64] The assessment of these IO artifacts suggests a number of points that must have contributed to the relative failure of this PSYOP and IO campaign. First, there appeared to be a fundamental lack of Afghan cultural literacy in the PSYOP and IO teams, as well as among military members as a whole. During the early phases of OEF-A, there were few cultural and area "experts" within the American military to be deployed with US operational units in Afghanistan. During the years 2001–4 there was relatively little effort on an institutional scale to train up a cadre of active duty military officers and enlisted members who could master appropriate languages and cultural cognizance to write and design successful messaging campaigns. In addition, the process for targeting hearts and minds to win the trust and confidence of the Afghan people revealed itself to be strategically shallow and culturally illiterate. Through shortage of time, message architects without the appropriate cultural training will not understand how to frame a succient visual and textual document and thereby will indirectly sabotage the campaign altogether. It is evident that a lack of intelligence (cultural and operational) about the target audience hindered the early IO and PSYOP effort in OEF-A.[65] In summary, the initial leaflet campaign of OEF-A was relatively unsuccessful at delivering informative and directive messages, much less messages that were effectively persuasive.

Later phases of OEF-A leaflets and other IO artifacts

During 2008, the United States turned to counter-insurgency (COIN) as their central tactic and objective in Afghanistan. Theoretically and consistent with US doctrine,[66] this new focus on COIN had significant implications for the US IO and PSYOP campaign, because information operations is theoretically considered as the key COIN "component" tying together the "three pillars of the COIN Framework: security, politics, and economics."[67] In 2009, President Obama ordered a surge of US military forces into Afghanistan in order to accomplish those counter-insurgency objectives. US and Coalition forces in Afghanistan at this time were under the command of General Stanley McChrystal. McChrystal tendered his resignation on 23 June 2010, two days before a controversial article on his leadership and policies was published in the magazine, *Rolling Stone*.[68] He was replaced by General David Petreaus, who in August 2010 issued his guidance for US counter-insurgency operations in Afghanistan, including the following two directives:[69]

Be first with the truth. Beat the insurgents and malign actors to the headlines. Preempt rumors. Get information to the chain of command, to Afghan leaders, to the people, and to the press as soon as possible. Integrity is critical to this fight. Avoid spinning, and don't try to "dress up" an ugly situation. Acknowledge setbacks and failures, including civilian casualties, and then state how we'll respond and what we've learned.

Fight the information war aggressively. Challenge disinformation. Turn our enemies' extremist ideologies, oppressive practices, and indiscriminate violence against them. Hang their barbaric actions like millstones around their necks.

The author was fortunate to receive the *345th TPS (A) "Product Book"* for 2009 and other IO work products that can be utilized to assess US IO and PSYOP during the height of the US COIN tactical approach in Afghanistan.[70] The assessment of IO and PSYOP artifacts deployed during 2009–10 is important for our analysis and comparison of US IO and Taliban IO for a number of reasons. First, referring back to the definition offered above that a counter-insurgency is basically an information war supported by military kinetics, the assessment of IO and PSYOP during this time period will tell us a lot about the overall success or failure of the US COIN tactics in Afghanistan in general. Second, after the early phases of OEF-A, it was assumed that PSYOP and IO efforts would gradually improve after years of producing ineffective and, in many cases, counterproductive products. Indeed, our preliminary examination of the PSYOP *Product Book* suggested that the authors of the product book had made significant efforts to generate well-crafted and colorful leaflets; however, most of the products were, in our opinion, created with little attention to Afghan cultural nuances, just as we saw above. For example, Afghans are generally practical and pragmatic people and have a tendency to pay less attention to complex and wordy messages.[71] If a banner in a village or an US IO artifact presents a picture of road-building and a message that says, "This is what the Government of the Islamic Republic of Afghanistan (GIRoA) does for you," there should be explicit "ground evidence" of roads being built in that area. In the absence of such, people will hardly believe the "blank promises," especially after nine or ten years of US occupation of Afghanistan.

The first observation concerning this PSYOP *Product Book* is the fact that the vast majority of the PSYOP and IO products appear not to be aimed at "persuasion" but rather "instruction" or the presentation of "information." This is an important finding that may suggest that US PSYOP and IO personnel had learned by 2009 that they, quite frankly, were not very adept at producing and deploying artifacts aimed at persuading the Afghan population or the Taliban to take certain actions. Very few of these messages "[hung the Taliban's barbaric] actions like millstones around their necks," as directed by General Petraeus' guidance for US counter-insurgency operations in Afghanistan.

Table 10.1: *345ᵗʰ TPS (A) "Product Book"* objectives

PSYOP objective	Number of PSYOP/IO artifacts
A: Increase support for Coalition partners	2
B: Decrease interference with CP (Command Post) operations	11
C: Increase support for GIRoA	26
D: Increase support for Afghan National Security Forces (ANSF)	45
E: Decrease support for insurgents	28
F: Increase support for Afghan National Security Forces (ANSF)[72]	35
H: Decrease insurgent activity	27
I: Increase support and participation in education system	17
J: Decrease incidents involving explosive devices	34
K: Increase safety and hygiene practices	19

Table 10.1 presents the explicit PSYOP and IO objectives presented in the PSYOP *Product Book* and the frequency of messages portraying each objective. We assume that the number of artifacts is an indicator of the priority of the particular objective; hence, the highest number being for the objective of increasing public support for the Afghan National Security Forces (ANSF), reflecting the priority of "Afghanization" of the war.

The next most "important" PSYOP and IO objective according to the metric emanating from Table 10.1 is decreasing the incidents of explosive devices. The years 2009 and 2010 saw a dramatic increase in IED fatalities in Afghanistan (see Figure 10.8). This increase in IED fatalities compounded by the public's growing disapproval of the war in Afghanistan[73] made it contingent that the US counteract the growing IED threat. For a COIN strategy to succeed, it is critical to have public support behind it. History has clearly shown that once the public loses confidence in the war effort, the probability of failure looms large.[74] And the American public since at least the Vietnam war has had little patience for increasing US casualties in a foreign war.

Figure 10.8: IED fatalities, 2001–11[75]

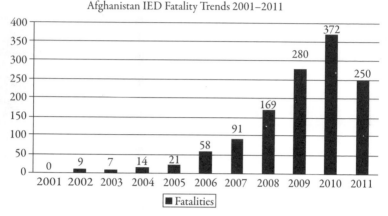

Afghanistan IED Fatality Trends 2001–2011

The leaflets and other products assessed below will, where relevant, be related to the associated PSYOP and IO objective from Table 10.1.

A: Increase support for Coalition partners

The leaflet shown in Figure 10.9 is yet another PSYOP product that was not well conceived. This leaflet shows an Afghan male dressed in usual attire—a

Figure 10.9: Hostilities will not be tolerated, AF09A02aaLF1569[76]

Figure 10.10: Report illegal weapons, AF09B02aaBB1063

shalwar kameez and woollen hat, or *pakol*—in the cross hairs of a weapon. While the man is wearing a bandolier and carrying automatic machine gun, this is also not uncommon in rural Afghanistan. There is nothing explicitly presented that suggests that this person is a Taliban or other insurgent/jihadist. The picture depicts a scene that is not necessarily threatening or hostile to the average rural Afghan. Even the person in the forefront using binoculars is not overly rare or unusual. Hence, the visual could be interpreted, based on the visual alone, as a threat to an average, rural Afghan. Moreover, the leaflet's message, "hostilities will not be tolerated," is very vague. What and whose hostilities are being referenced, when an invading force is by definition bringing hostilities? This is yet another example of a leaflet that had some purpose for the person who originated it, but the combination of selected image and pared down text creates too many ambiguities. Finally it is not at all clear how this leaflet supports the PSYOP objective of "increasing support for Coalition partners."

B: Decrease interference with CP (Command Post) operations

Figure 10.10 would make perfect sense to a literate Afghan, but relies too much on the text for an illiterate receiver of the leaflet. Had it been specifically designed to target urban, literate Afghans it could serve as a fairly useful mes-

Figure 10.11: Working for the future of Afghanistan, AF09B02aaHB 1069

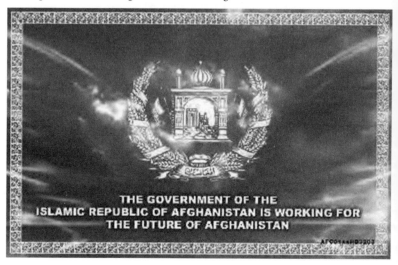

THE GOVERNMENT OF THE
ISLAMIC REPUBLIC OF AFGHANISTAN IS WORKING FOR
THE FUTURE OF AFGHANISTAN

sage; but in rural areas, where the literacy rate is low, it would not have suffi-
cient impact because the meaning of the message is not completely clear from
the visual alone. The text gives the options of speaking to an elder, as illustrated in the photo; or calling a Tipline, which most Afghans would feel more
comfortable with, for security reasons, when conveying information about
dangerous issues such as IEDs or weapons caches. So arguably the visual
should have illustrated the second option.[77]

C: Increase support for GIRoA

The leaflet shown in Figure 10.11 straightforwardly presents the objective
intended, but with no "story" at all. The static image gives no pictorial evidence of the message. The causes of Afghans' current political frustrations are
the massive corruption associated with the Kabul government and Afghan
urban elite, the lack of security experienced by most Afghans on a daily basis,
the lack of a creditable justice system, the relative absence of good, long-term
jobs, the fact that many Afghans view the Kabul government as a puppet of
the occupying power (the US), and many other reasons.[78] Hence, the official-
looking message probably fell on deaf ears: actions obviously speak much
louder than words, and most rural Afghans have not experienced a significant
improvement in their daily lives or standard of living. But these facts do not

exclusively apply to rural Afghans. Consider, for example, that Kandahar, the second largest city in Afghanistan, after thirteen years of American occupation (2001–14) and billions of dollars spent, still has only sporadic electricity.[79] Moreover, traditionally, local governments are much more important and have a greater impact on the average Afghan than the "central" government in Kabul. The majority of rural Afghans have never had much faith in, or understanding of, the central government in Kabul. Finally, "most Afghans feel increasingly frustrated with the term 'future'."[80] They are much more interested in day-to-day survival for themselves and their families. Finally, the leaflet's message is a very general statement that makes no specific promises. I would argue that this leaflet does not follow General Petraeus' instructions to "avoid spinning, and don't try to 'dress up' an ugly situation." This message should have been expanded with more explicit promises, e.g. "The Government of Afghanistan and its local government partners are working to answer your needs and improve your prosperity."

D: Increase support for Afghan National Security Forces (ANSF)

Figure 10.12 shows a leaflet that is purely instructional and warns Afghan drivers to "approach the checkpoint slowly and stop when told." While the text of the leaflet is self-explanatory to those who can read, the image is con-

Figure 10.12: Transport control protocols, AF09B02aaHB1495

Approach the checkpoint slowly and stop when told.

Figure 10.13: Billboard, AF09C01aaBB 1070

fusing and does not illustrate the text. The picture shows a car with an open trunk and open door while the message instructs the driver to drive slowly to the checkpoint. These types of errors that could easily be fixed with a better understanding of the importance of visual literacy do not give one confidence in the US PSYOP instructional campaign.

F: Increase support for Afghan National Security Forces (ANSF)

Figure 10.13 shows a PSYOP billboard that was deployed throughout pro-government areas of Afghanistan. Billboards, especially in the later phases of the US occupation of Afghanistan, became a popular PSYOP/IO messaging technique:

> The US military currently assists the Afghan government in constructing billboards aimed at undermining support to the insurgency... Billboards are a rarity in Afghanistan and receive special notice. The primary weakness of this method of dissemination is that billboards must be constructed in pro-Afghan government areas where the population is already sympathetic to the message ... from anecdotal evidence presented by PSYOP personnel, it seems that billboards reinforce the anti-Taliban sentiments of those who are already anti-Taliban and are ineffective in swaying pro-Taliban sectors, as they are seen simply as government propaganda on a big platform. Another possibility to consider is the effectiveness of billboards in areas where the Taliban has established a shadow government. In such cases, they

would probably serve to underscore the local's view of the government's self-delusion and inefficacy.[81]

The actual effectiveness of billboard messages has not been systematically studied. The billboard message presented in Figure 10.13 is primarily informational; it is not a persuasive message. It gives a rather rather prosaic statement that, "The Afghan National Army is protecting the citizens of Afghanistan." Part of the purpose might have been to counteract the fact that while the ANA is professional, its units' effectiveness are actually very uneven.[82] But the other part of the purpose was presumably to convey "protection", whereas the images of the two soldiers suggest hostility rather than protection of citizenry.[83] The choice of background pictures should have conveyed this dual message more effectively.[84]

Figure 10.14 is a leaflet aimed at educating the Afghan people concerning Article Twenty-Four of the Afghan Constitution, reproduced identically on both the front and back of the leaflet. Although the goal may be laudable, its practicality is questionable. As we have seen time and again with US PSYOP leaflets, the message is wordy and difficult for rural people to understand. Indeed, the interpretation and application of this constitutional article are difficult for any educated person to grasp completely. But most importantly, the majority of the Afghan population is more interested in the practicalities of their livelihood than in the Constitution's position on "liberty."

Figure 10.15 portrays an anti-opium poppy message and involves a very complex and controversial topic:

'The opium economy of Afghanistan is an intensely complex phenomenon. In the past, it reached deeply into the political structure, civil society and economy of the country. Spawned after decades of civil and military strife, it has chained a poor rural population—farmers, landless labour, small traders, women and children—to the mercy of domestic warlords and international crime syndicates that continue to dominate several areas in the south, north and east of the country. Dismantling the opium economy will be a long and complex process. *It cannot simply be done by military or authoritarian means.* That has been tried in the past, and was unsustainable. It must be done with the instruments of democracy, the rule of law, and development.'[85]

This is clearly a very contentious issue for the US to address in their PSYOP campaign because, as suggested in the quote above, Afghan peasant farmers have long cultivated opium for agronomic advantages and to support their family. It is estimated that Afghan farmers who grow opium make four times their former income.[86] While there is absolutely no argument concerning the

Figure 10.14: The Constitution of Afghanistan, AF09C08aaHB 1075

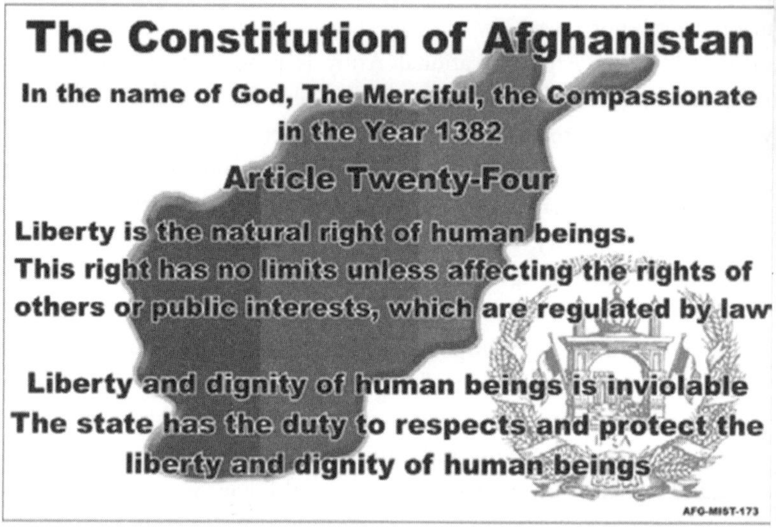

The Constitution of Afghanistan

In the name of God, The Merciful, the Compassionate
in the Year 1382

Article Twenty-Four

Liberty is the natural right of human beings.
This right has no limits unless affecting the rights of
others or public interests, which are regulated by law

Liberty and dignity of human beings is inviolable
The state has the duty to respects and protect the
liberty and dignity of human beings

AFG-MIST-173

BACK

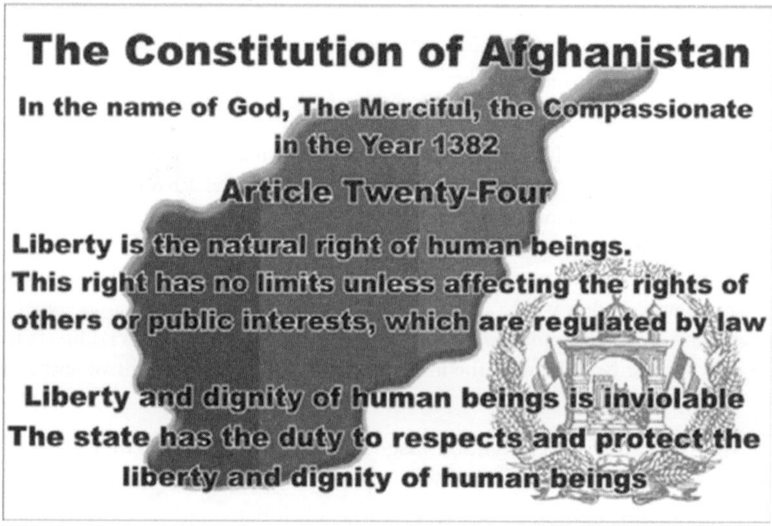

The Constitution of Afghanistan

In the name of God, The Merciful, the Compassionate
in the Year 1382

Article Twenty-Four

Liberty is the natural right of human beings.
This right has no limits unless affecting the rights of
others or public interests, which are regulated by law

Liberty and dignity of human beings is inviolable
The state has the duty to respects and protect the
liberty and dignity of human beings

Figure 10.15: Poppy eradication, AF09C09hhHB1487

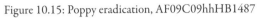

Figure 10.16: ANA continues to defeat Taliban

Mujahedeen's of the ANA are conducting military operations in your village. We are in search of the criminal Taliban who chose to harm and hurt the people we protect. During the operation, TB attacked the Mujahedeen. The ANA fought with courage and killed some of them. We apologize if we frighten you or your family in any way. The Taliban are here to cause death and destruction. The ANA will not let that happen. Thank you for your support.

disastrous effects that opium and heroin have on people's lives[87] and that the Taliban's taxes on opium production as well as trafficking increase their financial resources, opium cultivation is absolutely critical to hundreds of thousands of Afghan rural families' livelihood and existence. In fact, one the biggest concerns among rural Kandaharis interviewed in 2009 was the possibility of the eradication of their crops.[88] Hence, the leaflet's message presented in Figure 10.15 is not only extremely controversial and possibly counterproductive, it is also threatening, "The Islamic Government of Afghanistan will not tolerate the growing of Poppy...We will destroy your field." Afghan opium will not be eradicated by threatening people through IO messages. The tone of this message scarcely differs from many of the Taliban and other Afghan insurgents' intimidation campaigns, which have the effect of threatening and terrorizing the Afghan people.

E: Decrease support for insurgents

Figure 10.16 also has a title, not shown here, saying "Leave behind TB [Taliban] captured or killed." The front of the leaflet shows ANA soldiers firing at the Taliban with the message, the "ANA continues to defeat the Taliban." The back of the leaflet presents a lengthy message asking for Afghan villages to support the ANA fight against the Taliban, and includes an "apology" to the Afghan villagers if they were "frightened" by ANA actions against the Taliban.

The leaflet has several purposes. The request in the title that the Taliban leave their dead and fallen behind is a powerful message, especially considering Islamic burial traditions; and there is no reason given why this will support the declared purpose of "decreasing support for insurgents."

One question about the text superimposed on the front photo is whether it is a reflection of reality or else "spin," to use the term that General Petreaus' COIN guidance warns against.[89] In 2009–10, the Afghan National Army did not have a string of victories against the Taliban. In fact, during this period they rarely, if ever, played a forward role in fighting with the Taliban, and achieved few victories over the Taliban; that role was reserved for US or NATO forces, with the ANA serving as back-up force. A RAND study published during the relevant time period suggested:

> Evidence of operational proficiency is largely anecdotal, although there are some quantitative indicators. Numerous anecdotes attest to the operational capability of the ANA units. Quantitative ratings present a more restrained endorsement—for

Figure 10.17: Afghan National Police, AF09D02aaHB 1101

example, only seven of 42 infantry kandaks (17 per cent) have reached CM 1 [ability to operate totally independently]. Although progress is apparent, the ANA still has a long way to go.[90]

The back of the the leaflet (Figure 16) is an extremely wordy message that would only have a chance of being effective with literate Afghans. One interesting aspect of the message is that it refers to the ANA as "Mujahidin" (an

Arabic term meaning one who is engaged in jihad). The ANA implicitly describing their mission as a jihad has the potential of being ridiculed by the audience of the leaflet, because at the time the leaflet was deployed the ANA had not proven itself to be visibly effective or capable of confronting the Taliban without the support of foreign forces. This was a fact recognized by most Afghans. Moreover, jihad has a very specific meaning for Afghans and it is hard to argue that the ANA was actually involved in a "jihad".[91]

Figure 10.17 has a fairly simple and straightforward message: "[The] Afghan National Police serve and protect the people of the Government of the Islamic Republic of Afghanistan." The back of the leaflet suggest how to join the ANP.

The problem with this leaflet is again one of spin versus reality. Does the leaflet portray a reality that can be believed by the leaflet's Afghan target audience? Specifically, many Afghans view the ANP as an extremely corrupt and "extractive" organization. A US Institute of Peace "Special Report" published in 2009 (the same year as this leaflet was deployed) described the ANA as:

> riddled with corruption and generally unable to protect Afghan citizens, control crime, or deal with the growing insurgency... Beyond funding the Taliban, the explosion in Afghan narcotics production fueled widespread corruption in the Afghan government and police. Drug abuse by police officers became increasingly common as did other forms of criminal behavior.[92]

A variety of tribal leaders interviewed in Kandahar in 2008 and 2009 validated the USIP Special Report's findings concerning the ANP when they suggested that:

- They saw little difference between the conduct of ANP and Taliban in regards to extortion; some cited the ANP as being worse than the warlords of 1990s.
- The local ANP units continued to be viewed negatively by local residents and communities. Although some measures have purged violent and abusive officers, problems remain. Accusations of robbery, extortion, rape, drug trafficking, abductions and bribery were rampant.[93]

Whether or not these accusations could all be substantiated is in this context irrelevant; the perception among the locals was that the ANP were extractive predators, and in some cases the Taliban had exploited these grievances and bolstered their manpower and expanded recruitment efforts. Kandahari tribal leaders also suggested that serious consideration should have been given to the idea that ANA units should take the lead in protecting Kandahar City

Figure 10.18: Poster: The Taliban are cowards, AF09E02aaPS 1269

and other vital/critical areas. Although not all Kandaharis viewed the ANA positively, far more communities had pleasant experiences and respectful exchanges with ANA units when compared to the ANP, according to the leaders interviewed. The ANA had a reputation for fairness, respecting women, and resisting bribes.[94]

It is clearly difficult to produce and deploy a PSYOP or IO artifact asking for public support, much less recruiting, for an institution that is viewed as corrupt and held in disdain by the majority of a targeted audience. If it was even one of the most "hated" organizations in many areas of Afghanistan, then the "aspirational" purposes of the leaflet were maybe a step too far.

E/H: Decrease support for insurgents and their activities

Figure 10.18 is a PSYOP poster with the text: "The Taliban are cowards. They look and fight like women." And below, "The Taliban hide like women."

While there have been rumors of Taliban fighters being caught trying to travel clandestinely dressed in burqas, the authenticity of these rumors has been challenged, especially such images being posted on social media.[95] However, those who challenged these rumors were Pakistani media sources, and it is no secret that the Pakistani military and especially its Inter-Services Intelligence (ISI) directorate have supported, protected, and given refuge to the Afghan Taliban for decades.[96] This would suggest that the Pakistani media's attitude to the Taliban has to be questioned. The ISI have been accused of attempting to influence certain Pakistani media outlets and journalists, especially concerning issues of the Afghan Taliban and state-sponsored terrorism.[97]

The design of the poster in Figure 10.18 is cartoonish in style; but to those unused to graphic images, the sequence of action could be confusing. For a start, a Pashtun Afghan man seen dressing as a woman would seem devastating and a direct assault on Pashtunwali, bringing great shame (*sharam*) to the man's honor (*nang*), and extremely negative to his bravery and courage (*ghairat*).[98] But there is an additional implied slight on women as well: the poster suggests that Taliban are not actually very good fighters—they are as cowardly as women. So the audience should not respect their supposed bravery in the field. And a further accusation: they hide in a cowardly fashion, so the women's dress is synonymous with lack of courage.

Overall, the poster appears to be delivering a double negative of meaning. The Taliban are cowardly fighters; in fact so cowardly that they can be compared to women; and then they escape in the guise of women. This seems hardly the finest way to make a case against the insurgent Taliban.

Finally, Figure 10.19 has a similar objective but an opposite message: it derides the Taliban for their brutality, rather than their cowardice.

Part of this leaflet was originally designed by the author during the initial phase of OEF-A, and was discussed in the Preface of this book. The front of the leaflet carries the message, "The Taliban were annoying and beating with cables and whips. Do you want to receive the same fate or destiny?" While the picture seems self-evident, the message (at least in this English version) seems poorly worded. Is beating from the Taliban merely "annoying"? And why is the initial sentence in the past tense? Are the Taliban no longer practising such beatings? And if they are not, how will one experience this fate or destiny? Even allowing for mistranslations between the original text and this English version, the textual message is not as incisive as the image—a lost opportunity.

The back of the leaflet is a much better IO instrument, as the sequence of brutal images tell a powerful story; they are photos, suggesting authenticity;

Figure 10.19: Counter Taliban, AF09E01abHB1396

and the text is purely ancillary for anyone without a command of written language. The interrogative style draws in the reader to find answers. How can beating a person because of the length of his beard, or whipping a father or mother be Islamic? Also, the statements are personalized, referring to *my* father or mother.

Summary of US Afghan PSYOP and IO campaign in later phases of OEF-A

A critical analysis of the OEF-A leaflet campaign exposes a major shortfall in cultural awareness among leaflet preparers. It is important to say that not all the leaflets dropped during OEF-A were culturally deficient; however, a significant number ignored Afghan cultural nuances and thus demonstrated poor cross-cultural communication by US PSYOP and IO campaigns.

As noted, the US PSYOP and IO operations included artifacts other than leaflets, billboards, and posters: for example, radio broadcasts. Yet leaflets, billboards, and posters were the PSYOP/IO instruments that Afghans have seen most commonly over the course of the war. The radio messaging that we have heard seems more nuanced and effective than some other US PSYOP products; but even here the messages became problematic when the US attempted to address issues involving Islam or the Taliban's version of Islam, which many of them did. The US has little credibility in addressing these issues and many of the radio messages we have heard confirmed this.[99] The United States' inability to address issues of Islam has basically meant, as suggested above, that the US has had to concede a major portion of the IO and PSYOP battle space because this is an area, especially issues concerning the jihad, which is a primary focus of Taliban IO. And of course this is an issue not just of messaging; it is symptomatic of the US's struggle to justify their presence within this alien culture.

An IO or PSYOP campaign that relies heavily on leaflets, posters, or billboards suffers from the fact that it is geographically demanding to distribute them across the entire country, as the US did during the early phases of the war and also in later phases but not with the same frequency. Such instruments should be region-specific, reflecting the culture and lifestyle of that region, because Afghanistan is so culturally diverse. What works in one area, district, village or even valley will not necessarily work in an adjoining one. In fact, an IO artifact that may be effective in one area might be counterproductive in another because of ethno-linguistic, political, social, or other dynamics. For instance, some of the PSYOP and IO artifacts that we saw deployed in southern Afghanistan used photos or illustrations from the eastern regions of the country; it was evident that the people portrayed clearly did not come from the south. This can have a severe impact in how the message is viewed or interpreted by southern Afghans.

But the value of focusing on local concerns and matters is not only relevant with leaflets, posters, and billboards. Consider, for example, an ODA[100] IO initiative known as the "mobile mullah program" that used Afghan mullahs to address the Afghan population through a variety of means, including especially radio programs. Initial assessments suggested that the mobile mullah program suffered from a lack of willing participants, due to constant threats directed at the program. One mullah, for example, was fired for refusing to visit a particularly hostile village in Kandahar. Another mullah in the program who was to participate primarily in Kandahar was from Nangarhar and spoke a different dialect of Pashto, thus making it difficult to build trust among Kandahari Pashtuns who suspected his involvement with American PSYOP.[101] Hence, the mobile mullah program and network effectiveness suffered significantly because the vast majority of participating mullahs were perceived by Afghans as lackeys of the Americans. Moreover, the few mullahs who participated in the program were hesitant to travel to certain areas in fear of their life.[102]

The use of use local media can be very important. The US should have recruited local advocates, i.e. governors, district leaders, shura leaders, police chiefs, mullahs, who were involved with the local community and could present and could present Taliban counter-narratives.

Also, for many Afghans the leaflets' effectiveness relied heavily on people being able to read the textual messages. A stronger focus on selecting more appropriate visuals and more succinct texts would have helped convey messages in the rural battle space. "Less is more" is always the best message for punchy visual advertising or propoganda. For example, while serving as a COIN advisor to the Canadian Kandahar Task Force and spending considerable time in the Dand, Kandahar village, *Deh-e Bagh*—the initial village location of the Canadian's COIN operation *Kalay* (village) program[103]—during foot patrols, I witnessed on numerous occasions Afghans staring at the images of US PSYOP/IO leaflets which made no sense without the written message.[104] This was definitely an observation to relay to the troops.

Leaflets are in fact only rarely a productive format. They can easily be counterproductive if not effectively designed and vetted to reflect Afghan culture through a proper trial and review process. Moreover, many Afghans interviewed suggested they were afraid to hold onto them fearing the Taliban catching them with one. Finally and critically important, since the US lacked the linguistic competence to address Afghanis in their own language, they needed even more sophisticated skills to address them through images alone. And if they failed in this measure, they demonstrated publicly, in front of the insurgents, their inability to communicate why they were there at all.

Conclusion

The war in Afghanistan has always been a war of stories and narratives. The US has seemingly recognized this, with former Chairman of the Joint Chiefs of Staff Admiral Mike Mullen emphasizing the importance of strategic communication in an era where "the lines between strategic, operational and tactical are blurred beyond distinction."[105] However, the US military and the Afghan government have continually failed to offer a credible narrative or stories that resonate with the Afghan people. This has been the basic failing of the United States and allies' operations in Afghanistan, in my opinion. The Taliban, on the other hand, have crafted a strong, simple, and culturally relevant IO campaign to energize, coerce, and control the Afghan populace, fully recognizing that perceptions of strength and progress have always been crucial to determining the trust and confidence of Afghanistan's tribes and power brokers. The Taliban fluency in the Afghan linguistic and cultural space, in addition, has afforded them the opportunity to produce messages that resonate emotionally and shape the responses of their target audience, especially rural Pashtuns.

Above, we assessed a wide variety of US PSYOP/IO leaflets, posters, and billboards, and few of these products had enough substance to present a story that would resonate with the Afghan population. It is instructive to compare these leaflets to the only Taliban leaflet we know of and presented in Figure 2.2 (Chapter 2). This leaflet included enough vernacular text to offer an explicit story which would clearly resonate with the rural Afghan population.

In 2009 the author was invited to address a large meeting of professional personnel from military, intelligence, and diplomatic organizations intimately involved in US PSYOP and information operations in Afghanistan. At the conclusion of my presentation concerning Taliban IO, I asked the participants to name the main themes, stories, or narratives of their efforts in Afghanistan; to my utter disbelief, the large and senior crowd went silent. They could not offer me a *single* PSYOP or IO theme that they thought was critical to US efforts in Afghanistan. This vividly demonstrated to me that our efforts in Afghanistan were destined for failure. How could we succeed in our objectives if we did not have a single meaningful story to relate to the Afghan people as to why we had invaded and occupied their country?

In Iraq and especially Afghanistan, the US military was given the mission of persuading and influencing foreign audiences, but struggled to achieve viable and measurable success. Christopher Lamb's critique of the PSYOP operations of OEF-A and Operation Iraqi Freedom cited four main problems with PSYOP performance: first, the lack of national-level themes to guide message formulation; second, a slow product approval process that rendered some products irrelevant; third, questionable product quality with uncertain effects; and fourth, an overall lack of resources, including insufficient force structure.[106] Each of these four problems plagued PSYOP and IO personnel throughout OEF-A. This resulted, in part, in a failed persuasion campaign that targeted both short- and long-term Afghan behavior. Behavior psychologists advise that there is more success found in short-term persuasive campaigns than long-term, primarily because long-term persuasion requires logical versus emotional messages.[107] Human behavior pivots on reward cues and can change quickly, based on emotional triggers. Emotional arguments are more effective because most people want short-term gratification. Long-term persuasion efforts require an established relationship or at least a sophisticated understanding between the message transmitter (PSYOP/IO personnel) and receiver (Afghan target population).[108] A basic and fundamental misunderstanding of the Afghan target audience marred the US PSYOP and IO campaign. As has been suggested several times, the US is excellent at producing messages and pursuing strategies that make sense to those of similar language and culture, but not to an audience used to oral rather than written language, and Islamic values rather than military values.

All of Lamb's suggested problems could have been at least partially solved in Afghanistan if the Department of Defense (DoD) had invested heavily during the early stages of the war in making PSYOP and IO leaders and personnel competent speakers of the relevant target languages, and knowledgeable of about the cultural, political, social, and historical aspects of Afghanistan. Later in the war, the expansion of the military's Foreign and Regional Area Officers Program brought an improvement in the US military's knowledge of Afghan cultures and languages; but the damage caused by earlier uninformed PSYOP/IO personnel could not be overcome. Meanwhile, the Taliban dominated the strategic communication battle space and created a discourse due to their language and cultural familiarity, speed of information dissemination, and insider knowledge of how to conduct their information operations.

A coordinated IO campaign in Afghanistan would have had to account for the various tiers and factions within the insurgent network and carefully craft its message toward the demographics of particular areas. The local politics and local disposition of the people in an area are very important. With any IO campaign, a nuanced picture of the local tribal, political, and anthropological dynamics is very important. Withput a clearly developed picture, the US should have stuck to simple and clear messages that resonated especially within rural, Pashtun culture. The US should have used very narrow, simple, but resonating themes, filtered through local Pashtuns.

Possibly most damning for US information operations was the fact the US and their PSYOP and IO personnel did not have an adequate understanding of the Afghan discourse or narrative in their community context. As was argued in Chapters 1 and 2, narratives are a system of cognitive standards that allow messages to be interpreted. Narratives are the *means* by which humans interpret and prioritize information. Hence, a narrative becomes a lens through which people view their world; it can represent foundation beliefs that are often told and recalled as stories. Dupree's seminal work on Afghanistan suggests that such "framing" instruments performed a variety of significant functions to include "social control," where individuals are told by illustration what they should or should not do and what rewards or penalties they will incur for not following these norms.[109] This discourse or narrative primarily involved the Afghans' view of a *defensive jihad* and the Afghans' perceived obligation to support this defense of Islam and the Afghan way of life.

Nearly all Taliban communication—night letters (Chapter 5), sermons in mosques, public announcements, and the critical oral tradition (Chapter 2)—works as a cohesive whole to create an all-encompassing discourse of jihad or religious struggle. As we saw in earlier chapters and will be discussed in depth in the concluding chapter, the Taliban narrative and stories supporting it included:

1. Afghans and their religion/way-of-life are under attack by the international community, which is led by the United States.
2. Only the Taliban are fighting the oppressors of Islam.
3. If you are not supporting the Taliban, then you are supporting the infidel oppressors and apostates.
4. Afghans, as Muslims, must join with the Taliban to evict the invading army so that Shar'iah law can be re-established under the Islamic Emirate of Afghanistan (i.e. the Taliban government).

The US basically had to surrender to Taliban dominance within this discourse, meaning that the US efforts essentially refused to accept the cultural reality, especially of the Afghan peasant mental space, within which the US had to do battle in order to compete in the real world of ideas in rural

Afghanistan. And for a rural counter-insurgency this was devastating, because IO messages which did not fit within this discourse or narrative of how the struggle in Afghanistan was perceived by the peasant villager, who we earlier argued was the center of gravity of the war, were dismissed as nonsensical. The US could not credibly message in the jihadi narrative, for its messages were secular; so for the most part their messages were rejected as meaningless.

In order to message effectively within this discourse or message frame, four elements would have to be taken on board:

1. Language manipulation using Dari, Pashto, Urdu, and Arabic to convey certain emotions and select/mobilize target audiences.
2. Exploiting collective memory themes to evoke a strong sense of nationalism, an innate characteristic, as we saw earlier in Taliban messaging.
3. The critical role of the warrior poet in shaping respected cultural values as we saw in Chapter 7.
4. The nature of Pashtun folk tale transmission and the value system it reflects in cultural messaging.

But is it actually possible or pragmatic to adopt another country's culture to this degree?[110]

11

CONCLUSIONS

As we have seen throughout the previous chapters, the Taliban maintain simple objectives in their strategic communication, such as "forcing the invaders to withdraw" and re-establishing Shar'iah throughout Afghanistan. The objectives remain simple, for both the Taliban and other Afghan insurgent groups such as HIG, even if to Western perceptions the messages themselves look complex. *In fact, it is these simple objectives that have helped Afghan insurgents avoid convoluted messaging campaigns; they know that their target audience are typically rural, more adept in spoken than written communication, and conflict-fatigued.* The simplicity of their strategic aims was key to to their successes early on after their political creation in 1994, when they vowed to accomplish (and largely achieved) two highly desired objectives: establishing security and instilling law and order through swift Islamic-based justice.[1]

The Taliban's messaging spectrum and narrative universe is finite. The number of objectives, messages, and narratives can be identified and framed within a given outline. The Taliban are able to draw upon this information–message–narrative treasure chest and "plug it in" to the range of delivery systems available to them. Despite early misunderstandings of some technology, such as cell phones and the internet, the resurgent Taliban and other Afghan insurgent groups have keenly adopted modern communication and technology to their advantage. Video productions, internet web pages, text messaging, Twitter, Bluetooth dissemination of audio and video files are some of the modern delivery systems the Taliban now use to spread their views and statements, as we have seen, in addition to DVDs and CDs.

However, despite an aggressive effort from Afghan insurgent groups to exert control over territory, groups like the Taliban still lack the manpower and material needed to impose a large-scale occupation of territory inside Afghanistan. In 2008, the International Crisis Group suggested that the Taliban "still puts out contradictory messages that indicate internal rifts and the diffuse nature of the insurgency."[2]

The Taliban have been greatly aided in spreading their messages by the lack of significant government counter-attacks and the proliferation of jihadist messages through local and international media outlets. The Taliban have capitalized on this groundswell by producing multilingual websites as well as numerous militant publications that enable the Afghan insurgents to operate as a competitor for the "hearts and minds" in the general IO battle space.

The basic thesis of this book is that the war in Afghanistan represents a battle of narratives, and that the Taliban have been extremely successful in promoting a message to the Afghan people and the international community that the present as well as the future are theirs. As suggested above, the group has masterfully and consistently spread strong, simple, and culturally appropriate storylines that appeal to the deeply religious, cultural, and political sensibilities of tribal rural and many urban Afghans. Meanwhile, the Taliban have also strengthened their claim to legitimacy and demonstrated their potential for governance by creating administrative and legal bodies that now easily outperform the inefficient, corrupt, or absent institutions of the Kabul government. Finally, the Taliban has refocused its operations on the ground to demonstrate relentless resolve toward threatening Afghanistan's capital and surrounding areas, while also tempering and reforming their behavior toward Afghan villagers who have always been critical of the Taliban's brutal tactics and strict social restrictions. All these approaches combined have revealed that the Taliban are now telling all their various audiences that their return to power is imminent after US combat troops withdraw from Afghanistan, and that they will implement an Islamic regime that is inclusive and tolerant of all Afghans.

While the US military and the Afghan government have consistently failed to present a competitive narrative to the Afghan people since the rise of the Taliban insurgency, the chance to turn the tide has now expired. Nevertheless, as the United States prepares to draw down its forces and return the complete control of Afghanistan to its government and military, the time and the opportunity have never been more appropriate for the *Afghan government* to create a strong narrative of its own. After all, the storyline of the Taliban is full of inconsistencies and flaws that signal weaknesses in the group's true ability to overcome the Afghan government and the security forces, to remain a cohesive organization, and to move beyond their past brutality to form a government that is moderate and truly representative of the most commonly-held Afghan values. For Afghanistan to move forward, the government must focus on themes of real economic development and job creation, nationalism, reconciliation, unity, and hope; this could send a strong message that the Afghan government will someday provide a stable, peaceful, and prosperous future for its country.

In the introductory chapter of this book, a range of questions were raised that we believed would be useful in assessing the utility of Taliban narratives, such as:

1. Do Taliban narratives and stories provide an insight into the conceptual metaphors and other rhetorical techniques that are common in Afghanistan?
2. Does an analysis of Taliban narratives reveal some of the major contours of the Afghan/Taliban (Pashtun) worldview?

The answer to both of the questions as suggested by the data and analyses presented in this book posed above is "yes." For example, consider the Taliban's information operations and narratives in the important province of Kandahar (basically the Taliban's home province), where they address a wide variety of issues including the important dynamic of civilian casualties. And more often than not, these messages are grounded in language and terms that Kandaharis thoroughly understand and can relate to. The use of historical examples, poems, and chants—to name but a few—that Afghans can easily relate to is the modus operandi of Taliban information operations. The Taliban also have a basic message that they abhor civilian casualties and "collateral damage," but from their perspective this is less important ultimately than repelling the "crusaders" and "infidels" who want to destroy Islam and Afghan life.

It is important to note that many Afghans believe that the US is responsible for most civilian casualties in southern Afghanistan. Yet all reputable studies of civilian casualties suggest that the Taliban are responsible for the vast majority of civilian deaths.[3] The Taliban's messages to the Kandaharis suggest a very different story. For example, consider the terrible evening attack in Kandahar that killed dozens of people in the month of Ramadan in 2009; it was clearly carried out by the Taliban, according to knowledgeable American sources on the ground. And yet numerous interviews with Afghans reveal that they believe that the Americans carried out most of the attacks that caused civilian deaths. In regards to the Ramadan massacre of 2009, interviews clearly suggested that Afghans believe that US forces carried out the attack: they believe that a plane dropped a bomb or a cruise missile that killed the innocent civilians. When asked why they think so, the Afghans interviewed provided several reasons:

1. Some people "saw" a US plane flying over the area during the time of the massacre.
2. Some people saw a "big rocket with flames behind it," probably fired from the US base at the Kandahar Air Field (KAF).
3. They argued that the US and Kabul helped pay families of the dead, proving that the US was responsible for the civilian deaths.
4. No parts of a truck/tanker (the truck bomb that US and Kabul believe was the perpetrator of the attack) were found to prove it was a tanker loaded with explosives.
5. The Taliban did not claim responsibility for it.[4]

These interviews, in part, clearly demonstrate how Taliban messaging can have an impact that extends far beyond the initial message or story. That is, Taliban messaging can significantly impact on the perceptions of the Afghan population. As suggested by the numerous studies cited in Chapter 1, stories and narratives have a tremendous impact on how people view their environment, and this could be one explanation as to why Kandaharis have this seemingly incorrect view of US military actions.

Similarly many Afghans believe that the assassinations of prominent tribal elders and influential government officials who have considerable support among the public are the work of the US. For example, Abdul Majeed Babai, a famous Afghan poet and prominent figure in Kandahar, as well as head of the culture department, was assassinated in February 2010 while he was walking to his office.[5] Although most evidence suggested a Taliban assassination, his family believes that the Taliban did not carry out this attack because the Taliban went to his *Janazah* (ceremony or gathering after the funeral ceremony) and shared their condolences with his family. The Taliban also explicitly rejected any involvement in his killing.

According to interviews, there are other interesting conspiracy theories and counter-narratives concerning the US[6] that we believe are significantly influenced by the repetition of Taliban narratives and stories; for instance:

• Many Kandaharis, including many who are educated, believe that the 9/11 attacks were a plot by the US to give an excuse to expand its domination in the world.

- People believe that the US has massacred people in numerous Afghan villages. For example, one interviewee suggested that the US arrested around 160 people in Shahwalikot district and had "bags (hoods) placed over their heads." Many were later released (around 130, according to the interviewee), but the rest were killed ("blown up") while they were imprisoned in a house/room controlled by the Americans.
- Another interviewee suggested that when US forces come into an Afghan village, they "red stamp doors and later carry out raids during nights targeting these houses with killer dogs." We found this story was very common among students at schools—especially girls' schools in Kandahar. We found it surprising that even Afghan educated women's perceptions were influenced by Taliban propaganda.

This notion of messaging and narratives impacting on a person's perceptions, such as those presented above, is supported by those studies that posit that "information" such as that portrayed through Taliban messaging can impact on a person's motivations, judgment, attention, and thoughts.[7] "People use narratives to understand how their world works."[8]

Other discussions with Kandahar residents suggested that some mullahs in the city mosques and many mullahs in the village mosques were preaching against the government and in defense of the Taliban. We did not find this overly surprising because we recognized that the Taliban in the south got the mullahs to coordinate with their weekly messages, especially at *khutba* (Friday sermons and prayers).[9] One interviewee recalled a mullah in a mosque just a block away from UNAMA preaching against the Afghan government and the Americans. He also suggested that a mullah preaching a Friday prayer suddenly cried out that "yellow and white Taliban are fighting and martyring themselves for their religion"; he then said, "God swears that this is the time of jihad because red infidels have captured our soil."[10]

The examples above suggest that the Taliban are well aware that some of the most important messaging techniques are person-to-person interactions and whisper campaigns. Taliban mullahs play a prominent role in these techniques, and since religious and cultural themes are powerful among the public, the Taliban play this fact to the maximum. This is a testament to the success of the Taliban's *shabnamah*, *taranas*, poetry, circulars, radio messages, text messages, social media, and websites. Moreover, slickly produced DVDs showing interviews with Taliban commanders, battle footage, and misdeeds carried out by foreign forces and the Afghan government are widely available for sale in Afghanistan's urban cities and bazaars.

A summary of the stories, themes and vocabulary used by the Taliban

The Taliban stories

The ultimate goal of the Taliban since the US invasion has been the discrediting and removal of foreign forces from Afghanistan and the re-establishment of the Islamic Emirate of Afghanistan under Taliban rule. Associated with this narrative is the Taliban's consistent position over the years that they will never negotiate or reconcile until the foreign forces leave the country: "I will say very clearly, if they substitute their law with Islamic law and push out non-Afghan troops from our country, after this we will start negotiations with the government."[11] This has been a major component of their stories and narratives since 2002. What has *not* been part of their stories, however, has been a clear plan of governance for a future Afghanistan, other than the imposition of Shar'iah law.[12]

A second component of Taliban stories is their clear intention to confront and defeat the foreign, infidel invaders, just as their forefathers did earlier with the English and Soviets. The past history of Afghanistan is an important theme that the Taliban use for recruitment as well as to increase their popular support. We saw this explicitly in the Taliban leaflet presented in Chapter 2 (Figure 2.2). The inability or failure of the British and Soviet forces to conquer or subjugate Afghanistan is a common theme that is often emphasized: that the US and the international Coalition will share the same fate as those who invaded Afghanistan earlier. The Taliban's view of their own invincibility portrays the conflict as not one that the US will inevitably lose in the future, but one that they have already lost. Following Ramadan in 2008, Mullah Omar even urged the foreign forces to leave Afghanistan because he argued that in seven years they had failed to establish an effective government or make any significant progress.[13] In addition, the Taliban stories suggest that the longer the conflict draws on, the better off their fighting forces will become. For example, "the Mujahidin are becoming stronger by the passing days, and are gaining more experience in the fields of military, media, social issues and others."[14] They complement this sentiment with their belief that Afghanistan has never been, and in fact cannot be, conquered. Moreover, the Taliban view the conflict as a cosmic battle between "the just and unjust" that they *must* win; losing is not an option.[15]

A third component of Taliban stories is that they are selfless heroes who will do anything to protect Afghanistan from foreign infidels and Afghan apostates who are committed to destroying Afghanistan and the Afghans' way of life. Part of this trope is that the Taliban are patient, whereas the US and NATO's attributes are impatience and vanity. They speak of fighting for generations as an honor and a reward from Allah. The Taliban have ascribed *shaheed*, or martyrdom, to any of their fighters killed in combat against international or Afghan government forces, not just those who commit suicide bombings.

A fourth component of Taliban stories, of absolutely critical importance, relates to Islam and the supreme obligation of every Afghan to join, or at least support, their righteous jihad.[16] As we saw above and in numerous Taliban IO artifacts, Islam plays a central and explicit role in Taliban stories. Enfolding the Taliban's message in religion allows them to attract support from a variety of sources. Not only does it rally the Muslims of Afghanistan to their banner, but also perhaps more importantly it crosses borders and appeals to the international Muslim *Ummah*. By suggesting there is a threat against Islam, the Taliban are able to call for a defensive jihad that obliges all Muslims to support them against the international forces. As stated above, we conceive of the Taliban's war as basically an insurgency wrapped in the narrative of a jihad. The Taliban view themselves as fighting a noble battle against *fassād-e edāri* (administrative corruption), *fassād-e akhlāqī* (moral corruption), occupation (*eshghāl*), and oppression (*zolm*).

A fifth element of Taliban stories is the blatant corruption of the apostate Kabul government. Questioning the legitimacy of the Karzai government (and Ghani government) is also a common theme of Taliban stories. Hence the Kabul regimes are often portrayed as a puppet of the United States and the West. One statement compared the Karzai regime to past controversial regimes: "No difference between Shah Shuja, Babrak Karmal, and the rulers of the present Kabul administration. It is clear that all are equal when it comes to national and Islamic betrayal and treason and in their servitude to the interests of the occupiers and colonists." The statement goes further to derail the elections, declaring them to be nothing but a lie with the outcomes predetermined by the United States. It says these elected rulers are only figureheads and the power of action and decision lies in Washington; the expectation that these rulers could do anything other than what is in the interest of the US is pointless.[17] A statement by the late Mullah Omar not only urged employees of the Afghan government to stop serving the Afghan government and the occupation, but also threatened to kill any who rejected his warning.[18] This was the narrative that we saw in a number of the night letters assessed in Chapter 5. This sentiment, coupled with the rise of the Taliban's shadow governments and its ability to provide justice, further helps give their propaganda credence. Moreover, the Taliban have implemented Hezbollah-type strategies in areas of eastern Afghanistan and the south. That is, the Taliban offer social services that the government has for years failed to do. This was seen most clearly in their makeshift justice systems coordinated under shadow governments that provided "justice" in a matter of hours. During Afghanistan field research, the author also heard stories of the Taliban distributing medical supplies to villagers in need.[19] Such a practice undermined the US and Kabul policies of attempting to "impose" the legitimacy of the Afghan government on the people in these areas.

A sixth component of Afghan stories is the corruption of the ANSF, and especially the Afghan National Police (ANP). Local residents and communities viewed many local ANP units that we witnessed in southern Afghanistan very negatively.[20] Although some measures purged some violent and abusive officers, problems remained. Accusations of robbery, extortion, rape, drug trafficking, abductions, and bribery were rampant. Whether or not all these accusations could be substantiated was basically irrelevant; the perception among the local Afghan population was that the ANP were predators, and the Taliban exploited these grievances, bolstered their manpower, and expanded recruitment efforts. Corruption and the incapacity of local forces also make the population receptive to Taliban messages couched in local cultural terms. The Taliban play upon the suspicions and fears of the Afghan population by questioning the motives of the international forces as well as the Kabul government. Their stories portray the international military forces as imperialist invaders of Afghanistan with colonialist ambitions. Even immediately after the attacks of 11 September, statements attributed to Mullah Omar questioned the motives of the United States: "The United States' target is not Osama but the Taliban. The trouble started when we refused to cooperate with an American company for the gas pipeline project from Turkmenistan to Pakistan."[21] Other Taliban statements have mirrored this view, such as, "the occupying enemy does not want negotiations that'll end with Afghanistan's freedom and an end of the occupation, but they want negotiations that'll guarantee them the everlasting dirty occupation of Afghanistan."[22] The Taliban then take the threat one step further and imply that the United States' intentions are not only directed at Afghanistan but toward the entire region. For example, "The plans for expansionist imperialism in the region are being applied, and these plans have been facilitated in the name of economic assistance";[23] and "it is a strategy of colonialism aimed at securing interests of the American capitalists and it seems America has vast and protracted but wicked and hostile plans not only for Afghanistan but for the whole region."[24] They also described the metaphorical Global War on Terror (GWOT) as "imperialistic terminology" that the US used to justify its actions.

A seventh and extremely important component of the Taliban's narratives and stories is the collateral damage created by the international forces and the ANSF. The Taliban are well aware of the fact that if indirect fire or an errant bomb by the US or ANSF or their allies kills an innocent woman or child, that village is lost to Kabul forever. Such deaths play directly into Pashtunwali and the revenge society found throughout Afghanistan. In fact, it can be argued that a major combat strategy of the Taliban has been to "force" the Americans and others to make such mistakes:

Particularly problematic has been the careless use of U.S. air power, which has killed scores of civilians, and the apparent lack of sensitivity by U.S. troops to local perceptions, laws and customs. According to reports in the Afghan press, "U.S. Special Forces, during routine sweeps of Afghan villages searching for weapons and members of resistance groups, have physically abused villagers, damaged personal property, and subjected women to body searches, a major affront on a family's honor."[25] UN officials have commented that "This doesn't help us at all ... the people are basically pro-America. They want U.S. forces to be here. But American soldiers are not very culturally sensitive. It's hardly surprising that Afghans get angry when the Americans turn up and kick their doors in."[26]

There have been multiple episodes of U.S. and NATO counterinsurgency actions that have resulted in the death and injury of Afghan innocents. The implications of this are profound.[27] As suggested by the International Crisis Group (ICG) "when a child is killed in one of these villages, that village is lost for 100 years. These places run on revenge."[28]

Collateral damage and civilian casualties are common themes in the Taliban stories that further attempt to discredit the international military forces. Civilian deaths carry enormous repercussions, especially when considering the importance of honor and revenge within Pashtun and Afghan society in general. It is often stated that one innocent death creates ten future enemies. The Taliban aims to turn the Coalition into enemies by making provocative statements that incite these base ideals. For example, "the deceiver wants to carry out big bloody bombings in the name of martyrdom operations, in places of crowdedness like religious centers, and mosques and the likes,"[29] or "thousands of innocent Afghans have been killed in Nangarhar, Urozgan, Herat, Fara, Kunduz and Paktya provinces as a result of American and NATO blind bombardment."[30] The crossing of cultural boundaries is also an important aspect of collateral damage stories. For instance, international forces primarily consist of men and when they search houses or areas that are reserved for women in *purda* or physically search women themselves, it is a major cultural faux pas and creates reactive animosity among the Afghan population (again, see Figure 2.2 for an explicit example).

Finally, many Taliban stories are stories of intimidation and threat. Here the Taliban warn Afghans to join their jihad and quit working for or associating with the infidel Americans and the apostate Afghan government. A common trope of these stories is that "the Americans will not always be there" to protect those who choose to cooperate. Such stories deal with a litany of issues, such as the education of girls, the role of women (or lack thereof) in society, and many others.

Taliban themes and vocabulary

While analyzed in detail in earlier chapters, below we summarize the main themes and the vocabulary used by the Taliban in their messages and stories in a concluding effort to define the group's narratives and demonstrate how they attempt to influence or control the behavior of its primary indigenous audience, the rural Pashtuns, by appealing to their religion, culture, and tradition. Based on the data and analyses presented in previous chapters, the following tables summarize the main themes used by the Taliban (Table 11.1) and the most important vocabulary and its symbolism found in their messaging and narratives (Table 11.2).

Table 11.2 offers a list of terms used by the Taliban, which are very different from the Western meaning of these words.

In earlier chapters the importance of Afghan collective memory was analyzed; Table 11.1 presents a similar and valuable concept that is critical in assessing information operations in Afghanistan, especially those campaigns aimed at Afghan Pashtuns: the notion that Pashtuns represent a *memory-based society*. For example, for the average Pashtun the war against the Soviets is still very present in their minds, and the Afghan-Anglo wars are equally vivid; so it is not unusual to hear Americans referred to as both "Soviets" and "British." Pashtuns have a tendency to perpetuate memories of battles and inter-tribal or inter-clan fights and disputes. The relationship between the different sub-tribes and clans within the Pashtun confederacy as well as the relationship between the Pashtuns and other ethnic groups is thus affected importantly by past events.

Table 11.1: Themes used in Taliban narratives and stories

Theme	*Detail/Explanation*
Pashtunwali (*badal* and *izzat*)[31]	Refers to the Pashtun code of conduct used across Afghanistan. It is more than a set of rules to follow: it enables the Pashtuns to exist as a group and perpetuate their tribal structure. Its main concepts are: *badal* (revenge or retaliation), *nenawati* (protection or mediation), and *melmastia* (hospitality). The Taliban rely mainly on the concept of *badal* and *izzat* for the group's narrative. *Izzat* means honor, and Pashtuns follow the Pashtunwali to maintain their honor and resolve conflicts.
Historical events/Appeals to Pashtuns as a memory-based society	The Taliban draw upon the fact that the Pashtuns are a memory-based society. By systematically referring to the British and Soviet invasions when describing the US-led Coalition and the collateral damage caused by the Coalition forces, the Taliban ensure that the group will appeal to the population and thereby alter their interaction with foreign security forces or aid workers.
Religious rhetoric	The Taliban use extensively religious references to build their narrative. The group see the war against the US-led Coalition as a war of religion, which is expressed as a cosmic battle between the just and unjust. The role of Muslims is to reject the infidels and cooperate with the holy fighters, and Afghans have an obligation to join the jihad. The Taliban also use religious rhetoric to control the Afghans' behavior by designating what is Islamic or un-Islamic.

The Taliban, being part of this Pashtun society, are well aware of the attachment that Pashtuns and Afghans in general feel to the past. Consequently, the Taliban use this to their advantage, as can be seen in many of their information operation artifacts. In the *shabnamah*, for example, the Taliban sometimes make references to the Soviet invasion: "[A]s we and you rose against the Russian[s] with great manliness and passion, and with great fervor we extinguished their army from Afghanistan."[32] The Taliban represent the jihad

Table 11.2: Terms used in Taliban narratives and stories

Terms	Symbolism
Honor and manhood (*izzat*)	The Pashtuns follow Pashtunwali to maintain their honor, which is defined as the ability to control *zar* (gold), *zan* (women), *zamin* (land).[33] For the Taliban, honor and manhood are partly but importantly expressed by Afghans' willingness to collaborate with the Taliban fighters, join the jihad, seek revenge against the Coalition forces and reject any influence that the Taliban considers un-Islamic.
Revenge (*badal*)	According to Pashtunwali, in the case of murder or an offence to a woman, the family, clan and tribe are responsible for taking revenge by killing the offender or someone in his family, clan or tribe. The responsibility for implementing *badal* is collective, as is the punishment of the offender and his people. The Taliban uses the concept of revenge to push Afghan people to join the fight against the Coalition forces, as a result of the latter's un-Islamic influence and practices, aggression on the Afghans' holy land and religion, and collateral damage.
Jihad	The Taliban has a particular and puritanical interpretation of the Qur'an: for the Taliban, armed jihad is the most important duty for the Muslim and it is the only response in the context of the war. In the Qur'an, there are two types of jihad: the "greater jihad" which is the personal striving that Muslims go through to follow the way of God; and the "lesser jihad" which refers to the armed action that Muslims are allowed to take only after the authorization of a religious leader.
Mujahidin	This refers to fighters in a holy war or jihad. The term usually alludes to the Afghan resistance fighters who fought the Soviets. The Taliban call their fighters Mujahidin and believe that they serve as an example that the Afghan people should follow.
Infidels	In Taliban messaging, they refer to the security forces (foreign and Afghan) and foreign humanitarian workers as infidels and apostates.
Christian crusaders	The Coalition forces.
Slaves	Usually refers to the Afghan government and Afghan security forces, and also to any Afghan who collaborates or interacts with the infidels.

Personal and collective responsibility	The notion of collective responsibility is important in *badal*. Individuals have to comply with Pashtunwali or else they will expose their family or clan to the revenge of the person they offended. When the Taliban threaten an individual, they consider that the punishment or retaliation could be applied to the entire family or village. Also, once a person or village has been warned, that person is responsible for his own life. And if he gets hurt or killed by the Taliban, the person or his family has no right to complain.

against the US-led Coalition as a repetition of the jihad against the Soviets. There is little doubt that the resistance against the Soviet invasion was massive and is still present in the memories of many Afghans. This is not only because of the atrocities resulting from the war of attrition that the Soviets fought against the Afghan insurgency, but also because of the memories of past Afghan victories against invading and occupying forces. The Taliban use this reference strategically, hoping that it will encourage people to join the jihad and again defend their country from "infidel invaders." This is reinforced by the vocabulary used to designate the Coalition forces as congruent to the Soviets. As suggested above, the Taliban regularly refer to the US as "invaders," which strengthens the link between the Soviet invasion and American-led occupation of their country.

As suggested above, the Taliban also play on this aspect of Pashtun society when they denounce collateral damage caused by the Coalition forces: "[M]any time[s] they [Coalition forces] have placed the civilian areas under attack, and have killed a large number of our defenseless people including men, women, children, and have caused calamity and scar[s] [...] to many families [...] the filthy hands of the Christian invaders have been contaminated with our people's innocent blood."[34] The Taliban's narrative is aimed at influencing, arguably even controlling, the population's behavior by feeding propaganda through the loss of innocent lives caused by the "invaders." This ensures that people will remember these events and will consequently alter their interactions with foreign forces and workers. The Taliban, as suggested above, also use collateral damage to appeal to the most important aspect of Pashtun culture: Pashtunwali, and more specifically *badal* or revenge.

The information strategy of the Taliban was designed to degrade the will of the US Coalition to fight by remaining in the field despite exhaustive efforts to remove them by the Coalition. For the Taliban to remain in the field, support from the Afghan populations and external support from Arab and Pakistani populations was necessary. This support was cultivated through information campaigns directed at the Afghan people and at Arabs and Pakistanis. To succeed, the Taliban were adept at communicating with the Afghan population, and derived active or at least passive support from their local population. To achieve this, the Taliban needed a clear, concise "political objective, based on firm moral and ideological grounds that can be understood and accepted by the majority as the overriding 'cause' of the insurgency, desirable in itself and worthy of any sacrifice."[35]

The key to success for the Taliban lay in its ability to craft a resonant and persistent narrative in the minds of the Afghan and external populations. In 2005–6, the Taliban made information operations their main effort. Their campaign repeated five simple slogans in combination with the major themes presented in Table 11.1:

- Our party, the Taliban
- Our people and nation, the Pashtun
- Our economy
- Our constitution, the Shar'iah
- Our form of government, the Emirate

These simple slogans provided the Taliban with a political platform that spoke to the norms and apprehensions of their audience. They spoke to the themes of Pashtun nationalism, economic independence, and a deep-seated paranoia at foreign interference. "The Taliban's key strength mirrored the Coalition's key weakness—the capacity to synchronize physical activity in support of a unified information strategy."[36]

An effective method for communicating with the Afghan population is through direct intimidation. Chapter 5 described how night letters, a popular Taliban means of direct communication with the target Afghan audience to convey the insurgent narrative, dwelled on:

- Characterizing the Coalition as foreign invaders.
- Characterizing the Karzai or Kabul regime as a "puppet" of the West.
- Characterizing the Coalition as Crusaders.
- Glorifying the martyrdom concept.
- Saving the honor of the Afghan people.
- Prohibition against any Afghan supporting the enemy.

The first three themes are particularly problematic for the US and its Coalition because they are part of a narrative based on the reality of Afghan modern history. At least two generations of Afghans have lived in an Afghanistan destabilized by foreign influence and "puppet" governance, and the memory of the Soviet and Anglo-Afghan wars are not too remote to remain alive in oral folklore, as suggested above.

The Taliban also capitalize on the perceived injustices done to Muslims by the United States. The US detention center at Guantanamo Bay is a popular subject of Taliban propaganda, often with alleged letters from Taliban prisoners in Guantanamo appearing in popular Taliban magazines, as well as numerous poems and songs.[37]

Summary of Taliban information targets

The Taliban know the audience for their messages well. The two primary pillars of Taliban messages, as suggested above, have been Islamic jihad and Pashtunwali, and very often they are intertwined, so that the Pashtun custom of sanctuary is occasionally referred to as a Muslim custom. The two themes used to be mentioned in equal measure before the American-led invasion, but now Islam and jihad are given primacy in garnering support, whereas "Afghanness" or Pashtunwali take a back seat.

Almost all of the original Taliban leadership was Pashtun, with much of the original senior leadership of the Quetta Shura coming from the large Ghilzai tribe.[38] Inter-Pashtun tribal politics play into much of the Taliban's rhetoric, especially against the Karzai government. Clan and tribal politics in Afghanistan have been well analyzed in other works, but it is important to emphasize the rivalry between the late Mullah Omar's more numerous Ghilzai tribe and ex-President Karzai's more elite Durrani tribe. The modern origins of the conflict lie in the eighteenth century, when the Ghilzai briefly held power in Afghanistan, conquering as far as Isfahan in Persia, before the Durrani supplanted them as hereditary kings of Afghanistan.[39] This is not to suggest that many Durrani have not joined the Taliban, e.g. Mullah Abdul Ghani Berader, once head of the Taliban's Military Commander's Council, is a Popalzai Durrani; rather it is to suggest that tribal rivalries and dynamics are important in assessing the underlying structure of the Taliban and some of their narratives.

Table 11.3 summarizes the target audiences for Taliban messages and narratives, from Pashtuns to the global *Ummah* (community of Muslims), with their main emphases and lines of attack; although extremely rare, some narratives have even targeted non-Muslim support for the Taliban.[40]

Taliban transmissions can be loosely broken down into three periods, with three different sets of goals, obstacles, and religio-cultural references. The first period is roughly the period from the Taliban capture of Kabul until 9/11. The second period refers to the time between 9/11 and early 2004, when the Taliban insurgency in Afghanistan began to garner more support within Afghanistan and large swaths of the country became unsafe for Coalition forces and foreign aid organizations. The third period is ongoing, from early 2004 to the present. Table 11.4 summarizes the different goals, rhetorical devices, historical references, and methods of transmission transmission (see Chapter 3).

Table 11.3: Taliban narrative targets

Target Audience	Emphasis	Attacks
Ghilzai	Historical memory	Karzai and his family and clan/tribe
Pashtun	Pashtunwali	Karzai and the former Northern Alliance
Afghan	Recent history of foreign invasions	Foreign presence; "so-called Afghans," apostates
Ummah	Pan-Islamism; the flight of Mohammed from Mecca to Medina and his return	"Crusaders"
Global	Human rights, self-determination	Western troop presence
Coalition forces	Divisions; desire to avoid a protracted and dangerous deployment	Americans specifically

This follows the general trend of conflict in Afghanistan: before 9/11, the main enemy of the Taliban was the ethnic Uzbek and Tajik Northern Alliance. By appealing to a nationalist or ethnic solidarity through Pashtunwali-styled rhetoric, the Taliban hoped to marginalize the Northern Alliance and identify them with regimes generally hostile to the Taliban in Tashkent and Dushanbe, as well as Moscow by proxy. The continued presence of Osama bin Laden in Afghanistan was often explained with reference to the hospitality clause of Pashtunwali.[41] Many of the transmissions were in audio format, through radio or cassette.

After 9/11, as a new enemy entered Afghanistan, the Taliban were temporarily rendered relatively speechless. Taliban proclamations became relatively few compared to those during their time in Kabul. Since significantly re-emerging in late 2003,[42] however, new Taliban missives have appeared, showing a distinct shift in cultural markers, although keeping with a consistent chronology regarding the divine mission of the Taliban.

Shortly after 9/11, while waiting for the American military to invade Afghanistan, Mullah Omar was quoted as saying "the promise of God is that my land is vast. If you start a journey on God's path, you can reside anywhere on this earth and will be protected ... The promise of Bush is that there is no place on earth where you can hide that I cannot find you. We will see which one of these two promises is fulfilled."[43] This is "typical" of the Taliban messages immediately after 9/11: the accusation that Coalition forces, and American forces in particular, are directly opposed to the will of God.

Table 11.4: Temporal differentiation of Taliban messaging

	Pre-9/11	*9/11 to early 2004*	*Early 2004–*
Primary enemy	Northern Alliance	Coalition troops	American soldiers and the "puppet" regime in Kabul
Favored means of transmission	Audio	Night letters, poetry	Video, magazines, internet, social media, poetry, *taranas*, night letters, etc.
Primary target audience	Fellow Afghans and Pashtuns	Fellow Pashtuns and Ghilzais	Fellow Afghans, Muslims, and wavering coalition partners
Primary emphasis	Tribal, nationalist	Religious	Religious
Historical reference	The reign of Abdur Rahman ("the Iron Amir")	Russian invasion, British invasions, Durrani triumph over Ghilzai	Crusades
Desired outcome	Total control of Afghanistan, the existence of the Islamic Emirate	Local support, creation of insurgency groups	Broad Muslim support; fracturing of US-led Coalition

Interestingly, even before 9/11 the Taliban had begun to equate the Americans with *kafiri* and not simply *Al-i-kitab* or non-Muslim friends. In December 2000, as the Taliban regime found itself again prevented from taking Afghanistan's seat at the United Nations, it called for a jihad against all the "atheists" on the Security Council, singling out the United States.[44]

After President Bush was inaugurated, the Taliban seemed to take a more friendly tone towards the US and sent out at least two conciliatory messages to the new American president.[45] Not long after, however, the Taliban adopted a harsher tone. Speaking in Islamabad, the Taliban ambassador to Pakistan stated that the then current international call for bin Laden to be extradited was simply a way to cripple Afghanistan so that the US could more easily impose a pro-Western government. This also marks the first direct correlation between the Soviet Union and the US.[46] During the speech it was alleged that the US's goals in Afghanistan were twofold: to defeat the Soviet Union, and then to install a pro-Western government, a plan that the US was in 2001 still pursuing.

That this came out within a month of calls for renewed dialogue with the US is perplexing. In our opinion, there are two possible explanations. First, that the Taliban very quickly (especially for a nation with at that time very rudimentary access to media outlets) came to the conclusion that the Bush administration's policies toward the Taliban were not going to differ significantly from those of the Clinton administration. Or second, that perhaps the release of the speech (delivered on 25 January, but not published until a full three weeks later) was delayed until a more in-depth analysis of the Bush administration's Afghan policy could be undertaken. Regardless, the parallel drawn between the invasion of the Soviet Union and American activity in Afghanistan was one that would become extremely apt by the end of the year.

Much of the speech was also spent criticizing the Russian government's actions in supporting the Northern Alliance and trying to keep fundamentalist Islam out of Central Asia. The greater Muslim world was also appealed to for assistance in rebuilding Afghanistan. This appeal for assistance from fellow Muslims is something that the Taliban would use later in fighting the American-led Coalition forces, just as it had during the Soviet war.

In that same month, February 2001, the Taliban announced its decision to destroy the Bamiyan Buddhas. Originally it was announced that the decision had been made by the *ulema* (Islamic body of jurists),[47] but later in response to pressure from foreign governments and derision from other Islamic scholars, Mullah Omar used his trump card: the decision had come to him in a dream. Dreams are very important in both Islam and Pashtun culture, and one ignores a dream, at least according to Omar, at one's own peril. In Mullah Omar's dream, Allah chastised him for not removing false idols.[48]

Mullah Omar had used dreams before, such as when handling the cloak of the Prophet in Kandahar in 1996.[49] Through a dream, he said, he was invested with the authority to handle the cloak, and by so doing he invested himself with a greater authority than had been seen since Ahmad Shah Durrani originally brought the cloak to Afghanistan centuries before, while uniting the nation. Many, especially the Pashtuns, saw this as divine sanction for Mullah Omar's government.[50]

In summary, the Taliban's IO campaign had and has much strength. First, the Taliban created a simple, yet powerful narrative that resonated with the Afghan people. The use of songs and poetry played into the historical beliefs of many Afghans. Second, the Taliban were able to exploit cultural and tribal nuances because their insurgency was composed of Afghan locals who were intimately familiar with the language, culture, and people in their villages. Third, the Taliban found the most effective means to communicate their messages that were suited to the rural populace in the difficult geographic terrain of Afghanistan. Fourth, the Taliban could quickly get their message out to the media to exploit attacks, ambushes, and civilian casualties. Often it is the side that gets their story out first that is believed and can set the agenda, regardless of the facts. Fifth, the Taliban showed an increasing level of sophistication and use of technology to convey their narrative. Finally, the Taliban backed up their messages with credible threats to intimidate the population if they did not support their cause.

The Taliban's IO campaign also had many weaknesses that could have been exploited. First, the Taliban lacked broad genuine support in Afghanistan. Their initial basis of popular support was in the rural Pashtun population in eastern and southern Afghanistan and in the tribal areas of Pakistan. Yet eventually the Taliban gained support among other ethnic groups in other parts of the country. Second, the Taliban generally lacked a broad strategic overview with specifics as to how they would govern. The original Taliban leader Mullah Omar once even said, "Allah will take care of everything," when asked about how the Taliban would rule. Third, while the Taliban proved adept at spreading propaganda at the local Afghan level, they clearly lacked an understanding of how Western public opinion was formed, and consistently failed to exploit the international media at a strategic level. Finally, the Taliban consistently put out contradictory messages on issues such as attacking schools, poppy cultivation, and suicide bombings.[51] Some of this can be attributed to their decentralized organizational structure, with much of their IO depending on multiple spokesmen sending out different and confusing messages. More importantly, this showed up serious contradictions in the core beliefs of the Taliban narrative.

Overall, the Taliban's information campaign generated the perception, especially in the rural Pashtun areas, of a growing, unstoppable insurgency.

The Taliban narrative and stories have many strengths, as suggested throughout this book, and appealed to the common Afghan, but their stories also had some significant weaknesses which the US and Afghan government failed to exploit. In the end, the battle of the story was an important part of the Taliban strategy to retake Afghanistan, and they have proved adept at shaping local Afghan perceptions. And once perceptions are influenced, as Jowett and O'Donnell suggest, one can manipulate and control the environment.[52]

In conclusion, the Taliban's information operations as well as the process by which they were distributed, as witnessed by the author in Kandahar City in June 2009, represent almost a kind of metaphor for the problems that the United States and NATO/ISAF have faced in Afghanistan. That is, the West has attempted to apply methods and pursue policies in both military and civil–political domains without understanding the impact on individual Afghans. The West has clearly not understood the influences that sway and inspire Afghan behavior. The US and its NATO allies developed objectives based on *their* views and desires for Afghanistan, not based on the views and requirements of the common Afghan who represents the "center of gravity" for this conflict. The US and NATO then made promises that they did not deliver, at least in the eyes of Afghans (a disastrous and dangerous situation in Afghanistan). As a villager from Sperwan Ghar, Panjwayi district of Kandahar province suggested to the author, "they [the Coalition forces] promised to build, but they destroyed instead."

The US and NATO would have been well advised during the initial stages of Operation Enduring Freedom to ask simple questions about what Afghans—not just the elites in Kabul, technocrats, and expatriates—really wanted from the West's engagement. What are the messages and frames that motivate and influence Afghans? What is the best way to spread a message? Such questions were never systematically asked, resulting in many policies as well as strategies being misapplied in the eyes of the Afghan population. Many of the Taliban's information artifacts, on the other hand, appear to be deeply rooted in the Afghan psyche. They appeal to emotions that the West do not and have not tried to understand. This lack of understanding, in part, has ultimately doomed Western engagement in Afghanistan and contributed to the West losing the battle of the story in Afghanistan and, therefore, the war.

APPENDIX A

COMMUNAL STANDPOINTS: HOW AFGHANS IDENTIFY THE TYPES OF TALIBAN

Introduction

The intention of this Appendix is to provide an analytical snapshot of the Taliban's organizational construct, in theory and in practice, using captured Taliban documents and documents wilfully published by the militant organization, to help gain insight into how the Taliban view themselves. In particular, several of the Taliban's published "rules and regulations for Mujahidin", or *layeha* or code of conduct (see Chapter 8), have been cross-analyzed to help explain how local Afghan communities view and differentiate the many strains and types of Taliban operating throughout Afghanistan.

The elements presented in the appendix must be understood in the context of how local communities view and accept the Taliban. The framework indicates varying levels of involvement among individuals who engage in anti-government activities, nearly all of whom are designated "the Taliban" by Western sources and "enemies of Afghanistan" by Afghan government officials. Some of these groups, whether true Taliban, local gunmen, or begrudged tribesmen, are viewed with a sense of legitimacy and moral righteousness; others are viewed as criminal bandits and murderers. The following framework helps explain this seemingly complicated concept and helps identify different subtypes of Taliban fighters in a given community.[1]

TALIBAN NARRATIVES

Taliban Subtypes

Narzar (Disaffected)—Those who feel isolated, marginalized or excluded from the current politcial process.

Majburi (Forced)—Those individuals or clans abused or harassed by the central goverment, forced to leave their community. Are fighting for anti-government/revenge motives; also known as "anti-corruption" Taliban.

Taliban-e duzd (Thief Taliban)—Some are considered *zalam* (cruel) and abusive to locals.

Taliban-e Khana-neshin (Sitting at home Taliban)—Inactive, former Taliban regime members. Typically found in Quetta, Helmand, Kandahar, or Peshawar.

Taliban-e jangi (Fighting Taliban)—front-line fighters, full time insurgents, "addicted" to jihad.

Taliban-e mahali (Local Taliban)—fighters from the community, usually voluntary but can also include "blue collar" insurgents.

Makhtabi—Ideological, schooled Taliban.

Taliban-e asli (real Taliban) or *Taliban-e pak* (clean Taliban)—those considered "uncorrupted" and ideologically motivated.

Taliban subtypes and criteria for group solidarity (reconcilable)

Naraz (Disaffected)—Those who feel isolated, marginalized or excluded from the current political process.

- Sense of fear, hatred, moral outrage, revenge.
- Group is viewed as preserving the local way of life.
- Provides physical security against another armed group.

Taliban-e Khana-neshin (Sitting at home Taliban)—Inactive, former Taliban regime members. Typically found in Quetta, Helmand, Kandahar, or Peshawar.

- Sense of fear, hatred, moral outrage, revenge.
- Social status (honor/prestige).
- Admired leader/figure.
- Physical danger/threat from the group if support is withheld.

Taliban-e mahali (Local Taliban)—fighters from the community, usually voluntary but can also include "blue collar" insurgents.

- Group has local, tribal or ethnic ties.
- Group is viewed as indigenous and acceptable.
- Group is viewed as preserving the local way of life.
- Provides physical security aginst another armed group.
- Group may fulfill need for agression/adventure.

Taliban subtypes and criteria for group solidarity (reconcilable)

Majburi (Forced)—Those individuals or clans abused or harassed by the central government, forced to leave their community. Are fighting for anti-government/revenge motives; also known as "anti-corruption" Taliban.

- Need for justice/moral clarity/ideals.
- Sense of fear, hatred, moral outrage, revenge.
- Social status (honor/prestige).
- Sense of honor, identity, self-esteem.
- Provides physical security against another armed group.
- Group has local, tribal or ethnic ties.
- Group is viewed as indigenous and acceptable.
- Group is viewed as preserving the local way of life.
- Need for social relatedness; sense of belonging, loyalty.

286

APPENDIX A

Taliban subtypes and criteria for group solidarity (irreconcilable)

Taliban-e duzd (Thief Taliban)— Some are considered zalam (cruel) and abusive to locals.	• Group pays for assistance in conducting violent attacks. • Group shares resources and profits from criminal activities with members. • Physical danger/threat from the group if support is withheld.
Taliban-e Jangi (Fighting Taliban)— front-line fighters, full time insurgents, "addicted" to jihad.	• Friends or family are already members or encourage joining. • Need for aggression/adventure. • Social status (honor/prestige). • Physical danger/threat from the group if support is withheld. Group inspires members and provides deeper meanings to their lives. • Group uses religious justifications for violence to overcome social norms against it. • Group promises salvation to members who die for the ideology or religion.

Taliban subtypes and criteria for group solidarity (irreconcilable)

Taliban-e asli (real Taliban) or *Taliban-e pak* (clean Taliban)—thouse considered "uncorrupted" and ideologically motivated. *Makhtabi*—Ideological, schooled Taliban.	• Social status (honor/prestige). • Physical danger/threat from the group if support is withheld. Group inspires members and provides deeper meanings to their lives. • Group uses religious justifications for violence to overcome social norms against it. • Group promises salvation tom members who die for the ideology or religion. • Group has local, tribal or ethnic ties. • Group is viewed as indigenous and acceptable. • Provides physical security against another armed group. • Need for justice/moral clarity/ideals.

APPENDIX B

ILLUSTRATIVE EXAMPLE OF A FEW TALIBAN NIGHT LETTERS, 2008–10

(Data on all 279 Night Letters are available online at www.hurstpublishers.com/book/taliban-narratives)

Letter No.	Date	Location	Language	From	To	Purpose	Message	Audience
1	April 2008	Kunar Province, Kandi Village	Pashto	Mudir Muasib Bin Umair	Residents of Kandai Village	To warn residents working for Govt or Internationals to quite	Counter-collaboration	Undecided population
2	Unspecified	N/A	Pashto	Mujahedeen of Islamic Emirate	Said Usman Baba	Avoid activities and propaganda against Taliban	Counter-stability	Local personality
3	Unspecified	N/A	Pashto	Islamic Emirate of Afghanistan	All Muslim Brothers	1-Do not uncover Mujahidin wherever you see them. 2-Do not take tools related to Mujahidin 3-People who work for the Americans should quit their jobs. 4-People should keep quiet during the night operation by Mujahidin;	Counter-stability and Counter-collaboration	Govt workers and undecided population

#	Date	Location	Language	Issuer	Target	Message	Category	Audience
4	May 2008	Kundoz City, Kundoz	Pashto	Amir-ul-Momineen (Mullah Umar)	All Muslim Brothers	otherwise that person will become the main target. Stop any kind of support and friendship with the Western forces	Counter-collaboration	Undecided Population
5	June 2008	Murgha village	Pashto	Mujahedeen of Islamic Emirate	All Countryman and brothers	1- All those who work for the puppet government, such as Army, Police or Intelligence, should quit their jobs. 2- All mullahs should stop doing the funeral ceremony for those who die supporting the government.	Counter-collaboration	Undecided Population
6	Unspecified	Khost Province	Pashto	Khost military jihadi brigade	Khost Province population	1- Tribal leaders should not pass declarations against Mujahidin. 2- All those who work for the puppet government and the US should quit their jobs. 3- Do not stay close to the government and infidal army.	Counter-collaboration, Counter-mobility, Counter-stability	Undecided Population

4- Secure yourself during the assault on infidels and government army, and do not scream in support of their soldiers.

5- Our landmines and IEDs are live. We do not permit them to kill civilians, but you should not show them to our enemies.

6- Stay away when you see our enemies' carvans and do not move forward.

All mullahs should avoid participating in the funeral ceremonies of National Army, Police, Frontier Police and Intelligence personnel.

APPENDIX C

HIG OFFICIAL PEACE PROPOSAL AND TRANSLATION, DECEMBER 2010, *TANWEER*, VOL. 16

د ژغورنې ملي ميثاق

بِسْمِ اللهِ الرَّحْمٰنِ الرَّحِيمِ

د کابل حکومت د سولې عالي شورۍ له لورې له حزب اسلامي غوښتنه شوی چي د جګړې د پای ته رسېدو په اړه خپله طرحه هغوی ته وليږي، د حزب له لورې هغوی ته وویل شوی چي د کابل له حکومت سره مذاکرات په هغه صورت کي کېدلۍ دي او څه نتیجه ورکولۍ شي چي د متحده ایالاتو له لورې د کابل چاراوکو ته دا واک ورکړی شي چي له مجاهدینو سره د فوځونو د وتلو په اړه مذاکرات پیل کړي، او دا چي سپینه ماڼۍ به د افغاني لوریو ترمنځ د هر توافق درناوی کوي، موږ دا وضاحت هم ورته کړی چي مجاهدین به هیڅ توګه تر ۲۰۱۴ پورې د بهرنیو خواکونو له پاته کېدا سره توافق نه کوي. خو د دې لپاره چي د حزب دریخ د دوی او ټول افغان ولس ته واضح کړو؛ هغوی ته مو د ژغورنې ملي ميثاق مخکنی طرحه له معمولي تعدیل او تزنید سره په دې نوي بڼې کي وليږله:

موږ د افغان ولس او خپلو سیاسي ېلو په استازیتوب؛ د الله تعالی په نامه ژمنه کوو چي د روان دردناک حالت څخه د هېواد د ژغورلو لپاره یو بل ته لاس ورکوو چي د جګړه د تل لپاره پای ته ورسوو، په هېواد کي د پایښمن امنیت تامین کړو، له بهرنیو خواکونو فارغ او د پردیو له لاسوهنو خوندي افغانستان جوړکړو، خپل ملي وحدت لازیات مضبوط کړو او ملت ته دا موقع برابره کړو چي د خپلې خوښې زعامت غوره او د خپلي عقیدي او باور مطابق نظام جوړکري، دغو لورو او سپیڅلو اهدافو ته د رسېدو لپاره مو په لاندې طرحې توافق کړو:

۱. بهرنیو خواکونو دي د ۲۰۱۱ میلادي کال د جولای په میاشت کي له هېواده وتل پیل کړي او د شپږو میاشتو په ترخ کي د هغه بشپړ کړي.

۲. په دې مودي کي دي له بنارونو او ګڼ مېشتو سیمو ووخي او په عسکري مراکزو کي دې ځای په ځای شي.

۳. د امنیت چاري دي په بشپړه توګه ملي اردو او پولیس ته وسپارل شي، بهرني خواکونه به د افغانستان په هیڅ ګوټ کي او په هیڅ حالت کي په خپل سر د نظامي عملیاتو، د کورونو تلاشۍ او نیونو حق نه لري.

۴. قدرت دي یا یوه داسي موقت حکومت ته ولیږدول شي چي ټولو لوریو ته دمنلو وړ وي، که نور لوري دا نه شي منلی نو په اوسني حکومت کي دي داسي تعدیل راشي چي ټولو ته دمنلو وړ شي، خو په دې حکومت کي به متنازع فیه کسان چي په فساد، ملي خیانت، بې دیني او جنګي جنایاتو تورن کسان نه وي. همدارنګ د حکومت د دری ګونو امنیتي قواوو په مشرتابه کي به داسي کسان نه وي چي د یوې یوې ډلې په پلوي او د بلي ډلې په ضد جنګېدلۍ وي.

۵. د پارلمان پرځای به د ټولو افغاني لورو په اتفاق له داسي په نامه یوه کسیزه شورۍ جوړېږي چي په مهمو ملي مسایلو کي به د وروستۍ پرېکړې واک ورسره وي، د دي شورۍ مقر به په داسي ولایت کي وي چي امنیت نۍ په بشپړه توګه د افغاني خواکونو په لاس کي وي او هیڅ بهرني خواک په کي نه وي.

۶. د بهرنیو خواکونو له وتلو وروسته به د متناسب تمثیل پر بنسټ د جمهوري ریاست، ولسي جرګې او ولایتي شوراګانو لپاره یوخای، یوخل او همهال انتخابات ترسره شي.

۷. په دې انتخاباتو کي د حکومت د کابینې غړي او والیان یوازې په هغه صورت کي د برخي اخیستو حق لري د انتخاباتو تر نېټې دری میاشتي مخکي له خپلي دندي استعفا وکړي.

۸. په لومړي منتخب حکومت کي به د هر لوري برخه د هغه د آراوو د تناسب وي او له شورۍ به د اعتماد رایه ترلاسه کوي، خو تر دي وروسته به په بریمن لوري پردي مکلف نه دی چي انتلافي حکومت جوړ کري.

۹. هغه حزب یا انتخابي مجموعه به په بعدي انتخاباتو کي د برخي اخیستو حق لري چي په لومړي انتخاباتو کي د ترلس په سلو کي زیاتي رایې ترلاسه کړي.

۱۰. په دې مودي کي په به جګړو ته د ښکبلو لورو ترمنځ به د ښکبلو لورو ترمنځ به د اوربند بشیر اوربند تامین وي، ټول سیاسي بندیان به خوشي کېږي، ټول لوري به ژمنه کوي چي له دې وروسته به نه قدرت ته د رسېدو لپاره ناروا لاری لټوي او نه به دخپل حریف او رقیب لپاره د وسله کاروي.

۱۱. د لومړي منتخبه شورۍ به دا حق لري چي د دریو لورو له خوا اعلان شوي اساسي قوانین وڅیري او د هېواد د اساسي قانون په اړه وروستۍ پرېکړه وکړي.

۱۲. هیڅ بهرني خواک به دا حق نه لري چي په افغانستان کي زندان ولري، کوم افغان محاکمه او مجازات کړي، یا نی د محاکمې لپاره بهر ته انتقال او په بل ځای کي نی محبوس او محاکمه کړي.

۱۳. په اختلاس، د مخدره موادو قاچاق، د ملي شتمنیو په غصب او په جنګي جنایاتو تورن کسان به شرعي محکمي ته سپارل کېږي

او هیڅ لوري به له هغوي په خرګنده يا پټه توګه دفاع نه کوي.

۱٤. د بهرنيو خواکونو له وتلو وروسته به بهرني جنګياني هم په افغانستان کي نه وي.

۱٥. کوم کوني او بهرني لوري چي د د روغي جوړي له دي میثاق سره مخالفت او د جګړي پر دوام ټینګار وکړي موږ ټول به په ګډه او تر هغه د جنګ غوښتونکو مقابله کوو چي خپل هیواد او ولس د هغوی له شر او ضرر وژغورو.

والله علی مانقول وکیل

اوس باید ټولو ته واضح شوي وي چي نه بهرني خواکونه امنیت راوستی شي، نه د بهرنیو خواکونو تر چتر لاندي حکومت او نه نامشروع انتخابات او په درغلیو او تقلب ولار د اقلیت ممثل پارلمان، تبرو نامشروع او غلطو انتخاباتو وښودله چي نه یوازي ستونزي نشي حل کولي بلکي مزید ستونزي زیږوي، د اشغالګرو خواکونو د جهازونو او وزر لاندي انتخابات د هر انسان نه آزاد او عاقل انسان نه نظره ارزښت نه لري، وموليدل چي په وروستيو انتخاباتو کي د افغان ولس محدود شمیر خلکو برخه واخیسته، د انتخاباتو د کمیسیون د رسمي اعلان له مخي د ټولو بریالیو کاندیدانو د رایو شمیر نږدي یو ملیون او دوه سوه زره دی، یعني ټول په ګډه او راټولونکی پارلمان له مجموعه کي له هرو دبرشو افغانانو ځخه یوازي د یوه کس استازیتوب کوي، آیا داسي انتخابات او پارلمان ځه ارزښت لري!؟!! دا انتخابات نه له شرعي پلوه مشروعیت لري، ځکه قمار ته ورته دي، بی ځايه لګښتونه ایجابوي، داسي څوک پارلمان ته لار مومي چي د لګښتونو تامینولو لپاره لومري خان ته شتمنو بهرنیو خواکونو وپلوري، بیا په پارلمان کي خپل ضمیر، ایمان او ولس وپلوري، داسي مسخره انتخابات تل له درغلیو او تقلب سره توام وي، ټول نتایج او په خانګري توګه د غزني د انتخاباتو اعلان شوي نتایج یی بربنډ ثبوت دی، په غزني کي هغه مهال هم هزارګان یو اقلیت وو چي دای کندی هم ورسره یوخای وو، امریکایانو له دای کندي ببل ولایت جوړ کر، په دی سره په غزني ولایت کي د هزاره وو شمیر له شل سلني هم راټیټ شو، خو د انتخاباتو کمیسیون یولس نوماندان بریالي اعلان کړل چي په دوی کي یو پښتون هم نشته او ټول یه هزاره اقلیت پوري ترلی نوماندان دي!!

حزب اسلامي نه د هیواد د اشغال په حالت کي او د بهرنیو فوځونو د جهازونو او وزر لاندي انتخاباتو کي برخه اخلي او نه له داسي مسخره انتخاباتو سره توافق کولي شي چي بدي پایلي نی ښولو ته جوته شوی.

حزب اسلامي افغانستان

Translation[1]

National Convention of Rescue/Salvation

In the name of God, the Merciful, the Compassionate

The high peace council of the Kabul government requested HIG (Hezb-e-Islami Gulbuddin) to send them their proposal for ending war/conflict. HIG has told them that negotiations will be productive only when United States grants Kabul officials the authority of negotiating [US] forces' withdrawal. Also, the White House should respect all the decisions made by Afghan [peace talks] parties. We have clearly stated to them that HIG will never agree to the foreign forces remaining [in Afghanistan] until 2014. However, in order to highlight HIG stance to them [Afghan government] and the Afghan nation, we have sent them the National Convention of Salvation proposal with subtle changes and [here is] the new version [of the proposal].

Representing the Afghan nation and our political parties, we take an oath on the name of the great Allah that we will help each other to rescue our country from the ongoing heartbreaking situation, to end the conflict forever, to maintain security, to build an Afghanistan free of foreign forces and foreign interference, to strengthen our national unity, to provide an opportunity to this nation to choose their leadership and to build a state according to their beliefs.

To reach these holy objectives, we have agreed on the proposal below:

1. Foreign forces should begin withdrawing from the country starting from July 2011, and should complete the withdrawal process within 6 months.

2. Within this period, they [foreign forces] should withdraw from cities and populated areas and settle in military bases.

3. Security responsibilities should be immediately transferred to national army and national police. Foreign forces have no right to conduct unilateral military operations, house search, and arresting people in any corner of the country in any type of circumstances.

4. Power should be transferred to an interim government which is acceptable to all sides. If other parties do not accept this offer, changes should be brought to the current government that are acceptable to all sides. However, controversial, corrupt, traitor, infidel, and alleged war criminals should not be part of the [proposed] government.

5. With the consensus of all sides, there should be a national council which consists of 7 members that has the ultimate power of decision. The office of this council should be in a province over which Afghan forces have complete control and [the province] has no presence of foreign forces.

6. After the withdrawal of foreign forces, there should be presidential, parliamentary, and provincial council elections simultaneously.

7. In this election, members of the government cabinet and governors can only participate if they resign from their jobs three months ahead of the election.

8. In the first elected government, the role of each party should be based on the number of votes gained. These parties should receive a vote of confidence from the national council. In future elections after this one, the winning side is not obliged to form a coalition government.

9. Only those political parties or groups have the right to participate in the next election who have received over 10% of votes in the first election.

10. During this period [of peace negotiations], there should be a complete ceasefire among rival groups. All the political prisoners will be released. All sides will promise that neither use illegal ways to attain power, nor they will use weapons to defeat their rivals.

11. The first elected council will have the right to study constitutions presented by three sides and make the final decision on the country's constitution.

12. No foreign nation has the right to have prisoners in Afghanistan, to try or punish an Afghan citizen or transfer him abroad for trial and imprison him in other places.

13. All the alleged corrupt people, drug traffickers, illegal land seizers, and alleged war criminals should be taken to the Shar'iah court. No side should back them [criminals] secretly or in public.

14. After the withdrawal of foreign forces, no foreign fighters must stay in Afghanistan.
15. If any domestic or foreign players are against this peace convention and insist on the continuation of war, we will together confront these warlords until we rescue our country and nation.

God is the witness for what we have said

By now, it should be clear to all that neither foreign force can bring the security or the government under the shadow of foreign forces. Illegitimate elections, corrupt and minority representation parliaments, past illegitimate and wrong elections have shown that this does not solve problems, but creates more problems. Under the wing of occupying forces' jets, elections have no value to any free and wise human being. We saw that a limited number of people participated in the recent elections. According to the official announcement of the election commission, the total votes of all candidates were 1,200,000, meaning only 1 person out of every 30 Afghans. Does this type of election have any value? This election has no legitimacy based on Shar'iah, because it is similar to gambling. It depends entirely on expenses. People who sell themselves to rich foreign forces for their election expenses win the parliamentary election. Later, these people sell their integrity, beliefs, and nation in the parliament. Such joke elections are always accompanied by fraud and corruption. In particular the election result in Ghazni was clear evidence [of such fraud]. The Hazara were a minority even when Dai Kundi province was part of Ghazni province. The Hazara population fell below 20% after the establishment of Dai Kundi, a new province created by Americans. However, the electoral commission announced 11 Hazara candidates as winners and not even one Pashtun was among the winners. All the winners belong to the Hazara minority. HIG will not participate in an election held under occupation and under the wings of foreign forces' jets. It also does not agree with an election proven to have bad consequences.

NOTES

PREFACE

1. The views expressed in this book are the author's own and should not be construed as an official position or policy of the US Government, Department of Defense, Department of the Navy or Naval Postgraduate School.

2. For an image of this leaflet, see Herbert A. Freeman, "Psychological Operations in Afghanistan," http://www.psywarrior.com/Herbafghan.html or http://www.psy-warrior.com/afghanleaf04.html

3. I am well aware that this is a generalization and not all Afghans are xenophobic, but my experience in the rural Pashtun areas suggests that many of these communities, for geographic and historical reasons, have an initial, basic, and real distrust of foreigners and "outsiders."

4. This leaflet was dropped throughout the first year of the war in a variety of locations in Afghanistan. It is my understanding that it was intially dropped near Jalalabad and then in the Shomali Plain, north of Kabul.

5. Rzehak Lutz, "Doing Pashto: Pashtunwali as the ideal of honourable behavior and tribal life among Pashtuns," *Afghanistan Analyst Network*, p. 1, https://www.afghan-istan-analysts.org/wp-content/uploads/downloads/2012/10/20110321LR-Pash-tunwali-FINAL.pdf

6. http://www.psywarrior.com/Herbafghan.html

7. Herbert A. Friedman, "Psychological Operations in Afghanistan," http://www.psy-warrior.com/Herbafghan.html, describes the leaflet and validates the usefulness of this IO story: "On October 23 [2001], the Taliban showed that the leaflets and radio messages were having a result. A senior militia official announced from Kabul that the Afghan people in the eastern city of Jalalabad were burning [this] propa-ganda leaflet and radios being dropped by U.S. planes to turn the population against the Taliban. [This] leaflet [was] also reportedly dropped on the western neighbor-hoods of Kabul. Some Afghans said that they were afraid to pick up the leaflets and risk punishment by the Taliban."

8. DOD Directive 3600.01.

9. Thomas H. Johnson's interview with PSYOP officer, November 2015. He suggested a significant confusion between IO and PSYOP, as evidenced in many articles, white papers, and other research papers. Here are some examples: http://www.dtic.mil/dtic/tr/fulltext/u2/a575201.pdf http://www.rand.org/content/dam/rand/pubs/monographs/2012/RAND_MG1060.pdf, http://usatoday30.usatoday.com/news/military/story/2012–02–29/afghanistan-iraq-military-information-operations-usa-today-investigation/53295472/1

10. Thomas H. Johnson's interviews with numerous Afghans as well as Taliban commanders in Kandahar, August 2008 and September 2009.

11. Thomas H. Johnson's interview with US Army PSYOP officer, November 2015.

12. See the 2006–9 Afghan Field Research Trip Reports in Thomas H. Johnson, "Afghanistan Field Research Notebooks 3–6" (Monterey, CA, 2006–9).

13. Tim Foxley, "The Taliban's Propaganda Activities: How Well is the Afghan Insurgency Communicating and What is it Saying?" (Stockholm: SIPRI project paper, June 2007), p. 10; Azam Ahmed, "Taliban Justice Gains Favor as Official Afghan Courts Fail," *New York Times*, 31 January 2015, http://www.nytimes.com/2015/02/01/world/asia/taliban-justice-gains-favor-as-official-afghan-courts-fail.html?_r=0

14. Typically, Pashto, Dari, Arabic, Urdu, and English.

15. Robert Taber, *War of the Flea: The Classic Study of Guerrilla Warfare* (Washington, DC: Potomac Books, Inc., 2002), p. 12.

16. Greg Miller and Souad Mekhennet, "Inside the Surreal World of the Islamic State's Propaganda Machine," *Washington Post*, 20 November 2015, https://www.washingtonpost.com/world/national-security/inside-the-islamic-states-propaganda-machine/2015/11/20/051e997a-8ce6–11e5-acff-673ae92ddd2b_story.html

1. INTRODUCTION

1. http://9–11domorethenneverforget-stopislam.blogspot.com/2011/05/taliban-and-muslims-use-social-media-to.html

2. Helio Fred Garcia, *The Power of Communication: Skills to Build Trust, Inspire, Loyalty, and Lead Effectively* (Upper Saddle River, NJ: Pearson Education, Inc., 2012), p. 20.

3. T. E. Lawrence, quoted in B. H. Liddell Hart, *Lawrence of Arabia* (New York: DeCapo, 1989), p. 399.

4. Marshall McLuhan, *The Medium is the Message* (Berkeley, CA: Gingko Press, 2005).

5. Some information on other Afghan insurgents, such as the Haqqani Network, will be presented, but such groups are not a major focus of the research presented here. The Tora Bora group is a Taliban offshoot that operated in eastern Afghanistan's Nangarhar and Kunar provinces between 2006 and approximately 2010. The Tora Bora Military Front was created in 2006 and led by Anwar-ul Haq Mujahid, son of

the late Maulana Yunis Khalis, Emir of Hezb-e-Islami (Khalis faction, or HIK). Mujahid was reportedly arrested by Pakistani authorities in late 2009, other Afghan insurgents such as the Dadullah Front and Fidai Mahaz (Taliban splinter groups) will not be assessed.

6. See Daniel G. Bates and Fred Plog, *Cultural Anthropology*, 2nd edn (New York: Alfred A. Knopf, 1980), p. 7.

7. "Taliban" will be used as a plural noun (possessive form "Taliban's") throughout this book, because the Afghan insurgent/jihadist organization is not homogenous and consists of a variety of "types" of members, as well as units. See Appendix A for a description of the various types of Taliban.

8. For some general studies of the Taliban, see William Maley, *Fundamentalism Reborn?* (London: Hurst & Co., 1998); Ahmed Rashid, *Taliban: Militant Islam, Oil and Fundamentalism in Central Asia*, 2nd edn (New Haven, CT: Yale University Press; 2010); Wahid Muzhda, *Afghanistan va panj sal-i sultah-i taliban [Afghanistan Under Five Years of Taliban Sovereignty]* (2003); Iftikhar Murshed, *Afghanistan: The Taliban Years* (London: Bennett & Bloom, 2006); Husayn Ibn Mahmud, "Al-Rajul al-'Amlaaq: The Giant Man," 2005, http://www.archive.org/details/TheGiantMan; Sarah Chayes, *The Punishment of Virtue: Inside Afghanistan After the Taliban*, reprint edn (London: Penguin Books, 2007); Iftikhar Murshed, *Afghanistan: The Taliban Years*, 1st edn (London: Bennett & Bloom, 2006); Robert D. Crews and Amin Tarzi (eds), *The Taliban and the Crisis of Afghanistan* (Cambridge, MA: Harvard University Press, 2008); Antonio Giustozzi, *Decoding the New Taliban* (Oxford: Oxford University Press, 2012); Abdul Salam Zaeef, *My Life With the Taliban* (London: Hurst & Co., 2010); Hassan Abbas, *The Taliban Revival: Violence and Extremism on the Pakistan–Afghanistan Frontier* (New Haven, CT: Yale University Press, 2014); Graeme Smith, *The Dogs Are Eating Them Now: Our War in Afghanistan* (Toronto: Knopf Canada, 2013); Mufti Rasheed Ludhianvi, *Obedience to the Amir* (Berlin: First Draft Publishing, 2015); Anand Gopal, *No Good Men Among the Living: America, the Taliban, and the War through Afghan Eyes* (London: Picador, 2015); Mufti Rasheed Ludhianvi, ed. Michael Semple, trans. Yameema Mitha, *Obedience to the Amir: An early text on the Afghan Taliban Movement* (Berlin: First Draft Publishing, 2015); V. Sahay Comdt, *Taliban, Militant Islam and Afghanistan* (Delhi: Neha Publishers & Distributors, 2015); Mohammad Akbar Agha, ed. Alex Strick van Linschoten and Felix Kuehn, *I am Akbar Agha: Memories of the Afghan Jihad and the Taliban* (Berlin: First Draft Publishing, 2014); Sandy Gall, *War Against the Taliban: Why It All Went Wrong in Afghanistan* (New York: Bloomsbury, 2013); Alex Strick van Linschoten and Felix Kuehn, *An Enemy We Created: The Myth of the Taliban–Al Qaeda Merger in Afghanistan* (London, Hurst & Co., 2012); Carter Malkasian, *War Comes to Garmser: Thirty Years of Conflict on the Afghan Frontier* (London, Hurst & Co., 2013).

9. See David B. Edwards, *Heroes of the Age: Moral Fault Lines on the Afghan Frontier* (Berkeley, CA: University of California Press, 1996).

10. Mark Turner, *The Literary Mind* (New York: Oxford University Press, 1998), p. 1.

11. Edwards, *Heroes of the Age.*

12. Turner, *The Literary Mind*, p. 1.

13. See, for example, Alicia Juarero, *Dynamics in Action* (Cambridge, MA: MIT Press, 1999); Troy S. Thomas, Stephen D. Casebeer, and William D. Kiser, *Warlords Rising: Confronting Violent Non-State Actors* (Lanham, MD: Lexington Books, 2005); Troy S. Thomas and William D. Casebeer, "Violent Systems" (INSS Occasional Paper 52, 2004); A. C. Graesser and G. V. Nakamura, "The impact of a schema on comprehension and memory," in H. Bower (ed.), *The Psychology of Learning and Motivation* 16 (London: Academic Press, 1990), pp. 59–109; Maybel Chau-Ping Wong, "The effects of story schemata on narrative recall," https:// repository.ust.hk/dspace/handle/1783.1/1337 (2004); Daniel Dennett, "The Self as Center of Narrative Gravity," http://ase.tufts.edu/cogstud/papers/selfctr.htm (1992); William D. Casebeer, "Military Force and Culture Change: Systems, Narratives, and the Social Transmission of Behavior in Counter-Terrorism Strategy" (MA thesis, Naval Postgraduate School, 2006).

14. See D. A. Snow and R. Benford, "Ideology, Frame Resonance, and Participant Mobilization," in B. Klandermans, H. Kriesi, and S. Tarrow (eds), *From Structure to Action*, Vol. 1 (Greenwich, CT: JAI Press, 1988), pp. 197–217; Nick Paton Walsh, "Analysis: Afghanistan must recognize Taliban are winning," CNN, 21 April 2016, http://www.cnn.com/2016/04/20/asia/afghanistan-escalation-analysis/

15. For example, see Aish Ahmad and Roger Boase, *Pashtun Tales from the Pakistan–Afghan Frontier* (London: Saqi Books, 2003); Margaret A. Mills, *Rhetorics and Politics in Afghan Traditional Storytelling* (Philadelphia, PA: University of Pennsylvania Press, 1991); Amina Smith, *Tales of Afghanistan* (London: Octagon Press, 1982); Akram Osman, trans. Arley Loewen, *Real Men Keep Their Word: Tales from Kabul, Afghanistan* (Oxford: Oxford University Press, 2005); Henry George Raverty, trans., *Selections from the Poetry of Afghans: From the Sixteenth to the Nineteenth Century* (London: Forgotten Books, 2008).

16. This is particularly relevant to the Taliban's expansion into several districts including northern Baghlan, Kunduz, Takhar, Badghis, Jawzjan, Ghor, parts of Herat, and Nimroz.

17. This takes into account that Afghan insurgents often employ and entice members of society through financial and ideological means. Civilians willing to engage in militant activity are typically convinced through self-motivators like grievances, ethnic, tribal or business rifts, religious ideology, or opportunistic financial incentives.

18. The analyses reported in this book represent research in the spirit of Edwards' *Heroes of the Age*. Using oral narratives and other documentation, Edwards examined the lives of a variety of important Afghan figures, including Sultan Muhammad

Khan (a tribal chief), Amir Abdur Khan (the "Iron Amir" of Afghanistan), Najmuddin Akhundzada (the Mullah of Hadda), as well as the "the mad Fakir of Swat." His sophisticated and fascinating use of narratives and stories to uncover cultural artifacts and the underlying structure of the "moral systems" of these Afghan characters has served as the impetus and guide for the research presented here.

19. Anthony Trollope, *An Autobiography* (London: Penguin, 1996), p. 147.

20. Stephen King, *On Writing: A Memoir of the Craft* (London: Hodder and Stoughton, 2000), p. 184.

21. For more information see her website: www.wayofstory.com

22. Catherine Ann Jones, *The Way of Story: The Craft and Soul of Writing* (Ojai, CA: Prasana Press, 2004), p. 3.

23. Annette Simmons, *The Story Factor: Inspiration, Influence, and Persuasion through the Art of Storytelling* (New York: Basic Books, 2006), p. 108; idem, *Whoever Tells the Best Story Wins: How to Use Your Own Stories to Communicate with Power and Impact*, 2nd edn (New York: AMACOM, 2015).

24. Garth S. Jowett and Victoria O'Donnell, *Propaganda and Persuasion* (Thousand Oaks, CA: SAGE Publications, 1986), p. 16.

25. Ibid., pp. 153–4.

26. See Chapter 5.

27. William Safire, *Lend Me Your Ears: Great Speeches in History* (New York: W. W. Norton & Co., 1997), pp. 21–2.

28. George Lakoff and Mark Johnson, *Metaphors We Live By* (Chicago: University of Chicago Press, 1980), p. 3. See also Murray Knowles and Rosamund Moon, *Introducing Metaphor* (New York: Routledge, 2006), pp. 31–2.

29. Lakoff and Johnson, *Metaphors We Live By*, p. 5.

30. Casebeer, *Military Force and Culture Change*, pp. 34–5.

31. Ibid., p. 36.

32. Patrick Colm Hogan, *The Mind and its Stories* (Cambridge: Cambridge University Press, 2003), p. 83.

33. Ibid., p. 88.

34. Ibid., p. 94.

35. Ibid., p. 98.

36. Ibid., p. 204.

37. Ibid., p. 205.

38. Donald E. Polkinghorne, *Narrative Knowing and the Human Sciences* (Albany, NY: SUNY Press, 1988), p. 11.

39. Ibid.

40. Scott W. Ruston, *COMOPS Journal* (September 2009), http://comops.org/journal/2009/09/03/understand-what-narrative-is-and-does/ This online journal provides an interesting background on the concept of strategic communications, narratives, and audiences.

41. Steven R. Corman, Angela Trethewey, and Bud Goodall, *A 21st Century Model for Communication in the Global War of Ideas* (Consortium for Strategic Communication, Arizona State University, 2007), p. 4.

42. Ibid., p. 7.

43. John T. Cacioppo and Richard E. Petty, "Effects of Message Repetition on Argument Processing, Recall, and Presuasion," *Basic and Applied Social Psychology* 10:1 (1989): 3–12; see also George E. Belch, "The Effects of Television Commercial Repetition on Cognitive Response and Message Acceptance," *Journal of Consumer Research* 9:1 (June 1982): 56–65; George E. Belch and Michael A. Belch, "An Investigation of The Effects of Repetition on Cognitive and Affective Reactions to Humorous and Serious Television Commercials," *Advances in Consumer Research* 11 (1984): 4–10; Arie W. Kruglanski, Eric P. Thompson, and Scott Spiegel, "Bimodal Notions of Persuasion and Single-Process 'Unimodel'," in Shelly Chaiken and Yaacov Trope (eds), *Dual-Process Theories in Social Psychology* (New York: Guilford Press, 1999), p. 308; Lawson Abinanti, "Positioning Depends on Repetition and Consistency" (10 January 2016), http://www.messagesthatmatter.com/positioning-depends-on-repetition-and-consistency/

44. Jared Lewis and Demand Media, "Repetition as a Persuasive Strategy," *Houston Chronicle*, http://smallbusiness.chron.com/repetition-persuasive-strategy-26001.html

45. Gerald R. Miller, "On Being Persuaded: Some Basic Distinctions," in James Price Dillard and Michael Pfau (eds), *The Persuasion Handbook: Developments in Theory and Practice* (Thousand Oaks, CA: SAGE Publications, 2002).

46. Ibid., p. 4.

47. Ibid, p. 6.

48. H. C. Kelman, "Processes of Opinion Change," in *Public Opinion Quarterly* 25 (1961): 57.

49. Miller, "On Being Persuaded," p. 5.

50. Ibid.

51. Edgar Schein, *Coercive Persuasion: A Socio-Psychological Analysis of the "Brainwashing" of American Civilian Prisoners by the Chinese Communists* (New York: W. W. Norton & Co., 1961).

52. Martyn Carruthers, *Prevent Coercive Persuasion and Mind Control, Systemic Coaching*, http://www.systemiccoaching.com/coercion.htm (6 June 2011).

53. Milton Rokeach, *Beliefs, Attitudes, and Values* (San Francisco, CA: Jossey-Bass Inc, 1972), p. ix.

54. Edward L. Fink, Stan A. Kaplowitz, and Susan McGreevy Hubbard, "Oscillation in Beliefs and Decisions," in James Price Dillard and Michael Pfau (eds), *The Persuasion Handbook* (Thousand Oaks, CA: SAGE Publications, 2002), p. 18.

55. David R. Roskos-Ewoldsen, Laura Arpan-Ralstin, and James St Pierre, "Attitude Accessibility and Persuasion: The Quick and the Strong," in James Price Dillard

and Michael Pfau (eds), *The Persuasion Handbook* (Thousand Oaks, CA: SAGE Publications, 2002), p. 39.

56. Ibid., p. 42.
57. Steven Collins, "Mind Games," *NATO Review* online edn (2003), p. 1, http://www.iwar.org/uk/psyops/resources/iraq/mind-games.htm;   R.   Brown, "Information Operations, Public Diplomacy and Spin: The United States and the Politics of Perception Management," *Journal of Information Warfare*, 1:3 (2013), http://mcdia.leeds.ac.uk/papers/pmt/exhibits/32/JIW1_32.pdf#page=46
58. Christopher Lamb, *Review of Psychological Operations: Lessons Learned from Recent Operational Experience* (Washington, DC: National Defense University, 2005), p. 17; Arturo Munoz, "U.S. Military Information Operations in Afghanistan: Effectiveness of Psychological Operations 2001–2010," *National Defense Research Institute*   (2012),   http://www.rand.org/content/dam/rand/pubs/monographs/2012/RAND_MG1060.pdf
59. Carnes Lord, "Psychological–Political Instruments," in Audrey Kurth Cronin and James M. Ludes (eds), *Attacking Terrorism: Elements of a Grand Strategy* (Washington, DC: Georgetown University Press, 2004), p. 220.
60. Ibid., p. 222.
61. Lamb, *Review of Psychological Operations*, p. 10.
62. See James Watson, *Media Communication: An Introduction to Theory and Process* (New York: Palgrave Macmillan, 2008), pp. 14–24, 184–7, 199–203.
63. Albert C. Gunther, *The Persuasive Press Inference: Effects of Mass Media on Perceived Public Opinion* (Thousand Oaks, CA: SAGE Publications, 1998), http://crx.sagepub.com/content/25/5/486.full.pdf+html
64. Richard E. Petty, Joseph R. Priester, and Pablo Brinol, "Mass Media Attitude Change: Implications of the Elaboration Likelihood Model of Persuasion," in Jennings Bryant and Dolf Zillmann (eds), *Media Effects: Advances in Theory and Research* (Mahwah, NJ: Lawrence Erlbaum Associates, 2002), http://crx.sagepub.com/content/25/5/486.full.pdf+html
65. Ibid., p. 126.
66. Ibid.
67. Ibid., p. 127.
68. Ibid., p. 128.
69. See Mao Tse-tung (Samuel B. Griffith, trans.), *On Guerrilla Warfare* (University of Illinois Press, 2000; first published 1937).

2. AN OVERVIEW OF TALIBAN AND OTHER AFGHAN INSURGENT STORIES AND AN ASSESSMENT OF THEIR MASTER NARRATIVES

1. David Kilcullen, *The Accidental Guerrilla: Fighting Small Wars in the Midst of a Big One* (New York: Oxford University Press), p. 31.
2. Ibid.

3. Tim Foxley, "The Taliban's Propaganda Activities: How Well is the Afghan Insurgency Communicating and What is it Saying?" (Stockholm: SIPRI Project Paper, June 2007), p. 1.

4. Kilcullen, *The Accidental Guerrilla*, p. 31.

5. https://www.theguardian.com/technology/2016/apr/04/taliban-app-removed-from-google-play-store; James Titcomb, "Google bans Taliban app for hate speech," *Daily Telegraph*, 4 April 2016, http://www.telegraph.co.uk/technology/2016/04/04/google-bans-taliban-app-for-hate-speech/

6. See Chapters 4–9 for an in-depth discussion of Taliban delivery systems.

7. This is particularly relevant to the Taliban's expansion into several districts in northern Baghlan, Kunduz, Takhar, Badakhshan, Badghis, Jawzjan, and Sar-i-Pul and other provinces in the north as well as the west. This was vividly seen in Kunduz in late September 2015, when they took control of the city for over two weeks.

8. Mullah Akhtar Mansour confirmed in July 2015 that leader Mullah Omar had been dead for more than two years. The news was kept secret by a handful of Taliban leaders, apparently on tactical grounds. See Rod Nordland and Joseph Goldstein, "Taliban Leader Mullah Omar Died in 2013, Afghans Declare," *New York Times*, 29 July 2015, http://www.nytimes.com/2015/07/30/world/asia/mullah-omar-taliban-death-reports-prompt-inquiry-by-afghan-government.html?_r=0; "Mullah Omar: Taliban choose deputy Mansour as successor," BBC News, 30 July 2015, http://www.bbc.com/news/world-asia-33721074

9. Rohan Joshi, "The Taliban after Mullah Omar and the battle for Afghanistan," *Business Standard*, 11 August 2015, http://www.business-standard.com/article/punditry/the-taliban-after-mullah-omar-the-battle-for-afghanistan-115081000751_1.html

10. https://www.khaama.com/taliban-announce-summer-offensive-under-the-name-of-omari-operations-0622 and http://webcache.googleusercontent.com/search?q=cache:eLwcru8SUh8J:shahamat-english.com/statement-by-leadership-council-of-islamic-emirate-regarding-inauguration-of-spring-offensive-entitled-operation-omari/+&cd=1&hl=en&ct=clnk

11. Throughout the book we will present the explicit stories, as we perceive and interpet them, associated with the Taliban and other Afghan insurgent IO artifacts. We will make every effort to make these interpretations as Afghan-centric as possible.

12. This takes into account that insurgents employ and entice members of society through financial and ideological means. Civilians willing to engage in militant activity are typically convinced through self-motivators like grievances, ethnic, tribal or business rifts, religious ideology, or opportunistic financial incentives.

13. Literally "way" or code of the Pashtun; Pashtunwali is an informal and unwritten social code based around a series of various social identifiers and values, including *merana* (willpower and tenacity), *melmastia* (hospitality), *namus* (honor/reputa-

tion), *himmat* (ambitiousness), *sharam* (shame), and *badal* (literally "exchange," but also used to refer to one seeking revenge), *nenawati* (the provision of sanctuary), *ghairat* (bravery/courage), *nang* (honor, esteem). For sources on the Pashtun generally, see James W. Spain, *The Way of the Pathans* (Oxford: Oxford University Press, 1972); James W. Spain, *The People of the Khyber, the Pathans of Pakistan* (New York: Praeger, 1962); Akbar Ahmed, *Pukhtun Economy and Society* (London: Routledge, 1980); Sir Olaf Caroe, *The Pathans and Society* (Oxford: Oxford University Press, 1958); Brent Glatzer, "Being Pashtun–Being Muslim: Concepts of Person and War in Afghanistan," in Brent Glatzer (ed.), *Essays on South Asian Society, Culture and Politics II* (Berlin: Zentrum Moderner Orient, 1998), pp. 83–94; T. H. Holdich, "Swatis and Afridis," *Journal of the Anthropological Institute of Great Britain and Ireland* 29 (1899), http://links.jstor.org/sici?sici=0959–5295(1899)29%3A1%2F2%3C2%3ASAA%3E2.0.CO%3B2–2; Niloufer Qasim Mahdi, *Pukhtunwali: Ostracism and Honor Among the Pathan Hill Tribes* (New York: Elsevier, 1986), p. 1.

14. Ben Brandt, Mullah Omar's Conduct of Intelligence and Counterintelligence, *CTC Sentinel* 4:6 (June 2011): 19–23; Gilles Dorronsoro, Counterintelligence and Hill Tribes U.S. Needs to Wise Up, *US News*, 20 February 2009, http://www.usnews.com/opinion/articles/2009/02/20/taliban-strategy-in-afghanistan-is-smart-politics-so-us-needs-to-wise-up

15. "Da Kufar sara Jang dai" (Fight with Infidels) was credited to a singer named Shaheed Samiullah Shahid, http://alemarah-iea.net/Taranee/

16. Thomas H. Johnson, with Mumtaz Ahmad and Dietrich Reetz, *Who Speaks for Islam? Muslim Grassroots Leaders and Popular Preachers in South Asia*, NBR Special Report #22 (Seattle, WA: National Bureau of Asian Research, February 2010).

17. Thomas H. Johnson's interview with Canadian Military Intelligence Officer, September 2009.

18. This is not to suggest that ethnic and religious friction is non-existent in contemporary Afghanistan. Hazara and Pashtun divides, for instance, are particularly acute in areas where Pashtun nomads (Kochi) interfere with Hazara-owned pastures, namely in Ghazni, Wardak, Uruzgan, and Daikundi provinces.

19. Rod Nordland and Jawad Sukhanyar, "Taliban Are Said to Target Hazaras to Try to Match ISIS' Brutality, Afghans Declare," *New York Times*, 22 April 2015, http://www.nytimes.com/2015/04/23/world/asia/taliban-are-said-to-target-hazaras-to-try-to-match-isis-brutality.html; Mohammad Radmanesh, "Taliban violence reaches new peak after Hazara murders," *France 24 The Observers*, 11 November 2015, http://observers.france24.com/en/20151111-taliban-murder-women-children-hazara

20. "Suicide Attacks in Afghanistan (2001–2007)," UNAMA (9 September 2007), p. 68. See also Thomas H. Johnson, "Taliban Adaptations and Innovations," *Small Wars and Insurgencies* 24:1 (January 2013): 3–27.

21. During field research in Pakistan and Afghanistan in 1986–7, numerous Afghan

families approached the author to write compilations and stories about family members martyred during the anti-Soviet jihad.

22. Waigal district was attacked and overrun by insurgents in March 2011.

23. "Nick Paton Walsh reports on the reappearance of the Taliban to control one Afghanistan town near the Pakistan border," CNN, 22 June 2011.

24. See note 13 in this chapter.

25. See Thomas H. Johnson, "On the Edge of the Big Muddy: The Taliban Resurgence in Afghanistan," *China and Eurasian Forum Quarterly* 5:2 (2007): 93–129.

26. A US intelligence analyst found this Taliban leaflet in eastern Afghanistan in 2006, and gave it to the author in January 2007. The Taliban's use of leaflets is very rare; this is one of the few that I have ever seen.

27. *Namus* refers to a Pashtun man's responsibility to uphold the honor of his wife or wives, daughters, and his unmarried or widowed sisters. Importantly, the honor of an Afghan man and the honor of all females he is responsible for are interdependent values. *Ghairat* refers to the fundamental pride of an Afghan man's courage. If a person's courage is in question, he may no longer be called a man until he can prove it by showing it to people in practice. It could be participation in war, protection of village, family, and property or other activities that benefit people in the community. *Paighour* refers to taunting one's honor; it is a provoking reminder to a person whose acts have crossed or will cross the limits of community-accepted behavior.

28. In August 2009, the author was told that many Kandahari businessmen, the last people one would expect to support the Taliban, regularly went to Zangabar, Panjawyi to have water and land disputes resolved by the Taliban court and judges. The Karzai judicial system was viewed as slow, corrupt, and ineffectual.

29. During the Taliban's retreat and reconstitution phase, 2001–3, messaging primarily targeted Pashtun communities with threats against "collaborators" in the south and east as a way to re-establish influence, sympathy, and support among the locals. The years 2003–6 saw an increase in messaging that targeted Pashtun communities, in search of able-bodied recruits and helping to exploit communal grievances against the Afghan government and Coalition/NATO forces, including issues of tribal marginalization/isolation and losses from errant military strikes; it also tapped into the large pool of poor farming communities who were targets of the forced poppy eradication campaign.

30. "Taliban Strikes Back," CBS, 31 March 2003, http://www.cbsnews.com/stories/2003/04/03/attack/main547507.shtml

31. "Taliban chief calls for unity against U.S. troops," Reuters, 6 November 2005, http://www.redorbit.com/news/general/296445/taliban_chief_calls_for_unity_against_us_troops/index.html

4. TALIBAN AND AFGHAN INSURGENT MAGAZINES, CIRCULARS, AND NEWSLETTERS

1. Riaz Khan, "Pakistan arrests former Taliban spokesman," *The Independent*, 4 January 2009, http://www.independent.co.uk/news/world/asia/pakistan-arrests-former-taliban-spokesman-1224489.html
2. Muttaqi was the first Minister of Information and Culture before he was later reshuffled to serve as the regime's Minister of Education.
3. Joanna Nathan, "Reading the Taliban," in Antonio Giustozzi (ed.), *Decoding the New Taliban: Insights from the Afghan Field* (New York: Columbia University Press, 2009), p. 30.
4. Ibid., pp. 30, 40.
5. Ibid., p. 30.
6. Ibid., p. 30.
7. "Mukhbat biography," *Daily Shahadat*, http://dailyshahadat.com/mujale-show-page.php?id=340
8. "Selection List: Review of Pro-Taliban, Islamist Publications Oct/Nov 09," Open Source Center, SAP20091130950058, Caversham BBC Monitoring in English, 30 November 2009.

5. THE TALIBAN'S USE OF *SHABNAMAH* (NIGHT LETTERS)

1. This section is based, in part, on Thomas H. Johnson, "The Taliban Insurgency and an Analysis of *Shabnamah* (Night Letters)," *Small Wars and Insurgencies* 18:3 (September 2007): 317–44.
2. Louis Dupree, *Afghanistan* (New York: Oxford University Press, 1973), p. 129.
3. While many *shabnamah* are hand-written, typically in nearly illegible bad grammar, some *shabnamah* are typed and printed using modern computer and printer capabilities. Many of these are produced in Pakistan.
4. See Table 5.1 and its expanded definitions.
5. Appendix B (available online at www.hurstpublishers.com/book/taliban-narratives) presents a unique summary of 279 Taliban night letters/*shabnamah* from 2008–10 which the author and colleagues collected during field trips to Afghanistan, especially southern Afghanistan. Some of these letters were sent unsolicited to the author from US government personnel.
6. See Appendix B for night letters elaborating on these themes.
7. Dupree, *Afghanistan*, p. 114.
8. For example, see Doug McAdam, John D. McCarthy, and Mayer N. Zald (eds), *Comparative Perspectives on Social Movements: Political Opportunities, Mobilizing Structures, and Cultural Framings* (Cambridge: Cambridge University Press, 1996); Doug McAdam, Sidney Tarrow, and Charles Tilly, "Toward an Integrated Perspective on Social Movements and Revolution," in Mark I. Lichbach and Alan S. Zuckerman (eds), *Comparative Politics: Rationality, Culture and Structure* (Cambridge:

Cambridge University Press, 1997); Scott Mann, "Combat Story Telling," *Narrative Strategies*, 2 January 2016, http://www.narrative-strategies.com/scott-mann/combat-story-telling

9. The use of oral narratives for transmitting instructions and legends is crucial, especially in rural Afghanistan, considering that the vast majority of the rural population is illiterate. Night letters are generally posted at mosques or delivered to a literate village member and read to the community during a mass meeting.

10. See Chapter 7.

11. Hafizullah Emadi, *Culture and Customs of Afghanistan* (London: Greenwood Press, 2005), p. 98.

12. Sandy Gall, *Afghanistan: Agony of a Nation* (London: Bodley Head, 1988), p. 99.

13. Nelofer Pazira, *A Bed of Red Flowers: In Search of My Afghanistan* (New York: Free Press, 2005), p. 102.

14. For an example of a media account of night letters posted near the Spin Boldak border, see Ron Synovitz, "Afghanistan: U.S. Investigates Taliban 'Night Letters' Threatening Villagers," RadioLiberty, 10 March 2004, http://www.rferl.org/featuresarticle/2004/03/c47dc6f9–5e79–4213–8c0e-2430cf0557b5.html; also Jon Rabiroff, "Chilling 'night letters' from Taliban intimidate Afghans," *Stars and Stripes*, 30 November 2010, http://www.stripes.com/news/chilling-night-letters-from-taliban-intimidate-afghans-1.127043; and "Desperate Afghans pin asylum hopes on Taliban threat letters," *Dawn*, 15 September 2015, http://www.dawn.com/news/1207786

15. Aryn Baker, "Deadly Notes in the Night: How the Taliban are using a new kind of terrorist threat to intimidate Afghans," *Time Magazine*, 5 July 2006.

16. Ibid.

17. PYSOP officer interview by Captain Keely M. Fahoum, 14 June 2006. US PSYOP personnel have expressed frustration at their inability to respond to Taliban night letters in a timely, effective manner. While the Taliban could hand-deliver their communiqués to strategic points of contact within rural villages, US PSYOP planners have limited physical access or intimate knowledge of village politics and social structure. During Operation Enduring Freedom, PSYOP personnel and analysts struggled with bureaucratic red tape, which made it next to impossible to respond to Taliban propaganda efforts in a timely manner. (Personal communication with two PSYOP officers at the Naval Postgraduate School, May–July 2006.)

18. I would like to thank former NPS student Captain Keely M. Fahoum, USAF, for her outstanding support of the Taliban night letter analysis presented here. Captain Fahoum's earlier conceptualizations of Taliban *shabnamah* have been critical to my thinking on the subject.

19. This particular night letter was distributed and provided to the author in May 2006 by a government analyst returning from an Afghanistan deployment.

20. Translation provided from Amin Tarzi interview, 14 July 2006 and Farid Mohammad, September 2006.
21. Sir Percy Sykes, *A History of Afghanistan* (London: Macmillan, 1940), p. 367.
22. Dupree, *Afghanistan*, p. 314.
23. Ibid., p. 314.
24. Sir Olaf Caroe, *The Pathans and Society* (Oxford: Oxford University Press, 1958), pp. 15–19.
25. Caroe states that Ghilzais are descendants of Khalaj Turks who came with Attila and the Huns. Caroe also states that after several centuries these tribes became Pashtunized and they formed a unique dialect of Pakhtu with a heavy Turkish vocabulary. He also states that the word Ghilzai comes from Khalaj, which evolved through time from Khalaj to Khalji to Ghalji to Ghalzai or Ghilzai. Ibid., pp. 15–19.
26. See Thomas H. Johnson and W. Chris Mason, "Understanding the Taliban and Insurgency in Afghanistan," *Orbis: A Journal of World Affairs* 51:1 (2007).
27. James W. Spain, *The Pathan Borderland* (Karachi: Indus Publications, 1963), pp. 41, 57; Caroe, *The Pathans and Society*, pp. 15–19.
28. Dupree, *Afghanistan*, pp. 322–5; Frank Clements, *Conflict in Afghanistan: A Historical Encyclopedia* (Santa Barbara, CA: ABC-CLIO, 2003), p. 94.
29. The only period when the Pashtuns did not hold power in Afghanistan was briefly in 1929 when Habibullah Ghazi, a Tajik, took power until he was overthrown and Durranis returned to power Mohammad Najibullah Ahmadzai, who was a Soviet puppet during the USSR occupation of Afghanistan. Burhanuddin Rabbani, Tajik leader of the Jamiat-i-Islami, was an ineffectual Mujahidin president of pre-Taliban Afghanistan from June 1992 until the Taliban took Kabul in September 1996, and the present Afghan President Ashraf, Ashraf Ghani Ahmadzai. It is interesting to note that since becoming Afghan president in 2014, he is officially refered to as Mohammad Ashraf Ghani, dropping the name Ahmadzai, referring to his tribe from the Ghilzai conferation.
30. The competition and distrust between the Ghilzai and Durranis played a major role in the split of the PDPA when the Khalq (the people or masses) led by Nur Mohammed Taraki represented Ghilzai Pashtuns and the Parcham (Banner) led by Babrak Karmal represented the Durrani Pashtun, See Henry S. Bradsher, *Afghanistan and the Soviet Union*, 2nd edn (Durham, NC: Duke University, 1985).
31. From the hundreds of resistance groups which emerged to challenge the Soviet invasion and occupation, the Pakistani directorate for Inter-Services Intelligence (ISI), who played a central role arming and training Afghan resistance groups, recognized seven Sunni parties and established offices for them through which to channel covert support. Although most of these resistance groups had a strong religious ethos, the groups were organized primarily along ethno-linguistic and tribal lines. Significantly, while three parties were explicitly led by a Ghilzai, all

the "leaders" of the Peshawar parties except for one had Ghilzai tribal connections. Gulbuddin Hekmatyar, Abdul Rasoul Sayyaf, and Nabi Muhammadi were Ghilzais; Younis Khalis was from a neighboring eastern Pushtun tribe (the Khugiani); Pir Gailani and Sibghatullah Mujaddidi were from immigrant Sufi families whose religious and political links are largely with Ghilzais. Only Burhanuddin Rabbani has no intimate connection with Ghilzais. None of the Peshawar parties was led by the Durranis, who were deliberately marginalized by the ISI.

32. See Bradsher, *Afghanistan and the Soviet Union*.

33. Gailani's NIFA party often stood in for the royal family, partially because of the anomalous position of former King Zahir Shah.

34. Dupree, *Afghanistan*, p. 314.

35. Steve Coll, *Ghost Wars: The Secret History of the CIA, Afghanistan, and bin Laden, from the Soviet Invasion to September 10, 2001* (New York: Penguin Books, 2004), p. 238.

36. Jeffery J. Roberts, *The Origins of Conflict in Afghanistan* (Westport, CT: Praeger Publishing, 2003), p. xiii.

37. Fawaz A. Gerges, *The Far Enemy: Why Jihad went Global* (Cambridge: Cambridge University Press, 2005), p. 83.

38. Night letter provided by a government analyst deployed in Afghanistan in 2003, translated by Amin Tarzi and Farid Mohammad, October 2006.

39. Translation provided by Farid Mohammad, October 2006.

40. Thomas H. Johnson and M. Chris Mason, "Understanding the Taliban and Insurgency in Afghanistan."

41. Anna Badkhen, "Afghan government failure reopens door to the Taliban," *San Francisco Chronicle*, 17 September 2006, p. A4; David Jolly, "Afghanistan's Crippled Power Grid Exposes Vulnerability of Beseiged Capital," *New York Times*, 17 February 2016, http://www.nytimes.com/2016/02/18/world/asia/afghanistan-hardship-taliban-bombings.html?_r=0

42. Special Inspector General for Afghanistan Reconstruction (SIGAR), *Quarterly Report to the United States Congress* (Washington, DC: 30 July 2014).

43. See especially ch. 8 of Mark Juergensmeyer, *Terror in the Mind of God: The Global Rise of Religious Violence*, 3rd edn (Berkeley, CA: University of California Press, 2003).

44. See Bruce Lawrence (ed.), *Messages to the World: The Statements of Osama Bin Laden* (London: Verso, 2005); also "Bin Laden rails against Crusaders and UN," BBC News, 3 November 2001, http://news.bbc.co.uk/2/hi/world/monitoring/media_reports/1636782.stm; "Transcript of Bin Laden's October interview," CNN World, 5 February 2002, http://edition.cnn.com/2002/WORLD/asiapcf/south/02/05/binladen.transcript/; Bernard Lewis, "License to Kill: Usama bin Ladin's Declaration of Jihad," *Foreign Affairs*, Nov./Dec. 1998, https://www.for-

eignaffairs.com/articles/saudi-arabia/1998–11–01/license-kill-usama-bin-ladins-declaration-jihad; Doug Bandow, "Terrorism: Why They Want to Kill Us," *Huffington Post*, 25 May 2011, http://www.huffingtonpost.com/doug-bandow/terrorism-why-they-want-t_b_631942.html

45. Source: http://hrw.org/campaigns/afghanistan/2006/education/letter8.htm
46. Source: http://hrw.org/campaigns/afghanistan/2006/education/letter8.htm
47. A term of Persian origin, meaning an army, a camp; or one belonging to an army, a soldier.
48. Dupree, *Afghanistan*, p. 453.
49. Gerges, *The Far Enemy*, p. 83; "Taliban expands fight beyond Afghanistan's Kunduz," Aljazeera, 1 October 2015, http://www.aljazeera.com/news/2015/10/taliban-expands-fight-afghanistan-kunduz-151001172158686.html
50. He reportedly started the Taliban after a dream in which Allah came to him in the shape of a man, asking him to lead the faithful. In 1996 he made a risky but brilliant propaganda move, which again supports the notion of him being a charismatic leader, by taking the garment which Afghans believe to be the Prophet Mohammed's shroud or cloak out of Kandahar's royal mausoleum for the first time in sixty years and wearing it at a public rally as a way of identifying himself with the Prophet (Ahmed Rashid, *Taliban*, 1st edn (New Haven, CT: Yale University Press, 2001), p. 20.) The cloak is believed by many of the 90 per cent of Pashtuns who are illiterate to contain supernatural and mystical powers. This action also represented Omar's absolute faith in his perceived divine right to rule, and gave him legitimacy in his role as leader of the Afghan people ordained by Allah; soon after Omar was named Amir-ul Momineen or leader of the faithful, not just of the Afghans but of all Muslims. The cloak of the Prophet Mohammed had been folded and padlocked in a series of chests in a crypt in the royal mausoleum at Kandahar: "myth had it that the padlocks to the crypt could be opened only when touched by a true *Amir-ul Momineen*, a king of the Muslims." See Joseph A. Raelin, "The Myth of Charismatic Leaders," March 2003, http://www.findarticles.com/p/articles/mi_m0MNT/is_3_57/ai_98901483
51. Richard F. Nyrop and Donald M. Seekins (eds), *Afghanistan Country Study* (Washington, DC: American University, Foreign Area Studies, 1986), http://www.gl.iit.edu/govdocs/afghanistan/Family.html
52. Miles Bredin, "Class war: battle to educate Afghan girls and boys hindered by fear of Taliban retribution," *The Independent*, 12 September 2006; Simon Tomlinson, "Hundreds of Afghan girls poisoned by toxic gas at two schools in suspected attacks by Taliban militants opposed to their education," *Daily Mail*, 3 September 2015, http://www.dailymail.co.uk/news/article-3221073/Hundreds-Afghan-girls-poisoned-toxic-gas-two-schools-suspected-attacks-Taliban-militants-opposed-education.html; Abdullah Saljoqi, "Taliban burn down girls' school in Afghanistan," *France 24 The Observers*, 4 November 2015, http://observers.france24.com/en/20151104-taliban-shut-down-girls-school-afghanistan; for a similar type of attack by the Pakistani Taliban, see Sophla Salfi and Greg Botelho, "In Pakistan

school attack, Taliban terrorists kill 145, mostly children," *CNN World*, 17 December 2014,http://www.cnn.com/2014/12/16/world/asia/pakistan-peshawar-school-attack/

53. Source: Human Rights Watch, http://hrw.org/campaigns/afghanistan/2006/education/letter5.htm

54. Noor Khan, "Militants behead Afghan principal for educating girls: Taliban assaults cited in closing of schools," *Boston Globe*, 5 January 2006.

55. Human Rights Watch, http://hrw.org/campaigns/afghanistan/2006/education/letter3.htm

56. Source: Humans Rights Watch, http://hrw.org/campaigns/afghanistan/2006/education/letter3.htm

57. Esther Pan, "Afghanistan's New Security Threat," *Backgrounder*, Council on Foreign Affairs, 14 February 2006. See also Griff Witte, "Suicide Bombers Kill Dozens in Afghanistan, Violence in South is Seen as Message to NATO," *Washington Post Foreign Service*, 17 January 2006, p. A11.

58. See Thomas H. Johnson, "Taliban Adaptations and Innovations," *Small Wars and Insurgencies* 24: 1 (January 2013): 3–27.

59. For a chronology of suicide bombings in Afghanistan, compiled by Radio Liberty, see http://www.rferl.org/featuresarticle/2006/01/9ac36a59-d683–4189-a2b9–94fe5fbf32ad.html

60. Griff Witte, "Afghans Confront Surge in Violence: Foreign Support Seen Behind Attacks that Mimic Those in Iraq," *Christian Science Monitor*, 28 November 2005, p. 1; Ron Synovitz, "Afghanistan: Are Militants Copying Iraqi Insurgents' Suicide Tactics?" Radio Free Europe Radio Library, 17 January 2006, http://www.rferl.org/content/article/1064791.html

61. Associated Press, "Top Taliban military commander dismisses NATO casualty reports, warns journalists," *International Harold Tribune* (Asian and Pacific edition), 4 September 2006, internet version, http://www.iht.com/articles/ap/2006/09/04/asia/AS_GEN_Afghan_Taliban.php

62. Thomas H. Johnson, "Taliban Adaptations and Innovations."

63. Source: Humans Rights Watch, http://hrw.org/campaigns/afghanistan/2006/education/letter9.htm

64. Source: Humans Rights Watch, http://hrw.org/campaigns/afghanistan/2006/education/letter9.htm

65. Syed Saleem Shahzad, "In search of the Taliban's missing link," *Asia Times Online*, 16 September 2006, http://atimes.com/atimes/South_Asia/HI16Df01.html

66. Together these stories (frames) become an important Taliban narrative.

67. Charles Lindholm. "The Segmentary Lineage System: Its Applicability to Pakistan's Political Structure," in Ainslie T. Embree (ed.), *Pakistan's Western Borderlands: The Transformation of Political Order* (New Delhi: Vikas Publishing House, 1977), p. 60.

6. THE TALIBAN'S USE OF THE INTERNET, SOCIAL NETWORKING, VIDEOS, RADIO STATIONS, AND GRAFFITI

1. For instance, the 92,000 US military intelligence files "leaked" in the notorious Wikileaks controversy in the summer of 2010 denoted Pakistan's involvement in the Afghan conflict, namely the state-provided support for the Taliban and the Haqqani Network. See also Matt Waldman, "The Sun in the Sky: The Relationship Between Pakistan's ISI and Afghan Insurgents," Discussion Paper 18 (Carr Center for Human Rights Policy, Kennedy School of Government, Harvard University, June 2010); Peter Tomsen, *The Wars of Afghanistan: Messianic Terrorism, Tribal Conflicts, and the Failures of Great Powers*, 1st edn (New York: Public Affairs, 2011); Anand Gopal, *No Good Men Among the Living: America, the Taliban, and the War through Afghan Eyes* (London: Picador, 2015); Carlotta Gall, *The Wrong Enemy: America in Afghanistan, 2001–2014* (New York: Harcourt, 2014).

2. Some interviews include Taliban former "shadow" governors such as Qari Omar Farouq (Faryab 2009), Mauluvi Raz Haider (Balkh), Nur Mohammad (Wardak), Mawlawi Muhammad Muhsin Hashimi (Takhar), Mullah Shahabuddin Ghori (Herat, 2010), and Qari Mohammad Ismail Siraji (Jawzjan), among a few.

3. Ian Traynor, "NATO Afghanistan mission in doubt after Dutch withdrawal," *Guardian*, 22 February 2010; "Dutch government falls over Afghanistan mission," rnw media, https://www.rnw.org/archive/dutch-government-falls-over-afghani-stan-mission. Italy, Spain, and Germany have all suffered national political crises stemming from their NATO participation in Afghanistan.

4. International Crisis Group, "Taliban Propaganda: Winning the War of Words?" *Asia Report* 158 (July 2008): 15.

5. Internet World Stats: Afghanistan Country Profile, http://www.internetworld-stats.com/asia/af.htm; Index Mundi, Afghanistan: internet users, http://www.indexmundi.com/facts/afghanistan/internet-users; World Bank Data: Internet users (per 100 people), http://data.worldbank.org/indicator/IT.NET.USER.P2

6. Policy statement, Islamic Republic of Afghanistan, H. E. Mr Amirzai Sangin, Minister, Ministry of Communications and Information Technology (MCIT), http://www.itu.int/plenipotentiary/2010/statements/afghanistan/sangin.html

7. "SEAF-AGF & RANA Technologies Enterprises Partner to Expand Internet Service in Afghanistan," 24 January 2011, http://www.afghangrowthfinance.com/detail.asp?CatID=18&ContID=44

8. The official Taliban Twitter account is http://twitter.com/#!/alemarahweb and of this writing was last updated 19 June 2011.

9. Anecdotal reporting suggests that in 2006 the Taliban scattered hundreds of DVDs around the village of Niyazi, which is less than 3 miles from the center of Kabul. Ivan Watson, "Taliban Enlists Video in Fight for Afghanistan," *NPR*, 2 November 2006, http://www.wbur.org/npr/6423946/taliban-enlists-video-in-fight-for-afghanistan

10. Ibid., p. 11.

11. Amir Shah, "Ministry: Taliban Spokesman Arrested," Associated Press, 27 September 2007. Afghanistan's National Directorate of Security (NDS) claimed in May 2011 that Zabihullah Mujahid is the *nom de guerre* of Haji Ismail, a 42-year-old resident from Chaman Pakistan. Ray Rivera and Carlotta Gall, "Rebutting Afghan Spy Agency, Taliban Say Their Leader Isn't Dead," *New York Times*, 23 May 2011, http://www.nytimes.com/2011/05/24/world/asia/24omar. html

12. "Taliban Threatens to Kill Captured US Soldier," NBC News, 16 July 2009. "Taliban Dismisses Top Leader Mansoor Dadullah," Associated Press, 30 December 2007.

13. While conducting field research in southern Afghanistan in the summer of 2008, the author found it quite easy to make telephone contact with the Taliban spokesmen designated for southern Afghanistan (Qari Yousaf Ahmadi) and eastern Afghanistan (Zabihullah Mujahid) and spoke to them on two occasions.

14. Amin Tarzai, "Taliban radio back on the air," *Asia Times Online*, 11 March 2005, http://www.atimes.com/atimes/Central_Asia/GE11Ag01.html

15. "Afghanistan: Taliban Launch New Radio Station in South," *Xinhua*, 8 August 2009, republished at http://www.amicaltmedia.net/headlines-archive.php?pid= 316&year=2009. The Taliban were also reported to have broadcast three-hour programs in Ghazni as well.

16. Radioinfo.com.au, https://www.radioinfo.com.au/news/taliban-launch-secret-radio-station

17. Excerpt taken from OSC: Caversham BBC Monitoring in English (originally filed as SAP20091002950045).

18. Yochi J. Dreazen and Siobhan Gorman, "Pentagon James Web, Radio Links of the Taliban," *Wall Street Journal*, 18 April 2009, http://www.wsj.com/articles/ SB124001042575330715

19. Sher Ahmed Haider, "In Ghazni, Taliban FM radio goes on air," *Pajhwok Afghan News*, 8 August 2009, available at http://www.pajhwok.com/viewstory.asp?lng= eng&id=79248

20. See http://www.shahamat.org/

21. Ibid. Claire Truscott, "'Gooooood mornin' Afghanistan!' US fights Taliban on airwaves," AFP, 6 October 2009, available at http://www.google.com/hosted-news/afp/article/ALeqM5gygBjOcD9BhvtVR38JWQJFPS8PcA

22. Charles Lindholm. "The Segmentary Lineage System: Its Applicability to Pakistan's Political Structure," in Ainslie T. Embree (ed.), *Pakistan's Western Borderlands: The Transformation of Political Order* (New Delhi: Vikas Publishing House, 1977), pp. 41–66.

23. Early reports from the time when the Taliban were created indicated that the movement did not seek wider political authority than the re-establishment of law and order in Kandahar province.

24. International Crisis Group, "Taliban Propaganda: Winning the War of Words?" *Asia Report* 158, 24 July 2008.

25. Ibid., pp. 14–15.

7. THE AFGHANS' AND TALIBAN'S USE OF POETRY AND *TARANAS* AS AN EFFECTIVE COMMUNICATION TOOL

1. This chapter is based in part on Thomas H. Johnson and Wali Ahmed Shaaker, "The Taliban's Use of Poetry," unpublished manuscript, 2008).

2. See http://www.jahromchalipa.blogfa.com/cat-6.aspx

3. Louis Dupree, *The Afghans Honor a Muslim Saint* (New York: American Universities Field Staff, 1963), p. 12.

4. For the authoritative work on Taliban poetry, see Alex Strick van Linschoten and Felix Kuehn (eds), *Poetry of the Taliban* (London: Hurst & Co., 2012).

5. "A leader in Afghanistan must be a poet. It establishes his intellectual legitimacy. Without poetry, a man who aspires to leadership will be disregarded as intellectually inferior." Interview with an Afghan poet, 27 August 2009.

6. Shahid Afsar, Chris Samples, and Thomas Wood, "The Taliban: An Organizational Analysis," *Military Review* (May–June 2008): 59; Zachary Laub, "The Taliban in Afghanistan," *Council on Foreign Relations*, 4 July 2014, http://www.cfr.org/afghanistan/taliban-afghanistan/p10551

7. For a more in-depth analysis of why poetry resonates so strongly with Afghans, see Wali Shaaker, "Poetry: Why it Matters to Afghans," Culture and Conflict Studies Occasional Paper Series (Monterey, CA: Department of National Security Affairs, Naval Postgraduate School, August 2009).

8. As mentioned above, see van Linschoten and Kuehn (eds), *Poetry of the Taliban*.

9. Fawaz A. Gerges, *The Far Enemy: Why Jihad went Global* (New York: Cambridge University Press, 2005), p. 3.

10. Raymond Ibrahim (ed. and trans.), *The Al Qaeda Reader* (New York: Broadway Books, 2007), pp. 198–208.

11. Mark Juergensmeyer, *Terror in the Mind of God: The Global Rise of Religious Violence* (Berkeley, CA: University of California Press, 2003), p. 10.

12. Bernt Glatzer, "Being Pashtun–Being Muslim: Concepts of Person and War in Afghanistan," *Essays on South Asian Society: Culture and Politics II* (Zentrum Moderner Orient Arbeitshefte, 9) (Berlin: Das Arabische Buch, 1998), pp. 83–94.

13. A more detailed account of this event may be found in Sir Ewen Martin, *Afghanistan: A Short History of its People and Politics* (New York: Harper Collins, 2002).

14. All of the Taliban poems examined here can be found at http://www.toorabora.com/

15. *Takfir* is an Arabic word derived from the term *kufr* meaning impiety. In Islamic doctrine, this is a very serious accusation: that one who is or claims to be Muslim

is declared to be impure, is excommunicated in the eyes of the Community of the Faithful, may no longer benefit from the protection of the law, and is condemned to death. As per Gilles Kepel, *Jihad: The Trail of Political Islam* (Cambridge, MA: Harvard University Press, 2002), pp. 31–2.

16. Glatzer, "Being Pashtun–Being Muslim," pp. 83–94.

17. Aisha Ahmad and Roger Boase, *Pashtun Tales from the Pakistan–Afghan Frontier* (London: Saqi Books, 2008), p. 16.

18. Nimrod was the builder of the tower of Babel. He was said to have subverted the people away from honoring God in favor of honoring him. In the Book of Genesis, God punishes Nimrod and his people by sowing many languages in them so that they can no longer understand each other, thereby breaking up Nimrod's kingdom into many smaller multilingual factions. The idea conveyed by the poet is that the multilingual peoples of the world are all coming now to Afghanistan.

19. Forgiveness from God.

20. Belal lived 578–622. He was a slave from Abyssinia, whom Abubakr bought and released from slavery. He joined the army of Prophet Mohammad and, and as a committed Muslim and warrior, fought many wars. He was also the Mo'azen—the caller to prayers.

21. The third *Khalifa* of Islam.

22. The second *Khalifa* of Islam.

23. Reference to Khaled Ebni Walid, the conqueror of Spain.

24. The poet's last name.

25. The actual word is *Malang*, referring to a hermit, poor type of person.

26. The lover of Laila from the Laila and Majnon Afghan love story.

27. Born in the Khogyani district of Nangarhar, he was the leader of the Islamic Party-Khalis—one of the Peshawar-based resistant parties during the Soviet invasion of Afghanistan. He died in 2003.

28. People of religious authority and respect.

29. Western attire.

30. Not permissible according to Islamic law.

31. A clerical decree.

32. A cautionary reminder: due to the vast number of poets and diversity of opinions among the moderate poets, it could prove erroneous to categorize the moderates as pro- or anti-government. That the moderates do not encourage people to take up arms against the government does not necessarily mean that they support the government. However, a vast number of poets, essayists, and novelists are highly critical of the state. They often criticize institutional corruption, and accuse the government of inefficiency and incompetence in serving the public. It seems that what they aim to accomplish is to generate awareness among the general public, and initiate a discourse on social, economic, and political issues within the intellectual community. However, this does not necessarily translate into an attempt

to encourage a revolt against the government. What it does mean is that they are despondent regarding certain aspects of the current political and or economic state of affairs, and that they wish to contribute to positive social, political, and economic change in Afghanistan.

33. This section is based, in part on Thomas H. Johnson and Ahwad Waheed, "Analyzing Taliban *Taranas* (Chants): An Effective Afghan Propaganda Artifact," *Small Wars and Insurgencies* 22:1 (March 2011): 3–31. For an interesting and one of the few analysis of Taranas see: Michael Semple, "The Rhetoric of Resistance in the Talibans' Rebel Ballads," Carr Center Working paper, Harvard Kennedy School, March 2011.

34. Loy Kandahar is a common term used by Afghans to describe the contemporary provinces of Kandahar, Helmand, Uruzgan, and Zabul.

35. Thomas H. Johnson's interview with Kandahar City resident, June 2009.

36. See Hiromi Lorraine Sakata, *Music in the Mind: The Concept of Music and Musician in Afghanistan* (Kent, OH: Kent State University Press, 1983).

37. Hafizullah Emadi, *Culture and Customs of Afghanistan* (Westport, CT: Greenwood Press, 2005), p. 103.

38. A particularly important type of Afghan folk song is known as *nakhta*, usually sung by women to mourn death or in honor of heroic figures.

39. For overviews of Sufi history and philosophy, see Julian Baldick, *Mystical Islam: An Introduction to Sufism* (New York: New York University Press, 1989); Annnemarie Schimmel, *Mystical Dimensions of Islam* (Chapel Hill, NC: University of North Carolina Press, 1975); and J. Spencer Trimingham, *The Sufi Orders of Islam* (Oxford: Clarendon Press, 1971).

40. During the Afghan Mujahidin regime of Burhanuddin Rabbani (1992–6), music was heavily censored and discouraged. Musicians had to apply formally for special licenses, and only men could perform at private indoor ceremonies or gatherings. See John Baily, "The Censorship of Music in Afghanistan," http://www.rawa.org/music.htm

41. By 2009, analysts estimated that nearly 500 shops selling music CDs and cassettes had been burned and looted in the Swat region of Pakistan alone. Khushal Yousafzai, "Music has died in the Swat valley," Freemuse, 23 April 2009; "Taliban group issues new ban on sale of music," Freemuse, 23 August 2007.

42. Abubakar Siddique, "Understanding the Taliban's Campaign Against Music," Freemuse, http://www.freemuse.org/sw34252.asp; "British Ethnomusicologist, 'It Isn't Actually Correct to Say Taliban Have Banned Music'," Radio Free Europe/ Radio Liberty, 22 June 2009, http://www.rferl.org/content/British_Ethno-musicologist_Discusses_Talibans_Campaign_Against_Musicians/1753865.html

43. John Baily "'Can you stop the birds singing?' The censorship of music in Afghanistan," Freemuse, April 2001, http://www.freemuse.org/sw1106.asp

44. The Taliban usage of poetry follows the boundaries of *Ghazal*, which is arguably

the most popular classical form of poetry. We suspect that the Taliban use similar techniques in their creation of *taranas*.

45. Thomas H. Johnson's interviews with Kandahari residents (urban and rural), June–July 2009.

46. Thomas H. Johnson's interview with Kandahar City resident, August 2010.

47. Numerous conversations between Thomas H. Johnson and US government and military personnel in 2009 and 2010.

48. For Taliban magazines, see "Morchal Monthly Magazine," *Alemarah*, http://ia360709.us.archive.org/4/items/morchal-june-201/morchal-june-2010.pdf; "Shahamat," *Alemarah*, http://www.alemarah-iea.com/website/; "Sarak Monthaly Magazine," *Alemarah*, http://www.alemarah-iea.com/website/; "Taliban Tarana," http://www.getalyric.com/listen/sOZf78NLS00/taliban_tarana

49. For Taliban websites, see "Alemarah Taliban Poetry Section," *Alemarah*, http://www.alemarah-iea.com/index.php?option=com_content&view=category&id=7&Itemid=15; "Alemarah Taliban Tarana Section," *Alemarah*, http://www.alemarah-iea.com/

50. For a couple of YouTube examples, see "Taliban Pashto Nasheed Allah u Akbar," *You Tube*, http://www.youtube.com/watch?v=OAvz0g_e04Q&feature=related; "2010 Pashto Taran Taliban," *You Tube*, http://www.youtube.com/watch?v=ryo8mCMyKhk&feature=related

51. We are indebted to Alex Strick van Linschoten for graciously sharing CDs of Taliban chants, June 2009, Kandahar City.

52. All *taranas* were translated by Ahwad Waheed.

53. See Louis Dupree, *Afghanistan* (Princeton, NJ: Princeton University Press, 1978); Olivier Roy, *Islam and Resistance in Afghanistan*, 2nd edn (Cambridge: Cambridge University Press, 1990).

54. Olivier Roy, *Islam and Resistance in Afghanistan*, p. 242, defines a *qawm* as a "communal group, whose sociological basis may vary. It may be a clan (in tribal zones), a village, an ethnic group, an extended family, or a professional group."

55. David Isby, *Afghanistan: A New History of the Borderland* (New York: Pegasus Books, 2010), p. 47, my emphasis.

56. We are interested in how the chants relate to Pashtun values, and we use Hofstede's definition of value as "a broad tendency to prefer certain states of affairs over others." Geert Hofstede, *Culture's Consequences: International Differences in Work-Related Values* (Thousand Oaks, CA: SAGE Publications, 1980), p. 18.

57. Ibid.

58. For a discussion of "cosmic threats," see Mark Juergensmeyer, *Terror in the Mind of God* (Berkeley, CA: University of California Press, 2000).

59. For statements concerning an analysis of anti-US sentiments among the Afghan public, see for example: "NATO Forces in Afghanistan Can't Deny They Killed Civilians in Sangin Anymore," *You Tube*, http://www.youtube.com/watch?v=E4m6tQudSpI&feature=player_embedded; "TIME's Cover, the CIA and Afghan

Women," *Firedoglake*, http://firedoglake.com/2010/08/06/times-cover-the-cia-and-afghan-women/; Sayed Salahudin, "Karzai orders probe into Afghan civilian deaths reports," Reuters, 5 August 2010, http://www.reuters.com/article/idUS-TRE6741KP20100805; Carlotta Gall, "Afghans Want a Deal on Foreign Troops," *New York Times*, 25 August 2008, http://www.nytimes.com/2008/08/26/world/asia/26afghan.html

60. Based on interviews by Thomas H. Johnson in Kandahar City and the Dand and Panjwayi districts of Kandahar province, August 2010.

61. Based on discussions with Thomas H. Johnson and residents of Kandahar City, June 2010 and August 2010.

62. For example, Afghanistan qualified to play in the Cricket World Cup (ICC) World Twenty20 Tournament after achieving first position in a qualifying round in Dubai in February 2010. Afghanistan and Oman shared the Asian Cricket Council (ACC) Twenty20 Cup in November 2007; in winter 2007, Afghanistan participated in the Asian Winter Games held in Changchun, China; in 2007 the Afghan cricket team were finalists in the ACC U-19 Elite Cup; in 2008, Afghanistan competed at the Summer Olympics in Beijing, China. Rohullah Nikpai made history by winning Afghanistan's first Olympic medal. He defeated world champion Juan Antonio Ramos of Spain to take the bronze in the men's under 58-kilogram Taekwondo competition; in 2010, Afghanistan defeated Nepal to win for the first time the ACC Trophy Elite competition. In 2011 the Afghanistan Rugby Federation (ARF) was formed, and is registered with the National Olympic Committee and approved by the government of the Islamic Republic of Afghanistan. In 2015 Afghanistan held its first marathon; among those who ran the entire marathon was one woman, Zainab, age 25, who thus became the first Afghan woman to run in a marathon within her own country.

63. This chant is very different from others in referring to themselves not as Taliban, but rather Mujahidin. The Taliban initially did not use the term because of the perception it carried: it harkened back to the dark days of 1992–4 when the Mujahidin destroyed Kabul and killed thousands of Afghans. Now the Taliban openly refer to their loyalists as Mujahidin in an attempt to expand their base to include "all Afghans resistant to the Afghan government and ISAF" and probably encompasses independent factions as well, such as al Fath, Hezb-e-Islami, foreign fighters, Haqqani loyalists, Tora Bora Military Front, the Islamic Emirate of Nuristan fighters led by Sheikh Dost Mohammad, etc.

64. Jason Straziuso, "The Kabul Quagmire," Associated Press, 17 October 2009; Abdul Salam Zaeef, *My Life with the Taliban* (London, Hurst & Co., 2010).

65. Based on the Thomas H. Johnson's interviews with numerous Kandaharis, June 2009, Kandahar City.

66. Thomas H. Johnson, "Religious Figures, Insurgency, and Jihad in Southern Afghanistan," *Who Speaks for Islam? Muslim Grassroots Leaders and Popular*

Preachers in South Asia, NBR Special Report 22 (Seattle, WA: National Bureau of Asian Research, February 2010), p. 52.

67. It is interesting to note that "*gul*," meaning flower, is a common component in many Afghans' names, especially Afghan men (e.g. Gul Agha Sherzai, Gul Mohmand, etc.)

68. http://www.twincities.com/national/ci_15424622?source=rss&nclick_check=1; Thomas H. Johnson, "Religious Figures, Insurgency, and Jihad in Southern Afghanistan," p. 52.

69. Mullah Dadullah Mansour was also known as Shah Mansour Dadullah and Mullah Bakht Mohammad, and is the younger brother of slain Taliban strategist and "southern zone" commander Mullah Dadullah. Shah Mansour replaced his brother as southern zone commander following the latter's death in May 2007, and was later expelled from the Taliban movement following a public disagreement with the Taliban's supreme leader Mullah Omar in late 2007. Mullah Dadullah Mansour was subsequently shot and arrested by Pakistani authorities as he crossed into Baluchistan on 12 February 2008.

8. THE *LAYEHA*, THE TALIBAN CODE OF CONDUCT

1. This chapter is based in part on Thomas H. Johnson and Matthew DuPee, "Analysing the new Taliban Code of Conduct (*Layeha*): An Assessment of Changing Perspectives and Strategies of the Afghan Taliban," *Central Asian Survey* 31:1 (March 2012): 77–91.

2. For example, on the rise of the Taliban, see Ahmed Rashid, *Taliban: Militant Islam, Oil and Fundamentalism in Central Asia* (New Haven, CT: Yale University Press, 2001); Michael Griffin, *Reaping the Whirlwind: The Taliban Movement in Afghanistan* (London: Pluto Press, 2001); Stephen Coll, *Ghost Wars: The Secret History of the CIA, Afghanistan, and Bin Laden, From the Soviet Invasion to September 10, 2001* (London: Penguin Books, 2004); William Maley (ed.), *Fundamentalism Reborn? Afghanistan and the Taliban* (New York: New York University Press, 1998). On the Taliban generally, see citations in Chapter 1 footnote 8.

3. For an exception, see Kate Clark, "The Layha: Calling the Taleban to Account," Afghanistan Analysis Network Thematic Paper, 4 July 2011, https://www.afghanistan-analysts.org/publication/aan-papers/the-layha-calling-the-taleban-to-account/

4. Since the *Layeha* is published in Pashto, it is not strikingly apparent that the intention of the document was to convey messages solely to Western audiences.

5. For an assessment of the Taliban as an organization, see Abdulkader H. Sinno, *Organization at War in Afghanistan and Beyond* (Ithaca, NY: Cornell University Press, 2008).

6. On the post-2001 organization and how the Taliban evolved as an effective

insurgent force, see Thomas H. Johnson, "On the Edge of the Big Muddy: The Taliban Resurgence in Afghanistan," *China and Eurasian Forum Quarterly* 5:2 (2007): 93–129; Emma Sky, "Increasing ISAF's Impact on Stability in Afghanistan," *Defense and Security Analysis* 23:1 (March 2007): 7–25.

7. For a comparison of actual events pursed by the Taliban and the *Layeha*, see Afghanistan-Pakistan Center, *Taliban Violations of their Code of Conduct* (Tampa, FL: United States Central Command, 1 March 2011).

8. In late Mullah Abdul Rauf Alizai's 2014 pledged allegiance to Islamic State (IS). See Dan Lamothe, "Meet the shadowy figure recruiting for the Islamic State in Afghanistan," *Washington Post*, 13 January 2015.

9. The 2010 *Layeha* was published (and became "operational") on 9 May 2010. The copy assessed here was recovered by Coalition forces in the Sangin Valley, Helmand. Just how many fighters have a copy of this document on their person in Afghanistan, how many Taliban operators can even read the doctrine, and what implications this manual has for the overall insurgent infrastructure in Afghanistan is difficult, if not impossible, to ascertain. It is pertinent, however, to understand what the Taliban leadership is saying and how they are communicating within their own chain of command.

10. Berader was reportedly released by the Pakistanis in Fall 2010; see Syed Saleem Shahzad, "Pakistan frees Taliban commander," *Asia Times*, 16 October 2010, http://www.atimes.com/atimes/South_Asia/LJ16Df02.html; Praveen Swami, "Taliban deputy chief in high-stakes peace gamble: analysis," *Daily Telegraph*, 20 October 2010, http://www.telegraph.co.uk/news/worldnews/asia/afghanistan/8076284/Taliban-deputy-chief-in-high-stakes-peace-gamble-analysis.html

11. Numbers cited in Matthias Gebauer, "Special Forces Ratchet up Fight against Taliban," *Der Spiegel*, 28 August 2010.

12. Sami Yousafzai and Ron Moreau, "This Mullah Omar Show," *Newsweek*, 8 August 2010.

13. Thomas H. Johnson's interview with retired senior Pakistani official, October 2010; several reports widely circulated claimed Omar's detention. Afghan Television channel ToloTV, citing unnamed Pakistani government sources, also reported Omar's detention on 6 July, although the Taliban strongly denied the claims.

14. See J. Nathan, "Taliban Propaganda: Winning the War of Words?" *Asia Report* 158 (International Crisis Group, 2008), www.crisisgroup.org/en/regions/asia/south-asia/afghanistan/158-Taliban-propaganda-winning-the-war-of-words.aspx; also J. Nathan, "Reading the Taliban," in A. Giustozzi (ed.), *Decoding the New Taliban* (Oxford: Oxford University Press, 2012), pp. 23–42. Also consult earlier chapters of this book.

15. Territorial disputes, personality and ideological differences, cronyism, corruption, and even the presence or allegiance to foreign fighters is causing rifts among some

local Taliban fronts. Even among the much-vaunted Haqqani Network of eastern Afghanistan, ideological differences and corruption cause significant cleavages among various cells and commanders. Nevertheless, the extent of these differences and their significance is still open for judgment. For examinations of cleavages among Taliban factions, see Martine van Bijlert, "The Battle for Afghanistan Militancy and Conflict in Zabul and Uruzgan," *Counterterrorism Strategy Initiative Policy Paper*, New America Foundation, September 2010; Nasim Hotak, "Imam, rebel killed in Zabul," *Pajhwok Afghan News*, 14 November 2010; Ahmad Qureshi, "Commander killed in Taliban infighting," *Pajhwok Afghan News*, 10 March 2009; "Infighting leaves 5 Taliban dead, wounds 7 in W Afghanistan," *Xinhua*, 25 September 2009; Sher Ahmad Haider and Saboor Mangal, "Infighting leaves eight Taliban dead in Ghazni," *Pajhwok Afghan News*, 28 March 2008; Abdul Latif Ayubi, "Taliban infighting leaves one dead, four injured," *Pajhwok Afghan News*, 11 December 2008; Matthew C. DuPee, "Badghis Province: Examining the Taliban's Northwestern Campaign," *Culture and Conflict Review* 2:4 (December 2008); "Commander wounded as Taliban groups clash," *Pajhwok Afghan News*, 5 March 2006.

16. Stephen Carter and Kate Clark, *No Shortcut to Stability: Justice, Politics and Insurgency in Afghanistan* (London: Chatham House, Royal Institute of International Affairs, December 2010), pp. 20–22; Griff Witte, "Taliban establishes elaborate shadow government in Afghanistan," *Washington Post*, 8 December 2009, http://www.washingtonpost.com/wp-dyn/content/article/2009/12/07/AR2009120704127.html

17. It is important to note that different analysts translated the Pashto of the 2009 and 2010 *Layeha*, and where discrepancies in the language were found, an additional, senior translator was used to assess whether the translations were accurate. To receive copies of the 2009 and 2010 *Layeha* used in this analysis, please contact Thomas H. Johnson.

18. This *Layeha* comprised 29 rules of conduct.

19. The 2009 document had 13 chapters and 67 rules or laws.

20. Chapter 10, Health-Related Issues. The Islamic Emirate Health Commission has its own work plan for carrying out and coordinating its activities. Treatment of the Mujahidin will be done according to that work plan. Provincial representatives are bound to obey instructions of the commission in carrying out tasks related to health issues.

21. Michael Williams, "How the British presence in Sangin restored trust in government," *Guardian*, 20 September 2010; Robert Johnson and Timothy Clack, *At the End of Military Intervention: Hisotrical, Theoretical, and Applied Approaches to Transition, Handover, and Withdrawal* (Oxford: Oxford Univeristy Press, 2015), p. 331.

22. Chapter 1, rule 4 of the 2009 *Layeha* states, "If a person breaks his ties to the infi-

dels, and the Mujahidin gives him guarantees for full protection and this person is killed by a Mujahid or harmed in some way, then the person who committed the crime will not be supported by the Islamic Movement, and he will be dealt according to the laws of *Shar'iah*."

23. See note 13 in Chapter 2.

24. The Taliban beheaded six security personnel following a raid on their checkpoint in the northern province of Baghlan on 21 July 2010. Villager Lal Mohammad was mutilated (ears and nose cut off) in Daikundi for participating in the 2009 elections. For more, see "Taliban Behead Six Afghan Police," CNN, 22 July 2010; "Taliban behead 11 Shia Afghans," Press TV, 26 June 2010; and "The Man Who had His Ears and Nose Cut Off for Daring to Vote," *Mail Online*, 1 September 2009.

25. Reza Shirmohammadi, "Taliban Execute a Woman in Badghis," ToloTV, 9 August 2010; "Taliban publicly flog, execute pregnant woman for alleged adultery," *France 24 The Observers*, 9 August 2010, http://www.france24.com/en/20100809-aghanistan-taliban-publicly-flog-execute-pregnant-woman-alleged-adultery

26. "Commander of the Faithful."

27. In the 2009 *Layeha*, Mullah Omar is referred to as Imam in the document; Mullah Berader is referred to as Imam's Assistant.

28. The Emergency NGO runs several clinics in Afghanistan; however, the clinic in Lashkar Gah is directly tied to two controversial events in Afghanistan. The first was the mediation role that Emergency played in the prisoner exchange of five Taliban leaders in exchange for the kidnapped Italian journalist Daniele Mastrogiacomo in 2007. The Afghan doctor working at Emergency, Dr Rahmatullah, was imprisoned briefly for his role in the incident before being released. His two Afghan assistants, Sayed Agha and Ajmal Nasqbandi, were beheaded by militant Taliban fighters. The second incident occurred in April 2010 when Afghan authorities broke up a suspected assassination plot against Helmand's governor, which allegedly used the Emergency clinic as a logistics and facilitation hub for the attack. Afghan and British soldiers confiscated small and medium arms and explosives from the clinic following a tip-off. Zainullah Stanikzai, "Italian medics accused of complicity in murder," *Pajhwok Afghan News*, 17 April 2010.

29. Ahmad Rashid, *Descent into Chaos: The United States and the Failure of Nation Building in Pakistan, Afghanistan, and Central Asia* (New York: Viking, 2008), pp. 222–3.

30. Chapter 12, Recommendations, rules 59–60, 63.

31. Abdul Salam Zaeef, *My Life with the Taliban* (London: Hurst & Co., 2010); Jason Straziuso, "The Kabul Quagmire," Associated Press, 17 October 2009.

32. *Jabha-yi Muttahid-i Islami-yi Milli bara-yi Nijat-i Afghanistan*, or the United Islamic Front for the Salvation of Afghanistan, is most commonly known in the West by its simplistic moniker "the Northern Alliance."

33. The children abused for sexual relationships are referred to widely as *halekon*, *ashna*, or *bacha bereeshs*. While recent media efforts have focused attention on this heinous battlefield ritual, mostly confined to reports of *bacha bauzi* occurring in northern Afghanistan, this practice occurs widely throughout Afghanistan and among Afghanistan's diverse ethnic make-up. For more, see Rustam Qobil, "The sexually abused dancing boys of Afghanistan," BBC World Service, 7 September 2010; "The Dancing Boys of Afghanistan," PBS Frontline TV documentary, 20 April 2010; "Afghan boy dancers sexually abused by former warlords," Reuters, 18 November 2007.

34. Ahmed Rashid, *The Taliban: Militant Islam, Oil and Fundamentalism in Central Asia* (New Haven, CT: Yale University Press, 2001), p. 25.

35. Thomas H. Johnson's interviews with Afghan citizenry in Kandahar province, Afghanistan, August 2010.

36. The New America Foundation claims that the Taliban in Afghanistan and Pakistan have adopted kidnapping as a means to raise capital. Between 2008 and 2009, kidnappings in Pakistan increased two and half fold, and by 6 per cent in Afghanistan. Although only 10 per cent of kidnappings in Pakistan are attributed to the Taliban, the ransoms they receive are between $60,000 and $115,000, significantly more than what other insurgent groups receive in Pakistan. It is unclear how the money is distributed between Pakistan's Taliban network and Afghanistan's Quetta Shura. See Catherine Collins with Ashraf Ali, "Financing the Taliban: Tracing the Dollars Behind the Insurgencies in Afghanistan and Pakistan," Counterterrorism Strategy Initiative Policy Paper, *New America Foundation*, April 2010, p. 6; and National Counterterrorism Center, "2008 Report on Terrorism," 30 April 2009, p. 30; and National Counterterrorism Center, "2009 Report on Terrorism," 30 April 2010, p. 21.

37. Thomas H. Johnson's interviews with Afghan citizenry in Kandahar province, Afghanistan, August 2010.

38. Both Zabul and Ghazni provinces, hostile insurgent bastions south of Kabul, are prime examples of such activities. The Taliban in Zabul are frequently referred to as "thief Taliban" by Afghan observers, because they are viewed to be less motivated by ideology than they are by economic gain. For instance, an infamous dispute between two Taliban commanders in the Shah Joy district of Zabul erupted after a dispute over territory from which each commander wanted to collect taxes. Similar anecdotes have also occurred in Ghazni, Farah, and Badghis provinces, to name a few. Christoph Reuter and Borhan Yunus, "The Return of the Taliban in Andar: Ghazni," in A. Giustozzi (ed.), *Decoding the New Taliban: Insight from the Afghan Field* (New York: Columbia University Press, 2009), pp. 101–18; Abdul Awwal Zabulwal, "Taliban in Zabul: A Witness's Account," in A. Giustozzi (ed.), op. cit., pp. 179–89; Martine Van Biljert, "The Battle for Afghanistan: Militancy and Conflict in Zabul and Uruzgan," *New American Foundation*, Counterterrorism Strategy Initiative Policy Paper, September 2010, p. 16.

39. Ron Moreau, "America's New Nightmare," *Newsweek*, 3 August 2009; Rupert Hamer, "In bid to win Afghan hearts Taliban issue 'code of conduct,'" *Mirror*, 28 January 2012, http://www.mirror.co.uk/news/uk-news/in-bid-to-win-afghan-hearts-taliban-419862

40. "Commander of the Faithful," Mullah Mohammad Omar.

41. Rules 2, 4, 8, and 9 respectively of the 2009 *Layeha*; and rules 2, 6, 7, 10, 12 of the 2010 *Layeha*.

42. Generally, see Louis DuPree, *Afghanistan* (New York: Princeton University Press, 1980).

43. However, if the culprit is accused of something serious such as murder, the victim's family are usually obliged to fulfill their duty of *Qisaas*, a retaliatory form of condoned vigilante justice. International Legal Foundation, *The Customary Laws of Afghanistan* (2004), p. 10.

44. Rule 5 of 2010 *Layeha*.

45. Rule 6 of 2010 *Layeha*.

46. Rule 7 of 2010 *Layeha*.

47. The defecting group burned down their police post and left with their weapons, ammunition, food, and police truck. Dexter Filkins and Sharifullah Sahak, "Afghan Police Unit Defects en Masse to Taliban Side," *New York Times*, 1 November 2010, http://www.nytimes.com/2010/11/02/world/asia/02afghan.html?_r=1&ref=dexter_filkins; Julius Cavendish, "Afghan police unit defects after cutting deal with the Taliban," *The Independent*, 2 November 2010, http://www.independent.co.uk/news/world/asia/afghan-police-unit-defects-after-cutting-deal-with-the-taliban-2123564.html

48. As Filkins and Sahak suggest, "In the decades of war in Afghanistan, armed groups, whether fighting for the government or for someone else, have often changed sides to join the one they believe is winning." Rule 14 of the 2010 *Layeha* states: "Those soldiers or police who surrender to the Mujahidin or repent will not be killed, and if these soldiers bring some weapons with them or accomplish an achievement, then they should be praised."

49. Associated Press, "Afghanistan: Taliban Attack NATO Fuel Convoy, Killing 3," *New York Times*, 23 October 2010, http://www.nytimes.com/2010/10/23/world/asia/23briefs-ATTACK.html; Nick Schifrin and Habibullah Khan, "US Supply Line at Risk along Pakistan Border," ABC News, 10 November 2008, http://abcnews.go.com/International/story?id=6221453

50. See Warlord, Inc. Extortion and Corruption Along the US Supply Chain in Afghanistan, Report of the Majority Staff, Rep. John F. Tierney, Chair-Subcommittee on National Security and Foreign Affairs, Committee on Oversight and Government Reform, US House of Representatives, June 2010.

51. Rule 11 of 2010 *Layeha*.

52. Rule 19 of 2010 *Layeha*.

53. Rule 20 of 2010 *Layeha*.

54. Rule 25 of 2010 *Layeha*.

55. Rule 26 of 2010 *Layeha*.

56. Rules 15 and 16 of 2010 *Layeha*.

57. Rule 22 of 2010 *Layeha*.

58. Rule 27 of 2010 *Layeha*.

59. Ibid.

60. Rule 29 of 2010 *Layeha*.

61. During Thomas H. Johnson's research trips to Afghanistan in August–September 2008, May–June 2009, and July–September 2010, community leaders, village elders, and ordinary citizens confirmed the Taliban's creation of this parallel legal system and its popularity. Interviews with elders suggested that the shadow legal system organization and functions match the 2010 Taliban code of conduct rule on justice exactly.

62. The Taliban Court after being attacked by US Special Forces was moved from Zangabad to a location in the Zhari district.

63. Thomas H. Johnson's interviews with Afghan citizenry in Panjwayi, Kandahar, August 2010.

64. Based on Section 7, Internal Issues of the Mujahidin, rule 40: details how the chain of command works for the Taliban military force structure.

65. 2009 *Layeha*, article 2.

66. There is some debate as to whether the slaughter of ten aid workers on 5 August was carried out by the Taliban or if it was carried out by bandits, foreign fighters, or members of another insurgent organization. On 7 August, the Taliban spokesperson Zabihullah Mujahid claimed responsibility on Aljazeera through a written statement, accusing the medical team of proselytizing, although he later redacted the proselytizing claim and accused the NGO workers of spying. Hezbe-Islami also claimed responsibility for the attacks, whereas local Nuristani and Badakhshi Taliban deny responsibility. The sole survivor claims that the attackers had spoken Pashaye, a dialect common in Nuristan, and at least one used Pakistani words that are not common to Badakhshan. If the massacres were carried out by thieves, the subsequent massacre of foreign personnel is difficult to explain, as is the temporary kidnapping and release of the sole survivor. The ambush was carried out efficiently, which points away from simple criminal opportunists.

67. Afghan NGO Safety Office, 3rd Quarter Report 2010, p. 15.

68. Rupert Hamer, "In bid to win Afghan hearts Taliban issue 'code of conduct,'" *Mirror*, 28 January 2012, http://www.mirror.co.uk/news/uk-news/in-bid-to-win-afghan-hearts-taliban-419862; Ron Moreau, "America's New Nightmare," *Newsweek*, 25 July 2009.

69. The Taliban continue to operate an uneven "shadow government" structure, which varies widely in the strength given to regional differences. For instance, the Taliban

shadow government in the Andar and Deh Yak districts of Ghazni province remains robust, as "the Taliban runs 28 known schools; circulates public statements by leaflets at night; adjudicates land, water-rights and property disputes through religious courts; levies taxes on residents; and punishes Afghans labeled as collaborators." C. J. Chivers, "In Eastern Afghanistan, at War with the Taliban's Shadowy Rule," *New York Times*, 6 February 2011.

9. HEZB-E-ISLAMI GULBUDDIN (HIG) PROPAGANDA ACTIVITIES

1. I would like to thank Ahmad Waheed for his assistance in preparing this chapter.
2. BBC, "Afghan Hezb-e-Islami militants hold peace talks in Kabul," 22 March 2010, http://news.bbc.co.uk/2/hi/8579380.stm; "Special Representative Meets with Hezb-e-Islami Delegation in Kabul," United Nations Assistance Mission in Afghanistan, 25 March 2010, https://unama.unmissions.org/special-representative-meets-hezb-e-islami-delegation-kabul
3. Ron Moreau, "The Jihadi High School," *Newsweek*, 24 April 2011, http://www.newsweek.com/2011/04/24/the-jihadi-high-school.html
4. Moreau, "The Jihadi High School." See also Ch. 4.
5. ISI is the premier military-operated intelligence service of Pakistan.
6. Thomas H. Johnson conversations and correspondence with Ambassador Peter Tomsen, 27 and 29 April 2016. Ambassador Tomsen served as the US Special Envoy to Afghanistan 1989–92.
7. The pro-Hekmatyar Afghan News Agency does not exist today. It was most likely shut down by ISI after the Taliban overran Kabul and Hekmatyar fled to Iran. It was clear in 1994 that HIG was not the solution for Afghanistan, and Islamabad as well as the ISI shifted all its propaganda cadre and resources to the Taliban.
8. Peter Tomsen, *The Wars of Afghanistan: Messianic Terrorism, Tribal Conflicts, and the Failures of Great Powers*, 1st edn (New York: Public Affairs, 2011), p. 510.
9. Thomas H. Johnson's interviews with Afghan immigrants at the refugee camps in Pakistan, August 1986, September 1988.
10. Greg Bruno, Eben Kaplan, "The Taliban in Afghanistan," Council on Foreign Relations, 3 August 2009, http://www.cfr.org/afghanistan/taliban-afghanistan/p10551#p2
11. See original vernacular at http://www.tanweer.blogfa.com/post-2006.aspx
12. See Chapter 4 for a discussion of additional HIG magazines and printed media: *Mesaq-i-Esaar* (Covenant of Sacrifice), *Ihas* (Feelings), *Resalat* (Duty), and *Zamir* (Conscience).
13. HIG makes efforts to communicate with specific regions by using the appropriate dialect and language. For example, in *Tanweer* vol. 16, December 2010, Gulbuddin Hekmatyar issued a statement "Message to Panjshir Mujahidin from

Gulbuddin Hekmatyar," in Dari to target the Dari-speaking audience in Panjshir province.

14. BBC, "Afghan Hezb-e-Islami militants hold peace talks in Kabul," BBC, 22 March 2010, http://news.bbc.co.uk/2/hi/8579380.stm; "Special Representative Meets with Hezb-e-Islami Delegation in Kabul," United Nations Assistance Mission in Afghanistan, 25 March 2010, https://unama.unmissions.org/special-representative-meets-hezb-e-islami-delegation-kabul

15. Abdul Mueed Hashmi, "Militants overrun remote district in Nuristan," *Pajhwok Afghan News*, 25 May 2011, http://www.pajhwok.com/en/2011/05/25/militants-overrun-remote-district-nuristan

16. Abdul Moeed Hashmi, "Fuel trucks come under attack," *Pajhwok Afghan News*, 15 December 2009, http://www.pajhwok.com/en/2009/12/15/fuel-trucks-come-under-attack

17. Khan Wali Salarzai, "A commander among 4 fighters killed in Kunar," *Pajhwok Afghan News*, 31 October 2010, http://www.pajhwok.com/en/2010/10/31/commander-among-4-fighters-killed-kunar

18. "Shaheed Habibullah Shabab Hekmatyar" video was uploaded to YouTube on 4 June 2011 by user Ghazy66: http://www.youtube.com/user/Ghazy66#p/u/17/Tbm0yP2GrIo. Habibullah Shabab Hekmatyar was the son of Gulbuddin's brother, Shabuddin, and died after a US airstrike hit a militant position in the Nerkh district of Wardak province on 22 April 2011. Mohammad Farid Karimi, "Hekmatyar's nephew killed in NATO-led raid," *Pajhwok Afghan News*, 22 April 2011. http://www.pajhwok.com/en/2011/04/22/hekmatyars-nephew-killed-nato-led-raid; "How large is the caravan we have?" video was uploaded to YouTube on 21 August 2011 by user Ghazy66: http://www.youtube.com/user/Ghazy66#p/u/4/d5Kn2xLUPkU

19. *Oqab*, "statement to Loy Paktiya."

20. It includes Paktiya, Paktika, and Khost provinces of Afghanistan.

21. It is important to note that the Taliban also claimed credit for the attack. "We claim responsibility for the attack, and it was carried out at a time when foreigners were shopping, including the head of a security company," Taliban spokesman Zabiullah Mujahid was quoted as telling Reuters.

22. "Hezb-e-Islami killed 2 Afghans and 8 foreigners," *TOLO News*, 7 August 2010, http://tolonews.com/en/afghanistan/235-hezb-e-islami-killed-2-afghans-and-8-foreigners

23. Jafar Tayar, "HIA claims killing medics," *Pajhwok Afghan News*, 7 August 2010, http://www.pajhwok.com/en/2010/08/07/hia-claims-killing-medics; Jason Motlagh, "Will Aid Workers' Killings End Civilian Surge?" *Time*, 9 August 2010, http://content.time.com/time/world/article/0,8599,2009399,00.html

24. It is a traditional Pashtun expression used to indicate pride in the individual, family, or tribe.

25. Religious verdict by clerics.

26. HIG statements, *Oqab*.

27. Original vernacular can be found here: http://www.oqab1.com/index.php? option=com_content&view=article&id=273:2011–02–24–06–12– 36&catid=18:2010–11–09–19–39–36&Itemid=108

28. http://dailyshahadat.com/showstory.php?id=7658

29. "Afghan Election," *Oqab*, http://www.oqab1.com/index.php?option=com_ content&view=article&id=267:2011–02–15–02–12–19&catid=22:2010-11- 09-19-47-37&Itemid=110

30. "Afghan Election," *Oqab*, http://www.oqab1.com/index.php?option=com_ content&view=article&id=91:2011-01-04-23-28-11&catid=22:2010-11-09– 19–47–37&Itemid=110

31. See Appendix C for the original form of the HIG peace proposal as published in *Tanweer*, December 2010, vol. 16.

32. Hezb-e-Islami Hekmatyar delegates interviews and debates during their visit to Kabul, http://www.youtube.com/watch?v=MjPiypmAytE&feature=related, http://www.youtube.com/watch?v=89gfVkER34Y&feature=related, http:// www.youtube.com/watch?v=gqZuc1QZ5IY&feature=related

33. Arian TV interview with Daoud Abedi, uploaded 13 August 2010, http://www. youtube.com/watch?v=M5udzTSdhP4, http://www.youtube.com/watch?v=- Du8c29CBp8

34. HIG senior official interview with an Afghan TV channel operating in the US, uploaded 3 May 2011, http://www.youtube.com/watch?v=SxHriMK5lJs&featu re=related

35. "Hezb-e-Islami National Agreement," *Oqab*, http://www.oqab1.com/index. php?option=com_content&view=article&id=267:2011-02-15-02-12-19& catid=22:2010-11-09-19-47-37&Itemid=110

36. Mukhilsyar, "Proud of the youth emotions and devotions," *Daily Shahadat*, 21 April 2010, http://dailyshahadat.com/safha_e_jawanan-story.php?id=40

37. See original vernacular at http://www.tanweer.blogfa.com/post-2006.aspx

38. http://dailyshahadat.com/mujale-show-page.php?id=345

39. See original vernacular at http://www.tanweer.blogfa.com/post-2006.aspx

40. See note 13 in Chapter 2.

41. Maiwand as suggested above, is one of the major historical locations where the fight between the Afghans and the British Empire forces took place during the nineteenth century. Most Afghans refer to it as a symbol of Afghan resistance against foreign invading forces and the sacrifice of men and women to gain their country's independence.

42. http://dailyshahadat.com/mujale-show-page.php?id=345

10. THE UNITED STATES' AFGHAN INFORMATION AND PSYOP CAMPAIGN AND A COMPARISON TO THE TALIBAN'S CAMPAIGN

1. The Afghan operation was intially called "Operation Infinite Justice," but was changed when it was brought to the planners' attention that the concept of "infinite justice" was, according to Muslim experts, a prerogative of God, and not of man. The name was changed to Operation Enduring Freedom. This was a precursor of mistakes in information operations that would soon follow.

2. OEF-A lasted from 7 October 2001 to 31 December 2014 and was part of the overall Global War on Terrorism (GWOT). OEF-A was succeeded by Operation Freedom's Sentinel.

3. For example, see Anthony H. Cordesman, "Losing the 'Forgotten War': The Need to Reshape US Strategy in Afghanistan, Pakistan, and Central Asia," (Washington DC: Center for and International Studies, 6 October 2014), http://csis.org/files/publication/141006_Losing_the_Forgotten_War_Final.pdf; and Gian P. Gentile, "A Strategy of Tactics: Population-centric COIN and the Army," *Parameters* (Autumn 2009): 5–17.

4. For general works on counter-insurgency (COIN) and US COIN tactics in Afghanistan, see David Kilcullen, *Counterinsurgency* (New York: Oxford University Press, 2010); David Kilcullen, *The Accidental Guerrilla: Fighting Small Wars in the Midst of a Big One* (New York: Oxford University Press, 2009); Thomas H. Johnson and Barry Zellon (eds), *Culture, Conflict and Counterinsurgency* (Palo Alto, CA: Stanford University Press, 2014); *The US Army/Marine Corps Counterinsurgency Field Manual* (Chicago: University of Chicago Press, 2007), http://permanent.access.gpo.gov/lps79762/FM_3–24.pdf; Anand Gopal, *No Good Men Among the Living: America, the Taliban, and the War through Afghan Eyes* (New York: Henry Holt & Co., 2014); Carlotta Gall, *The Wrong Enemy: America in Afghanistan, 2001–2014* (New York: Harcourt, 2014).

5. For an example of some of these leaflets, see http://www.psywarrior.com/Afghanleaflinks.html and below.

6. Thomas H. Johnson interviews with various Afghans in Kandahar City and Panjwayi district in Kandahar province, August 2009.

7. *CIA World Factbook*, https://www.cia.gov/library/publications/the-world-factbook/geos/af.html. The illiteracy rate has significantly improved since 2002, but not in many rural, hinterland areas of Afghanistan.

8. For an excellent discussion of "narratives" and war, see Jill Lepore, *The Name of War: King Phillip's War and the Origins of American Identity* (New York: Alfred A. Knopf, 1998); and Douglas Porch, *The Conquest of Morocco* (New York: Farrar, Straus and Giroux, 2005). For Afghan narratives, see Thomas H. Johnson, "The Taliban Insurgency and an Analysis of *Shabnamah* (Night Letters)," *Small Wars and Insurgencies* 18:3 (September 2007): 317–44 and Chapter 1 of this book.

9. *CIA World Factbook*, https://www.cia.gov/library/publications/the-world-factbook/geos/af.html

10. See note 2 in Preface.

11. http://www.dailymail.co.uk/news/article-2035160/Most-Afghans-know-9–11-according-disturbing-poll.html#ixzz47doJf7yp

12. Col. Francis Scott Main, US Army Reserve, Psychological Operations Support to Strategic Communications in Afghanistan, Carlisle Barracks, PA: US Army War College, strategy research project, 24 March 2009, p. 2.

13. Arturo Munoz, *US Military Information Operations in Afghanistan: Effectiveness of Psychological Operations 2001–2010*, (Santa Monica, CA: RAND National Defense Research Institute, 2012), p. 33, http://www.rand.org/content/dam/rand/pubs/monographs/2012/RAND_MG1060.pdf

14. US Deputy Secretary of Defense, Implementation of the DOD Strategic Communication Plan for Afghanistan, 12 September 2007.

15. Ibid.

16. Based on Thomas H. Johnson's field research in Afghanistan, 2006–10.

17. Thomas H. Johnson, "Religious Figures, Insurgency, and Jihad in Southern Afghanistan," *Who Speaks for Islam? Muslim Grassroots Leaders and Popular Preachers in South Asia*, *NBR Special Report 22* (Seattle, WA: National Bureau of Asian Research, February 2010), pp. 41–65.

18. Originally written in *Joint Forces Quarterly* and cited in Daniel Nasaw, "Mullen blasts US 'strategic communication' efforts in Afghanistan," *Guardian*, 28 August 2009, http://www.theguardian.com/world/2009/aug/28/mullen-afghanistan-communication

19. Col. Francis Scott Main, US Army Reserve, "Psychological Operations Support to Strategic Communications in Afghanistan," 2009, p. 5.

20. http://www.transparency.org/research/cpi/overview

21. During a research trip to Afghanistan in 2008 (July–August), I heard countless complaints from the provincial council and governor of Nangarhar, Gul Agha Sherzai, about how they felt powerless and even willing to resign if they were not put into the authorizing loop when it came to night operations.

22. For an extensive review of the Haqqani Network and its criminal activities, see Vahid Brown and Don Rassler, *Fountainhead of Jihad: the Haqqani Nexus, 1973–2012* (New York: Columbia University Press, 2013); Thomas Ruttig, "The Haqqani Network as an Autonomous Entity," in Antonio Giustozzi (ed.), *Decoding the New Taliban: Insights from the Afghan Field* (New York: Columbia University Press, 2009), pp. 57–88; and Matthew DuPee, "Afghanistan's Conflict Minerals: The Crime-State-Insurgent Nexus," *CTC Sentinel*, 12 February 2012, https://www.ctc.usma.edu/posts/afghanistans-conflict-minerals-the-crime-state-insurgent-nexus

23. Consult the Special Inspector General for Afghan Reconstruction (SIGAR)'s numerous reports for specific details.

24. Chief of Staff, Supreme Headquarters Allied Powers Europe, NATO/ISAF Strategic Communication 2011, https://info.publicintelligence.net/NATO-STRATCOM-Afghanistan.pdf

25. http://www.army.mil/standto/archive_2015–03–13/?s_cid=standto

26. RSM Fact Sheet, "Essential Function 8: Maintain Internal and External Strategic Communication Capability," http://www.rs.nato.int/article/rs-news/rsm-essential-function-8-strategic-communication.html

27. Ivan Arreguín-Toft, *How the Weak Win Wars: A Theory of Asymmetric Conflict* (Cambridge: Cambridge University Press, 2005), p. 45.

28. Robert Taber, *War of the Flea: The Classic Study of Guerrilla Warfare* (Washington, DC: Potomac Books, 2002), p. 19.

29. A common Afghan Taliban statement is that "the US may have the watches, but we have the time."

30. Joanna Nathan, "Reading the Taliban," in A. Giustozzi (ed.), *Decoding the New Taliban: Insights from the Afghan Field* (New York: Columbia University Press, 2009), p. 25.

31. This section, especially the discussion of early US OEF-A leaflets, is partially based on Thomas H. Johnson and Keely M. Fahoum, "Successes and Failures of the United State's Initial Leaflet Campaign in Operation Enduring Freedom," unpublished research paper (Monterey, CA: Naval Postgraduate School, July 2006), and Thomas H. Johnson's direct experience with the very early OEF leaflet campaign (see this book's Preface).

32. Philip M. Taylor, "Psychological Operations During Operation Enduring Freedom," Paper presented at the University of Leeds, UK, 2002.

33. See Chapter 5.

34. Keely M. Fahoum, personal communication with PSYOP officer involved in initial OEF-A leaflet campaign, 14 June 2006, cited hereafter as "PSYOP officer interview."

35. Keely M. Fahoum interview with Bruce Clingman, member of 1st IO command FST during the start of OEF, 13 June 2006.

36. "'Solo' Tells Afghans They Aren't Alone," *Indian Express*, 19 October 2001.

37. PYSOP officer interview, 14 June 2006.

38. Ibid.

39. Ibid., 14 June 2006. See Chapter 7 for an elaboration of this argument.

40. PYSOP officer interview, 14 June 2006.

41. The author witnessed this while working in OSD on the intial OEF-A IO campaign.

42. Craig Storti, *Cross-Cultural Dialogues: 74 Brief Encounters with Cultural Difference* (Yarmouth, ME: Intercultural Press, 1994), p. 4.

43. http://www.psywarrior.com/Herbafghan.html

44. http://www.psywarrior.com/afghanleaf31.html

45. Personal anecdote relayed to Herbert Friedman by PSYOP officer, http://www.psywarrior.com/Herbafghan02.html

46. http://www.psywarrior.com/Herbafghan.html

47. Gilles Dorronsoro, *Revolution Unending: Afghanistan, 1979 to the Present* (New York: Columbia University Press, 2005), footnote 10, p. 340.

48. http://www.psywarrior.com/Herbafghan.html

49. Ibid.

50. General Carl von Clausewitz, *On War: The Complete Edition* (Wildside Press, LLC, 2009).

51. See Chapter 2 footnote 13.

52. http://www.psywarrior.com/Herbafghan.html

53. Ibid.

54. See footnote 11.

55. http://www.psywarrior.com/Herbafghan.html

56. Gopal, *No Good Men Among the Living: America, the Taliban, and the War through Afghan Eyes*, p. 104.

57. http://www.psywarrior.com/Herbafghan.html

58. In an interview concerning bin Laden, Mutawakkil stated, "Osama bin Laden has been hated because he is accused of killing innocent people." Yasmin Jiwani, "Colluding Hegemonies: Constructing the Muslim Other Post-9/11," in Jasmin Zine (ed.), *Islam in the Hinterlands: Muslim Cultural Politics in Canada* (Toronto: UBC Press, 2012), p. 127.

59. Jan Ahmad, *The Baloch Cultural Heritage* (Karachi: Royal Book Company, 1982), pp. 140–41.

60. http://www.psywarrior.com/Herbafghan.html

61. Eid is an important Islamic religious holiday marking the end of Ramadan, the Islamic holy month of fasting (*sawm*).

62. The Prophet Muhammad recommended that Muslims break their fasting during Ramadan (*iftar*) with dates.

63. http://www.psywarrior.com/Herbafghan.html

64. For a fairly robust analyis of the IO leaflets used by the US during the early phases of Operation Enduring Freedom, see Herbert A. Friedman, "Psychological Operations in Afghanistan," http://www.psywarrior.com/Herbafghan.html or http://www.psywarrior.com/afghanleaf02.html

65. Christopher Lamb, *Review of Psychological Operations: Lessons Learned from Recent Operational Experience* (Washington, DC: National Defense University, 2005).

66. *The US Army/Marine Corps Counterinsurgency Field Manual.*

67. See David J. Kilcullen, "Three Pillars of Counterinsurgency," Remarks delivered at the US Government Counterinsurgency Conference, Washington, DC, 28 September 2006, http://www.au.af.mil/au/awc/awcgate/uscoin/3pillars_of_counterinsurgency.pdf

68. Michael Hastings, "The Runaway General," *Rolling Stone*, 22 June 2010, http://www.rollingstone.com/politics/news/the-runaway-general-20100622

69. COMISAF's Counterinsurgency Guidance, 1 August 2010, http://www.stripes.com/polopoly_fs/1.113197.1280774784!/menu/standard/file/COMISAF%27s%20COIN%20Guidance%2C%201Aug10.pdf

70. All the leaflets examined in this section are from the *345th TPS (A) "Product Book,"* May 2009, as well as other IO work products given to Thomas H. Johnson by senior officers of the Combined Joint PSYOP Task Force (CJPOTF), Bagram Airforce Base, May 2009. All these materials are unclassified and unrestricted.

71. Based on numerous interviews by Thomas H. Johnson with Afghans living in the east and south of the country, 2006–10.

72. This objective is obviously mislabled in the *Product Book* because it is a repeat of objective D. Most of the PYSOP/IO artifacts associated with this objective, in fact, relate to "wanted posters" of various Taliban insurgents, propositions concerning the evil of Taliban, and the need for the Afghan population to support the ANSF. Also note that the copy of the *Product Book* received had no objective G.

73. A 25-nation Pew Global Attitudes survey conducted in June 2009 found that the war in Afghanistan was unpopular in most nations and that most publics wanted American and NATO troops out of Afghanistan. See "25-Nation Pew Global Attitudes Survey," http://www.pewglobal.org/files/pdf/264.pdf

74. Generally, see, David Galula, *Counterinsurgency Warfare: Theory and Practice* (Westport, CT: Praeger Security International, 2006).

75. Ian S, Livingston and Michael O'Hanlon, "Afghanistan Index" (Washington, DC: Brookings Institute, 24 April 2012), p. 12, http://www.brookings.edu/foreign-policy/afghanistan-index.aspx

76. All the written messages associated with the PSYOP/IO leaflets or other products will be presented in English. The actual deployed leaflets' messages were written in either Pashto or Dari, or both.

77. Thomas H. Johnson interview with Kandahari Afghan, August 2009.

78. Generally, see Graeme Smith, *The Dogs Are Eating Them Now: Our War in Afghanistan* (Toronto: Knopf Canada, 2013).

79. For example, see Jennifer Glasse, "Ice cream and dreams melt as Kandahar's electricity falters," AlJazeera America, 23 June 2015, http://america.aljazeera.com/watch/shows/compass/articles/2015/6/23/kandahar-electricity.html

80. Ibid.

81. Arturo Munzo, *U.S. Military Information Operations in Afghanistan: Effectiveness of Psychological Operations 2001–2010* (Santa Monica, CA: RAND Corporation, 2012), pp. 103–4.

82. For an excellent assessment of the Afghan National Army, see Antonio Giustozzi, *The Army of Afghanistan: A Political History of a Fragile Institution* (London: Hurst & Co., 2016).

83. Thomas H. Johnson interview with Kandahari Afghan, August 2009.

84. Ibid.

85. UN Office on Drugs and Crime, *The Opium Economy in Afghanistan: An International Problem* (New York: United Nations, January 2003), my emphasis.

86. Sean Carberry and Sultan Faizy, "Afghan Farmers: Opium is the Only Way to Make a Living," NPR Morning Edition, 14 November 2013, http://www.npr.org/sections/parallels/2013/11/14/245040114/afghan-farmers-opium-is-the-only-way-to-make-a-living

87. "The United States estimates that there as many as 1.6 million drug users in Afghan cities—about 5.2 percent of the population—up from 940,000 in 2009. As many as 3 million more are believed to be in the countryside." Pamela Constable, "Heroin addition spreads with alarming speeds across Afghanistan," *Washington Post*, 8 January 2015, https://www.washingtonpost.com/world/asia_pacific/heroin-addiction-spreads-with-alarming-speed-across-afghanistan/2015/01/06/2cbb61ea-94e7-11e4-aabd-d0b93ff613d5_story.html

88. Thomas H. Johnson interview with Panjwai Afghan farmers, August 2009.

89. See note 69 in this chapter.

90. Obaid Younossi et al., *The Long March: Building an Afghan Army* (Santa Monica, CA: RAND Corporation, 2009), p. 48.

91. See Thomas H. Johnson, "Religious Figures, Insurgency, and Jihad in Southern Afghanistan."

92. Robert M. Perito, "Afghanistan's Police: The Weak Link in Security Sector Reform," *United States Institute of Peace Special Report 227* (Washington, DC: USIP, August 2009), p. 1.

93. Thomas H. Johnson interview with Tribal elders in Kandahar, June 2008 and August 2009.

94. Ibid.

95. Kashif Aziz, "Waziristan Taliban caught in Burqa? Social Media Propaganda exposed," *Chowrangi*: Pakistan Politics, Current Affairs, Business and Lifestyle, 7 July 2014, http://www.chowrangi.pk/waziristan-taliban-caught-burqa-social-media-propaganda-rise.html

96. Among many sources available, generally see Carlotta Gall, *The Wrong Enemy: America in Afghanistan, 2001–2014* (New York: Harcourt, 2014); Peter Tomsen, *The Wars of Afghanistan: Messianic Terrorism, Tribal Conflicts, and the Failures of Great Powers* (New York: Public Affairs, 2011), pp. 517–58. Hassan Abbas, *The Taliban Revival: Violence and Extremism on the Pakistan-Afghanistan Frontier* (New Haven, CT: Yale University Press, 2014); Bruce Riedel, "Pakistan, Taliban and the Afghan Quagmire" (Washington DC: Brookings Institute, 24 August 2013, http://www.brookings.edu/research/opinions/2013/08/26-pakistan-influence-over-afghan-taliban-riedel; Aleem Maqbool, "Pakistan helping Afghan Taliban—NATO," BBC News, 1 February 2012, http://www.bbc.com/news/world-asia-16821218

97. Malik Siraj Akbar, "Mounting Tensions Between Pakistan Media and Military," *Huffpost Media*, 24 June 2014, http://www.huffingtonpost.com/malik-siraj-akbar/mounting-tensions-between-press-freedom_b_5195628.html; Jon Boone, "Geo TV's face-off with the ISI spy agency—a subplot of a larger tussle in Pakistan," *Guardian*, 27 April 2014, http://www.theguardian.com/world/2014/apr/27/geo-tv-isi-spy-agency-pakistan-military; Declan Walsh, "Press battle in Pakistan feeds into larger conflict: Government vs. Military," South Asia Media Net: A News and Views Website of South Asia, 25 May 2014, http://www.south-asianmedia.net/sam-monitors/pakistan-media-crisis/press-battle-in-pakistan-feeds-into-larger-conflict-government-vs.-military-story; Neha Anssari, "Not Fit to Print: An Insider Account of Pakistani Censorship," Foreign Policy: South Asia Channel, 20 November 2014, http://foreignpolicy.com/2014/11/20/not-fit-to-print-an-insider-account-of-pakistani-censorship/

98. See Chapter 2 and note 13.

99. See *345ᵗʰ TPS (A) "Product Book,"* May 2009.

100. ODA is Operational Detachment-Alpha, the standard 12-member teams of US Army Special Forces operators once known as A-Teams.

101. Thomas H. Johnson interview with ODA personnel, Camp Bastion, Afghanistan, June 2006.

102. Ibid.

103. An innovative Canadian counter-insurgency program that deployed a company of Canadian soldiers to live in an Afghan village and work with the villagers on a daily basis to improve the Afghans' daily lives and security through repairing a Dand District Center that resided near the village, make improvements to the village bazzar, build new irrigation canals for the village, repair and improve village mosques, and various other humanitarian and agricultural programs. A key objective of the program was to improve the security of the village and reduce the appeal of the Taliban to the villagers. See Gerald Meyerie, Megan Katt, and Jim Gavrillas, *On the Ground in Afghanistan: Counterinsurgency in Practice* (CAN and Marine Corp University Press, 2012), pp. 156–60.

104. Observation of Thomas H. Johnson, Deh-e Bagh village, Dand, Kandahar, June–August 2009.

105. Arturo Munoz, *US Military Information Operations in Afghanistan: Effectiveness of Psychological Operations 2001–2010*, p. 4.

106. Christopher Lamb, *Review of Psychological Operations: Lessons Learned from Recent Operational Experience*, p. 3.

107. Gerald R. Miller, "On Being Persuaded: Some Basic Distinctions," in James Price Dillard and Michael Pfau (eds), *The Persuasion Handbook: Developments in Theory and Practice* (Thousand Oaks, CA: SAGE Publications, 2002).

108. Ibid.

109. Louis Dupree, *Afghanistan* (New York: Oxford University Press, 1973).

110. Further research is needed to evaluate successes, failures, and measures of effectiveness for PSYOP and IO campaigns; more specifically, it is vital to evaluate the degree to which PSYOP and IO planners can be integrated into short-notice military operations on the ground. Some research has been conducted into one measure of effectiveness, Value Focused Thinking (VFT), but it would behoove the DoD to apply studies such as VFT to cultural messaging within IO and PSYOP operations in order to craft the most effective and powerful tactics to meet military and strategic objectives. There are endless possibilities for future research into this area, but the bottom line remains clear: persuasion strategies must be viewed within an anthropological context and not a Western context of creative advertising. The PSYOP campaign should focus on themes and stories that are vetted by and make sense to Afghans. A value model captures the concerns (values) of a decision-maker in a particular situation, and then requires a decision to capture quantitative results (from qualitative information), enabling analysts to measure whether or not a particular campaign met the goals of a PSYOP Detachment Commander. The Value Focused Thinking method provides one strategy to measure the effectiveness of a PSYOP campaign. Captain Philip M. Kerchner, Dr Richard F. Deckro, LTC (Retd) Jack M. Kloeber, Jr, "Valuing Psychological Operations," *Military Operations Research* 6:2 (2001): 45–65.

11. CONCLUSIONS

1. Early reports from the time when the Taliban were created indicated that the movement did not seek wider political authority than the re-establishment of law and order in Kandahar province.
2. "Taliban Propaganda: Winning the War of Words?" *International Crisis Group*, Asia Report 158, 24 July 2008.
3. For example, see Gulabudin Ghubar, "Rights Body Slams Taliban for High Civilian Death Toll," *Tolo News*, 15 February 2016, http://www.tolonews.com/en/afghanistan/23793-rights-body-slams-taliban-for-high-civilian-death-toll; David Jolly, "Afghanistan had Record Civilian Casualties in 2015, UN Says," *New York Times*, 14 February 2016, http://www.nytimes.com/2016/02/15/world/asia/afghanistan-record-civilian-casualties-2015-united-nations.html?_r=0
4. Ahmad Waheed's interviews with numerous Kandaharis, Spring 2014.
5. BBC, "Afghan official killed by gunman," 24 February 2010, http://news.bbc.co.uk/2/hi/8533629.stm; Keith B. Richburg, "Kandahar slides into lawlessness as Taliban attacks force government to retreat," *Washington Post*, 14 March 2010, http://www.washingtonpost.com/wp-dyn/content/article/2010/03/13/AR2010031300574.html
6. Ahmad Waheed's interviews with numerous Kandaharis, Spring 2014.

7. See Jonathan R. Zadra and Gerald L Clore, "Emotions and perception: the role of affective information," Wiley Interdisciplinary Reviews, *Cognitive Science* 2:6 (November–December 2011): 676–85.

8. See note 40 in Introduction.

9. Thomas H. Johnson's interview with a Taliban commander in Kandahar City, September 2008.

10. Ahmad Waheed's interview with Kandaharis, Spring 2014.

11. Thomas H. Johnson's interview with Taliban commander in Kandahar City, July 2009.

12. The parts, components, and/or themes of the Afghan stories are not necessarily presented in their order of importance to the Taliban.

13. Open Source Center, "Terrorism: Taliban Chief Mullah Omar Offers Foreign Forces Safe Exit from Afghanistan," Jihadist websites: OSC Summary in Arabic, 30 September 2008, https://www.opensource.gov/portal/server.pt/gateway/PTARGS_0_0_200_217_51_43/content/Display/GMP20080930479002

14. NEFA Foundation, "In Celebration of Eid al-Adha," released 25 November 2009, http://www.nefafoundation.org/miscellaneous/nefa_mullahomar1109.pdf

15. Generally, see Mark Juergensmeyer, *Terror in the Mind of God* (Berkeley, CA: University of California Press, 2000).

16. Tim Foxley, "The Taliban's Propaganda Activities: How Well is the Afghan Insurgency Communicating and What is it Saying?" (Stockholm: SIPRI project parer, June 2007), p. 6; Abdulhadi Hairan, "A Profile of the Taliban's Propaganda Tactics," *World Post*, 25 May 2011, http://www.huffingtonpost.com/abdulhadi-hairan/a-profile-of-the-talibans_b_442857.html.

17. Open Source Center, "Terrorism: Taliban Leader Congratulates Muslims on Id, Urges Boycotting 'Deceptive Elections,'" Jihadist websites: OSC Summary in Arabic, 7 December 2008, https://www.opensource.gov/portal/server.pt/gateway/PTARGS_0_0_200_217_51_43/content/Display/GMP20081209054013

18. Open Source Center, "Al-Jazirah: Mullah Omar Urges Afghan Employees Not to Serve Govt, 'Occupation,'" Al-Jazirah Satellite Channel Television in Arabic, 1419 GMT 12 October 2007, https://www.opensource.gov/portal/server.pt/gateway/PTARGS_0_0_200_217_51_43/content/Display/GMP20071012640001; Golnar Motevalli, "Taliban targeting Afghan women and government workeres, UN report finds," *Guardian*, 19 February 2013, http://www.theguardian.com/world/2013/feb/19/taliban-targeting-women-un-report

19. Thomas H. Johnson interviews with Kandaharis in Kandahar City, August and September 2009.

20. Observations of Thomas H. Johnson in Kandahar, August–September 2008 and May–August 2009. See 2006–9 Trip Reports in Thomas H. Johnson, *Afghanistan Field Research Notebooks 4–6* (Monterey CA, 2008–9); Catherine Norman, "What do Afghans want from the police? Views from Helmand province," CNA (January 2012), p. 5.

21. Open Source Center, "Afghanistan: Mullah Omar Claims US After Taliban, Not Usama," Islamabad *Ausaf* in Urdu, 27 September 2001, https://www.opensource. gov/portal/server.pt/gateway/PTARGS_0_0_200_217_51_43/content/Display/ SAP20010928000057

22. NEFA Foundation, "In Celebration of Eid al-Adha," 25 November 2009, http:// www.nefafoundation.org/miscellaneous/nefa_mullahomar1109.pdf

23. Ibid.

24. NEFA Foundation, "Regarding Obama's New Strategy," 2 December 2009, http:// www.nefafoundation.org/miscellaneous/nefa_talibanobamasurge1209.pdf

25. Jim Loney, "Civilian deaths undermine West's Afghan mission," Reuters, 22 May 2007, http://in.today.reuters.com/news/newsArticle.aspx?type=worldNews& storyID=2007–05–22T184642Z_01_NOOTR_RTRJONC_0_India-299435–1.xml&archived=False

26. Luke Harding, "Heavy Hand of America Fans the Taliban Embers into Life," *Guardian*, 18 June 2003, http://www.guardian.co.uk/afghanistan/story/ 0,1284,979617,00.html

27. Thomas H. Johnson, "On the Edge of the Big Muddy: The Taliban Resurgence in Afghanistan," *China and Eurasian Forum Quarterly* 5:2 (2007): 123–4.

28. International Crisis Group, "Afghanistan: The Problem of Pashtun Alienation," ICG Asia Report 62, August 2003.

29. NEFA Foundation, "In Celebration of Eid al-Adha," released 25 November 2009, http://www.nefafoundation.org/miscellaneous/nefa_mullahomar1109.pdf

30. NEFA Foundation, "Taliban: Obama, Following in Bush's Steps," released 8 December 2009, http://www.nefafoundation.org/miscellaneous/nefaTaliObamaBush1209.pdf

31. See note 13 in Chapter 2.

32. A Taliban night letter from 2009.

33. Vern Liebl, "Pushtuns, Tribalism, Leadership, Islam and Taliban: A Short View," *Small War and Insurgencies* (September 2007): 498.

34. A Taliban night letter from 2010.

35. Robert Taber, *War of the Flea: The Classic Study of Guerrilla Warfare* (Washington, DC: Potomac Books, 2002), pp. 154–5.

36. David Kilcullen, *The Accidental Guerrilla: Fighting Small Wars in the Midst of a Big One* (New York: Oxford University Press, 2009), pp. 50–58.

37. Joanna Nathan, "Reading the Taliban," in Antonio Giustozzi (ed.), *Decoding the New Taliban: Insights from the Afghan Field* (New York: Columbia University Press, 2009), p. 35.

38. Thomas H. Johnson and M. Chris Mason, "Understanding the Taliban and Insurgency in Afghanistan," *Orbis: A Journal of World Affairs* 51:1 (2007).

39. Brent Glatzer, "Afghanistan: Ethnic and tribal disintegration?" in William Maley (ed.), *Fundamentalism Reborn? Afghanistan and the Taliban* (New York: New York University Press, 1998).

40. One message from 2006, apparently originating from the late Taliban spokesman Mullah Dadullah, was aimed at North Korea. Matthew DuPee, "The Specter of Mullah Dadullah," Afgha.com, 13 June 2006, http://www.afgha.com/?q= node/520

41. "Taliban Deny Osama Granted Afghan Nationality to Move," *Islamabad Al-Akbar* (Urdu language), 29 September 1998; Tim McGirk, "On bin Laden's Trail," *National Geographic*, December 2004, http://ngm.nationalgeographic.com/features/world/asia/pakistan/pashtun-text/1

42. See generally Thomas H. Johnson, "On the Edge of the Big Muddy: The Taliban Resurgence in Afghanistan."

43. "Mullah Omar—in his own words," *Guardian*, 26 September 2001, http://www.guardian.co.uk/g2/story/0,3604,558076,00.html

44. Foreign Broadcast Information Service, "Islamic/Aegean Terrorism Review," Daily London Bureau Roundup, 17 January 2001; Guillaume Debre, "Taliban asks: What does it take to join the UN club?" *Christian Science Monitor*, 26 September 2000, http://www.csmonitor.com/2000/0926/p7s1.html

45. "Press Release," Afghan Islamic Press News Agency, 22 January 2001; Zahid Hussain, "Taleban offers US deal to deport bin Laden," *Times of London*, 5 February 2001, http://www.newsint-archive.co.uk/pages/main.asp?T=1

46. "Afghan Ambassador's 25 January Speech on Sanctions, Usama," *Islamabad Khabra* (Urdu language), 15 February 2001.

47. "Afghan Taliban leader orders destruction of ancient statues," *Agence France-Press*, 26 February 2001, http://www.rawa.org/statues.htm; Ahmed Rashid, "After 1,700 years, Buddhas fall to Taliban dynamite," *Daily Telegraph*, 12 March 2001, http://www.telegraph.co.uk/news/worldnews/asia/afghanistan/1326063/After-1700-years-Buddhas-fall-to-Taliban-dynamite.html

48. Robert Marquand, "The Reclusive Ruler who Runs the Taliban," *Christian Science Monitor*, 10 October 2001, http://www.csmonitor.com/2001/1010/p1s4-wosc. html; Brenda Shaffer, *The Limits of Culture: Islam and Foreign Policy* (Cambridge, MA: MIT Press, 2006), p. 286.

49. Norimitsu Onishi, "A Tale of the Mullah and Muhammad's Amazing Cloak," *New York Times*, 19 December 2001, http://select.nytimes.com/gst/abstract.html?re s=F00E1FFA395A0C7A8DDDAB0994D9404482&n=Top%2fReference%2 fTimes%20Topics%2fPeople%2fO%2fOmar%2c%20Muhammad

50. Ahmed Rashid, *Taliban: Militant Islam, Oil and Fundamentalism in Central Asia* (New Haven, CT: Yale University Press, 2001); Kevin Sieff, "A fight for Afghanistans most famous artifact," *Washington Post*, 29 December 2012, https://www.washingtonpost.com/world/a-fight-for-afghanistans-most-famous-artifact/2012/12/29/ab2dc394–51cb-11e2–835b-02f92c0daa43_story.html

51. Tim Foxley, "The Taliban's Propaganda Activities: How Well is the Afghan Insurgency Communicating and What is it Saying?" (Stockholm: SIPRI project

paper, June 2007), pp. 13–16; International Crisis Group, "Taliban Propaganda: Winning the War of Words?" *Asia Report* 158 (July 2008): 25–8.

52. Garth S. Jowett and Victoria O'Donnell, *Propaganda and Persuasion* (Thousand Oaks, CA: SAGE Publications, 1986), p. 16.

APPENDIX A

1. Adopted from Antonio Giustozzi (ed.), Decoding the New Taliban: Insights from the Afghan Field (New York: Columbia University Press, 2009).

APPENDIX C

1. Translation by Ahmad Waheed, January 2016.

BIBLIOGRAPHY

345th TPS (A) "Product Book," May 2009.

Abbas, Hassan, *The Taliban Revival: Violence and Extremism on the Pakistan-Afghanistan Frontier* (New Haven, CT: Yale University Press, 2014).

Abinanti, Lawson, "Positioning Depends on Repetition and Consistency" (10 January 2016), http://www.messagesthatmatter.com/positioning-depends-on-repetition-and-consistency/.

Arreguín-Toft, Ivan, *How the Weak Win Wars: A Theory of Asymmetric Conflict* (Cambridge: Cambridge University Press, 2005).

Afsar, Shahid Chris Samples, and Thomas Wood, "The Taliban: An Organizational Analysis," *Military Review* (May–June 2008).

Agence France-Press, "Afghan Taliban leader orders destruction of ancient statues," 26 February 2001, http://www.rawa.org/statues.htm.

Agha, Mohammad Akbar, Alex Strick van Linschoten and Felix Kuehn (eds.), *I am Akbar Agha: Memories of the Afghan Jihad and the Taliban* (Berlin: First Draft Publishing, 2014).

Afghan Ambassador, "25 January Speech on Sanctions, Usama," *Islamabad Khabra* (Urdu language), 15 February 2001.

Afghan Islamic Press News Agency "Press Release," 22 January 2001.

Ahmad, Aisha and Roger Boase, *Pashtun Tales from the Pakistan-Afghan Frontier* (London: Saqi Books, 2008).

Ahmad, Jan, *The Baloch Cultural Heritage* (Karachi: Royal Book Company, 1982).

Ahmed, Akbar, *Pukhtun Economy and Society* (London: Routledge, 1980).

Ahmed, Azam, "Taliban Justice Gains Favor as Official Afghan Courts Fail," *New York Times*, 31 January 2015, http://www.nytimes.com/2015/02/01/world/asia/taliban-justice-gains-favor-as-official-afghan-courts-fail.html?_r=0.

Akbar, Malik Siraj, "Mounting Tensions Between Pakistan Media and Military," *Huffpost Media*, 24 June 2014, http://www.huffingtonpost.com/malik-siraj-akbar/mounting-tensions-between-press-freedom_b_5195628.html.

BIBLIOGRAPHY

Aljazeera, "Taliban expands fight beyond Afghanistan's Kunduz," 1 October 2015, http://www.aljazeera.com/news/2015/10/taliban-expands-fight-afghanistan-kunduz-151001172158686.html.

Anssari, Neha "Not Fit to Print: An Insider Account of Pakistani Censorship," *Foreign Policy: South Asia Channel*, 20 November 2014, http://foreignpolicy.com/2014/11/20/not-fit-to-print-an-insider-account-of-pakistani-censorship/.

Associated Press, "Afghanistan: Taliban Attack NATO Fuel Convoy, Killing 3," *New York Times*, 23 October 2010, http://www.nytimes.com/2010/10/23/world/asia/23briefs-ATTACK.html

—— "Top Taliban military commander dismisses NATO casualty reports, warns journalists," *International Harold Tribune* (Asian and Pacific edition), 4 September 2006, internet version, http://www.iht.com/articles/ap/2006/09/04/asia/AS_GEN_Afghan_Taliban.php.

—— "Taliban Dismisses Top Leader Mansoor Dadullah," Associated Press, 30 December 2007.

Ayubi, Abdul Latif, "Taliban infighting leaves one dead, four injured," *Pajhwok Afghan News*, 11 December 2008.

Aziz, Kashif, "Waziristan Taliban caught in Burqa? Social Media Propaganda exposed," *Chowrangi: Pakistan Politics, Current Affairs, Business and Lifestyle*, 7 July 2014, http://www.chowrangi.pk/waziristan-taliban-caught-burqa-social-media-propaganda-rise.html.

Badkhen, Anna, "Afghan government failure reopens door to the Taliban," *San Francisco Chronicle*, 17 September 2006, p. A4.

Baily, John "'Can you stop the birds singing?' The censorship of music in Afghanistan," Freemuse, April 2001, http://www.freemuse.org/sw1106.asp.

—— "The Censorship of Music in Afghanistan," http://www.rawa.org/music.htm.

Baker, Aryn, "Deadly Notes in the Night: How the Taliban are using a new kind of terrorist threat to intimidate Afghans," *Time Magazine*, 5 July 2006.

Baldick, Julian *Mystical Islam: An Introduction to Sufism* (New York: New York University Press, 1989).

Bandow, Doug, "Terrorism: Why They Want to Kill Us," *Huffington Post*, 25 May 2011, http://www.huffingtonpost.com/doug-bandow/terrorism-why-they-want t_b_631942.html.

Bates, Daniel G. and Fred Plog, *Cultural Anthropology*, 2nd edn (New York: Alfred A. Knopf, 1980).

BBC News, "Mullah Omar: Taliban choose deputy Mansour as successor," 30 July 2015, http://www.bbc.com/news/world-asia-33721074.

—— "Afghan official killed by gunman," 24 February 2010, http://news.bbc.co.uk/2/hi/8533629.stm.

—— "Afghan Hezb-e-Islami militants hold peace talks in Kabul," 22 March 2010, http://news.bbc.co.uk/2/hi/8579380.stm.

—— "Bin Laden rails against Crusaders and UN," 3 November 2001, http://news. bbc.co.uk/2/hi/world/monitoring/media_reports/1636782.stm.

Belch, George E., "The Effects of Television Commercial Repetition on Cognitive Response and Message Acceptance," *Journal of Consumer Research* 9:1 (June 1982): 56–65.

Belch, George E. and Michael A. Belch, "An Investigation of The Effects of Repetition on Cognitive and Affective Reactions to Humorous and Serious Television Commercials," *Advances in Consumer Research* 11 (1984): 4–10.

Boone, Jon, "Geo TV's face-off with the ISI spy agency—a subplot of a larger tussle in Pakistan," *Guardian*, 27 April 2014, http://www.theguardian.com/world/2014/ apr/27/geo-tv-isi-spy-agency-pakistan-military.

Bradsher, Henry S., *Afghanistan and the Soviet Union*, 2nd edn (Durham, NC: Duke University, 1985).

Brandt, Ben, "Mullah Omar's Conduct of Intelligence and Counterintelligence," *CTC Sentinel* 4:6 (June 2011): 19–23.

Bredin, Miles, "Class war: battle to educate Afghan girls and boys hindered by fear of Taliban retribution," *The Independent*, 12 September 2006.

Brown, R., "Information Operations, Public Diplomacy and Spin: The United States and the Politics of Perception Management," *Journal of Information Warfare*, 1:3 (2013), http://media.leeds.ac.uk/papers/pmt/exhibits/32/JIW1_32.pdf#page= 46.

Brown, Vahid and Don Rassler, *Fountainhead of Jihad: the Haqqani Nexus, 1973– 2012* (New York: Columbia University Press, 2013).

Bruno, Greg and Eben Kaplan, "The Taliban in Afghanistan," Council on Foreign Relations, 3 August 2009, http://www.cfr.org/afghanistan/taliban-afghanistan/ p10551#p2.

Cacioppo, John T. and Richard E. Petty, "Effects of Message Repetition on Argument Processing, Recall, and Presuasion," *Basic and Applied Social Psychology* 10:1 (1989): 3–12.

Carberry, Sean and Sultan Faizy, "Afghan Farmers: Opium is the Only Way to Make a Living," NPR Morning Edition, 14 November 2013, http://www.npr.org/sec-tions/parallels/2013/11/14/245040114/afghan-farmers-opium-is-the-only-way-to-make-a-living.

Caroe, Sir Olaf, *The Pathans and Society* (Oxford: Oxford University Press, 1958).

Carruthers, Martyn, *Prevent Coercive Persuasion and Mind Control, Systemic Coaching*, http://www.systemiccoaching.com/coercion.htm (6 June 2011).

Carter, Stephen and Kate Clark, *No Shortcut to Stability: Justice, Politics and Insurgency in Afghanistan* (Chatham House: Royal Institute of International Affairs, December 2010).

Casebeer, William D., *Military Force and Culture Change: Systems, Narratives, and the Social Transmission of Behavior in Counter-Terrorism Strategy* (MA thesis, Naval Postgraduate School, 2006).

Cavendish, Julius, "Afghan police unit defects after cutting deal with the Taliban," *The Independent*, 2 November 2010, http://www.independent.co.uk/news/world/asia/afghan-police-unit-defects-after-cutting-deal-with-the-taliban-2123564.html.

CBS, "Taliban Strikes Back," CBS, 31 March 2003, http://www.cbsnews.com/stories/2003/04/03/attack/main547507.shtml.

Chayes, Sarah, *The Punishment of Virtue: Inside Afghanistan After the Taliban*, reprint edn (London: Penguin Books, 2007).

Chief of Staff, Supreme Headquarters Allied Powers Europe, NATO/ISAF Strategic Communication 2011, https://info.publicintelligence.net/NATO-STRATCOM-Afghanistan.pdf.

Chivers, C. J., "In Eastern Afghanistan, at War with the Taliban's Shadowy Rule," *New York Times*, 6 February 2011.

Central Intelligence Agency, *CIA World Factbook*, https://www.cia.gov/library/publications/the-world-factbook/geos/af.html.

Clark, Kate, "The Layha: Calling the Taleban to Account," *Afghanistan Analysis Network Thematic Paper*, 4 July 2011, https://www.afghanistan-analysts.org/publication/aan-papers/the-layha-calling-the-taleban-to-account/.

Clements, Frank, *Conflict in Afghanistan: A Historical Encyclopedia* (Santa Barbara, CA: ABC-CLIO, 2003).

CNN, "Nick Paton Walsh reports on the reappearance of the Taliban to control one Afghanistan town near the Pakistan border," 22 June 2011.

―――― "Taliban Behead Six Afghan Police," 22 July 2010.

CNN World, "Transcript of Bin Laden's October interview," 5 February 2002, http://edition.cnn.com/2002/WORLD/asiapcf/south/02/05/binladen.transcript/.

Coll, Steve *Ghost Wars: The Secret History of the CIA, Afghanistan, and bin Laden, from the Soviet Invasion to September 10, 2001* (New York: Penguin Books, 2004).

Collins, Catherine with Ashraf Ali, "Financing the Taliban: Tracing the Dollars Behind the Insurgencies in Afghanistan and Pakistan," *Counterterrorism Strategy Initiative Policy Paper*, New America Foundation, April 2010.

Collins, Steven, "Mind Games," *NATO Review* online edn (2003), p. 1, http://www.iwar.org/uk/psyops/resources/iraq/mind-games.htm.

Comdt, V. Sahay, *Taliban, Militant Islam and Afghanistan* (Delhi: Neha Publishers & Distributors, 2015).

COMISAF's, *Counterinsurgency Guidance*, 1 August 2010, http://www.stripes.com/polopoly_fs/1.113197.1280774784!/menu/standard/file/COMISAF%27s%20COIN%20Guidance%2C%201Aug10.pdf.

Pamela Constable, "Heroin addition spreads with alarming speeds across Afghanistan," *Washington Post*, 8 January 2015, https://www.washingtonpost.com/world/asia_pacific/heroin-addiction-spreads-with-alarming-speed-across-afghanistan/2015/01/06/2cbb61ea-94e7-11e4-aabd-d0b93ff613d5_story.html.

Cordesman, Anthony H., "Losing the 'Forgotten War': The Need to Reshape US

Strategy in Afghanistan, Pakistan, and Central Asia," (Washington DC: Center for and International Studies, 6 October 2014), http://csis.org/files/publication/141006_Losing_the_Forgotten_War_Final.pdf.

Corman, Steven R., Angela Trethewey, and Bud Goodall, *A 21st Century Model for Communication in the Global War of Ideas* (Consortium for Strategic Communication, Arizona State University, 2007).

Crews, Robert D. and Amin Tarzi (eds), *The Taliban and the Crisis of Afghanistan* (Cambridge, MA: Harvard University Press, 2008).

Daily Shahadat, "Mukhbat biography," http://dailyshahadat.com/mujale-show-page.php?id=340.

Dawn, "Desperate Afghans pin asylum hopes on Taliban threat letters," 15 September 2015, http://www.dawn.com/news/1207786.

Debre, Guillaume, "Taliban asks: What does it take to join the UN club?" *Christian Science Monitor*, 26 September 2000, http://www.csmonitor.com/2000/0926/p7s1.html.

Dennett, Daniel, "The Self as Center of Narrative Gravity," http://ase.tufts.edu/cogstud/papers/selfctr.htm (1992).

Dorronsoro, Gilles, *Revolution Unending: Afghanistan, 1979 to the Present* (New York: Columbia University Press, 2005).

—— Counterintelligencence and the Hill Tribes: U.S. Needs to Wise Up, *US News and World Report*, 20 February 2009.

Dreazen, Yochi J. and Siobhan Gorman, "Pentagon James Web, Radio Links of the Taliban," *Wall Street Journal*, 18 April 2009, http://www.wsj.com/articles/SB124001042575330715

DuPee, Matthew C., "Afghanistan's Conflict Minerals: The Crime-State-Insurgent Nexus," *CTC Sentinel*, 12 February 2012, https://www.ctc.usma.edu/posts/afghanistans-conflict-minerals-the-crime-state-insurgent-nexus.

—— "Badghis Province: Examining the Taliban's Northwestern Campaign," *Culture and Conflict Review* 2:4 (December 2008).

—— "The Specter of Mullah Dadullah," Afgha.com, 13 June 2006, http://www.afgha.com/?q=node/520.

Dupree, Louis *Afghanistan* (New York: Oxford University Press, 1973).

—— *The Afghans Honor a Muslim Saint* (New York: American Universities Field Staff, 1963).

Edwards, David B., *Heroes of the Age: Moral Fault Lines on the Afghan Frontier* (Berkeley, CA: University of California Press, 1996).

Emadi, Hafizullah, *Culture and Customs of Afghanistan* (London: Greenwood Press, 2005).

Fink, Edward L., Stan A. Kaplowitz, and Susan McGreevy Hubbard, "Oscillation in Beliefs and Decisions," in James Price Dillard and Michael Pfau (eds), *The Persuasion Handbook* (Thousand Oaks, CA: SAGE Publications, 2002).

BIBLIOGRAPHY

Foxley, Tim, "The Taliban's Propaganda Activities: How Well is the Afghan Insurgency Communicating and What is it Saying?" (Stockholm: SIPRI project paper, June 2007).

France 24, "Taliban publicly flog, execute pregnant woman for alleged adultery," *The Observers*, 9 August 2010, http://www.france24.com/en/20100809-aghanistan-taliban-publicly-flog-execute-pregnant-woman-alleged-adultery.

Freeman, Herbert A., "Psychological Operations in Afghanistan," http://www.psy-warrior.com/Herbafghan.html or http://www.psywarrior.com/afghanleaf04.html.

Filkins, Dexter and Sharifullah Sahak, "Afghan Police Unit Defects en Masse to Taliban Side," *New York Times*, 1 November 2010, http://www.nytimes.com/2010/11/02/world/asia/02afghan.html?_r=1&ref=dexter_filkins.

Foreign Broadcast Information Service, "Islamic/Aegean Terrorism Review," Daily London Bureau Roundup, 17 January 2001.

Gall, Carlotta, *The Wrong Enemy: America in Afghanistan, 2001–2014* (New York: Harcourt, 2014).

——— "Afghans Want a Deal on Foreign Troops," *New York Times*, 25 August 2008, http://www.nytimes.com/2008/08/26/world/asia/26afghan.html.

Gall, Sandy, *War Against the Taliban: Why It All Went Wrong in Afghanistan* (New York: Bloomsbury, 2013).

——— *Afghanistan: Agony of a Nation* (London: Bodley Head, 1988).

Galula, David, *Counterinsurgency Warfare: Theory and Practice* (Westport, CT: Praeger Security International, 2006).

Guardian, "Mullah Omar—in his own words," 26 September 2001, http://www.guardian.co.uk/g2/story/0,3604,558076,00.html.

Garcia, Helio Fred, *The Power of Communication: Skills to Build Trust, Inspire, Loyalty, and Lead Effectively* (Upper Saddle River, NJ: Pearson Education, Inc., 2012).

Gebauer, Matthias, "Special Forces Ratchet up Fight against Taliban," *Der Spiegel*, 28 August 2010.

Gentile, Gian P., "A Strategy of Tactics: Population-centric COIN and the Army," *Parameters* (Autumn 2009): 5–17.

Gerges, Fawaz A., *The Far Enemy: Why Jihad went Global* (Cambridge: Cambridge University Press, 2005).

Giustozzi, Antonio, *The Army of Afghanistan: A Political History of a Fragile Institution* (London: Hurst & Co., 2016).

——— *Decoding the New Taliban* (Oxford: Oxford University Press, 2012).

Ghubar, Gulabudin, "Rights Body Slams Taliban for High Civilian Death Toll," *Tolo News*, 15 February 2016, http://www.tolonews.com/en/afghanistan/23793-rights-body-slams-taliban-for-high-civilian-death-toll.

Glasse, Jennifer, "Ice cream and dreams melt as Kandahar's electricity falters," *AlJazeera America*, 23 June 2015, http://america.aljazeera.com/watch/shows/compass/articles/2015/6/23/kandahar-electricity.html.

Glatzer, Brent, "Afghanistan: Ethnic and tribal disintegration?" in William Maley (ed.), *Fundamentalism Reborn? Afghanistan and the Taliban* (New York: New York University Press, 1998).

—— "Being Pashtun-Being Muslim: Concepts of Person and War in Afghanistan," in Brent Glatzer (ed.), *Essays on South Asian Society, Culture and Politics II* (Zentrum Moderner Orient Arbeitshefte, 9) (Berlin: Das Arabische Buch, 1998).

Gopal, Anand, *No Good Men Among the Living: America, the Taliban, and the War through Afghan Eyes* (London: Picador, 2015).

Graesser, A. C. and G. V. Nakamura, "The impact of a schema on comprehension and memory," in H. Bower (ed.), *The Psychology of Learning and Motivation* 16 (London: Academic Press, 1990), pp. 59–109.

Griffin, Michael, *Reaping the Whirlwind: The Taliban Movement in Afghanistan* (London: Pluto Press, 2001).

Gunther, Albert C., *The Persuasive Press Inference: Effects of Mass Media on Perceived Public Opinion* (Thousand Oaks, CA: SAGE Publications, 1998), http://crx.sage-pub.com/content/25/5/486.full.pdf+html.

Haider, Sher Ahmed, "In Ghazni, Taliban FM radio goes on air," *Pajhwok Afghan News*, 8 August 2009, http://www.pajhwok.com/viewstory.asp?lng=eng&id=79248.

Haider, Sher Ahmad and Saboor Mangal, "Infighting leaves eight Taliban dead in Ghazni," *Pajhwok Afghan News*, 28 March 2008.

Hamer, Rupert, "In bid to win Afghan hearts Taliban issue 'code of conduct,'" *Mirror*, 28 January 2012, http://www.mirror.co.uk/news/uk-news/in-bid-to-win-afghan-hearts-taliban-419862.

Hairan, Abdulhadi, "A Profile of the Taliban's Propaganda Tactics," *World Post*, 25 May 2011, http://www.huffingtonpost.com/abdulhadi-hairan/a-profile-of-the-talibans_b_442857.html.

Harding, Luke, "Heavy Hand of America Fans the Taliban Embers into Life," *Guardian*, 18 June 2003, http://www.guardian.co.uk/afghanistan/story/0,1284,979617,00.html.

Hart, B. H. Liddell, *Lawrence of Arabia (New York: DeCapo, 1989)*.

Hashmi, Abdul Mueed, "Militants overrun remote district in Nuristan," *Pajhwok Afghan News*, 25 May 2011, http://www.pajhwok.com/en/2011/05/25/militants-overrun-remote-district-nuristan.

—— "Fuel trucks come under attack," *Pajhwok Afghan News*, 15 December 2009, http://www.pajhwok.com/en/2009/12/15/fuel-trucks-come-under-attack.

Hastings, Michael, "The Runaway General," *Rolling Stone*, 22 June 2010, http://www.rollingstone.com/politics/news/the-runaway-general-20100622.

Hofstede, Geert, *Culture's Consequences: International Differences in Work-Related Values* (Thousand Oaks, CA: SAGE Publications, 1980), p. 18.

Hogan, Patrick Colm, *The Mind and its Stories* (Cambridge: Cambridge University Press, 2003).

BIBLIOGRAPHY

Holdich, T. H., "Swatis and Afridis," *Journal of the Anthropological Institute of Great Britain and Ireland* 29 (1899), http://links.jstor.org/sici?sici=0959–5295(1899) 29%3A1%2F2%3C2%3ASAA%3E2.0.CO%3B2–2.

Hotak, Nasim, "Imam, rebel killed in Zabul," *Pajhwok Afghan News*, 14 November 2010.

Human Rights Watch, http://hrw.org/campaigns/afghanistan/2006/education/letter3.htm.

Hussain, Zahid, "Taleban offers US deal to deport bin Laden," *Times of London*, 5 February 2001, http://www.newsint-archive.co.uk/pages/main.asp?T=1.

Ibrahim, Raymond (ed. and trans.), *The Al Qaeda Reader* (New York: Broadway Books, 2007), pp. 198–208.

Indian Express, "'Solo' Tells Afghans They Aren't Alone," 19 October 2001.

International Crisis Group, "Taliban Propaganda: Winning the War of Words?" *Asia Report* 158, 24 July 2008.

———— "Afghanistan: The Problem of Pashtun Alienation," ICG Asia Report 62, August 2003.

Internet World Stats: Afghanistan Country Profile, http://www.internetworldstats.com/asia/af.htm.

Isby, David, *Afghanistan: A New History of the Borderland* (New York: Pegasus Books, 2010).

Islamabad Al-Akbar, "Taliban Deny Osama Granted Afghan Nationality to Move," (Urdu language), 29 September 1998.

Jiwani, Yasmin, "Colluding Hegemonies: Constructing the Muslim Other Post-9/11," in Jasmin Zine (ed.), *Islam in the Hinterlands: Muslim Cultural Politics in Canada* (Toronto: UBC Press, 2012).

Johnson, Robert and Timothy Clack, *At the End of Military Intervention: Hisotrical, Theoretical, and Applied Approaches to Transition, Handover, and Withdrawal* (Oxford: Oxford Univeristy Press, 2015).

Johnson, Thomas H. "Taliban Adaptations and Innovations," *Small Wars and Insurgencies* 24:1 (January 2013): 3–27.

———— "Religious Figures, Insurgency, and Jihad in Southern Afghanistan," *Who Speaks for Islam? Muslim Grassroots Leaders and Popular Preachers in South Asia*, *NBR Special Report* 22 (Seattle, WA: National Bureau of Asian Research, February 2010).

———— *Afghanistan Field Research Notebooks 4–6* (Monterey CA, 2008–9).

———— "Afghan Field Research Trip Reports," in *Afghanistan Field Research Notebooks 3–6*, (Monterey, CA, 2006–9).

———— "The Taliban Insurgency and an Analysis of *Shabnamah* (Night Letters)," *Small Wars and Insurgencies* 18:3 (September 2007): 317–44.

———— "On the Edge of the Big Muddy: The Taliban Resurgence in Afghanistan," *China and Eurasian Forum Quarterly* 5:2 (2007): 93–129.

Johnson, Thomas H. with Mumtaz Ahmad and Dietrich Reetz, *Who Speaks for Islam? Muslim Grassroots Leaders and Popular Preachers in South Asia*, NBR Special Report #22 (Seattle, WA: National Bureau of Asian Research, February 2010).

Johnson, Thomas H. and Matthew DuPee, "Analyzing the New Taliban Code of Conduct (*Layeha*): An Assessment of Changing Perspectives and Strategies of the Afghan Taliban," *Central Asian Survey* 31:1 (March 2012): 77–91.

Johnson, Thomas H. and Keely M. Fahoum, "Successes and Failures of the United State's Initial Leaflet Campaign in Operation Enduring Freedom," unpublished research paper (Monterey, CA: Naval Postgraduate School, July 2006).

Johnson, Thomas H. and W. Chris Mason, "Understanding the Taliban and Insurgency in Afghanistan," *Orbis: A Journal of World Affairs* 51:1 (2007).

Johnson, Thomas H. and Wali Ahmed Shaaker, "The Taliban's Use of Poetry," unpublished manuscript, 2008).

Johnson, Thomas H. and Ahwad Waheed, "*Taranas* (Chants): An Effective Afghan Propaganda Artifact," *Small Wars and Insurgencies* 22:1 (March 2011): 3–31.

Johnson, Thomas H. and Barry Zellon (eds), *Culture, Conflict and Counterinsurgency*, with Barry Zellen (Palo Alto, CA: Stanford University Press, 2014).

Jolly, David, "Afghanistan's Crippled Power Grid Exposes Vulnerability of Beseiged Capital," *New York Times*, 17 February 2016, http://www.nytimes.com/2016/02/18/world/asia/afghanistan-hardship-taliban-bombings.html?_r=0.

—— "Afghanistan had Record Civilian Casualties in 2015, UN Says," *New York Times*, 14 February 2016, http://www.nytimes.com/2016/02/15/world/asia/afghanistan-record-civilian-casualties-2015-united-nations.html?_r=0.

Jones, Catherine Ann, *The Way of Story: The Craft and Soul of Writing* (Ojai, CA: Prasana Press, 2004).

Joshi, Rohan, "The Taliban after Mullah Omar and the battle for Afghanistan," *Business Standard*, 11 August 2015, http://www.business-standard.com/article/punditry/the-taliban-after-mullah-omar-the-battle-for-afghanistan-115081000751_1.html.

Jowett, Garth S. and Victoria O'Donnell, *Propaganda and Persuasion* (Thousand Oaks, CA: SAGE Publications, 1986).

Juarero, Alicia, *Dynamics in Action* (Cambridge, MA: MIT Press, 1999).

Juergensmeyer, Mark, *Terror in the Mind of God: The Global Rise of Religious Violence*, 3rd edn (Berkeley, CA: University of California Press, 2003).

Karimi, Mohammad Farid, "Hekmatyar's nephew killed in NATO-led raid," *Pajhwok Afghan News*, 22 April 2011. http://www.pajhwok.com/en/2011/04/22/hekmatyars-nephew-killed-nato-led-raid.

Kelman, H. C., "Processes of Opinion Change," in *Public Opinion Quarterly* 25 (1961).

Kepel, Gilles *Jihad: The Trail of Political Islam* (Cambridge, MA: Harvard University Press, 2002).

Kilcullen, David, *The Accidental Guerrilla: Fighting Small Wars in the Midst of a Big One* (New York: Oxford University Press, 2009).

—— *Counterinsurgency* (New York: Oxford University Press, 2010).

—— "Three Pillars of Counterinsurgency," Remarks delivered at the US Government Counterinsurgency Conference, Washington, DC, 28 September 2006, http://www.au.af.mil/au/awc/awcgate/uscoin/3pillars_of_counterinsurgency.pdf.

King, Stephen, *On Writing: A Memoir of the Craft* (London: Hodder and Stoughton, 2000).

Khan, Noor, "Militants behead Afghan principal for educating girls: Taliban assaults cited in closing of schools," *Boston Globe*, 5 January 2006.

Khan, Riaz "Pakistan arrests former Taliban spokesman," *The Independent*, 4 January 2009, http://www.independent.co.uk/news/world/asia/pakistan-arrests-former-taliban-spokesman-1224489.html.

Kerchner, Captain Philip M., Dr Richard F. Deckro, LTC (Retd) Jack M. Kloeber, Jr, "Valuing Psychological Operations," *Military Operations Research* 6:2 (2001).

Knowles, Murray and Rosamund Moon, *Introducing Metaphor* (New York: Routledge, 2006).

Kruglanski, Arie W. Eric P. Thompson, and Scott Spiegel, "Bimodal Notions of Persuasion and Single-Process 'Unimodel'," in Shelly Chaiken and Yaacov Trope (eds), *Dual-Process Theories in Social Psychology* (New York: Guilford Press, 1999).

Lakoff, George and Mark Johnson, *Metaphors We Live By* (Chicago: University of Chicago Press, 1980).

Lamb, Christopher, *Review of Psychological Operations: Lessons Learned from Recent Operational Experience* (Washington, DC: National Defense University, 2005).

Lamothe, Dan, "Meet the shadowy figure recruiting for the Islamic State in Afghanistan," *Washington Post*, 13 January 2015.

Laub, Zachary, "The Taliban in Afghanistan," *Council on Foreign Relations*, 4 July 2014, http://www.cfr.org/afghanistan/taliban-afghanistan/p10551.

Lawrence, Bruce (ed.), *Messages to the World: The Statements of Osama Bin Laden* (London: Verso, 2005).

Lepore, Jill, *The Name of War: King Phillip's War and the Origins of American Identity* (New York: Alfred A. Knopf, 1998).

Lewis, Bernard, "License to Kill: Usama bin Ladin's Declaration of Jihad," *Foreign Affairs*, Nov./Dec. 1998, https://www.foreignaffairs.com/articles/saudi-arabia/1998-11-01/license-kill-usama-bin-ladins-declaration-jihad.

Lewis, Jared and Demand Media, "Repetition as a Persuasive Strategy," *Houston Chronicle*, http://smallbusiness.chron.com/repetition-persuasive-strategy-26001.html.

Liebl, Vern, "Pushtuns, Tribalism, Leadership, Islam and Taliban: A Short View," *Small War and Insurgencies* (September 2007): 498.

Lindholm. Charles, "The Segmentary Lineage System: Its Applicability to Pakistan's Political Structure," in Ainslie T. Embree (ed.), *Pakistan's Western Borderlands: The Transformation of Political Order* (New Delhi: Vikas Publishing House, 1977).

Livingston, Ian S, and Michael O'Hanlon, *Afghanistan Index* (Washington, DC: Brookings Institute, 24 April 2012), http://www.brookings.edu/foreign-policy/afghanistan-index.aspx.

Loney, Jim, "Civilian deaths undermine West's Afghan mission," Reuters, 22 May 2007, http://in.today.reuters.com/news/newsArticle.aspx?type=worldNews&storyID=2007–05–22T184642Z_01_NOOTR_RTRJONC_0_India-299435-1.xml&archived=False.

Lord, Carnes, "Psychological–Political Instruments," in Audrey Kurth Cronin and James M. Ludes (eds), *Attacking Terrorism: Elements of a Grand Strategy* (Washington, DC: Georgetown University Press, 2004).

Ludhianvi, Mufti Rasheed, *Obedience to the Amir* (Berlin: First Draft Publishing, 2015).

—— (ed.), Michael Semple, trans. Yameema Mitha, *Obedience to the Amir: An early text on the Afghan Taliban Movement* (Berlin: First Draft Publishing, 2015).

Lutz, Rzehak, "Doing Pashto: Pashtunwali as the ideal of honourable behavior and tribal life among Pashtuns," *Afghanistan Analyst Network*, https://www.afghanistan-analysts.org/wp-content/uploads/downloads/2012/10/20110321LR-Pashtunwali-FINAL.pdf.

Mahdi, Niloufer Qasim, *Pukhtunwali: Ostracism and Honor Among the Pathan Hill Tribes* (New York: Elsevier, 1986).

Mahmud, Husayn Ibn, "Al-Rajul al-'Amlaaq: The Giant Man," 2005, http://www.archive.org/details/TheGiantMan.

Mail Online, "The Man Who had His Ears and Nose Cut Off for Daring to Vote," 1 September 2009.

Main, Col. Francis Scott, US Army Reserve, Psychological Operations Support to Strategic Communications in Afghanistan, *Strategy Research Project* (Carlisle Barracks, PA: US Army War College), 24 March 2009.

Maiwandi, Abdul Satar (ed.), *Alemarah* or the *Voice of Jihad* (Taliban official website), http://9–11domorethenneverforget-stopislam.blogspot.com/2011/05/taliban-and-muslims-use-social-media-to.html.

Maley, William, *Fundamentalism Reborn? Afghanistan and the Taliban* (New York: New York University Press, 1998).

Malkasian, Carter *War Comes to Garmser: Thirty Years of Conflict on the Afghan Frontier* (Oxford: Oxford University Press, 2013).

Mann, Scott, "Combat Story Telling," *Narrative Strategies*, 2 January 2016, http://www.narrative-strategies.com/scott-mann/combat-story-telling.

Marquand, Robert "The Reclusive Ruler who Runs the Taliban," *Christian Science Monitor*, 10 October 2001, http://www.csmonitor.com/2001/1010/p1s4-wosc.html.

Maqbool, Aleem "Pakistan helping Afghan Taliban—NATO," BBC News, 1 February 2012, http://www.bbc.com/news/world-asia-16821218.

Martin, Sir Ewen, *Afghanistan: A Short History of its People and Politics* (New York: Harper Collins, 2002).

McAdam, Doug Sidney Tarrow, and Charles Tilly, "Toward an Integrated Perspective on Social Movements and Revolution," in Mark I. Lichbach and Alan S. Zuckerman (eds), *Comparative Politics: Rationality, Culture and Structure* (Cambridge: Cambridge University Press, 1997).

McAdam, Doug, John D. McCarthy, and Mayer N. Zald (eds), *Comparative Perspectives on Social Movements: Political Opportunities, Mobilizing Structures, and Cultural Framings* (Cambridge: Cambridge University Press, 1996).

McGirk, Tim, "On bin Laden's Trail," *National Geographic*, December 2004, http://ngm.nationalgeographic.com/features/world/asia/pakistan/pashtun-text/1.

McLuhan, Marshall, *The Medium is the Message (Berkeley, CA: Gingko Press, 2005).*

Meyerie, Gerald Megan Katt, and Jim Gavrillas, *On the Ground in Afghanistan: Counterinsurgency in Practice* (CAN and Marine Corp University Press, 2012).

Miller, Gerald R., "On Being Persuaded: Some Basic Distinctions," in James Price Dillard and Michael Pfau (eds), *The Persuasion Handbook: Developments in Theory and Practice* (Thousand Oaks, CA: SAGE Publications, 2002).

Miller, Greg and Souad Mekhennet, "Inside the Surreal World of the Islamic State's Propaganda Machine," *Washington Post*, 20 November 2015, https://www.washingtonpost.com/world/national-security/inside-the-islamic-states-propaganda-machine/2015/11/20/051e997a-8ce6-11e5-acff-673ae92ddd2b_story.html.

Mills, Margaret A., *Rhetorics and Politics in Afghan Traditional Storytelling* (Philadelphia, PA: University of Pennsylvania Press, 1991).

Mukhilsyar, "Proud of the youth emotions and devotions," *Daily Shahadat*, 21 April 2010, http://dailyshahadat.com/safha_e_jawanan-story.php?id=40.

Ron Moreau, "The Jihadi High School," *Newsweek*, 24 April 2011, http://www.newsweek.com/2011/04/24/the-jihadi-high-school.html.

——— "America's New Nightmare," *Newsweek*, 3 August 2009.

Motevalli, Golnar, "Taliban targeting Afghan women and government workeres, UN report finds," *Guardian*, 19 February 2013, http://www.theguardian.com/world/2013/feb/19/taliban-targeting-women-un-report.

Motlagh, Jason, "Will Aid Workers' Killings End Civilian Surge?" *Time*, 9 August 2010, http://content.time.com/time/world/article/0,8599,2009399,00.html.

Munoz, Arturo, "U.S. Military Information Operations in Afghanistan: Effectiveness of Psychological Operations 2001–2010," *National Defense Research Institute* (2012), http://www.rand.org/content/dam/rand/pubs/monographs/2012/RAND_MG1060.pdf.

Murshed, Iftikhar, *Afghanistan: The Taliban Years* (London: Bennett & Bloom, 2006).

Muzhda, Wahid, *Afghanistan va panj sal-i sultah-i taliban [Afghanistan Under Five Years of Taliban Sovereignty]* (2003).

Nasaw, Daniel "Mullen blasts US 'strategic communication' efforts in Afghanistan," *Guardian*, 28 August 2009, http://www.theguardian.com/world/2009/aug/28/mullen-afghanistan-communication.

Nathan, Joanna, "Reading the Taliban," in Antonio Giustozzi (ed.), *Decoding the New Taliban: Insights from the Afghan Field* (Oxford: Oxford University Press, 2012

—— "Taliban Propaganda: Winning the War of Words?" *Asia Report* 158 (International Crisis Group, 2008), www.crisisgroup.org/en/regions/asia/south-asia/afghanistan/158-Taliban-propaganda-winning-the-war-of-words.aspx.

National Counterterrorism Center, *"2008 Report on Terrorism," 30 April 2009.*

—— *"2009 Report on Terrorism," 30 April 2010.*

NBC News, "Taliban Threatens to Kill Captured US Soldier," 16 July 2009.

NEFA Foundation, "In Celebration of Eid al-Adha," 25 November 2009, http://www.nefafoundation.org/miscellaneous/nefa_mullahomar1109.pdf.

—— "Regarding Obama's New Strategy," 2 December 2009, http://www.nefafoundation.org/miscellaneous/nefa_talibanobamasurge1209.pdf.

—— "Taliban: Obama, Following in Bush's Steps," 8 December 2009, http://www.nefafoundation.org/miscellaneous/nefaTaliObamaBush1209.pdf.

Nordland, Rod and Joseph Goldstein, "Taliban Leader Mullah Omar Died in 2013, Afghans Declare," *New York Times*, 29 July 2015, http://www.nytimes.com/2015/07/30/world/asia/mullah-omar-taliban-death-reports-prompt-inquiry-by-afghan-government.html?_r=0.

Nordland, Rod and Jawad Sukhanyar, "Taliban Are Said to Target Hazaras to Try to Match ISIS' Brutality, Afghans Declare," *New York Times*, 22 April 2015, http://www.nytimes.com/2015/04/23/world/asia/taliban-are-said-to-target-hazaras-to-try-to-match-isis-brutality.html.

Norman, Catherine, "What do Afghans want from the police? Views from Helmand province," CNA (January 2012).

Nyrop, Richard F. and Donald M. Seekins (eds), *Afghanistan Country Study* (Washington, DC: American University, Foreign Area Studies, 1986), http://www.gl.iit.edu/govdocs/afghanistan/Family.html.

Onishi, Norimitsu, "A Tale of the Mullah and Muhammad's Amazing Cloak," *New York Times*, 19 December 2001, http://select.nytimes.com/gst/abstract.html?res=F00E1FFA395A0C7A8DDDAB0994D9404482&n=Top%2fReference%2fTimes%20Topics%2fPeople%2fO%2fOmar%2c%20Muhammad.

Open Source Center, "Selection List: Review of Pro-Taliban, Islamist Publications Oct/Nov 09," SAP20091130950058, Caversham BBC Monitoring in English, 30 November 2009.

—— "Terrorism: Taliban Chief Mullah Omar Offers Foreign Forces Safe Exit from Afghanistan," Jihadist websites: OSC Summary in Arabic, 30 September 2008, https://www.opensource.gov/portal/server.pt/gateway/PTARGS_0_0_200_217_51_43/content/Display/GMP20080930479002.

—— "Terrorism: Taliban Leader Congratulates Muslims on Id, Urges Boycotting 'Deceptive Elections,'" Jihadist websites: OSC Summary in Arabic, 7 December 2008, https://www.opensource.gov/portal/server.pt/gateway/PTARGS_0_0_200_217_51_43/content/Display/GMP20081209054013.

—— "Al-Jazirah: Mullah Omar Urges Afghan Employees Not to Serve Govt, 'Occupation,'" Al-Jazirah Satellite Channel Television in Arabic, 1419 GMT 12 October 2007, https://www.opensource.gov/portal/server.pt/gateway/PTARGS_0_0_200_217_51_43/content/Display/GMP20071012640001.

—— "Afghanistan: Mullah Omar Claims US After Taliban, Not Usama," Islamabad *Ausaf* in Urdu, 27 September 2001, https://www.opensource.gov/portal/server.pt/gateway/PTARGS_0_0_200_217_51_43/content/Display/SAP2001092800 0057. *Oqab*, "Afghan Election," http://www. oqab1.com/ index.php?option=com_content&view=article&id=267:2011–02–15–02–12–19&catid=22:2010–11–09–19–47–37&Itemid=110.

Osman, Akram, Arley Loewen (trans.), *Real Men Keep Their Word: Tales from Kabul, Afghanistan* (Oxford: Oxford University Press, 2005).

Pajhwok Afghan News, "Commander wounded as Taliban groups clash," 5 March 2006.

Pan, Esther, "Afghanistan's New Security Threat," *Backgrounder*, Council on Foreign Affairs, 14 February 2006.

Pazira, Nelofer, *A Bed of Red Flowers: In Search of My Afghanistan* (New York: Free Press, 2005).

PBS Frontline TV documentary, "The Dancing Boys of Afghanistan," 20 April 2010.

Petty, Richard E., Joseph R. Priester, and Pablo Brinol, "Mass Media Attitude Change: Implications of the Elaboration Likelihood Model of Persuasion," in Jennings Bryant and Dolf Zillmann (eds), *Media Effects: Advances in Theory and Research* (Mahwah, NJ: Lawrence Erlbaum Associates, 2002), http://crx.sagepub.com/content/25/5/486.full.pdf+html.

Pew, "25-Nation Pew Global Attitudes Survey," http://www.pewglobal.org/files/pdf/264.pdf.

Polkinghorne, Donald E., *Narrative Knowing and the Human Sciences* (Albany, NY: SUNY Press, 1988).

Porch, Douglas, *The Conquest of Morocco* (New York: Farrar, Straus and Giroux, 2005).

Press TV, "Taliban behead 11 Shia Afghans," 26 June 2010.

Qobil, Rustam, "The sexually abused dancing boys of Afghanistan," BBC World Service, 7 September 2010.

Qureshi, Ahmad, "Commander killed in Taliban infighting," *Pajhwok Afghan News*, 10 March 2009.

Rabiroff, Jon, "Chilling 'night letters' from Taliban intimidate Afghans," *Stars and Stripes*, 30 November 2010, http://www.stripes.com/news/chilling-night-letters-from-taliban-intimidate-afghans-1.127043.

Radio Free Europe/Radio Liberty, "British Ethnomusicologist, 'It Isn't Actually Correct to Say Taliban Have Banned Music'," 22 June 2009, http://www.rferl.org/content/British_Ethnomusicologist_Discusses_Talibans_Campaign_Against_Musicians/1753865.html.

Radioinfo.com.au, https://www.radioinfo.com.au/news/taliban-launch-secret-radio-station.

Radio Liberty, "Afghanistan: A Chronology Of Suicide Attacks Since 2001," January 17, 2006, http://www.rferl.org/featuresarticle/2006/01/9ac36a59-d683-4189-a2b9-94fe5fbf32ad.html.

Radmanesh, Mohammad, "Taliban violence reaches new peak after Hazara murders," *France 24 The Observers*, 11 November 2015, http://observers.france24.com/en/20151111-taliban-murder-women-children-hazara.

Raelin, Joseph A., "The Myth of Charismatic Leaders," March 2003, http://www.findarticles.com/p/articles/mi_m0MNT/is_3_57/ai_98901483.

Rashid, Ahmed, *Taliban: Militant Islam, Oil and Fundamentalism in Central Asia*, 2nd edn (New Haven, CT: Yale University Press; 2010).

—— *Descent into Chaos: The United States and the Failure of Nation Building in Pakistan, Afghanistan, and Central Asia* (New York: Viking, 2008), pp. 222–3.

—— "After 1,700 years, Buddhas fall to Taliban dynamite," *Daily Telegraph*, 12 March 2001, http://www.telegraph.co.uk/news/worldnews/asia/afghanistan/1326063/After-1700-years-Buddhas-fall-to-Taliban-dynamite.html.

—— *Taliban*, 1st edn (New Haven, CT: Yale University Press, 2001).

Raverty, Henry George (trans.), *Selections from the Poetry of Afghans: From the Sixteenth to the Nineteenth Century* (London: Forgotten Books, 2008).

Richburg, Keith B. "Kandahar slides into lawlessness as Taliban attacks force government to retreat," *Washington Post*, 14 March 2010, http://www.washingtonpost.com/wp-dyn/content/article/2010/03/13/AR2010031300574.html.

Riedel, Bruce, "Pakistan, Taliban and the Afghan Quagmire" (Washington DC: Brookings Institute, 24 August 2013), http://www.brookings.edu/research/opinions/2013/08/26-pakistan-influence-over-afghan-taliban-riedel.

Reuter, Christoph and Borhan Yunus, "The Return of the Taliban in Andar: Ghazni," in A. Giustozzi (ed.), *Decoding the New Taliban: Insight from the Afghan Field* (New York: Columbia University Press, 2009).

Reuters, "Afghan boy dancers sexually abused by former warlords," 18 November 2007.

Reuters, "Taliban chief calls for unity against U.S. troops," Reuters, 6 November 2005, http://www.redorbit.com/news/general/296445/taliban_chief_calls_for_unity_against_us_troops/index.html.

Rivera, Ray and Carlotta Gall, "Rebutting Afghan Spy Agency, Taliban Say Their Leader Isn't Dead," *New York Times*, 23 May 2011, http://www.nytimes.com/2011/05/24/world/asia/24omar.html.

RSM Fact Sheet, "Essential Function 8: Maintain Internal and External Strategic Communication Capability," http://www.rs.nato.int/article/rs-news/rsm-essential-function-8-strategic-communication.html.

RNW Media, "Dutch government falls over Afghanistan mission," https://www.rnw.org/archive/dutch-government-falls-over-afghanistan-mission.

Roberts, Jeffery J., *The Origins of Conflict in Afghanistan* (Westport, CT: Praeger Publishing, 2003).

Rokeach, Milton, *Beliefs, Attitudes, and Values* (San Francisco, CA: Jossey-Bass Inc, 1972).

Roskos-Ewoldsen, David R. Laura Arpan-Ralstin, and James St Pierre, "Attitude Accessibility and Persuasion: The Quick and the Strong," in James Price Dillard and Michael Pfau (eds), *The Persuasion Handbook* (Thousand Oaks, CA: SAGE Publications, 2002).

Roy, Olivier, *Islam and Resistance in Afghanistan* (Cambridge: Cambridge University Press, 1988).

Ruston, Scott W. *COMOPS Journal* (September 2009), http://comops.org/journal/2009/09/03/understand-what-narrative-is-and-does/.

Ruttig, Thomas "The Haqqani Network as an Autonomous Entity," in Antonio Giustozzi (ed.), *Decoding the New Taliban: Insights from the Afghan Field* (New York: Columbia University Press, 2009).

Safire, William, *Lend Me Your Ears: Great Speeches in History* (New York: W. W. Norton & Co., 1997).

Sakata, Hiromi Lorraine, *Music in the Mind: The Concept of Music and Musician in Afghanistan* (Kent, OH: Kent State University Press, 1983).

Salahudin, Sayed, "Karzai orders probe into Afghan civilian deaths reports," Reuters, 5 August 2010, http://www.reuters.com/article/idUSTRE6741KP20100805.

Salfi, Sophla and Greg Botelho, "In Pakistan school attack, Taliban terrorists kill 145, mostly children," CNN World, 17 December 2014, http://www.cnn.com/2014/12/16/world/asia/pakistan-peshawar-school-attack/.

Salarzai, Khan Wali "A commander among 4 fighters killed in Kunar," *Pajhwok Afghan News*, 31 October 2010, http://www.pajhwok.com/en/2010/10/31/commander-among-4-fighters-killed-kunar.

Saljoqi, Abdullah "Taliban burn down girls' school in Afghanistan," *France 24 The Observers*, 4 November 2015, http://observers.france24.com/en/20151104-taliban-shut-down-girls-school-afghanistan;.

Schein, Edgar, *Coercive Persuasion: A Socio-Psychological Analysis of the "Brainwashing" of American Civilian Prisoners by the Chinese Communists* (New York: W. W. Norton & Co., 1961).

Schifrin, Nick and Habibullah Khan, "US Supply Line at Risk along Pakistan Border," ABC News, 10 November 2008, http://abcnews.go.com/International/story?id=6221453.

Schimmel, Annnemarie, *Mystical Dimensions of Islam* (Chapel Hill, NC: University of North Carolina Press, 1975).

Sieff, Kevin, "A fight for Afghanistans most famous artifact," *Washington Post*, 29 December 2012, https://www.washingtonpost.com/world/a-fight-for-afghanistans-most-famous-artifact/2012/12/29/ab2dc394–51cb-11e2–835b-02f92c0daa43_story.html.

Shaaker Wali, "Poetry: Why it Matters to Afghans," *Culture and Conflict Studies Occasional Paper Series* (Monterey, CA: Department of National Security Affairs, Naval Postgraduate School, August 2009).

Shaffer, Brenda, *The Limits of Culture: Islam and Foreign Policy* (Cambridge, MA: MIT Press).

Shah, Amir, "Ministry: Taliban Spokesman Arrested," Associated Press, 27 September 2007.

Shahzad, Syed Saleem, "Pakistan frees Taliban commander," *Asia Times*, 16 October 2010, http://www.atimes.com/atimes/South_Asia/LJ16Df02.html.

———— "In search of the Taliban's missing link," *Asia Times Online*, 16 September 2006, http://atimes.com/atimes/South_Asia/HI16Df01.html.

Shirmohammadi, Reza "Taliban Execute a Woman in Badghis," ToloTV, 9 August 2010.

Siddique, Abubakar "Understanding the Taliban's Campaign Against Music," Freemuse, http://www.freemuse.org/sw34252.asp.

Simmons, Annette, *Whoever Tells the Best Story Wins: How to Use Your Own Stories to Communicate with Power and Impact*, 2nd edn (New York: AMACOM, 2015).

———— *The Story Factor: Inspiration, Influence, and Persuasion through the Art of Storytelling* (New York: Basic Books, 2006).

Sinno, Abdulkader H., *Organization at War in Afghanistan and Beyond* (Ithaca, NY: Cornell University Press, 2008).

Sky, Emma, *"Increasing ISAF's Impact on Stability in Afghanistan," Defense and Security Analysis 23:1 (March 2007): 7–25.*

Smith, Amina, *Tales of Afghanistan* (London: Octagon Press, 1982).

Smith, Graeme, *The Dogs Are Eating Them Now: Our War in Afghanistan* (Toronto: Knopf Canada, 2013).

Snow, D. A. and R. Benford, "Ideology, Frame Resonance, and Participant Mobilization," in B. Klandermans, H. Kriesi, and S. Tarrow (eds), *From Structure to Action*, Vol. 1 (Greenwich, CT: JAI Press, 1988), pp. 197–217.

Spain, James W., *The Way of the Pathans* (Oxford: Oxford University Press, 1972).

———— *The Pathan Borderland* (Karachi: Indus Publications, 1963).

———— *The People of the Khyber, the Pathans of Pakistan* (New York: Praeger, 1962).

Special Inspector General for Afghanistan Reconstruction (SIGAR), *Quarterly Report to the United States Congress* (Washington, DC: 30 July 2014).

Stanikzai, Zainullah, "Italian medics accused of complicity in murder," *Pajhwok Afghan News*, 17 April 2010.

Storti, Craig, *Cross-Cultural Dialogues: 74 Brief Encounters with Cultural Difference* (Yarmouth, ME: Intercultural Press, 1994), p. 4.

Straziuso, Jason, *"The Kabul Quagmire," Associated Press, 17 October 2009.*

Swami, Praveen, "Taliban deputy chief in high-stakes peace gamble: analysis," *Daily Telegraph,* 20 October 2010, http://www.telegraph.co.uk/news/worldnews/asia/afghanistan/8076284/Taliban-deputy-chief-in-high-stakes-peace-gamble-analysis.html.

Sykes, Sir Percy, *A History of Afghanistan* (London: Macmillan, 1940).

Synovitz, Ron, "Afghanistan: Are Militants Copying Iraqi Insurgents' Suicide Tactics?" Radio Free Europe Radio Library, 17 January 2006, http://www.rferl.org/content/article/1064791.html.

——— "Afghanistan: U.S. Investigates Taliban 'Night Letters' Threatening Villagers," RadioLiberty, 10 March 2004, http://www.rferl.org/featuresarticle/2004/03/c47dc6f9–5e79–4213–8c0e-2430cf0557b5.html.

Taber, Robert, *War of the Flea: The Classic Study of Guerrilla Warfare* (Washington, DC: Potomac Books, Inc., 2002).

Tarzai, Amin, "Taliban radio back on the air," *Asia Times Online,* 11 March 2005, http://www.atimes.com/atimes/Central_Asia/GE11Ag01.html.

Tayar, Jafar, "HIA claims killing medics," *Pajhwok Afghan News,* 7 August 2010, http://www.pajhwok.com/en/2010/08/07/hia-claims-killing-medics.

Taylor, Philip M., "Psychological Operations During Operation Enduring Freedom," Paper presented at the University of Leeds, UK, 2002.

Thomas, Troy S., William D. Casebeer, and Stephen D. Kiser, *Warlords Rising: Confronting Violent Non-State Actors* (Lanham, MD: Lexington Books, 2005).

Thomas, Troy S. and William D. Casebeer, "Violent Systems" (INSS Occasional Paper 52, 2004).

Tierney, Rep. John F., Chair-Subcommittee on National Security and Foreign Affairs, *Warlord, Inc. Extortion and Corruption Along the US Supply Chain in Afghanistan,* Report of the Majority Staff, Committee on Oversight and Government Reform, US House of Representatives, June 2010.

Titcomb, James, "Google bans Taliban app for hate speech," *Daily Telegraph,* 4 April 2016, http://www.telegraph.co.uk/technology/2016/04/04/google-bans-taliban-app-for-hate-speech/.

TOLO News, "Hezb-e-Islami killed 2 Afghans and 8 foreigners," *7 August 2010, http://tolonews.com/en/afghanistan/235-hezb-e-islami-killed-2-afghans-and-8-foreigners.*

Tomlinson, Simon, "Hundreds of Afghan girls poisoned by toxic gas at two schools in suspected attacks by Taliban militants opposed to their education," *Daily Mail,* 3 September 2015, http://www.dailymail.co.uk/news/article-3221073/Hundreds-Afghan-girls-poisoned-toxic-gas-two-schools-suspected-attacks-Taliban-militants-opposed-education.html.

BIBLIOGRAPHY

Tomsen, Peter, *The Wars of Afghanistan: Messianic Terrorism, Tribal Conflicts, and the Failures of Great Powers*, 1st edn (New York: Public Affairs, 2011).

Traynor, Ian, "NATO Afghanistan mission in doubt after Dutch withdrawal," *Guardian*, 22 February 2010.

Trimingham, J. Spencer, *The Sufi Orders of Islam* (Oxford: Clarendon Press, 1971).

Trollope, Anthony, *An Autobiography* (London: Penguin, 1996).

Truscott, Claire, "'Gooooood mornin' Afghanistan!' US fights Taliban on airwaves," AFP, 6 October 2009, http://www.google.com/hostednews/afp/article/ALeq M5gygBjOcD9BhvtVR38JWQJFPS8PcA.

Tse-tung, Mao, (Samuel B. Griffith, trans.), *On Guerrilla Warfare* (University of Illinois Press, 2000; first published 1937).

Turner, Mark, *The Literary Mind* (New York: Oxford University Press, 1998).

United Nations Assistance Mission in Afghanistan, "Special Representative Meets with Hezb-e-Islami Delegation in Kabul," 25 March 2010, https://unama.unmissions.org/special-representative-meets-hezb-e-islami-delegation-kabul.

—— "Suicide Attacks in Afghanistan (2001–2007)," (9 September 2007).

United Nations Office on Drugs and Crime, *The Opium Economy in Afghanistan: An International Problem* (New York: United Nations, January 2003).

United States Army/Marine Corps. *Counterinsurgency Field Manual* (Chicago: University of Chicago Press, 2007), http://permanent.access.gpo.gov/lps79762/FM_3-24.pdf.

United States Central Command, Afghanistan-Pakistan Center, *Taliban Violations of their Code of Conduct* (Tampa, FL: 1 March 2011).

United States Deputy Secretary of Defense, *Implementation of the DOD Strategic Communication Plan for Afghanistan*, 12 September 2007.

van Biljert, Martine, "The Battle for Afghanistan Militancy and Conflict in Zabul and Uruzgan," *Counterterrorism Strategy Initiative Policy Paper*, New America Foundation, September 2010.

van Linschoten, Alex Strick and Felix Kuehn, *An Enemy We Created: The Myth of the Taliban-Al Qaeda Merger in Afghanistan* (Oxford: Oxford University Press, 2012).

van Linschoten, Alex Strick and Felix Kuehn (eds), *Poetry of the Taliban* (London: Hurst & Co., 2012).

von Clausewitz, General Carl, *On War: The Complete Edition* (Wildside Press, LLC, 2009).

Waldman, Matt, "The Sun in the Sky: The Relationship Between Pakistan's ISI and Afghan Insurgents," *Discussion Paper 18* (Carr Center for Human Rights Policy, Kennedy School of Government, Harvard University, June 2010).

Walsh, Declan, "Press battle in Pakistan feeds into larger conflict: Government vs. Military," South Asia Media Net: A News and Views Website of South Asia, 25 May 2014, http://www.southasianmedia.net/sam-monitors/pakistan-media-crisis/press-battle-in-pakistan-feeds-into-larger-conflict-government-vs.-military-story.

Walsh, Nick Paton, "Analysis: Afghanistan must recognize Taliban are winning," CNN, 21 April 2016, http://www.cnn.com/2016/04/20/asia/afghanistan-escalation-analysis/.

Watson, Ivan, "Taliban Enlists Video in Fight for Afghanistan," *NPR*, 2 November 2006, http://www.wbur.org/npr/6423946/taliban-enlists-video-in-fight-for-afghanistan.

Watson, James, *Media Communication: An Introduction to Theory and Process* (New York: Palgrave Macmillan, 2008).

Williams, Michael, "How the British presence in Sangin restored trust in government," *Guardian*, 20 September 2010.

Witte, Griff, "Taliban establishes elaborate shadow government in Afghanistan," *Washington Post*, 8 December 2009, http://www.washingtonpost.com/wp-dyn/content/article/2009/12/07/AR2009120704127.html.

——— "Suicide Bombers Kill Dozens in Afghanistan, Violence in South is Seen as Message to NATO," *Washington Post Foreign Service*, 17 January 2006, p. A11.

——— "Afghans Confront Surge in Violence: Foreign Support Seen Behind Attacks that Mimic Those in Iraq," *Christian Science Monitor*, 28 November 2005, p. 1.

Wong, Maybel Chau-Ping, "The effects of story schemata on narrative recall," https://repository.ust.hk/dspace/handle/1783.1/1337 (2004).

Xinhua, "Afghanistan: Taliban Launch New Radio Station in South," 8 August 2009, republished at http://www.amicaltmedia.net/headlines-archive.php?pid=316&year=2009.

Xinhua, "Infighting leaves 5 Taliban dead, wounds 7 in W Afghanistan," 25 September 2009.

Younossi, Obaid et al., *The Long March: Building an Afghan Army* (Santa Monica, CA: RAND Corporation, 2009).

Yousafzai, Khushal, "Music has died in the Swat valley," *Freemuse*, 23 April 2009.

Yousafzai, Sami and Ron Moreau, "This Mullah Omar Show," *Newsweek*, 8 August 2010.

Zadra, Jonathan R. and Gerald L Clore, "Emotions and perception: the role of affective information," Wiley Interdisciplinary Reviews, *Cognitive Science* 2:6 (November–December 2011): 676–85.

Zaeef, Abdul Salam, *My Life With the Taliban* (London: Scribe Publications, 2010).

Zabulwal, Abdul Awwal, "Taliban in Zabul: A Witness's Account," in A. Giustozzi (ed.), *Decoding the New Taliban: Insight from the Afghan Field* (New York: Columbia University Press, 2009.

INDEX